Archaic Greece

Archaic Greece

The Age of New Reckonings

Brian M. Lavelle

WILEY Blackwell

This edition first published 2020
© 2020 Brian M. Lavelle

Registered Office
John Wiley & Sons, Inc., 111 River Street, Hoboken, NJ 07030, USA

Editorial Office
101 Station Landing, Medford, MA 02155, USA

For details of our global editorial offices, customer services, and more information about Wiley products visit us at www.wiley.com.

Wiley also publishes its books in a variety of electronic formats and by print-on-demand. Some content that appears in standard print versions of this book may not be available in other formats.

Library of Congress Cataloging-in-Publication Data
Names: Lavelle, Brian M., author.
Title: Archaic Greece : the age of new reckonings / Brian M. Lavelle.
Description: Hoboken, NJ : John Wiley & Sons, 2020. | Includes bibliographical references and index. |
Identifiers: LCCN 2018022258 (print) | LCCN 2018032104 (ebook) | ISBN 9781119370451 (Adobe PDF) |
   ISBN 9781119369943 (ePub) | ISBN 9781405198592 (hardcover) | ISBN 9781405198608 (pbk.)
Subjects: LCSH: Greece–History–To 146 B.C. | Greece–Civilization.
Classification: LCC DF214 (ebook) | LCC DF214 .L34 2018 (print) | DDC 938/.02–dc23
LC record available at https://lccn.loc.gov/2018022258

Cover Design: Wiley
Cover Image: © Paul Fearn/Alamy Stock Photo

Set in 10/12pt Warnock by SPi Global, Pondicherry, India
Printed in Singapore by C.O.S. Printers Pte Ltd

10 9 8 7 6 5 4 3 2 1

For my Nancy, without whose saving smiles
and gentle touch
this book could not have been written.

Sempre e per sempre ti amo.

Contents

Figures and Source-Acknowledgments *xiii*
Preface *xvii*
Acknowledgments *xix*
Abbreviations and Citations *xxi*
Maps *xxiii*

1   Sources for the Archaic Period *1*
1.1   Introduction *1*
1.2   Archaeology and the Material Remains *1*
1.2.1 Pottery *2*
1.2.2 Burials *4*
1.2.3 Inscriptions *5*
1.2.4 Other Types of Material Evidence *7*
1.2.5 Problems of Interpretation *7*
1.3   Literary Sources *8*
1.3.1 Archaic Greek Poets *9*
1.3.2 Prose Writers *10*
1.4   Managing the Muses *11*
1.4.1 Evaluating and Deploying the Evidence *11*
       Notes *13*
       Further Reading *13*

2   A Brief Overview of the Archaic Period *15*
2.1   Introduction *15*
2.2   The Environment and Greek Life *16*
2.2.1 The Land and the Sea *16*
2.2.2 The Greeks and Others *17*
2.3   The Early Archaic Period *18*
2.4   The Seventh Century BCE: Expansion and Change *19*
2.4.1 Colonies *19*
2.4.2 Law Codes *20*
2.4.3 Tyranny *21*

2.5   The Sixth Century BCE: Conflict and Creation   *21*
2.5.1   The Kingdom of Lydia   *21*
2.5.2   The Empire of the Persians   *22*
2.5.3   Greek Culture in the Sixth Century BCE   *24*
2.6   The Early Fifth Century BCE: The Defeat of Persia   *24*
2.7   Sparta and Lakonia   *25*
2.8   Athens and Attika   *26*
        Notes   *27*
        Further Reading   *27*
        Brief Timeline for the Archaic Period   *29*

3   ***Polis* and Politics in Archaic Greece**   *31*
3.1   Introduction   *31*
3.2   Origins and Nature of the Early *Polis*   *31*
3.3   Transformations of Leadership and Governance
        in the Archaic *Polis*   *34*
3.3.1   *Basileis* and *Aristoi*   *35*
3.3.2   Archaic Greek Tyrants and Tyranny   *38*
3.3.3   Lawgivers and Law Codes   *40*
3.4   *Demokratia*   *42*
3.4.1   Background   *42*
3.4.2   Kleisthenes and His Reforms   *43*
3.5   The Evolution of Politics and Government in Archaic Greece: A Summary   *45*
3.6   Politics and the Archaic Greek Farmer   *46*
        Notes   *47*
        Further Reading   *48*

4   **War and Violence in Archaic Greece**   *51*
4.1   Introduction   *51*
4.1.1   "Homeric" Warfare   *51*
4.2   Land Warfare in the Early Archaic Period   *53*
4.2.1   "Servant of the War-God"   *53*
4.2.2   Hoplites and the Phalanx   *56*
4.3   Land Warfare in the Later Archaic Period   *61*
4.3.1   Sparta, the *Polis* of War   *61*
4.4   Epilogue: The Causes of War   *64*
4.5   Summary   *64*
4.5.1   The Land War Experience in the Archaic Period   *64*
4.6   Conflict at Sea   *66*
4.6.1   Early Sea Travel and Piracy   *66*
4.6.2   Archaic Greek Ship-Guilds   *66*
4.6.3   Archaic Greek Ships   *68*
4.6.4   The Archaic Greeks and the Sea: A Summary   *70*
        Notes   *71*
        Further Reading   *71*

5   Archaic Greek Myth and Religion   73
5.1   Introduction   73
5.2   The Gods of Hesiod and Homer   76
5.2.1   Hesiod   76
5.2.2   Homer   79
5.2.3   Xenophanes' Complaint   81
5.3   Sanctuaries and Seers   82
5.3.1   Sacred Space   82
5.3.2   Seers, Prophets, and Sibyls   84
5.3.3   Dodona and Delphi   85
5.4   Gods and *Poleis*   86
5.4.1   Cult and Identity   86
5.5   The Archaic Greeks and Their Gods: A Summary   87
5.5.1   Law, Order, and Justice in the *Kosmos*   87
5.6   The Olympians   89
         Notes   91
         Further Reading   91

6   Early Greek Science   93
6.1   Darkness and Lumination   93
6.2   A Farmer's Handbook: Hesiod's *Works and Days*   94
6.3   The Near East, Miletos, and Science   95
6.3.1   Thales, *Physikos kai Astronomikos*   97
6.3.2   Anaximandros, Hekataios, and the World Imagined   100
6.3.3   Milesian Science: A Summary   102
6.4   "Wonders"   102
6.4.1   The Evolution of Archaic Greek Temples   102
6.4.2   Tunnels, Moles, and Bridges   104
6.5   Medicine   106
6.6   "Civilians," Science, and Technology   107
         Notes   108
         Further Reading   109

7   Archaic Greek Philosophy   111
7.1   Introduction   111
7.2   Hesiod and Zeus   112
7.3   Ionian Philosophy   114
7.3.1   The Milesians and the *Kosmos*   114
7.4   Skeptics, Critics, and Epistemology   116
7.4.1   Xenophanes   116
7.4.2   Herakleitos   118
7.5   Mathematics and the Mystical   120
7.5.1   Pythagoras   120
7.6   Summary   123
7.6.1   Early Philosophers and the Archaic Greeks   123

Notes   *124*
Further Reading   *124*

8   **The Art of the Archaic Greeks**   *127*
8.1   Introduction   *127*
8.2   Archaic Pottery-Painting   *128*
8.2.1   Later Geometric Pottery   *128*
8.2.2   Early Archaic Pottery: Orientalizing, Proto-Corinthian, and Proto-Attic   *129*
8.2.3   Later Archaic Pottery: Black-Figure and Red-Figure Ware   *131*
8.3   Archaic Greek Sculpture   *137*
8.3.1   Introduction   *137*
8.3.2   Later Geometric Sculpture   *137*
8.3.3   Archaic Architectural Sculpture   *138*
8.3.4   *Kouroi*   *142*
8.3.5   *Korai*   *145*
8.4   Summary   *149*
8.4.1   Archaic Greek Art and Archaic Greeks   *149*
Notes   *149*
Further Reading   *150*

9   **Archaic Greek Literature**   *151*
9.1   Introduction   *151*
9.2   Homer   *151*
9.2.1   *Iliad*   *153*
9.2.2   *Odyssey*   *155*
9.3   Hesiod   *157*
9.4   Early Greek Lyric and Elegaic Poets   *157*
9.4.1   Archilochos   *158*
9.4.2   Semonides   *160*
9.4.3   Tyrtaios   *160*
9.4.4   Mimnermos   *162*
9.5   Later Lyric and Elegaic Poets   *163*
9.5.1   Sappho   *163*
9.5.2   Solon   *165*
9.5.3   Anakreon   *167*
9.5.4   Simonides   *169*
9.5.5   Pindar   *173*
9.6   Summary   *174*
Notes   *175*
Further Reading   *176*

10   **Festivals and Games of the Archaic Greeks**   *179*
10.1   Introduction   *179*
10.1.1   Pre-Olympic Festivals and Games   *179*
10.2   The Olympic Festival and Games   *181*

10.2.1   Origins and Arrangements   *181*
10.2.2   *Agones*   *182*
10.2.3   *Nike* ("Victory")   *188*
10.2.4   The Panhellenic Ideal   *191*
10.3   Other Games and Festivals   *191*
10.3.1   The Pythian, Nemean, and Isthmian Games   *191*
10.4   Local and Regional Festivals   *194*
10.4.1   *Panathenaia*   *194*
10.4.2   Other Local and Regional Festivals   *196*
10.5   Festivals and Culture   *197*
10.5.1   *Dionysia* and Drama at Athens   *197*
10.5.2   The Dithyramb, Thespis, and Attic Tragedy   *197*
10.6   Summary   *199*
         Notes   *199*
         Further Reading   *200*

11   **Cultural Identity, Social Forces, Values, and Behaviors**   *203*
11.1   Introduction   *203*
11.1.1   *Philochoria*   *204*
11.2   Honor, Fame, and Good Repute   *205*
11.2.1   *Kleos* and *Arete:* Old Standards and New Benchmarks   *205*
11.2.2   Adjustments and Modifications to Standards and Expectations   *207*
11.2.3   Right Conduct: Constructive and Destructive   *209*
11.2.4   *Philia*   *211*
11.3   Excess and Moderation   *212*
11.3.1   The Seven Sages and the Delphic Maxims   *213*
11.4   Competition   *214*
11.4.1   The Pursuit of Wealth   *215*
11.4.2   The *Agon* of Politics and Display   *216*
11.5   Old Allegiances and New Realities   *217*
11.5.1   *Aristos* and *Demos*   *217*
11.6   Summary   *218*
         Notes   *219*
         Further Reading   *219*

12   **Gender and Sexuality in Archaic Greece**   *221*
12.1   Introduction   *221*
12.2   Archaic Greek Females   *221*
12.2.1   The Problem of Male Sources: Pandora, Helen, Clytemnestra, Penelope   *221*
12.2.2   Voices of Archaic Greek Women   *224*
12.2.3   Childhood and Maidenhood   *229*
12.2.4   Marriage and Family   *231*
12.2.5   Ritual and Religion   *233*
12.2.6   Summary   *234*
12.3   Archaic Greek Males   *236*

12.3.1   Childhood and Youth   *236*
12.3.2   Marriage and Family   *237*
12.3.3   Ritual and Religion   *238*
12.3.4   Social Life: *Philia* and *Symposia*   *238*
12.3.5   Summary   *239*
12.4   Sex, Gender, and Archaic Greek Society   *239*
12.4.1   Introduction: "Secret Sex" and Open Encounters   *239*
12.4.2   *Eros*   *240*
12.4.3   Same-Sex Relationships   *241*
12.5   Summary   *243*
       Notes   *243*
       Further Reading   *244*

13   **Epilogue: The Common and the Extraordinary**   *247*
       Notes   *253*

       Glossary of Greek Terms   *255*

       Index: Literary Citations   *259*
       Index   *265*

Figures and Source-Acknowledgments

Map 1   The Eastern Mediterranean. *xxiii*
Map 2   Greece and the Aegean. *xxiv*

1.1   The "Cup of Nestor." Late Geometric *kotyle, c.* 750–740 BCE. Image of cup and inscription by kind permission of Museo Civico Archeologico di Pithecusae. *Source:* Museum online site.   *3*
1.2   The Law of Dreros. Rendering of schist inscription, *c.* 650–600 BCE, Dreros, Crete, Museum of Agios Nikolaos, Crete. *Source:* Author.   *6*
2.1   Central Greece landscape. View from Osios Loukas, near Distomo, south-east toward Mount Helikon, summer 2015. *Source:* Author.   *17*
4.1   Melee fighting. Drawing from a Late Geometric amphora, Paros, *c.* 730–700 BCE. Archaeological Museum of Paros, 3524. *Source:* Drawing by Leah Lavelle, Urban Wild Studio.   *56*
4.2   Fighting over Patroklos' body. Attic Black-Figure *kalyx krater, c.* 530 BCE. National Museum, Athens, 26746. *Source:* Art Resource: alb1469481.   *58*
4.3   Archaic Greek hoplites about to engage. The Chigi Vase: proto-Corinthian *olpe, c.* 650–640 BCE, detail. Villa Giulia Museum, 22679. *Source:* Art Resource: ART79507.   *59*
4.4   Modern Greek fishing boat, Agios Nikolaos, Crete, summer 2017.   *69*
5.1   Olympian gods. Partially restored fragments of Attic Black-Figure neck amphora, Princeton Painter (?), *c.* 540 BCE, *Source:* Metropolitan Museum of Art, New York, 1991.11.2.   *74*
5.2   Zeus or Poseidon of Artemision. Bronze statue, *c.* 470–460 BCE. *Source:* Art Resource: 61981.   *75*
6.1   Achilles bandages Patroklos' upper arm. Rendering of Attic R-F *kylix tondo*, Sosias, *c.* 500 BCE. Berlin Antikensammlung F 2278. *Source:* Art Resource: AR922049.   *106*
7.1   Tetractys.   *122*
8.1   Dipylon Amphora. Dipylon Master, *c.* 750 BCE. *Source:* Art Resource: ART383136.   *128*
8.1a   Dipylon Amphora: detail: *Prothesis. Source:* Art Resource: ART531993.   *129*
8.2   Corinthian *olpe*, Sphinx Painter, 630–610 BCE. *Source:* Metropolitan Museum of Art, 96.18.38.   *130*

8.3   Nessos Amphora. Proto-Attic B-F amphora. Nessos Painter, *c.* 620 BCE National Museum, Athens 1002. *Source:* Art Resource: ART 98979.   *130*

8.3.a   Nessos Amphora: detail: Herakles and Nessos. Nessos Painter, 620 BCE National Museum, Athens 1002. *Source:* Art Resource: ART28240.   *131*

8.4   François Vase, Attic B-F volute krater. Kleitias, *c.* 570 BCE. *Source:* Florence Museum 4209. By permission of Florence Museum.   *132*

8.4a   François Vase: detail: Aias and Achilles. *Source:* Florence Museum 4209. By permission of Florence Museum.   *133*

8.5   Suicide of Aias, Attic B-F amphora, Exekias, *c.* 530 BCE. *Source:* Boulogne Museum AN 558. By kind permission of the Boulogne Museum.   *134*

8.6   Achilles and Penthesilea, Attic B-F amphora, Exekias, *c.* 530 BCE. *Source:* British Museum B 210. By permission of the British Museum.   *135*

8.7   Three Old Revelers, Attic R-F amphora. Euthymides, *c.* 510–500 BCE. *Source:* Munich Antikensammlungen 2307. By permission of the Munich Antikensammlungen.   *135*

8.8   Youthful Revelers, Attic R-F *skyphos*. Brygos Painter, *c.* 490–480 BCE. *Source:* Louvre G 156. By permission of the Louvre Museum.   *136*

8.9   Figure of a woman, ivory carving, Athens, *c.* 730 BCE, National Museum, Athens 776. *Source:* Art Resource: ART383141.   *137*

8.10   Mantiklos, bronze figure, Thebes, *c.* 700 BCE. *Source:* Boston Museum of Fine Arts 03.997. By permission of the Boston Museum of Fine Arts.   *138*

8.11   Cattle Raid of the *Dioskouroi*, metope, Sikyonian Treasury, Delphi, *c.* 560 BCE, Delphi Museum 1322. *Source:* Art Resource: ART424935.   *139*

8.12   Gigantomachy, relief sculpture, Siphnian Treasury, Delphi, North Ionic frieze, *c.* 530 BCE, Delphi Museum. *Source:* Art Resource: ART6437.   *140*

8.13   Herakles leaping on the Keryneian Hind, metope, Treasury of the Athenians, Delphi, *c.* 490 BCE, Delphi Museum. *Source:* Art Resource: ART392383.   *141*

8.14   New York *kouros*, marble statue, Attica, *c.* 590–580 BCE. *Source:* Metropolitan Museum of Arts, NYC, 32.11.1.   *142*

8.15   Kleobis and Biton, *kouroi*, marble statues. Delphi, *c.* 580–570 BCE, Delphi Museum 467, 1524. *Source:* Art Resource: orz107774.   *143*

8.16   Kroisos, *kouros*, marble statue. Anavysos, Attica, *c.* 530 BCE, National Museum, Athens 3851. *Source:* Art Resource: ART123355.   *144*

8.17   Aristodikos, *kouros*, marble statue, Athens, *c.* 500 BCE, National Museum, Athens 3938. *Source:* Art Resource: ART383176.   *144*

8.18   Kritios Boy, marble statue, Athens, *c.* 490–475 BCE. *Source:* Akropolis Museum, Athens 698. By permission of Akropolis Museum.   *145*

8.19   Nikandre, *kore*, marble statue, Delos, *c.* 640 BCE, National Museum, Athens 1, *Source:* Art Resource: ART383140.   *146*

8.20   Berlin *Kore*, marble statue, Attika, *c.* 570–560 BCE, Berlin Museum 1800. *Source:* Art Resource: ART71821.   *147*

8.21   Phrasikleia, *kore*, marble statue, Merenda, Attika *c.* 540 BCE, National Museum, Athens 4889. *Source:* Art Resource: ART535186.   *148*

8.22   *Kore* 674, marble statue, Akropolis, Athens, *c.* 510–500 BCE. *Source:* Akropolis Museum 674. By permission of the Akropolis Museum.   *148*

9.1   Woman playing a lyre. Attic R-F squat *lekythos*. *c.* 470 BCE. *Source:* Metropolitan Museum of Art, NYC, 41.162.169.   *153*

10.1   The *Altis* at Olympia: the Philippeion and Temple of Hera. *Source:* Author.   *181*

10.2   The *stadion* at Olympia. *Source:* Author.   *183*

10.3   Runners in a foot race. Attic B-F Panathenaic amphora, attributed to the Euphiletos Painter, *c.* 530 BCE. *Source:* Metropolitan Museum of Art, NYC, 14.130.12.   *184*

10.4   *Pankration*, Attic B-F *skyphos*, attributed to the Theseus Painter, *c.* 500 BCE. *Source:* Metropolitan Museum of Art, NYC, 06.1021.49.   *188*

10.5   Chariot-racing, Attic B-F Panathenaic amphora, attributed to Group of Copenhagen 99, *c.* 530 BCE. *Source:* Metropolitan Museum of Art, NYC, 56.171.5.   *189*

10.6   Delphi: Theatre and Temple of Apollo. *Source:* Author.   *192*

10.7   Panathenaic amphora, Attic B-F vase, attributed to the Princeton Painter, *c.* 550–540 BCE. *Source:* Metropolitan Museum of Art, NYC, 53.11.1.   *196*

12.1   Wedding procession, Attic B-F *lekythos*, attributed to the Amasis Painter, *c.* 550–530 BCE. *Source:* Metropolitan Museum of Art, NYC, 56.11.   *233*

12.2   Women at fountain house, Attic B-F *Hydria*, attributed to the class of Hamburg 1917.477, *c.* 510–500 BCE. *Source:* Metropolitan Museum of Art, NYC, 06.1021.77.   *236*

12.3   Youth playing a lyre, Attic Red-Figure *chous*, attributed to the Berlin Painter, *c.* 510–500 BCE. *Source:* Metropolitan Museum of Art, NYC, 22.139.32.   *237*

Preface

This aim of this book is to introduce students and interested others to the Archaic period of Greek history and civilization. It is an era when, after the relative dimness of the post-Mykenaian Dark Ages, *c.* 1150–750 BCE, the lights come blazing on again almost all at once. Archaic Greeks seem to be in action everywhere in the Mediterranean as well as at home: colonizing, trading, learning and adapting new and better things from older civilizations to the east; over-hauling institutions or developing new ones, challenging old beliefs and allegiances while accepting new ones; and moving rather boldly toward broader and deeper understanding of themselves and their world.

As a kind of primer, the book aims to stimulate and so to encourage students and others to probe the Archaic period more deeply and to come to grips with more of its primary evidence. A title like "Archaic Greece" might suggest the "whole story," but an "introduction" by definition can neither be all-encompassing nor exhaustively detailed. Economy imposes limitations on subject-matter and treatment. The goal in sight has always been a concentrated, yet agreeable compendium of essential evidence and careful interpretation that will engage students new to the period and stimulate a desire to go on to learn more about this fascinating, extremely significant period in ancient and world history.

Acknowledgments

For her kindness, acumen, and extraordinary patience throughout the lengthy process of producing this book, I thank above all Haze Humbert, Acquisitions Editor for John Wiley & Sons. I am very grateful to Deirdre Ilkson, who as early Contact Editor assisted greatly in the book's development by contributing many helpful comments. Thanks, too, to Allison Kostka, Jen Bray, and Denisha Sahadevan for their efforts and comments. Lastly, very deep and sincere thanks to Janani Govindankutty and Rajalakshmi Nadarajan who have helped so very much to see this book into print.

I am especially indebted to the anonymous readers of the draft manuscript, all but one of whom offered very valuable and constructive comments. That helpful advice was indispensable in crafting the revision of the initial manuscript. I also thank my colleague, Dr. Laura Gawlinski, Chair of the Department of Classical Studies, Loyola University Chicago, for advice and assistance at a critical juncture of production.

Finally, it would have been impossible to write this book without the love and support of, in particular, my beloved wife Nancy. There are no words sufficient to express my gratitude to or to approach description of the depths of my feelings for my closest friend, my dearest companion, and the love of my life.

Abbreviations and Citations

Unless otherwise specified, all fragments of Greek poetry derive from M.L. West, ed. *Iambi et Elegi Graeci, I and II* (Oxford, 1971). Other Greek texts derive from Oxford Greek editions. All translations are the author's.

CA	P. Rhodes, trans. [Aristotle]. *The Athenian Constitution* (London, 1984).
Campbell	D. Campbell, *Greek Lyric Poetry* (London, 1967).
CEG	P. Hansen, *Carmina Epigraphica Graeca* (Berlin, 1983, 1989).
D-K	W. Kranz, ed. H. Diehls, *Die Fragmente der Vorsokratiker*⁶ (Berlin, 1951).
Dillon & Garland	M. Dillon and L. Garland, *Ancient Greece: Social and Historial Documents from Archaic Times to the Death of Alexander*³ (London, 2010).
FrGrHist	F. Jacoby, ed. *Die Fragmente der Griechischen Historiker, I–IV* (Leiden, 1950–59).
Graham	D. Graham, ed. *The Texts of Early Greek Philosophy* (Cambridge, 2010).
IG	*Inscriptiones Graecae* (Berlin, 1924–).
M&L	R. Meiggs and D. Lewis, *A Selection of Greek Historical Inscriptions to the End of the Fifth Century B.C.* (Oxford, 1975).
Marm. Par.	F. Jacoby, ed. *Chronicum Parium* (Berlin, 1904).
Neer	R. Neer, *Greek Art and Archaeology: A New History, c. 2500–c. 150 BCE* (New York, 2012).
PMG	D. Page, ed. *Poetae Melici Graecae* (Oxford, 1962).
S&A	D. Page, *Sappho and Alcaeus* (Oxford, 1959).
SEG	*Supplementum Epigraphicum Graecum* (Leiden, 1923–).

Abbreviations and Citations

Maps

The Eastern Mediterranean

Neapolis

Thasos

Mt Olympos

Lemnos

Troy

Sigeion

Dodona

Kerkyra

Lesbos

Iolkos

Thessaly

Mytilene

Skyros

Chios

Phokaia

Thermopylai

Sardis

Abai

Euboia

Delphi

Smyrna

Chalkis

Boiotia

Eretria

Teos

Ithaka

Askra Thebes

Kolophon

Plataia

Marathon

Ephesos

Sikyon

Megara

Athens

Samos

Corinth

Isthmia

Mykale

Nemea

Salamis

Miletos

Olympia

Mykenai

Didyma

Argos

Keos

Hysiai

Delos

Halikarnassos

Messenia

Sparta

Paros

Naxos

Kos

Amorgos

Kythera

Rhodes

**GREECE and
the Aegean**

Crete

Dreros

Karphi

Gortyn

100 km

1

Sources for the Archaic Period

1.1 Introduction

The Archaic period (*c.* 750–480 BCE) is such an important one in the study of ancient Greece, it is unfortunate that there are no contemporary accounts available to tell us accurately and in detail what we would like to know about it. "History," "archaeology," and "anthropology," as we know them today, were quite beyond the conceptual grasp of Archaic Greeks. These were certainly interested in the past, who their ancestors were and what they did; they were engaged in their present and were quite conscious of the future. But they did not comprehend the need for carefully observing, evaluating, and then recording past events, details of their present conditions, or distinctive features of their culture for posterity as historians, social scientists, and others do today. As a consequence, we have relatively little solid information about the Archaic period.

The nature of the evidence available, which derives primarily from material remains and ancient literary sources, only adds to the difficulty of knowing about it. While such remains sometimes offer invaluable information, depending upon their condition, they can also be almost valueless. Literary sources that pertain to Archaic Greece are diverse in nature and content, often very problematic in themselves, and frequently date much later than the period. These sources range from the layered epics of Homer and the nuanced or allusive verses of Archaic lyric poets to the fifth-century BCE complexities of Herodotos' *Histories* and the sometimes baffling bricolage of Plutarch. Archaic historians must make sense of these sources, arranging disparate, difficult information into a coherency. What follows is a brief survey of the types of sources available for the Archaic period, what they provide, some of the problems attending them, and how they may be interpreted.

1.2 Archaeology and the Material Remains

Material remains provide the most credible evidence for a study of the Archaic period. These are usually discovered above ground, unearthed by excavation, or drawn up from the sea. If such remains are recoverable, in reasonable condition and in datable contexts, they can provide very useful, first-hand information. They might tell us, for example, where and how Archaic Greeks actually lived, including sometimes precisely what they ate and drank; possibly whom or what and how they worshipped; and perhaps even intimate details of their personal lives

Archaic Greece: The Age of New Reckonings, First Edition. Brian M. Lavelle.
© 2020 Brian M. Lavelle. Published 2020 by John Wiley & Sons Ltd.

among other things. Archaeology, the study which incorporates the recovery, description, cataloguing, and explication of material remains, has yielded indispensable information about Archaic Greece.

1.2.1 Pottery

The most abundant material remains for the Archaic period are pieces of pottery, ranging from whole objects to broken bits called shards. These may be found in many different contexts, for example, strewn over habitation sites, in concentrated dumps of broken pots, or mostly or even completely intact in such places as burials. Pottery can provide evidence about levels of technology and proficiency in craftsmanship as well as of artistic expression attained by potters and pottery-painters in their time. Vase paintings also tell us about what painters and their patrons were interested in, how they thought about those interests, and how they portrayed their conceptions. Archaic Greek painters frequently depict humans in vase paintings – sometimes in mythical scenes, sometimes in mundane ones. The distribution of Archaic Greek pottery from Spain to Syria and from southern Russia to North Africa attests to its attractiveness and desirability as a trade commodity. Black-Figure and Red-Figure pottery, produced primarily in Athens in the sixth century BCE, was so prized by the Etruscans, the ancient people who dwelt in modern-day Tuscany north of Rome, that they placed Attic painted pottery in tombs with their dead, presumably for the deceased to enjoy in the afterlife.

Perhaps the best example of Greek pottery as material evidence for the early Archaic period is the "Cup of Nestor" (Figure 1.1). It tells us about Greek colonials in their settlement in Italy around the mid-eighth century BCE (Box 1.1).

How do historians and archaeologists go about interpreting such a modest but intriguing piece of pottery? First, before moving and inspecting it more closely, they consider its context, both general and specific. Where in the burial is the object in relation to the boy's body? What could that spatial relationship mean? What else was in the grave? How is it to be dated? What might all of the things in the grave taken together and then separately tell us about the boy, his kin, and the burial? In such cases, archaeologists carefully measure and photograph the grave and its contents.

Then they thoroughly examine the individual piece. What is the cup's size, shape, material, color, decoration? How did it function exactly? Was it produced locally or imported? Are there any comparable pieces from elsewhere? The "Cup of Nestor" resembles pottery made on the island of Rhodes for the same period and, if produced on Rhodes, was obviously shipped to Ischia.

Ischia is not a large island and was not settled by Greeks for its fertility. Rather, valuable mineral deposits on the adjacent mainland controlled by the indigenous Italians there seem to have attracted the settlers. Obviously some of the Greeks at Pithekoussai, perhaps including the boy's family, were traders, established on Ischia exchanging goods for the metal ore of the mainland. A Rhodian cup implies that the Ischians traded with other Greeks as well as with the indigenous Italians around the Bay of Naples. Or perhaps the boy's kin were smiths who worked the Italian ore. Mounds of metal waste on Ischia suggest the presence of metal workers there. There were many such Greek colonies throughout the Mediterranean in the eighth century BCE functioning as transit trade locales. Pithekoussai tells us more about the nature of these.

Box 1.1 The "Cup of Nestor"

Figure 1.1 The "Cup of Nestor." Late Geometric *kotyle*, *c.* 750–740 BCE.

Nestor's I am, the easy-to-drink-from wine-cup:

whoever drinks from this cup will straightway
be taken over by a longing for beautifully crowned Aphrodite.[1]

The ***kotyle*** ("small, two-handled cup") was discovered at Pithekoussai on Ischia, an island lying just off the north coast of the Bay of Naples. Dated *c.* 750–740 BCE, the cup was found in the grave of a young boy, possibly the child of Greek parents dwelling there. The crudely made cup is by no means outstanding among other Greek pottery of its period, but its context and inscription, which suggest that it had special meaning to the child or his kin, are of considerable significance.

The inscription scratched into its surface in Greek letters announces that it is to be linked to a primary character in Homer's *Iliad*, the old warrior-mentor Nestor who counsels the younger Achaian kings at Troy. Nestor himself possessed a far more impressive drinking vessel (*Iliad* 11.632–637) than this crude little earthen cup. The inscription playfully departs from the epic lines it seems to reference by declaring that whoever drinks from it will become sexually aroused immediately.

The "Cup's" light-hearted inscription, which may have been scratched in on the island, implies that the Greeks inhabiting the island could read and perhaps write. They seem to have appreciated humor. The "Cup's" reference to Nestor bespeaks their familiarity with Homer's *Iliad* or, at least, the myth which gave rise to the Homeric passage about Nestor's drinking vessel. The "Cup" has in fact been used by some scholars to date the *Iliad*. While the inscription represents an attempt by an individual or group to establish a link to the old Trojan War hero, it seems to parody the Homeric passage irreverently drawing attention to drinking, sex, and music, the essential ingredients of the **symposion** ("male convivial drinking-together"). This crude little cup boasts that it actually outdoes Nestor's own golden one!

The "Cup of Nestor" also gives evidence of culture shared between the colonists and other Greeks of the time. Was it a cherished possession during the boy's lifetime? Or did someone older who valued it part with it as a last loving token for the dead boy? This humble little piece of pottery offers a wealth of information about very early Archaic Greek trade, literacy, and burial custom – and even provides a glimpse into personal feelings. It gives us further ground to speculate a bit about the culture shared by the Greeks of the mid-eighth century BCE.

Different pots or pottery pieces provide other types of evidence. A Proto-attic *loutrophoros* by the Analatos painter (*c.* 675 BCE) offers relatively little about Archaic Greek life or history for its period.[2] It does, however, help to chart a significant transition in pottery decoration from vases crammed with geometric decoration to ones adorned with depictions of human, floral, and animal motifs. Sphinxes, a piper and dancers, and charioteers driving chariots are distinctively presented on the vase in registers amid fillers of geometric design, painted in, around, and between the figures. The decoration on the vase looks backward to Geometric antecedents and forward to Black-Figure ware and its interests in human figures in action.

Steady progress in artistic expression in Archaic Greek vase paintings may be observed from the less sophisticated pieces of the very early seventh century BCE to the sublime Attic Red-Figure pottery produced through the late Archaic period. The latter is characterized by deft and expressive line-drawing detailing human and other figures, reserved against a black background. Archaic Greek pottery from datable contexts shows that pottery painters sought to render figures, activities, and actions in increasingly realistic ways through the period. Other Archaic Greek pottery may thus be placed in an evolutionary chart which sometimes enables even a minute fragment of painted pottery to be dated stylistically. Pottery pieces may be further analyzed in relation to other pottery from the same or even different contexts having the same or similar material, shape, paint, painted figures, or other designs. Thus, even a very small piece may provide just a bit more information about the Archaic Greeks.

Even pottery fragments discovered by surface surveying, though lacking context, can be useful. Types of pottery can date a site's habitation. Shards might inform us about the site's relative wealth or poverty. Pottery fabric might reveal if a pot was made locally or imported and thus whether and with whom the habitants traded. Its decoration might tell us about the abilities of the Greek artists and craftsmen of the time, but also about preferences of buyers.

1.2.2 Burials

The "Cup of Nestor" shows how just a single item from a single burial can provide important information about Greeks living in a colony late in the Geometric period. Graves themselves may provide a good deal of material data and not just because they often contain artifacts that have remained undisturbed since the time of the burial. Data may range from grave-types, including inhumation, entombment, or cremation, grave-numbers and their distribution, to the number and disposition of the dead interred in them. Grave goods might include anything from simple iron straight pins or small figurines of ivory imported from the Near East to whole bronze suits of armor. Many Archaic graves were marked above ground by pottery, painted or incised wood or marble *stelai* ("upright slabs"), or sculpture in stone, sometimes of monumental size. Graves can tell us much about the wealth and social standing of individuals and, by extension, the economy, culture, and beliefs of their communities.

In Athens, burials occurred in what became the market-assembly place of the *polis* ("settlement-center") until the eighth century BCE when they were moved outside it. Archaic Greeks did not live over or around burials, but rather interred their dead outside of their settlements. From this practice, scholars have concluded that Athens was a collection of villages until the eighth century, each village burying its dead outside its boundaries. When the villages coalesced into one *polis* and the settlement size increased, the burial grounds were moved beyond the enlarged *polis* area. That the number of graves in Athens multiplied in the eighth century BCE has led to an assumption about a rise in population then. That rise seems to be supported by an increase in the number of settlements in the countryside during the same period: presumably, the overflow population was moving into the Attic hinterland. But could the rise in the number of graves actually imply more deaths because of plague, famine, or some other type of crisis increasing mortality?

There are different ways of evaluating grave numbers. One hypothesis is that formal burial before the eighth century was the prerogative of elites by birth who had monopolized it to that time. Around 750 BCE, however, a substantial change occurred in the Greek world enabling others formerly not privileged to bury as the elites had. The appearance of more graves at the time has been linked to abruptly altered social and political circumstances or, more precisely, to the rise of the *polis* which is generally dated to right around this time. New political conditions disrupted the social order and empowered non-elites to bury as the elites had. Around 700, however, the latter seized back their ancient prerogatives at Athens at least and began to demonstrate wealth and power in ever more elaborate ways. These demonstrations involved especially above-ground funeral displays, which continued until they were curbed by Solon, *c.* 600.

The recent discovery of an extensive Archaic Age cemetery at Phaleron, Athens' old port, has provided a rich new source for information about Archaic Athens and Attika.[3]

1.2.3 Inscriptions

The "Cup of Nestor" has already introduced us to epigraphy, the study of inscriptions. Archaic Greek inscriptions, far less abundant than pottery or burials, are invaluable because they speak to us directly from the period. Writing can be inscribed on various surfaces, as the scratched-in letters on the "Cup of Nestor" show. Inscriptions carved in stone are more durable and usually more legible than scratched-in or painted ones. The oldest Greek legal inscription, that of the Law of Dreros (Figure 1.2) in eastern Crete, dates to the early Archaic period (Box 1.2).

The provenience of the Dreros inscription is noteworthy. It was not only displayed prominently in the *polis* center, but as part of a sacred building. Apollo was associated by ancient Greeks with law, and the Drerian law gained authority by being written into the wall of the god's "house." The prominent location of the inscription as part of the temple near the *agora* ("market-place/assembly-place") suggests that the limitations for Drerian officials were of great concern to the people of Dreros.

Box 1.2 The Law of Dreros[4]

Figure 1.2 The Law of Dreros. Rendering of schist inscription, *c.* 650–600 BCE.

> … The *polis* has resolved the following: when (a man) has been *kosmos*, the same man will not be *kosmos* again for ten years. If he does become *kosmos*, when he judges, he will owe double, and he will be useless [barred from office? without civic rights?], as long as he lives, and whatever he did as *kosmos* will be as nothing. The *kosmos* and the *damioi* and the twenty of the *polis* are swearers.

The inscription was carved into a block of schist set into the wall of the temple dedicated to Apollo some time in the last half of the seventh century BCE. Restrictions are imposed upon the **kosmos** ("arranger"), presumably the community's most significant official, who apparently also functioned as a judge. To become *kosmos* again before the ten-year limit had elapsed meant a heavy fine for the offender, a lifetime ban from office or loss of civic rights, it appears, and voiding of all his judgments. In addition to the (new?) *kosmos*, the **damioi** ("those of the people") and the "twenty of the *polis*" play a prominent part in ensuring the penalties.

Mention of the *polis* in the Drerian inscription provides evidence that that most crucial of Archaic Greek political institutions was functioning even in this relatively out-of-the-way place for some time before the law was inscribed. The word *polis* here applies to the collective identity of its inhabitants, the participant-overseers of the law are its articulated representatives. Although the precise meaning of the word *damioi* is unclear, it is surely rooted in **damos/demos** – "the people." The *kosmos*, the *damioi*, and "the twenty of the *polis*" appear to be the leading officials of the community: they have been identified respectively as one of the **aristoi** ("the best people, nobles"), representatives of the *demos*, and council members. That three governing entities will swear to the law implies a balance of power within the *polis*. If that is so, may we construe the Drerian law as an attempt to resolve political tensions between *aristoi* and *demos* by a sharing of power? Evidence from other literary sources – and the interpretation of burials at Athens offered above – support the assumption that such tensions were widespread in Archaic Greece around this time.

Publication of the law by inscription implies that the Drerian *demos* was able to read it. That implication is supported by the "Cup of Nestor," dated nearly a century earlier. Reading and perhaps writing in early Archaic Greece were not confined to class or status, but fairly widespread even by the later eighth century BCE. The articulation, inscription, and publication of the Drerian law checking the ambitions of aristocratic office-holders fit together with other evidence of laws being written down and published on behalf of the *demos* and limitations being imposed upon *aristoi* in other Greek *poleis* during the seventh century BCE.

1.2.4 Other Types of Material Evidence

Material evidence may range from small shards of unpainted, coarse-ware pots, which, as parts of intact vessels in their time, were used every day for drinking, cooking, or storing, to bits of bronze votives scattered, for example, over the ancient site of Olympia. It might include wooden dowel- and mortise-holes from sunken ships such as that discovered off Pabuç Burnu near ancient Halikarnassos (modern Bodrum), the pins and fibulae of Abai (near modern Kalapodi) in ancient Phokis, and the sparse remains of ever-enlarging sacred buildings all over the Greek world created during the Archaic period.

Archaic Greek temples resulted from the desires of Greek communities to construct "houses" for their deities. These were foci of common belief, but also shared identity. They illustrate the abilities of Archaic Greeks to conceive of the buildings as functioning edifices and permanent community symbols, to underwrite them financially, to plan and build them systematically, and so to cooperate in common cause over time for the betterment of the community. Constructing a temple, a source of collective pride for the community, helped to cement local and group identity.

1.2.5 Problems of Interpretation

For all that material remains might offer, archaeologists and historians must interpret them very carefully with their limitations fully in view. Such evidence is usually incapable by itself of telling us what we want to know about the Archaic Greeks. It certainly can be misunderstood or misconstrued. The "Cup of Nestor" informs us about the Greeks on Ischia *c.* 750 BCE, but what *exactly* does it say? Its provenience was the grave of a Greek child. Its type and inscription date it to around the mid-eighth century BCE and indicate that at least some Ischian Greeks could read and probably write. Whoever made the inscription knew the myth of Nestor and his apparently famous drinking vessel, they may have known the *Iliad*. However, the "Cup" cannot tell us anything more certain about the child, his parents, or the colony. It cannot explain precisely why it is of the type that it is or why it was buried with the boy. It cannot provide more precise information about what the Greeks actually did in that colony, where they came from, or what life was really like on Ischia for them.

Does the Law of Dreros actually typify conditions throughout Archaic Greece? What exactly was a *kosmos* in Archaic Crete? Was he really an *aristos*? Who precisely are the *damioi* and the "twenty of the *polis*"? What brought about this restriction on the *kosmos* and his political possibilities? Some scholars have taken the *damioi* to be financial supervisors, rather than "of the people," whereas the "twenty of the *polis*" have been understood as a representative group of the popular assembly of the town, a group from a town council, or the council itself. What actually produced the significant division of authority in the little mountain-top *polis* of Dreros?

Similarly, burials: interpreting patterns of burials can be highly speculative. Archaeological evidence has often been construed in light of theories or methodologies transferred from other newer archaeologies to ancient Greece. Are we justified in doing that or in attaching to the burials the significances that we do?

While we may carefully and reasonably extrapolate from an object or an inscription, set it in relation to other contemporary remains, and consider it from different angles, after all, the concrete conclusions that may be drawn from such evidence must ultimately be limited to the objects, their conditions, and their contexts. Incautious speculations, overly imaginative conjectures, or surmises that take us too far from the evidence are to be avoided. Though they may be datable to the Archaic period, scattered fragments of uninscribed or otherwise unpainted pots or portions of buildings, for example, frequently tell us no more than what they are when and as we see them. The effects of age and wear-and-tear on material objects from the ancient world can sometimes destroy them as evidence. Inscriptions carved into stone blocks have been lost because the stones have been repurposed and the writing worn beyond recognition. Caution and reason must always guide the interpretation of ancient material evidence. Similarly, the written evidence.

1.3   Literary Sources

Literary sources for the period pose several problems of interpretation. Archaic literature is mostly poetry, which, by its very nature, communicates more obliquely than directly. Poetry is governed by aesthetics, including meter and diction, more than fact; most Archaic Greek poetry was sung rather than spoken. Authors intended their poems to inform, educate, inspire, or entertain their audiences, but also to engage the aesthetic sensibilities, intellect, and emotion of their audiences sometimes in turn, sometimes, it appears, simultaneously. Every poem or fragment possesses its own individual complexities. Although, like archaeological evidence, Archaic Greek poetry is best placed and interpreted in context, preconceptions informed by modern literary and other theories and scholarly tendencies have influenced interpretation.

Archaic Greek poetry nevertheless contains information relating to society, politics, religion, and even the psychology of individuals and groups. Hesiod, who lived *c.* 700 BCE, tells of troubles with his brother Perses, about bad judges, and conditions affecting farmers in his poem *Works and Days*. Many of the extant poems and fragments of Solon, who lived about a century after Hesiod, center upon political turmoil at Athens, while the focus of interest for Archilochos, a Parian warrior of the early seventh century, is himself in his world. In the *Homeric Hymns*, many of which were composed during the Archaic period, we read invocations and appeals to the Olympian gods, as well as stories about them.

Not all Archaic literature is poetry. Some of the Ionian philosopher-scientists and ***logographoi*** ("chroniclers") of the Archaic period wrote prose, although Greek prose seems really to begin with the Greek historians of the fifth century BCE. Important oral traditions from the Archaic period kept by individuals or families emerge in Herodotos' *Histories*. However, whether the priests of Apollo at Delphi, noble Athenian families like the Alkmeonids, or the Greek "man in the marketplace," none of them was interested in historical objectivity more than in conveying their own thoughts, beliefs, and interests. The accounts of later Greek prose authors, some of whom, like Plutarch, provide considerable information about the Archaic period, are even more vexed because of the quality of sources used from the intervening years. That vexation is compounded by the ancient authors' own apparent inability to make distinctions between better and worse information written down before their times. Notwithstanding such contaminations, even much later sources can preserve precious bits of plausible information pertaining to Archaic Greece.

1.3.1 Archaic Greek Poets

The ancient Greeks attributed the *Iliad* and the *Odyssey* to Homer, an **aoidos** ("singer") of epic poems, believing his home to be either Smyrna (Izmir) in modern Turkey or just off its coast on the island of Chios. Scholars estimate that the *Iliad* and the *Odyssey* were composed some time between 750 and 650 BCE and were owed to an oral epic tradition that was rooted in the Bronze Age. Details such as the boars' tusk helmet, which were not used in Greece after the Mykenaians exist alongside descriptions of what seem to be fighting tactics contemporary with Homer's own time. According to ancient sources, the text of the *Iliad* was not written down before *c.* 525 BCE; in fact, what we have today of both epic poems is owed, in the first instance, primarily to the great Alexandrian scholar-editors of the third and second centuries BCE.

The *Iliad* concerns the anger of the great Greek hero, Achilles, and the destruction that it creates; the war at Troy is a backdrop to that story. The *Odyssey* is about the struggles of another hero, Odysseus, to return home from Troy at the war's end. Though the poems' contents span many centuries, both have an important bearing on the Archaic period, in no small part because of the values and social relations they depict. Competition, pride, and shame, the pursuit of **arete** ("excellence, virtue") and **kleos** ("fame, glory"), and obtaining and keeping higher status in the community motivate the Homeric heroes in the *Iliad* to risk death in battle. Such behaviors were grounded in persistent Greek social standards. The *Odyssey* ennobles the struggle of Odysseus to survive amidst many perils, using cunning, wit, audacity, and duplicity – an aim which the Archaic Greeks could well appreciate, though the means to achieve it are utterly rejected by such as Achilles. The Greeks themselves considered that the *Iliad* captured the Greek ethos so well that it became the cornerstone for the education of their youth through antiquity. The *Iliad* and the *Odyssey* also portray relations between men and women, older and younger, within families and outside of them, and between gods and humans, all of which reflect to some degree beliefs and conditions in Archaic Greece.

Hesiod composed the *Theogony*, literally meaning "the coming-into-being of the gods," and the *Works and Days*, both very different from the Homeric poems. In the latter, the poet attempts to instruct his brother Perses, but also a larger audience of contemporaries, about the virtues and benefits of hard work as well as the costs of idleness. He sings of justice and injustice and of such practical matters as farming. A large part of the *Works and Days* is about how to live and prosper in harmony with the seasons. Both poems, composed *c.*725–680 BCE, are pointedly instructive in nature, unlike the *Iliad* and *Odyssey*.

Lyric poetry, the hallmark literary genre of the Archaic period, is quite distinct from epic poetry in form and content. Archilochos (*c.* 665 BCE) is the first Greek author of whom we know to focus extensively on his own actions, thoughts, and emotions. A self-described "servant of the War-god" and one "who knows the Muses' lovely gift" (F 1), Archilochos refuses to sentimentalize the life of an Archaic warrior – the life he seems to have lived. His verse is sharp-edged and he sometimes castigates others, but he also speaks about his own errors. Archilochos is frank and very vivid when it comes to sex and **eros** ("sexual desire"). Laying bare his feelings about himself and others so candidly and humanly, he seems to be speaking to us almost as a modern poet would.

Archilochos was by no means the lone individual voice of Archaic Greece. Sappho of Lesbos (*c.* 600 BCE) was famous among the Greeks for her erotic poems. These often reflect a deep awareness of emotional and physical responses to *eros* produced by acute observation of herself and others. Archilochos and Sappho appear to have broken new ground in their emphases on personal emotion: both were self-analytical and candid and may well have been encouraged by changes affecting Archaic Greeks more generally in the seventh century.

Other lyric poets are less personal. The verses of Tyrtaios of Sparta (*c.* 650 BCE) are about war and warfare; in them, he tells Spartan men what they should do to fight better and so stop losing battles. In the early sixth century, Solon speaks extensively of **stasis** ("civil strife") at Athens and how people should behave to end it, whereas, in the later sixth century, Anakreon of Teos crafted charming apolitical diversions for his Greek tyrant patrons. A generation later, Pindar of Thebes lavished praise on tyrant-victors in Panhellenic contests, while his contemporary, Simonides of Keos, renowned for his prodigious memory, offered verses in a number of genres on a wide array of subjects, from lyric to epigram and from war to philosophy.

1.3.2 Prose Writers

Herodotos composed his *Histories c.* 450–420 BCE. His avowed purpose was to record and so commemorate past events and human achievements, including those of non-Greeks. In particular, he wanted to account for and memorialize the great Persian War, the cataclysmic event that marked the end of the Archaic period in Greece. Although Herodotos was only incidentally interested in the Archaic period, the *Histories* contain a good measure of information on the sixth century BCE especially. Yet, while some of what he writes is surely factual, it is largely based on various oral traditions kept by non-objective sources. As a result, although Herodotos was aware of the difference between myth and history to some degree, his best reporting on the past before his own time could be no better than what he was told by his "civilian" sources. Herodotos is really more of a storyteller – or rather a relayer of stories – especially when he recounts the events of times much before his own. His account of the Persian War, something that occurred in the not-too-distant past, is more solid by contrast.

The **Athenaion Politeia** ("Constitution of the Athenians") (*CA*) was attributed to the fourth-century BCE Greek philosopher Aristotle, but was likely composed by another, perhaps a student of his. Beginning in Athens' mythical prehistory, the work traces the *polis*' political development to the author's own time, *c.* 320 BCE. Much of what appears in the *CA* is based upon **Atthides** ("local chronicles of Athens"), compiled from the end of the fifth century. For information about Archaic Athens, like Herodotos, the *Atthides* depended largely upon Athenian oral traditions. While there is a good deal of myth and story in the *Atthides*, there is also plausibly factual content in them as well.

Finally, later Greek prose authors are much removed in time from Archaic Greece but nevertheless supply some useful information about it. Plutarch, who lived in the later first century CE, furnishes us with a biography of Solon, the Athenian lawgiver, in his *Lives of the Noble Greeks and Romans*. But while the biography is valuable in places and seems to preserve some facts about Solon in his time, it is literally awash with spurious content. The contamination includes embellishments, inferences, half-truths, and outright falsehoods, many of which derive from ancient authors of varying credibility who wrote about Solon between the lawgiver's lifetime and Plutarch's. As a result, Plutarch's *Life of Solon* is a complicated narrative of fact and fiction laced together without any real critical discretion. The *Life of Solon* also includes fragments of Solon's poetry, which most scholars have taken to be authentic and not unduly tampered with.[5] Other late sources, such as Diodoros of Sicily, Athenaios of Naukratis in Egypt, and the Byzantine lexicon, the *Suida*, among others, also provide information about the Archaic period based upon a variety of earlier prose and poetry sources. How shall we go about using these literary sources?

1.4 Managing the Muses

1.4.1 Evaluating and Deploying the Evidence

In the *Theogony* (1–35), Hesiod describes an encounter with the Muses on Mount Helikon near Askra as he was tending sheep. The Muses are the divine, very beautiful, maiden daughters of Zeus and Memory. After scoffing at the sordidness of humanity, the Muses tell Hesiod that it is in their power to tell many lies that seem like the truth, but also the truth itself, if they so choose. They present Hesiod with a staff of laurel and breathe a voice into him, enabling him to instruct others by telling them of things they could not possibly know otherwise. Hesiod then proceeds to recount the story of creation, how things came into being, including the gods, and how and why the Olympians came to rule the world.

The Muses' "gifts" and their capacity to tell truth or lies about the past provide a useful metaphor summing up the nature of evidence for Archaic Greece. There is both "truth" and "lies" in the evidence, some of it more obvious, some less so. How do we make distinctions and what criteria do we employ to sort things out? By what methodology do we accept or reject what has come down to us about the Archaic period so as to understand it better?

The sources we possess limit us and, at best, we may only hope to draw nearer to the truth of things. Though we may aspire to isolate what appears to be the real or factual, set it apart from obvious falsity, embellishment, or ambiguity, there are of course no guarantees that such isolation will result in veritable truth. As we have seen, interpreting archaeological data from the period has its pitfalls; Archaic literature is often more difficult to construe. Yet, Archaic Greeks did not seek purposefully to obscure their thoughts and meanings when they communicated them, but rather to convey the truth of things as they understood them to be true. A new "common sense" based on observation and experience, signs of which may be found in the quasi-science of Hesiod and Archilochos, stimulated Archaic Greeks to begin to distinguish more distinctly between truth and fiction. Early Greek science had strong practical ends, fundamentally united with which was the belief that knowing the truth of things could actually be profitable. While there were still no standards of objectivity among the Archaic Greeks to approach modern ones and selective inclusion, omission, and embellishment were embedded in their culture, affecting how they communicated and so much of the evidence we have, there is no good reason to think that what Archaic Greeks communicated was generally intended to be false or misleading.

So how do we begin to "manage the Muses," evaluate and deploy the evidence? First, the material record, especially what is datable, contextualized, and informative. Epigraphic documents stand high up on the list of material sources. As we have seen, the "Cup of Nestor" and the Law of Dreros are single examples that offer useful information about early Archaic Greeks in smaller communities in the Greek world. Other examples include the Nikandre inscription from Delos (*c.* 640 BCE), the law of Chios (600–575 BCE), the inscription from the gravestone of Phanodikos from Sigeion (*c.* 550 BCE), and the Athenian archon-list (527–521 BCE).[6]

Other archaeological material offers information of varying value. The fairly extensive Archaic remains at Delphi and the Samian Heraion are informative, but even a single set of limestone blocks datable to the Archaic period may provide something of importance. Because early Greek stone temples are mostly rectangular, even meager remains permit fairly precise reconstructions, sometimes as far as the entablature. Temples dedicated to Apollo *Delphinios* at Dreros and Apollo *Daphnephoros* at Eretria provide valuable evidence about early Archaic Greeks' sacred buildings. These, in turn, become "texts" that can shed more light on contemporary technology, religion, and aesthetics – and upon other, even less well-preserved edifices. The prototypes for the first large-scale stone statues of Archaic Greece, depicting human males and females, were Egyptian. The technology for making these will have come first to Ionia, the staging area for Archaic Greeks traveling to Egypt beginning in the mid-seventh century BCE. It is of course possible that the first Greek *kouroi* ("nude male youth statues") were actually worked from stone by Egyptians, not Greeks, and that other skills and technologies were imported into the Greek world by migrating non-Greeks.

How do we evaluate the literary evidence? Some is non-controversial and generally accepted as factual without question. For example, we read that Sparta underwent profound social and political change in the mid-seventh century BCE; that Greek lawgivers wrote down the laws for the first time in various Greek *poleis* around the same time; and that Lydia and Ionia were subjugated by the Persians in the mid-sixth century. That Sparta underwent such change appears to be reflected in the material record, which seems to diminish as Sparta became more militaristic, as well as in the contemporary poems of Tyrtaios. That law codes were written down in the seventh century is corroborated by the Law of Dreros and supported by various examples attested in literature as, for example, the law codes of Lykourgos of Sparta and Drakon of Athens. Finally, a Babylonian chronicle independently attests the Persian conquest of Lydia *c.* 547 BCE, thus complementing Greek ones about that event. These are given first place for credibility in the list of literary evidence.

Other more controversial information must be treated more carefully. Sources tell us that the profound changes affecting Sparta in the mid-seventh century came about because of wars with Messenia (plausible) and the journey of the Spartan lawgiver, Lykourgos, to Apollo's shrine at Delphi in central Greece (controversial). One source says that it was not clear if Lykourgos was a man or a god! As to the Persian conquest of Ionia, Herodotos declares that it was caused by an overly aggressive Kroisos of Lydia attacking the Persians simply because the Lydian had misinterpreted a Delphic oracle. Was that the real cause of the attack? It seems much likelier that these powerful empires were inevitably headed for collision and that the final clashes occurred for significant territorial and economic reasons.

Insights into Archaic Greek society and social values can derive from contemporary literary sources. For both Hesiod and Solon, *dike* ("justice") is all-important: both seek to educate their contemporaries about it, since they do not seem to know its true nature. But was justice as important a topic to their Archaic Greek contemporaries as it was to Solon and Hesiod? Semonides of Amorgos composed a notorious diatribe about women, but were his sentiments widespread? Are his verses to be taken completely seriously? Checks may be imposed upon such sources as Solon and Semonides based on other information from the period and even later. Greek tragic poets of the fifth century BCE, for example, seem very concerned with justice; Euripides seems keenly interested in gender issues. Such continuous discourse suggests that these subjects were of lasting interest to Archaic and Classical Greeks alike.

The evidence we have about the Archaic period in Greece when it is not partial or absent altogether can be further complicated by too concise, inexplicit, or otherwise obscure expressions. Notwithstanding, certain of it seems relatively secure and even allows us some reasonable reconstructions of the deficient parts. Although gaps will remain and prevent us from restoring the complete "tapestry," we may nonetheless endeavor to reconstruct by consciously observing the possibilities and limitations of what resources we have, by careful consideration of what they provide, and finally by scrupulous deployment of the evidence that results.

Notes

1 M&L 1.
2 Louvre *CA* 2985; cf. Neer, p. 107.
3 J. Lobell, "Ancient Athens' other cemetery: Excavations at Phaleron," *Archaeology* 71 (2018) pp. 48–53.
4 M&L 2; Dillon and Garland, pp. 31–32.
5 Some authors have questioned the authenticity of Solon's poems (e.g., A. Lardinois, "Have We Solon's Verses?" in J. Blok and A. Lardinois eds., *Solon of Athens: New Historical and Philological Perspectives* [Leiden, 2006], pp. 13–35), but offer little more than speculation as grounds for doubt.
6 For discussion of the Nikandre inscription, see Jeffery, p. 291; E. Bowie, "Epigram as Narration," in M. Baumbach, A. Petrovic, and I. Petrovic, eds. *Archaic and Classical Greek Epigrams* (Cambridge, 2010), pp. 339–340; see also Chapters 8.3.5 and 12.2.2 in this volume. On the Law from Chios, see E. Robinson, *The First Democracies: Early Popular Government Outside Athens* (*Historia Einzelschriften* 107) (Stuttgart, 1997), pp. 90–92; M&L 8; C. Fornara, *Translated Documents of Greece and Rome*, Vol. 1: *Archaic Times to the End of the Peloponnesian War* (Cambridge, 1983), p. 24. Phanodikos, see Jeffery, 366–367, 371; Fornara, 25. The Athenian archon list, see *IG* I³ 1031a; M&L 6; Fornara, pp. 27–28; Dillon & Garland, pp. 330–331.

Further Reading

Archaic Greece

J. Hall, *A History of the Archaic Greek World*² (Oxford, 2014).
R. Osborne, *Greece in the Making, 1200–479 BC*² (London, 2009).

Archaeological Evidence

J. Boardman, "The Material Culture of Archaic Greece," *The Cambridge Ancient History* III.1² (Cambridge, 1982), pp. 442–462.
J. Whitley, *The Archaeology of Ancient Greece* (Cambridge, 2001), pp. 77–268.

Methodology

J. Davies, "The Historiography of Archaic Greece," in K. Raaflaub and H. van Wees, eds. *A Companion to Archaic Greece* (Oxford, 2009), pp. 3–21.

On burial: I. Morris, *Burial and Ancient Society: The Rise of the Greek City-State* (Cambridge, 1987).

On the "Cup of Nestor": D. Ridgway, *The First Western Greeks* (Cambridge, 1992), pp. 55–57.

On the Law of Dreros: M. Gagarin, *Writing Greek Law* (Cambridge, 2008), pp. 45–49, 76–79.

Epigraphic Evidence

L. Jeffery, *The Local Scripts of Archaic Greece* (Oxford, 1990).

Literature

A. Dalby, "Homer's Enemies: Lyric and Epic in the Seventh Century," in N. Fisher and H. van Wees, eds. *Archaic Greece: New Approaches and New Evidence* (London, 1998), pp. 195–212.

2

A Brief Overview of the Archaic Period

2.1   Introduction

Scholarly consensus dates the Archaic period to between *c.* 700 and 480 BCE, but our study must begin somewhat earlier. Greeks were active in the eastern and western Mediterranean by the early eighth century BCE, trading with Syrians and Phoenicians at Al Mina and scouting sites for colonies in Sicily and southern Italy that were founded by mid-century. A Greek alphabet had been adapted from the Phoenician one, and reading and writing were fairly widespread among Greeks around the same time, as the "Cup of Nestor" attests. The *polis*, that distinctive regional, social, and political focus of Archaic and Classical Greece, was already functioning in many places, it seems. The first glimmerings of natural science are discernible in Hesiod's *Works and Days*, dated to the end of the eighth century BCE. Trade and colonization, literacy, political transformation, and science among other factors created new conditions that greatly impacted Archaic Greece.

Momentum for change increased in the seventh century BCE. A new style of massed fighting; social, economic, and political turbulence in many Greek *poleis* that led in some cases to tyrannies; the permanent opening of Egypt to the Greeks; and finally the appearance of actual science in Ionia altered Greek society fundamentally. Archilochos and Sappho convey personal realities in verses that differ dramatically from those of the epic poets before them. Greeks seem already to be thoroughly absorbed in what it is to be human. Vases decorated in the seventh century lose the densely packed designs of the Geometric period in favor of the bands of animals, floral motifs, and stylized humans of the Orientalizing period. The first large stone statues of humans appear in Greece after 650 BCE. By the end of the century, Ionian philosopher-scientists have begun to offer more objective hypotheses about the enigmas of the cosmos.

The sixth century BCE is an age of continuing social, economic, and political upheaval in the Greek world, but also one of cultural and intellectual advancement. Ionia, the headwaters of Greece's cultural and scientific rebirth, was repeatedly assailed by the Lydians and finally completely subjugated by the Persians. The shockwaves of the Persian conquest reverberated throughout the Greek world. Yet despite all of that destruction, displacement, fear, and apprehension, those such as the poet Anakreon, the philosophers Herakleitos and Pythagoras, and the mostly anonymous creators of statues and temples and pottery-painters of the period carried on pursuing their interests, honing their crafts, and producing monuments of thought and masterpieces of art and architecture. By the end of the Archaic period in the early fifth century BCE, the Greek world was in many ways a very different place from what it had been in 700 BCE.

2.2 The Environment and Greek Life

Two prominent aspects of the Aegean environment permanently affected the Greeks, their society and history. First, Greece consists of many islands; most of the mainland borders on or is proximate to the sea. Second, the mainland is sectioned by impressive mountain ranges, which, while partitioning the land, are traversable. These factors help to illustrate the geo-political paradoxes affecting Greece until its conquest by the Romans. While Greeks were regionally focused and identified themselves with where they dwelt, separated by land and water, they were by no means immobile, isolated, or detached from other Greeks. To the contrary, they were united by a common language, common values, customs, practices, and beliefs – and they moved around a lot. The forces of localism and regional differences, on the one hand, and commonalities of attitudes and culture, on the other, pulled the ancient Greeks in opposing directions throughout their history.

2.2.1 The Land and the Sea

From the earliest times through the Classical period, most Greeks were primarily small-holding farmers who lived in basic dwellings, worked the land, ate and drank mostly plain foods and liquids, and led simple, unadorned lives. Archaic Greeks' food consisted of grain, barley, and wheat, made into bread or cakes; olives, honey, figs, and nuts; beans and vegetables such as cucumber and celery; fruits like apples, pomegranates, and lemons; goat and lamb meat and cheeses; fish when they could get it; and wine. Archaic Greeks congregated in settlements of various sizes and walked to their lands when they did not dwell upon them. Typically, houses were constructed of mud brick or stone. Greeks traveled regularly to local market-sites, coming together to exchange produce for other goods. They congregated at places of common worship and political discussion in their home regions. Adventurous Greeks sailed overseas, joining other Greeks in colonies and trading sites throughout the Mediterranean and Black Sea regions. Archaic Greeks also traveled to attend Panhellenic festivals, such as those at Olympia and Delphi. When they fished, they did so in simple boats; when they voyaged to trade alone or with others, they did so in ships with sails and from two to 30 or even 50 oars.

Much of the soil of mainland Greece is poor and difficult to work. Except for large arable tracts in the Peloponnesos, central Greece, and Thessaly, and much smaller ones scattered here and there, the land requires intensive labor to make it productive (Figure 2.1). Ionia was very fertile, but Greeks there were hemmed in along a narrow strip of the coast by Lydians and Karians, their backs to the sea. In the *Works and Days*, Hesiod says that those who till the land must labor all day, every day, haunted by the relentless specters of poverty and hunger. Though impoverished, land remained the most highly prized and important commodity an Archaic Greek could possess. Initially, a farmer's share – and right to share – in his community and its affairs depended upon what land he held.

Figure 2.1 Central Greece landscape.

Weary farmers were forced by "grinding poverty" to find ways to supplement their incomes, and Hesiod implies that Greeks risked going to sea to trade because of the insufficiency of agriculture. A calm sea provided ready enough passage for short hopping from shore to shore: on a good day, the visible land lying opposite seems easily reached. But storms can come up at any time in the Aegean Sea, and sea travel in ancient times was always especially dangerous. Of course, many Greek communities were located right on the sea and, for islanders like Archilochos or Simonides, journeying by sea was unavoidable.

Piracy, the eternal concomitant of sea trade and sea travel in the Mediterranean, became a compelling occupation for Greeks desperate to acquire any kind of wealth. Thucydides (1.5) says that, in Homer's time, pirates were everywhere in Greece, and that what they did was so common and impressive that they were even respected by their countrymen. But piracy is, after all, a hit-or-miss affair, and real profits lay in regular contact and fair exchange with steady trading partners, as seems to have been the case with the Greek settlers on Ischia. Hesiod indicates the benefit of such trade when he encourages his brother Perses to "load a suitable cargo" onto a ship if he wants to profit (*Works and Days*, 631–632).

2.2.2 The Greeks and Others

Sustained trading contacts, especially with the Near East and Egypt, brought Greeks into the orbits of older civilizations, superior technologies, and better ways of living. Archaic Greeks in Egypt and Phoenicia encountered sophisticated metal and stone working, written law codes, and superior ship-building, among other technologies. They apparently "borrowed" the basics of new style weaponry from their Karian neighbors in Ionia, who had gotten them in turn from the Assyrians. The concept of "tyranny" came from the Lydians, but became uniquely Greek by adaptation. Greek mathematics, geometry, and even theology, all of which stimulated science and philosophy in Ionia, originated in the Near East and Egypt. One of the most obvious examples of eastern influence on the Greeks in the seventh century BCE is the Orientalizing style of vase painting characterized by lush registers of exotic animals or composite creatures and elaborate vegetal and floral designs.

Archaic Greeks were receptive to innovation, especially if it entailed practical advantage. Although encouraged by the hard life that Greek farmers led, their receptivity was also stimulated by Greece's position in the Mediterranean – in between the more advanced societies of the east and the rich resources of the west that easterners coveted. Beholden to those much older civilizations, the Greeks nevertheless adapted what they learned to suit their own purposes and tastes, putting their own uniquely Hellenic stamps on their "borrowings."

Notwithstanding contacts with other peoples, Archaic Greeks strongly distinguished themselves from non-Greeks. These distinctions are apparent in Homer, who first uses a compound of *barbaros* ("foreign/foreigner") to describe non-Greeks, and later in Herodotos who often polarizes "Greeks" and "non-Greeks" in terms of customs and values. This polarization was intensified by the conflict of Greeks and Persians in the early fifth century BCE. Athenians who considered themselves to be Ionians but also "sprung from the land itself" conceived that they were much different from the Dorians who had migrated into the Peloponnesos after the Bronze Age. The Dorians spoke a different Greek dialect from the Ionians and both spoke differently to the Aeolians.

Yet similarities and differences were not always so clear-cut. Though the Athenians worshipped essentially the same gods as the Dorians and Aeolians, they did so in their own distinctive ways. Dorians were actually barred from the temple of Athena on Athens' *akropolis* ("high settlement-center") *because* they were Dorians. Affinities, on the other hand, did not count for much, and wars were fought in the Archaic period over border lands with no regard to ethnicity. Spartans and Argives, both Dorians, were the bitterest of enemies. Dorians warred with Dorians, Ionians with Ionians. On the other hand, despite their differences, Greeks could participate in such alliances as the Delian *Amphiktyonia* ("league of neighbors"), centered on the cult of Artemis and Apollo on Delos, or the Delphic *Amphiktyonia* whose focus was Apollo's oracle at Delphi. Archaic Greeks, whether Dorian, Ionian, or Aeolian, came together peacefully for the Olympic, Isthmian, and Nemean festivals, all in the mostly Dorian Peloponnesos, to watch competitors from every region of the Greek world.

2.3 The Early Archaic Period

Our main literary sources for the early Archaic period are Homer and Hesiod. The tradition of the Homeric epic poems stretches back to the Bronze Age, but also possesses information up to the time of composition. Hesiod's *Works and Days* portrays conditions apparently affecting Greek farmers in his own time. The poem, which reads in some places like a farmer's almanac, is overcast by a tone of deep pessimism that seems to reflect the mood of contemporary Greek farmers: life is hard and the gods don't really help at all. Whereas Hesiod's poem depicts a hard agrarian world ruled by mostly indifferent, sometimes quite vengeful gods, it also describes some of the workings of the *polis* which supplement what little Homer tells us.

While the Mykenaians seem to have used the word *p(t)olis* to describe their strongholds, by the eighth century BCE, the *polis* was very different from what it had been in the Bronze Age. For Homer, the *polis* was the scene of significant community social, legal, and political interactivity; its *agora* was where the people assembled and important community decisions were made. Because of its growing political importance, the *polis* would become a theatre for *stasis* between factions in communities reacting to changing conditions. The Law of Dreros could be construed as sign of such reaction.

A substantial population increase is indicated in the material record for the eighth century which apparently stimulated unrest within *poleis* as well as colonization. One type of colonization was local. In Attika, for example, new sites appear in inland regions, implying to some scholars that settlers from crowded communities were "colonizing" formerly unused tracts in their home-regions. Overseas colonies also relieved overpopulation. Pithekoussai was among the first of many Greek colonies founded in Italy and Sicily. Euboians founded Kymai on the mainland adjacent to Ischia (*c.* 740 BCE), Corinthians Syrakusa in Sicily in 734 BCE, and Taras (Tarento) in south-eastern Italy was settled by Spartans *c.* 706 BCE. Populations were not necessarily restricted to colonists from mother-*poleis*, but could include Greeks from elsewhere.

The earliest presence of the Greeks in the eastern Mediterranean after the Bronze Age appears to have been Al Mina in south-eastern Turkey at the mouth of the Orontes River. The material remains of this **emporion** ("trading station") offer only an impression of more substantial trading ties that had developed between Greeks, Syrians, and Phoenicians by the end of the ninth century. It may have been at a place like Al Mina that the Greeks learned and adapted the Phoenician alphabet. On the other hand, could it be that Phoenicians themselves were responsible for introducing the Greek alphabet to the Greeks?[1]

2.4 The Seventh Century BCE: Expansion and Change

2.4.1 Colonies

Archilochos of Paros, a poet and warrior, was also a sailor, colonist, and traveler. In his verses, he mentions Siris in southern Italy, Gortyn on Crete, the islands of Lesbos and Euboia, and the shore of the Black Sea. He describes life on Thasos and fighting the Thracians on the mainland opposite the island. Archilochos' time in the north seems to have been miserable not only because he had been forced out of Paros but also because of constant warfare waged by Greeks against the savage Thracians. The poet paints a rather unhappy picture of his colonial experience. How typical of seventh-century Greek colonists was that experience?

Greek colonists journeyed far afield for wealth, even to dangerous places like Thrace. Procuring metals was a paramount aim, but the Parians and Thasians, who were after gold and silver on the Thracian mainland, had to fight to get it. Colonists wanted land to work as well. Greek settlers imported Greek laws, customs, and religious practices and sought to live their lives abroad approximating how they lived at home – at least initially. Change was inevitable, however, and, while Greek colonists kept their ties with their mother-*poleis*, for practical reasons, many Greek males married native women. Subsequent generations were affected by differences in practices and beliefs. Over time, colonists acquired their own identities which, in some cases, could be distinct from where they had come. Some, like the Spartan settlers of Taras in southern Italy, were permanently exiled from their home, while others could return to their mother-*poleis*.

Archilochos and his fellow Parians were Ionians. Ionia proper was a narrow strip of coastal land in the south-western part of modern Turkey. According to tradition, Athens dispatched colonists there at the end of the Bronze Age; their main Ionian colony was Miletos. During the Archaic period, Miletos became the principal *polis* of the Ionians, its chief market-town, a vigorous colonizer, and a powerful naval presence in the Mediterranean. It was the port of departure and return for Greek traders traveling the Anatolian coast, but also for Phoenicia and Egypt. It was the terminus of an important land route through Anatolia to the Aegean coast. Miletos owed its power to trade and colonization and so could resist the mainland Lydians as no other Ionian *polis* could.

A joint expedition of Greeks and Karians sailed to Egypt from Ionia in 664 BCE. Its achievements were profound. Greeks had never beheld such remarkably fertile land, impressive cities, or awe-inspiring architecture. When they returned, they brought back tales of Egypt's wonders, but also news of its science and technology. The first stone temples make their appearance in Greece after 650 BCE; among the Ionians, these become monumental. Temples in stone and the first large Greek stone statues, the *kouroi*, were copied from contemporary Egyptian prototypes. Any Greek male willing to fight for the pharaoh might travel to Egypt and enlist in the pharaoh's army as a mercenary. Archilochos seems to note that Karian-Ionian expedition (F 216) and may himself have become a mercenary soldier there. The Greeks in Egypt, soldier-traders really, journeyed back and forth from Greece, as others did from their colonies.

2.4.2   Law Codes

Law codes, which date to the second millennium BCE in the Near East, were rather late arriving in the Greek world. In Homer's time, trials were adjudicated by councils of judge-elders, presided over by a senior member, quite possibly a **basileus** ("king"). In the *Works and Days* (38–40), Hesiod alludes to a similar panel which decided the inheritance case involving his brother Perses and himself. These "gift-eating *basileis*" ruled in favor of Perses, quite unfairly in Hesiod's opinion, because they were bribable. Such injustices, undoubtedly repeated in other cases, will have prompted general demands for fairer judgments and immutable legal codes that deprived "gift-eaters" of their arbitrary powers.

In the seventh century BCE, many *poleis* delegated the writing-down of laws to lawgivers. One of these, Drakon of Athens (*c.* 622/621 BCE), specifies in his homicide law precisely what judges are to do. The code of Lykourgos of Sparta seems to have been formulated during the crisis of the Second Messenian War (*c.* 650 BCE) and became Sparta's Constitution. Pittakos of Mitylene on Lesbos, an "elected" tyrant, made laws for his fellow-citizens at the end of the seventh century. Law codes reined in the powers of rulers and judges, who had before been drawn traditionally from the *aristoi*, and so favored the non-aristocratic, such as Hesiod. Some scholars have detected distinct similarities between lawgivers and tyrants, both of whom seemed to have favored the *demos*.

2.4.3 Tyranny

The Greek word **tyrannos** ("tyrant") derived from Lydia where rulers were monarchs in the truest sense. Greek **tyrannis** ("tyranny, rule of one man") was different in that it usually resulted when an ambitious *aristos* prolonged an established office illegally, seized power by coup, or was essentially granted it. Tyrants often came to power with the consent of the *demos* and sometimes even the *aristoi*. But why would Archaic Greek **politai** ("citizens of a *polis*") who sought to limit the exercise of individual power as at Dreros consent to the rule of a single person?

In fact, many tyrannies came into being because of crises with which traditional *polis* leaders could not cope. Some tyrannies resulted from military or other emergencies, others arose from *stasis*. *Politai* supported strongmen who could solve crises. Prospects of peace, security, and material gain were more compelling than individual freedoms – at least temporarily. Tyrannies nevertheless disrupted traditional patterns of governance and established new political precedents rather abruptly. While Archaic Greek *tyrannis* was a transitory political phenomenon, its effects could be permanent – as they seemed to have been at Athens.

A new style of warfare, adopted by the Greeks from around the mid-eighth century BCE, may have further stimulated the rise of tyrannies. It was based upon the **hoplon** ("round shield"), spear, and sword; a warrior might also possess a heavy bronze helmet and body-armor. While such metal was expensive and only the wealthiest Greeks could afford a panoply, a full set of armor, even Greeks who possessed relatively little could acquire a *hoplon* and a jabbing spear and short sword. By the mid-seventh century, large numbers of adult Greek males were armed with the standard equipment of the Greek **hoplite** ("shield-warrior") through the Classical Period.

Concomitantly, the adoption of the **phalanx**, the massed formation of hoplites marching and attacking in unison, replaced individual melee fighting. Phalanx fighting is tactically superior, since as long as the phalanx remains coherent, adversaries fighting individually cannot withstand its massive onslaught. To survive the attacks of aggressive neighbors or others, Greeks were forced to adopt the hoplite phalanx and *poleis* to muster as many men into the formation as were available to fight. Every man who could wield a shield and spear was needed, regardless of economic or social status. The drilling and discipline that phalanx fighting required and battles that ensued muted distinctions of class and wealth and created a new cohesiveness centered on the formation, common cause and risk, and the *polis*. While the landless or very impoverished males of the community may have been excluded from hoplite ranks, those who possessed *hoplon* and spear now took their place in line next to the traditional fighters – and so in *polis* assemblies. Archaic Greeks recognized that those who put their lives on the line to defend the community should have a stake in public affairs. How could the old ruling and fighting elites justly deny these new warriors a share in *polis* governance?

2.5 The Sixth Century BCE: Conflict and Creation

2.5.1 The Kingdom of Lydia

The kingdom of Lydia, just to the east of Ionia, posed a constant threat to the Ionian Greeks from the time of Gyges, *c.* 685 BCE. The Lydians were famous horse-mounted warriors, who carved out a kingdom that ultimately encompassed all of Anatolia west of the Halys River (modern Kizilirmak). It was Gyges who began sustained attacks against the Ionian *poleis*, and these continued under his successors for over a century. The wealth and power of the Lydian kingdom, which impressed the Greeks as fabulous, were founded upon the gold that washed down from Mount Paktolos above the Lydian capital of Sardis.

Though Greeks considered them *barbaroi*, Lydian kings were attracted to Greek culture and, in particular, Greek oracles. Even while attacking the Greeks, Gyges was also placating the Greek gods, bestowing rich gifts of gold and silver, in particular, on Apollo at Delphi. His successors continued the donations, but, by far, the most impressively generous was Kroisos, the last and most fabled of the Lydian kings (*c.* 560–547 BCE).

The Greeks thought Kroisos so wealthy that he could part easily with vast amounts of gold. According to Herodotos (6.125.2–5), Kroisos allowed an Athenian named Alkmeon to take as much gold dust as he could carry from the king's treasure-room. The lucky fellow, rewarded for doing the king good service, proceeded to fill his pockets, the most capacious boots he could find, the folds of his tunic, to sprinkle his hair, and even to pack his mouth with gold dust. The sight of the misshapen man weighted down and waddling out of his treasury so delighted Kroisos that he doubled the amount of gold the man was carrying on the spot! Or so the Greek story went.

Kroisos' many gifts to Apollo were breathtaking even to later Greeks. Herodotos was overwhelmed by the Lydian gold and silver votives to be seen at Delphi in his time. Kroisos wanted to display his wealth, but he also seems to have genuinely believed in the credibility of Apollo's oracle. In fact, in Herodotos at least, Kroisos seems rather more Greek than barbarian. Of course, the Greek image of Kroisos says more about the Greeks than it does the historical Kroisos.

The Lydians presented an intriguing double standard to the Greeks. On the one hand, for all their hostile efforts to capture the Ionian *poleis*, they were sometimes friendly, certainly wealthy, and quite luxurious. Kroisos was admirable to the Archaic Greeks because his riches allowed him the freedom from the toil that they believed they could not escape. Lydian kings were capable of acquiring their hearts' desires, something that the Greeks imagined was available only to the gods. Kroisos, the richest man in the world, was envied as most blest by many.

Yet Archaic Greeks also believed that too much wealth could lead to a very bad end. Someone like Kroisos might think that he had it all and so somehow possessed immunity from what might befall him. For the Greeks, such a man was ripe for destruction because of his **hybris** ("arrogance, sin caused by arrogance"). Wealth and luxury, they believed, could overwhelm the senses and extinguish good judgment. Too much wealth also softened men, making them effete. And that is exactly how the Greeks explained the subsequent Persian subjugation of the Lydians: too rich, too decadent, too soft. Of course, it was an Archaic Greek, Solon of Athens, who vainly attempted to point out to Kroisos that being "blest" really meant ending one's life well rather than being supremely wealthy (Herodotos 1.32.5). Would all Archaic Greeks have thought the same?

2.5.2 The Empire of the Persians

Persia's heartland was the upland plateau of modern Iran. Persian armies overwhelmed their opponents by massed attacks of men armed with curved swords, wicker shields, and bows and arrows. They could field thousands of warriors for any battle.

The Persian Empire was built upon that of the Medes, their neighbors to whom the Persians were related and at first tributary. However, under their first king, Kyros, they rose up and subjugated the Medes. Kroisos feared the Persians' growing power and attacked them across the Halys River. The battle beyond the river was fought to a draw, but Kroisos' retreating army was followed back to Sardis by Kyros and the Persians. After a short siege, Sardis fell and Kroisos was taken prisoner.

The defeat of the Lydians brought the Persians to the shores of the Aegean and into contact with the Ionian Greeks. According to Herodotos (1.141.3), before the war, Kyros dispatched emissaries to the Ionian *poleis*, requesting those formerly allied to Kroisos to join with him. Blinded by Kroisos' visible wealth and power, the Ionians believed the odds favored the Lydian. Kroisos was philhellenic after all and had even contributed to the construction of the great temple of Artemis at Ephesos, whereas the Persians were truly *barbaroi*. The Milesians alone reached an accord with Kyros. After the capture of Sardis, Kyros' general, Harpagos, reduced the Ionian *poleis* to Persian rule one by one.

According to Thucydides (1.16), Ionia was on its way to "great things" when it was conquered by the Persians. Kroisos' defeat and Ionia's conquest were certainly shocks to the system. Rather than face Persian rule, however, many Ionians simply abandoned their homes. Herodotos says that about one half of the Phokaians (1.164–165) and all of the inhabitants of Teos (1.168) left their *polei*s in the face of Persian domination. Other *poleis* resisted, but were captured in turn until the entire Anatolian coast, Miletos excepted, was in Persian hands. The remaining Ionians became the ***douloi*** ("slaves") of the Persian "great king."

Xenophanes of Kolophon, a poet and philosopher, witnessed the Persian conquest and speaks of it in F 8. He was 25 years old when he left Kolophon and then 67 years "tossed about" in the Greek world, eventually settling in Elea in southern Italy. In another fragment he asks, "How old were you when the Mede (*sc.* Harpagos) came?"[2] The implication is that, like 9/11, Pearl Harbor, and other well-known dates aligned with collective traumas, the arrival of the "Mede" was an indelible catastrophe for Ionians, even as Thucydides implies. Xenophanes apparently could never go home again; Herodotos says that other Ionians simply resolved not to. Many refugees fled to Athens, their mother-*polis*.

Miletos' position and its precarious relationship to the major powers of the mainland, first Lydia, then Persia, fostered a culture of innovation born of necessity. Ingenuity appears to be a Milesian hallmark, as the ruse of the tyrant Thrasyboulos suggests (Herodotos 1.21–22). During a Lydian siege, Thrasyboulos tricked Alyattes, Kroisos' father, into thinking that Miletos was much stronger than it actually was and so it survived Alyattes' determined assault. Because Miletos of all Ionian *poleis* made a pact with the Persians, it survived again. But its luck ran out when Miletos chose to lead a rebellion of Ionian *poleis* from Persia in 499 BCE. It was a disastrous choice: when Miletos fell in 494, it was razed to the ground by the vengeful Persians.

Samos, the large island adjacent to the Mykale promontory of south-western Turkey, was Miletos' chief rival in the later Archaic period. It flourished *c.* 530 largely due to the tyrant Polykrates who had established sovereignty over much of the eastern Aegean with a powerful navy. The wealth and power of Samos even before Polykrates are attested by a succession of huge temples dedicated to Samian Hera beginning in the seventh century BCE. Unfortunately, we know so much less about Polykrates, the Samians, and the Ionians in general during the later Archaic period than we would like to. The brilliance of Ionia, which was dimmed by the Persian conquest and all but extinguished by the Ionian revolt, passed to Athens.

2.5.3   Greek Culture in the Sixth Century BCE

Though Archaic Ionian Greeks were traumatized by events in Anatolia, the sixth century BCE was a time of increasing cultural refinement. Imposing temples with ornate and intricate decoration and urbane poetry portray not only the sophistication of Ionian culture, but also the elevated tastes of broadening audiences. Artemis' temple at Ephesos, *c.* 550 BCE, was the largest ever built by Greeks and became one of the wonders of the ancient world.

Around the mid-sixth century BCE, however, cultural focus shifts to Athens. Attic painted pottery made high art available to mass audiences at home and abroad. The static decorative registers of later Orientalizing pottery were abandoned by the early sixth century in favor of figures and stories portrayed first in leaner Attic Black-Figure and then elegant Red-Figure style. Athens' beautifully painted pottery was only one facet of its great cultural leap forward from the mid-sixth century BCE.

Athens under its tyrants became a magnet for celebrated poets, whose verses differed from those of their predecessors. Their poems were self-consciously created: they were witty, elegant, and highly polished. Their authors intended them for select and sophisticated audiences like the Peisistratids who could appreciate the urbanity of their poetry – and reward them for their efforts. Anakreon and Simonides were retained as ornaments for the Peisistratid court. The tastes of the Athenian *demos*, whose refinement is evident in the complexities of the Attic tragedies of the fifth century BCE, were undoubtedly stimulated by these poets in residence and their poetry.

In spite of Athens' growing urbanity, Sparta's increasing isolationism, and the mercantile energies of the Corinthians and other *poleis*, rural Greece remained much the same as before, largely populated by the same type of farmers as Hesiod addresses in *Works and Days*. Many regions in mainland Greece underwent little apparent change during the Archaic period. Farmers continued to plow, to sow, and to reap in season, as they'd always done and would do. Greek *poleis* and regions evolved at different rates, some faster, some more slowly. Because of the nature of the evidence for the Archaic period, our focus must be fixed disproportionately on Athens and Sparta. But we must remember, too, that these were only two among many other Archaic Greek *poleis* about which we unfortunately know all too little.

2.6   The Early Fifth Century BCE: The Defeat of Persia

No greater cataclysm befell the Archaic Greeks than the Persian War of the early fifth century BCE. Dareios' lightning expedition to Marathon in 490 BCE was defeated by the Athenians and Plataians, but ten years later, the Persians came again. Quite contrary to expectation, the allied Greeks vanquished them, first by sea at Salamis (480 BCE), and then again on land at Plataia (479 BCE). Xerxes, the son of Dareios, who had accompanied his seemingly unstoppable forces to Greece, departed hastily after Salamis, rushing back to manage his now restive empire. After Plataia, the remnant of the Persian land force fled back to Asia overland the way they had come. Persian arms would never again threaten Greece. But though the invaders were expelled from Greece, they changed the Greeks forever. The harsh realities of the war and the opportunities presented in its aftermath ensured that change.

Much of mainland Greece was destroyed during the Persian advance, including Athens. The invaders respected neither man nor god during their invasion, razing temples as readily as houses, stealing what they could, destroying what they could not steal. Greece was left a desolation. But Athens and other *poleis* rose again by the will of their people. The end of hostilities on the mainland in 479 BCE marks the end of the Archaic period.

2.7 Sparta and Lakonia

Of Athens and Sparta, only the latter could be considered pre-eminent in the Archaic period. By the sixth century BCE, Sparta was wholly oriented toward war, its adult male citizens comprising a standing army. To ensure that army's superiority, every male Spartan was expected to train for war from childhood. That training produced the finest hoplites in Greece and, in fact, the Spartans were the main reason for the Persian defeat at Plataia. But how did Sparta become the renowned military society we know of today?

The Dorian ancestors of the Spartans were settled in the Eurotas valley between Mounts Taygetos and Parnon in the southern Peloponnesos by the mid-tenth century BCE. They may have come in two distinct groups: at least, they were ruled thereafter by two kings. Spartan expansion began in earnest in the eighth century BCE. Amyklai, perhaps a Bronze Age survivor-community just south of Sparta, was incorporated and the Spartans absorbed some of the culture and practices of the Amyklaians.[3] The festival called the *Hyakinthia*, centered upon the cult of Apollo Hyakinthos, became an element of Spartan state religion. A cult involving Menelaos and Helen was established by the eighth century BCE at Therapne, on an outcrop overlooking the Eurotas very near to what had been a Mykenaian villa.

After expanding down the valley, the Spartans turned toward Messenia, a broad and fertile land west of Mount Taygetos. When the long First Messenian War ended *c.* 720–710 BCE, the Spartans occupied all Messenia from Mount Ithome to the Messenian Gulf. The first subjugation was tenuous, however, and, when the Messenians revolted *c.* 680–670 BCE, the Spartans found themselves in a life-or-death struggle. After several losses to the Messenians and weakened by a major defeat at Hysiai north-east of Lakonia at the hands of the Argives, *c.* 669 BCE, Sparta was in desperate straits.

It was at this pass apparently that Spartan society changed and began to take the form famous in antiquity and today. Although new leadership was desperately needed for the crisis, the Spartans did not turn to tyranny or revolution. It was perhaps now that Lykourgos introduced the "Great **Rhetra** ("Covenant"), which he had obtained from Delphi. The *Rhetra* confirmed the kings in their power and a council of elders, but also that "power" was to belong to the "*damos*," that is the assembly of citizen-soldier equals. Lykourgos is said to have introduced other reforms, among them the profoundly altering institution of the **agoge** ("Spartan military training program").

At length, the Spartans defeated the Messenians, reducing them again to being **helots** ("serfs"). These worked the fertile land of Messenia to feed the Spartan "equals" and so free them up to train for war. The Second Messenian War was such a near-run thing, however, that the Spartans never forgot how closely they had come to ruin. They remained constantly fearful that such a threat might materialize again and that their beautiful land might be taken from them. The Spartans' utter dedication to war thenceforth led to repeated victories and, by the end of the sixth century BCE, domination of most of the Peloponnesos. It was Sparta's reputation for victory that made it the leader of the Greeks in the Persian War.

The sacrifice made at Thermopylai by Leonidas and his escort of three hundred Spartans cemented Sparta's reputation for valor and, simultaneously, created a sense of nation for the Greeks that transcended parochial boundaries. Though the Spartans did not really participate in the naval victory at Salamis, they were most responsible for the land victory at Plataia that sealed the Greek victory over the Persians. Sparta lacked ambitions outside of the Peloponnesos at this juncture and so kept to Lakonia, initially ceding to Athens the possibilities created by the Persian defeat and withdrawal from the Aegean and its eastern shore.

2.8 Athens and Attika

Athens was very different from Sparta, and the differences begin with location. While Sparta lies deep within the Peloponnesos, surrounded by mountains, Attika's position in central Greece is at a crossroads. The Attic peninsula stretches out toward the Cyclades; its eastern coast lies opposite the great island of Euboia. Western Attika is within sight of the Peloponnesos; its neighbors are Megara and Boiotia. Attika is naturally situated for movement to and through it both by land and by sea.

Unlike the Spartans who had migrated from north-central Greece, the Athenians prided themselves upon their autochthony and the fact that they had never been conquered by foreigners. Rather, they thought that Athens had become the staging point for Achaians heading east at the end of the Bronze Age. Athens' claim to being the mother of Ionian *poleis* was never denied by the Ionians, and the Athenians maintained strong ties of kinship with the Ionians through the Archaic and Classical periods.

Though there is material evidence of individual wealth at Athens before the Archaic period, the seventh century BCE appears to have been a regressive time for Athens. A long war with Megara begun *c.* 650 BCE may be most to blame. The lowest point in the war came when the Megarians occupied the Athenian *akropolis* with the help of Kylon, a traitor and would-be tyrant, *c.* 636 BCE. No invader had ever accomplished this before – at least according to Athenian mythology. The occupation produced a deep shock, but the ensuing slaughter of Kylon's followers amounted to sacrilege and only made matters worse. The war continued amidst internal crisis.

Though Drakon was authorized to codify laws for Athens *c.* 622/621 BCE and presumably to relieve the ongoing crisis, it fell to Solon to solve Athens' abiding political and economic problems (594–592 BCE). Solon grasped that concessions had to be made to the *demos*. He abolished debts and opened up the offices of the *polis* to those who qualified on the basis of wealth instead of aristocratic standing. An aristocrat at heart, however, Solon did not go far enough in the view of the *demos*.

Athens relapsed into *stasis* after Solon's laws were enacted and the Megarian War continued until Peisistratos, theretofore an obscure figure from eastern Attika, took over command of the Athenian war effort. He ended it in victory for Athens *c.* 565 BCE, then parlayed the popularity he had gained into a tyranny. By accepting Peisistratos and then his sons as tyrants, the Athenians lost self-determination, but gained a measure of peace and prosperity for over three decades from *c.* 546 BCE.

The Peisistratids were expelled from Athens in 511/510 BCE, and *stasis* ensued once more. Yet another lawgiver emerged dramatically to alter Athens' government. Kleisthenes conceded absolute political power to the *demos*: the ***ekklesia*** ("assembly") of all male *politai* was recognized as sovereign in all matters. What Kleisthenes achieved was the most radical political change of the Archaic period, one that had profound consequences. Athens became the first *polis* governed by ***demokratia*** ("rule of the people").

Although the Athenians won an exhilarating victory over the Persians at Marathon in 490 BCE, the *polis* was destroyed in 480 BCE. But because they had invested in ships and seapower after Marathon, the Athenians were able not only to preserve themselves by evacuating to Salamis, but also to play the decisive role in the defeat of the Persian fleet off the island. Victory over the Persians fostered a desire for retribution especially among the Greeks who had suffered during the invasion. Led by a vengeful Athens and at first encouraged by the Spartans who happily hung back in the Peloponnesos, Greeks swept into the void created by the contraction of Persian forces after the war. Ionia was liberated, and its *poleis*, as well as the islanders of the Aegean, joined a mutual defense league centered on Delos. Because of its massive plurality of ships, Athens attained a privileged position among the league-members, first as leader of the Delian alliance and then, rather rapidly, as outright hegemon. Athens' rise in the early fifth century BCE was directly due to its part in the Persian War and the opportunities that it seized afterwards. The Athenians came to rival the Spartans in the Classical period.

Athens, now very wealthy, attracted artists, scientists, poets, philosophers, teachers, and other thinkers and creators from all around Greece. Stimulated by innovation and subsidized by new money flowing in from its leadership of the Delian League *poleis*, the Athenians indulged their collective tastes, especially in public works. At length, the Athenians would construct the *Parthenon* in honor of Athena "the Maiden," the most beautiful of all Doric-style edifices. That building and the sculpture of the period which came to be called "classical" were blends of science and aesthetics – the flowering of inspiration owed to Archaic Greeks, to their cultural legacies, and to the increasing sophistication of the Athenians themselves.

Notes

1 Cf. S. Stockwell, "Before Athens: Early Popular Government in Phoenician and Greek City States," *Geopolitics, History, and International Relations* 2 (2010), pp. 123–135.
2 F 18 (Campbell).
3 Kennell (2010, p. 31) offers grounds to doubt the pre-Dorian nature of Amyklai.

Further Reading

Environment

C. Thomas, "The Mediterranean World in the Early Iron Age," in K. Raaflaub and H. van Wees, eds. *A Companion to Archaic Greece* (Oxford, 2009), pp. 22–40.

Eighth Century BCE

J. Crielaard, "Cities," in K. Raaflaub and H. van Wees, eds. *A Companion to Archaic Greece* (Oxford, 2009), pp. 349–372.

I. Morris, "The Eighth Century Revolution," in K. Raaflaub and H. van Wees, eds. *A Companion to Archaic Greece* (Oxford, 2009), pp. 64–80.

On the *polis*, J. Hall, "*Polis*, Community, and Ethnic Identity," in H. Shapiro, ed. *The Cambridge Companion to Archaic Greece* (Cambridge, 2007), pp. 40–60.

Colonization

C. Antonaccio, "Colonization: Greece on the Move, 900–480," in H. Shapiro, ed. *The Cambridge Companion to Archaic Greece* (Cambridge, 2007), pp. 201–224.

I. Malkin, "Foundations," in K. Raaflaub and H. van Wees, eds. *A Companion to Archaic Greece* (Oxford, 2009), pp. 373–394.

Greeks and Egypt

M. Austin, *Greece and Egypt in the Archaic Age* (Cambridge, 1970).

T. Braun, "The Greeks in Egypt," *Cambridge Ancient History*[2] III.3 (Cambridge, 1982), pp. 32–56.

Archaic Greek Law

R. Osborne, "Law and Laws: How Do We Join Up the Dots?" in L. Mitchell and P. Rhodes, eds. *The Development of the Polis in Archaic Greece* (London, 1997), pp. 74–82.

J. Whitley, "Literacy and Law-Making: The Case of Archaic Crete," in N. Fisher and H. van Wees, eds. *Archaic Greece: New Approaches and New Evidence* (London, 1998), pp. 311–331.

Archaic Tyranny

A. Andrewes, *Greek Tyrants* (New York, 1956).

E. Stein-Hölkeskamp, "The Tyrants," in K. Raaflaub and H. van Wees, eds. *A Companion to Archaic Greece* (Oxford, 2009), pp. 100–116.

Hoplite/Phalanx Warfare

P. Krentz, "Warfare and Hoplites," in H. Shapiro, ed. *The Cambridge Companion to Archaic Greece* (Cambridge, 2007), pp. 61–84.

H. van Wees, *Greek Warfare: Myths and Realities* (London, 2004), pp. 47–52.

Ionia

A. Greaves, *The Land of Ionia: Society and Economy in the Archaic Period* (Oxford, 2010).

G. Huxley, *The Early Ionians* (New York, 1966).

Miletos

V. Gorman, *Miletos, the Ornament of Ionia: A History of the City to 400 B.C.E.* (Ann Arbor, 2001) pp. 13–145.

A. Greaves, *Miletos: A History* (New York, 2002) pp. 74–130.

Sparta and Lakonia

N. Kennell, *Spartans. A New History* (London, 2010).
M. Nafissi, "Sparta," in K. Raaflaub and H. van Wees, eds. *A Companion to Archaic Greece* (Oxford, 2009), pp. 117–137.

Athens and Attika

S. Houby-Nielsen, "Attica: A View from the Sea," in K. Raaflaub and H. van Wees, eds. *A Companion to Archaic Greece* (Oxford, 2009), pp. 189–211.
M. Stahl and U. Walter, "Athens," in K. Raaflaub and H. van Wees, eds. *A Companion to Archaic Greece* (Oxford, 2009), pp. 138–161.

Demokratia

G. de St. Croix, *Athenian Democratic Origins: And Other Essays* (Oxford, 2004).
K. Raaflaub, J. Ober, and R. Wallace (with P. Cartledge and C. Farrar), *Origins of Democracy in Ancient Greece* (Berkeley, 2008).

Greeks and Persians

J. Wiesehöfer, "Greeks and Persians," in K. Raaflaub and H. van Wees, eds. *A Companion to Archaic Greece* (Oxford, 2009), pp. 162–185.

Brief Timeline for the Archaic Period

Date BCE	Event
c. 800–700	*Late Geometric (Proto-Archaic) Period*
c. 800	Euboian pottery at Al Mina (south-eastern Turkey); reading and writing throughout the Greek world
c. 776	Olympic Games: first recorded victor (Elis, Peloponnesos)
c. 775–750	Pithekoussai on Ischia settled (Bay of Naples)
c. 750–675	Homer's *Iliad* and *Odyssey* composed
c. 750–725	"Nestor's Cup" (Pithekoussai)
c. 740	Kymai founded (near Naples)
c. 740/730–720/710	First Messenian War: Spartans vs. Messenians
c. 733	Syrakusa founded (Sicily)
c. 725–680	Hesiod's *Theogony* and *Works and Days* composed
c. 700–600	*Earlier Archaic Period*
c. 685–652	Gyges rules Lydia (western Turkey)
c. 680/670	Second Messenian War begins: Sparta vs. Messenians
c. 669	Pheidon, tyrant of Argos (Peloponnesos); Battle of Hysiai: Argives defeat Spartans

c. 664/663	Greeks and Karians become mercenaries for Psammetichos, settle in Egypt in garrisons; Archilochos of Paros
c. 660–650?	Reforms of Lykourgos at Sparta
c. 650	Megarian War begins: Athenians vs. Megarians. Sparta triumphant in Messenian War
c. 650–600	Law of Dreros; stone temples appear in Greece
c. 650–499	Miletos prospers
c. 636 (or 632)	Kylon and partisans seize Athens' *akropolis*
c. 622/21	Law code of Drakon at Athens
c. 610–560	Alyattes rules Lydia, attacks Miletos
c. 600–479	*Later Archaic Period*
c. 600	Sappho of Lesbos
594–592	Solon of Athens institutes reforms
c. 560–547	Kroisos rules Lydia
c. 550	Sparta constitutes the Peloponnesian League
547/546	Persians conquer Lydia, most of Ionia; Peisistratids rule in Athens for 36 years
508/507	Kleisthenes introduces *demokratia* in Athens
499–494	Miletos leads Ionian revolt, but is destroyed by Persians (494)
490	Victory of Marathon (Attika): Athenians defeat Persians
481–479	Persian invasion of Greece
480	Thermopylai (Lokris): death of Leonidas and the 300. Salamis (Attika): Greek ships defeat Persian fleet
479	Plataia (Boiotia): Greeks led by Sparta defeat last Persian army
478/477	League of Delos established; Athens leads

3

Polis and Politics in Archaic Greece

3.1   Introduction

Greek communities appear to have been dominated by *basileis* or associations of *aristoi* through the Dark Ages (roughly 1150–750 BCE) and into the Archaic period. The emergence of the Archaic Greek *polis* in the eighth century BCE implies that Greeks had come together in some numbers in these settlement-centers and that new political and social conditions resulted. Certainly, by the early seventh century BCE there is evidence of growing dissatisfaction with the political status quo, resulting in tension and then changes in government in many places in the Greek world. The reasons seem clear enough: hereditary leaders, *basileis* and *aristoi*, were simply not up to coping with the evolving social, economic, and political conditions in Archaic Greek *poleis*. The stubborn entrenchment of the *aristoi* in their ages-old governing prerogatives didn't help matters. Of course, things were not the same everywhere in Greece: Sparta, for example, retained its kings, and governments in other places appear to have gone on not much differently from before.

3.2   Origins and Nature of the Early *Polis*

The *polis* is key to understanding the political lives of Archaic and Classical Greeks, but its precise nature has long been controversial. Its origins may be traced to the Bronze Age inasmuch as the Mykenaians seem to have used *p(t)olis* to describe their the citadel-palaces. An elite few dwelt in these stoutly walled castles, their status and power arranged in pyramid form from the **wanax** ("high king") at the top to minor officials and skilled workers. The regional population, the *damos*, dwelling outside the citadels on the lands around them, seem to have been at the very bottom of the pyramid.

Mykenaian citadels have been called "redistributive centers, into which commodities moved from territory to center in the form of taxes, obligatory donations, trade and gifts."[1] By "redistributive," we should understand flow and counter-flow of exchangeable goods, for in addition to being repositories, the Mykenaian *poleis* also possessed manufactories wherein artisans crafted objects of great skill and value. Markets presumably came into being for exchange outside the citadel-walls. The citadels were also cult places where rituals were overseen by high kings, and

Archaic Greece: The Age of New Reckonings, First Edition. Brian M. Lavelle.
© 2020 Brian M. Lavelle. Published 2020 by John Wiley & Sons Ltd.

political centers where laws were made and justice dispensed. If the Mykenaian citadels were not the direct progenitors of Archaic Greek *poleis*, they functioned in similar ways.

Agora is a word closely associated with *polis* in many Greek sources. While Mykenaian *a-ko-ra* seems to mean "flock, collection" or perhaps "gathering," Homer and Hesiod knew the *agora* to be a "market-place" and "assembly-place" for the *demos* and their leaders. Presumably Bronze Age *agorai* were designated spaces for trading, but also for gatherings that allowed the Mykenaian *demos* to come together with the citadel-elites on matters of secular or religious significance. At Athens, originally a Mykenaian site, the *agora* of the Archaic and Classical periods was outside the Bronze Age citadel of the *akropolis*. It was also where Archaic Athenians assembled for political and religious occasions.

In his description of the "*polis* of Peace" on the "Shield of Achilles" in the *Iliad*, Homer gives more information about *polis* and *agora* in his time (Box 3.1).

The most prominent feature of Homer's "*polis* of Peace" *is* its *agora*. Here political and legal events occur as the masses – also frequently called *demos* by Homer – assemble to hear pronouncements by judges on a homicide case. Seemingly, at no great distance from the *agora*, a celebratory wedding procession takes place.

In the *Odyssey* (6.262–269), Nausikaa describes the Phaiakian *polis* to Odysseus. Around it are lofty, towered walls approached by a narrow road. Oared ships are drawn up along that road. The *agora* is near Poseidon's precinct and paved with stones; there sailors and fishermen sort out their catches and cargoes after voyaging. Not every Greek *polis* was so near the sea and the Phaiakian one is something of a fantasy, in some ways hearkening to Mykenaian citadel-centers. But it was undoubtedly recognizable to Homer's contemporary audience and so does tell us more about early Archaic Greek *poleis*. The *agora* is outside the walls; Scheria's sailors put in to trade there.

Box 3.1 The *Polis* of Peace

On [the shield] he [*sc.* Hephaistos] made *poleis* of men who are gifted with speech, beautiful. In one [*polis*] …
The ***laoi*** ["masses"] of people were in the *agora* in a crowd. There, a quarrel had arisen: two men were contending for the sake of blood money for a man who had been killed. And the one vowed to give everything due, declaring it to the *demos*, but the other refused to take anything.
Both wanted a judge to make an end of it.
The masses shouted approval for both sides, there were advocates for both.
Heralds held back the masses; the judge-elders sat on polished stone-seats in the sacred circle holding the wands of the loud-voiced heralds in their hands.
With these they stood up smartly and in succession gave judgment.
There lay in the middle two talents of gold, to give to him who spoke out the straightest judgment among them.

(Homer, Iliad *18.490–491, 497–508*)

Homer's "*polis* of Peace" is both real and imagined: real in that Homer wanted his audience to see affinities between it and what they knew of *poleis* and activities in them; but unreal in that the *polis* is part of a divinely-wrought shield-decoration, its *agora* within the walls.

In the *Iliad*, the *agora* is also where community leaders speak to inform the *politai* assembled and gain consent for policy. Agamemnon addresses the Achaian army in the *agora* near the ships (*Iliad* 2.92–95), ostensibly to lay out his plan for the warriors' hearing and approval. Agamemnon cannot simply order the soldiers to do his bidding, but rather must persuade them with words. When he tries to incite the Greeks to fight harder against the Trojans by telling them that they are returning to Greece, his plan backfires: the war-weary Achaian warriors stampede for the ships. Only with the greatest difficulty can Agamemnon's captains reverse the tide, shepherding the men back to the assembly – again by persuasion, not by force. Of course, there is no true Greek *polis* at Troy, but there is an *agora* in which the masses of soldiers assemble to hear leaders and others speak and to decide.

Similarly in the *Odyssey* (2.7–10), the heralds summon the masses of Ithaka to the *agora* where Telemachos address them. However, before he begins, an old man named Aigyptios speaks out (Box 3.2).

Aigyptios specifies why the assembly would have been called: news of some army coming or "some other matter" affecting the community. He implies that, while a *basileus* usually summons an assembly, it can also be called when someone else has something important to say. It is thus not the *basileus*' sole privilege to summon and apprise the *demos* of what it needs to know. Significant community matters demand prompt attention and action, and Aigyptios blesses that man who informs the community about them. In Homer's world, common interests supersede even kingly prerogatives, and *politai* must consult and act together for the community's well-being. *Demos* and *basileus* are thus partnered for the good of the *polis*. We note that only adult males are present in the assemblies, apparently the rule for assembly-attendance generally in Archaic Greece.

During the near-disastrous assembly summoned by Agamemnon, Thersites also speaks out (*Iliad* 2.211 ff.). One of the common soldiers, he rises before the assembled Greeks and, with clear voice and blistering words, excoriates Agamemnon for wronging Achilles. Though Thersites suffers bodily injury for speaking out at the hands of the *basileus* Odysseus, he is no stranger to public address. Rather he is practiced at speaking – and accustomed to being allowed

---

Box 3.2 Aigyptios and the Homeric Assembly

Hear me now, you men of Ithaka, what I say.
Not once has our *agora* come about nor an assembly, since that time when godlike Odysseus sailed in the hollow ships.
But now who summons us? What urgency so moves one of the young men, or of those who are older?
Has he heard some message of an army coming that he might tell us of accurately, seeing that he heard of it earlier?
Or is it some other matter for the people he is telling or announcing?
This is an excellent man, I think, a blessed man.
May Zeus grant him a good thing, whatever abides in his heart!

(Homer, Odyssey, 2.25–34)

Aigyptios is permitted to speak in the assembly not merely because he is an elder or even because "he knew ten thousand things" (*Odyssey* 2.16), but rather because he is a member of the community, a *polites*, and has something of significance to say.

to speak – in such assemblies. When, at length, Odysseus' scepter came down hard upon his back, it was not because Thersites spoke out, but because he did so unconstructively and so, in the view of the assembly, uselessly. Thersites' own comrades-in-arms approve his chastisement because he has wasted the assembly's time. The *demos* apparently has the power to approve or disapprove of what it hears, just as it does listening to the judge-elders on the "Shield of Achilles."

In Homer's world, kings do not decide and then command nor do the people merely hear and obey. Aristocratic leaders formulate policy but must propose it to the *demos* for approval.[2] The *demos* must be persuaded to assent to the leaders' policies, even if, in the poet's time, it is denied the right to provide leaders from its own ranks. A common man may address the assembly and, like Thersites, speak until his speech is deemed useless. It is for community good that aristocrat or non-aristocrat speakers alike provide counsel. For Homer, a *polis* is a place of community, the *agora* a place of assembly where public affairs are conducted by the *politai*.[3]

3.3 Transformations of Leadership and Governance in the Archaic *Polis*

The Classical Greek *polis* was the focus of regional identity and interactivity. It was a locale for trade and commerce, festivals and religious worship, law and legal processes, and for the *politai* to gather to hear and decide about community-affecting issues in its *agora*. It was also a place of social concourse. Although *poleis* differed in size, situation, and physical circumstances throughout Greece, they were usually located either on or clustered around a higher defensible ground; those inhabiting the land around it, varying in extent and number, were its *politai*. (*Polis* is frequently modernly translated as "city" or "city-state," but the modern connotations of "city" and "city-state" render such translations misleading, even for the Classical period.[4])

Early Archaic *poleis* cannot have been much different from the Homeric ones before them. Some were on or very near what had been Mykenaian citadel-sites. Athens was one such and strongly tied to its Mykenaian past by myth and religious ritual. Athenians worshipped Athena "of the *polis*" whose Bronze Age cult was primary on the *akropolis* – the Mykenaian *polis*.[5] Other *polis*-sites such as Sparta and Corinth did not occupy former Mykenaian ones, it appears.

Archaic *poleis* seem to have resulted from the coalescences of smaller settlements. According to Thucydides (2.15.1–2), Athens' greatest hero, Theseus, created the *polis* in its prehistory by the **synoikesis** ("settling-together") of several Attic towns. While the Athenian festival of the founding of the *polis*, the **Synoikia**, was very old by the fifth century BCE, scholars now generally accept that such amalgamation occurred much later than the Bronze Age, perhaps even after the Dark Ages. As we have seen, there is support for Athens' *synoikesis* in the material record for the eighth century BCE. It was then, too, that the five villages of Sparta came together.

Archaic and Classical Greek *poleis* were fusions of place, identity, institutions, and politics. *Polis*-centric nationality derived from habitation proximate to the *polis* site, but also from shared efforts and activities centered on it. Common customs, rites, beliefs, practices – and experiences – reinforced that identity. While the Archaic *polis* may have been based on Bronze Age foundations, it was also reactive to changing social and political conditions and so evolved over time. It is unfortunate that we have so little information for the rest of Greece for *polis* formation, but Athens at least allows some further insight into the evolution.

What follows is based upon literary sources that date later than the Archaic period.

3.3.1 *Basileis* and *Aristoi*

By the end of the eighth century BCE, political power in many places in Greece had shifted from single leaders to *gene* ("clans"), such as the Bakhiadai of Corinth, or to confederations of aristocrats united by common interests. If, as it seems, Archaic *poleis* in Greece arose from smaller communities coalescing into larger ones during the eighth and seventh centuries, then it is likely that leaders of those smaller communities – the many local *basileis* of Homer's *Odyssey*, for instance – became the new *aristoi* of the larger *polis* entities. In so doing, they kept their local connections, but also achieved status and a share of power in the coalesced *polis*. These were achieved at the expense of the hereditary *basileis* of the *poleis* cores who were incapable of maintaining their monarchies in the enlarged *poleis*.

Further evidence for change to aristocratic governance in Dark Age *poleis* may be found in *CA* 3.3. King Akastos of Athens is said to have voluntarily laid down his kingship for a lifetime archonship. That any king would abdicate his ages-old prerogatives without pressure is unlikely. Life-time archonships at Athens gave way to ten-year elective archonships around the mid-eighth century BCE and annual archonships by 683/682 BCE.[6] The last, the archonship eponymous, became the most important political office in Archaic Athens, eclipsing that most ancient of Athenian offices, the archon *basileus* (*CA* 3.2). It seems also to have overshadowed that of the **polemarchos** ("war-leader"), an office invented during the Dark Ages to provide the war-leadership hereditary kings could no longer manage (*CA* 3.2). The **thesmothetai** ("law-establishers") were instituted in the seventh century BCE apparently to ensure that laws were observed (*CA* 3.5).

The last office complements other evidence of further political evolution in Archaic Greece. It is in keeping with the needed correctives implied by Hesiod's complaints that the *basileis*, as judge-elders for his community, were "bribe-eaters" who rendered "crooked" judgments. So, too, the later fragmentary Chian law of *c.* 575–550 BCE which mentions *basileis*, "guarding the *rhetra* for the *demos*," fines for misbehaving officials, "leaders of the *demos*," and a people's council which heard appeals – presumably involving "crooked" judgments delivered at existing lower courts.[7] Such limitations and guardian offices benefitted the *demos* by curbing or correcting aristocratic abuses. As we have seen, the contemporary Law of Dreros apparently did the same thing for similar reasons. Restrictions on the old prerogatives of the *aristoi* also benefitted those nobles who might have been excluded from a share of power and office-holding.

Changes in the governance structure at Athens occurred ostensibly as practical responses to ineffective leadership in view of evolving *polis* needs. Traditional offices were retained through the Classical period but lost most of their political significance. The archon *basileus* continued as a religious functionary, presiding over homicide trials involving blood-guilt and pollution. The archon eponymous became mostly honorific by the late sixth century BCE after the establishment of democracy.

The Council of the Areopagos at Athens was composed of former archons and elected officials. It convened on the "Hill of Ares," a bald rocky outcrop adjacent to Athens' *akropolis*, and functioned as a court and body advisory to serving archons. Lifetime membership of elected officials in the Council of the Areopagos provided honor and status for some, but not as many as wanted them. Elections inevitably encouraged rivalry, contentiousness, and *stasis* among the *aristoi* seeking the highest offices and honors. Yet these conditions also favored the people, since at least some *aristoi* understood that the *demos* constituted a significant political force and appealed to it for its support.

Archaic *poleis* possessed a **prytaneion** ("town-hall"), where holy fire, the very essence of the *polis*, burned upon a sacred hearth. The *prytaneion's* features are reminiscent of the Dark Age "chieftain's house" at Nichoria in Messenia, notable for its size, central location in the community, and large hearth. It appears to be where the *basileus* resided and may have ritually feasted with others.[8] The participation of the Athenian archon *basileus* in an ancient ritual mating near the *prytaneion* further implies that it was the residence of the Dark Age *basileus* (*CA* 3.5.).

In the Archaic period, the town-hall quartered the **prytaneis** – earlier, "lords," but from the Archaic period "presiders" or "leaders," who comprised colleges of *aristoi* apparently governing the *polis*. In Athens, the *prytaneion* became the headquarters for the archon eponymous who gave his name to his archon year; in Miletos, the annually elected *prytanis* was eponymous for the year. The Athenian *prytaneion* may have been the seat of **prytaneis ton naukraron** ("leaders of the ship-guild members"), community chiefs, it seems (Herodotos 5.71). Tyrants, too, resided in *prytaneia* in the Archaic period. In Miletos, according to Aristotle (*Politics* 5. 1305a, 19), a *prytanis* became tyrant.

Archaic associations of *aristoi* are described by the epic poets. The judge-elders of the "Shield of Achilles" and the *basileis* of Hesiod are peers, not underlings dominated by a *basileus* or a supreme *prytanis*.[9] Homer's judge-elders pronounce separately and independently in a "sacred circle," each speaking in turn holding a herald's wand. Hesiod also refers to the *basileis*-judges collectively. For whatever they may have claimed as birthright, their powers were delegated by their communities whose members sanctioned their decisions, as the *demos* does in Homer's "*polis* of Peace." Loss of credibility, trust, and so the authority of these evoked corrective responses, one of which, an Eretrian law from *c.* 525 BCE, strictly specifies that "the judge shall judge the penalty after he has taken an oath."[10] Similar conditions would seem to have produced the laws of Dreros and Chios and the institution of the Athenian *thesmothetai*, all of them involving stricter standards for governance, judging, and justice.

The rule of the aristocratic few was challenged in many places in Archaic Greece by non-aristocrats, but also by members of their own class who were willing to act apart from them in their own interests. In Megara, Theognis, an aristocratic Archaic poet, laments that the sway of *aristoi* had been weakened both by the advent of newcomers and by the willingness of "old blood" to mingle with new (193–196). Outlanders sought new status by intermarrying with amenable *aristoi*, to Theognis' great irritation (53–58). One of the earlier upstarts may have been Theagenes, who parlayed Megara's crises of the mid-seventh century BCE into a tyranny.[11] Some *poleis* continued to be ruled by "the few," however: Corinth reinstated oligarchy after a period of tyranny, while Sparta retained its dual monarchy for nearly all of its history. In other *poleis*, however, *aristoi* were very willing to break altogether with tradition and become tyrants – or, at least, to throw in with them.

Theognis was by no means alone in his outrage. Elsewhere the "well-born" were loath to concede to "the base-born," a disparagement they attached to the *demos*. Their disdain was hallmarked by arrogance, abusiveness, and sometimes even violence. The *demos*, for its part, looked to dissident *aristoi* who were willing to lead it. According to Solon, an *aristos* who seems to have done just that, politicians regularly addressed the Athenian *demos*, seeking to win favor by promising it gain. By the end of the seventh century BCE, political speeches aimed at persuading the assembled *demos* constituted an essential element of Athenian politics. Of course, as we have seen, assemblies of the *laos* and persuasive speeches in them were at least as old as Homer.

Political conflict triggered *stasis*. At Mitylene, the noble Penthilidai were opposed by other nobles: violence, murder, and tyranny resulted.[12] Much less is clear about the "Maidens' Sons," a pejoratively named group who were expelled from Sparta at the end of the eighth century

BCE and founded Taras in southern Italy.[13] At Miletos, wealthy and working-class factions clashed, suggesting economically based conflict. The result was the sovereignty of "the powerful," presumably the wealthy.[14]

We know most about Archaic period *stasis* at Athens from Solon's poems. Factions were arrayed along class and economic lines, *aristoi* and *demos*. An *aristos* himself, Solon appeared in a time of crisis, *c.* 600 BCE. Engaged in prolonged war with Megara, the *polis* was dominated by apparently inept aristocratic leaders, the poor weighed down by crippling indebtedness. Both sides turned to Solon to resolve the crisis. Though acknowledged as a righteous man, because he was a noble, Solon had to work hard to win over the *demos*. Many of his political poems seem to be addressed to the Athenians in assembly (Box 3.3).

Box 3.3 Solon and Political Crisis at Athens, *c.* 600 BCE

I know it and, within my soul, grief lays heavy,
  looking on that eldest land of Ionia
wasting …
                                    (F 4a)

You there, quell that unyielding heart in your breast,
  you who have pushed your way to excessive wealth,
moderate that haughty spirit. For neither will we
  obey you, nor will you have these matters as you want them.
                                    (F 4c)

So would the *demos* best heed its leaders.
  neither act too freely nor being forced too much:
excess breeds *hybris*, whenever too much wealth attends
  men whose minds are not straight.
                                    (F 6)

Each one of you alone walks in the fox's tracks,
  but all of you together have an empty mind:
For you look to the tongue and the word of a deceitful man
  but see nothing of what he does.
                                    (F 11, 5–8)

… As it is, you are all angry with me,
and glare at me with hateful looks as if I were an enemy.
You shouldn't. For the things I said (I'd do), by the gods I did …
                                    (F 34, 4–6)

On account of those things for which I brought together
the *demos*, from which of them did I leave off before it was done?
  … These things with authority,
harnessing might and right,
I acted upon and accomplished, just as I promised to do.
                                    (F 36, 1–2, 15–17)

In F 4a, Solon expresses sadness for what *stasis* has done to Athens. In F 4c, he attempts to win the *demos* by scolding the wealthy, distancing himself from them. But he also scolds the *demos* for falling under the spell of politicians who speak to it seductively (F 11). Solon implies that the Athenians are easily fooled by speakers. Solon's promises are implicit in his defense of what he had done – and not done. The *demos* was not buying it, however (Frs. 34, 36).

By the time of Solon's appearance on the political scene, politicians were already making false promises to the *demos*. But the tradition of deceit in public speaking was old by Solon's day: we remember that Agamemnon addressed the assembly of Greek warriors deceitfully, attempting to manipulate the *laos* by lying.

Solon's poems imply that the "old order" was trying to hold on to its prerogatives and disregard the *demos*' discontentment. Its apparent intransigence in the face of real crises afflicting the *polis* and misunderstanding of conditions and realities simply underscored its inability to adjust and govern effectively. These incapacities help to explain the decay of aristocratic power and prestige in the Archaic period. Solon was an unusual *aristos* whose sensibilities were not so hidebound – and he was not alone. There were others who understood that the real basis of political power in the changing *polis* was the *demos* and they aimed at securing its support for their own ends. For all his painstaking efforts, Solon's reforms failed. Not much later, Peisistratos made himself tyrant at Athens.

3.3.2 Archaic Greek Tyrants and Tyranny

Greek tyranny may be defined as monarchy established and maintained through extra-legal means. Tyrants' paths to power in the Archaic period were prepared in several ways: by economic, military, or other crises; by *stasis* which over time proved intolerable to the majority of *politai*; and, more generally, by the failure of existing governments to solve essential problems. Pheidon of Argos, said by Aristotle (*Politics* 1310b, 26–27) to have been a hereditary *basileus* who exchanged his kingship for *tyrannis*, was the first Archaic Greek tyrant of whom we know. On appearances, Pheidon was a military leader who may have defeated the Spartans in battle at Hysiai in Argive territory around 669 BCE. He then led the Argives to the conquest of the northern Peloponnesos, ending with the capture of Olympia and control of its prestigious games. Kypselos of Corinth, Theagenes of Megara, Pittakos of Mytilene, and Peisistratos of Athens all came to their tyrannies either during military crises or as war-heroes who had addressed the crises successfully.

There were other paths to power. Some tyrants were elected officials who simply prolonged their offices. Damasias of Athens held on to his archonship for two years and was expelled in the third year (*CA* 13.2). Phalaris of Akragas in Sicily parlayed his commission as temple-builder into a tyranny. Others such as Kleoboulos of Lindos on Rhodes and Tynnondas of Euboia were conceded tyrannies because of their wisdom. Some tyrants were handed tyranny, while others simply took it. Peisistratos' first tyranny came about when the *demos* voted him a bodyguard with which he seized the *akropolis*. Pittakos was also an "elected tyrant," a war-hero, and renowned for his intelligence. Tyrants were usually opposed by the *aristoi*, whose real power and prerogatives were nullified by them, even if traditional offices were continued. At Athens, the Peisistratids kept the old offices alive, but controlled them by "always taking care that one of their own men" was in them (Thucydides 6.54.6).

Tyrants did more than address crises, however. Pheidon reportedly introduced a system of weights and measures to the Peloponnesos, an innovation facilitating trade and so economic growth there. The first coined money circulated in Greece was also attributed to him. (Scholars have doubted both attributions.) Athens' first coins were apparently minted during Peisistratos' final tyranny. Tyrants also subsidized public buildings. Theagenes and Peisistratos provided fountain-houses for their *poleis*. Far less modest were the monumental edifices of Polykrates on Samos and the younger Peisistratids at Athens. Giant temples such as the Samian Heraion and the Athenian Olympeion were not just symbols of tyrannical power or vanity, but also work-projects for the employment of citizens. These monuments were meant to shore up popularity, but also perpetually to proclaim prosperity, god-favor, and so the tyrant's good fortune, the latter much envied by Archaic Greeks. Even the symbols on Peisistratos' small "heraldic" coins could remind those lucky enough to obtain one of them of his success.

The images of god-favor and wealth were important aspects of Archaic tyranny, and victories in contests at Olympia, Delphi, and elsewhere helped to prove that divine patronage was actual. Kylon based his bid for power at Athens in 636 BCE on the notion that his Olympic victory, gained through the gods' goodwill, would win the Athenians' support for a tyranny. They rejected him altogether, however, because he introduced Dorian Megarians onto the Athenian *akropoli*s. Another Athenian, Kimon won the chariot competition at Olympia three times running during the later sixth century BCE and was then slain apparently by the Peisistratids.[15] Such victories could kindle tyrannical ambitions, even as they had for Kylon, and the Peisistratids apparently feared that Kimon would try to capitalize on his truly extraordinary success. Tyrants could also add to their own prestige through the Panhellenic Games. Pheidon, Polykrates, the Peisistratids, and Kleisthenes of Sikyon controlled games outright, but victories burnished the "brand" best of all. Winning the Pythian chariot-race in games that Kleisthenes helped re-establish in 582 proved his good fortune and so helped to efface the stigma of his lowly birth.

At least some Archaic tyrants understood very well the benefits of further publicity. Polykrates, the Peisistratids, and the Thessalian Skopadai retained poets to sing their praises. Pindar was most famous for his odes of praise for tyrant-victors at the Panhellenic Games. The messages of such publicity were not only that the tyrant was "blest" and happy, but also that *politai* were very right to concede government to such as these who could benefit them.

The cost of tyranny to the populace was loss of political determination, and most tyrannies lasted no longer than two generations. When *politai* realized that they really were not being served by tyrants anymore, that tyrants' first allegiances were to themselves and their families after all (Thucydides 1.17.1), and that new government was necessary, tyrannies ended. What provided welcome security in crisis became oppressive when crises passed. Second-generation *tyrannoi* alienated *politai* even more since their behavior was especially influenced by flattery, arrogance, and paranoia about usurpers or assassins. Phalaris of Akragas seems to have become psychopathic. He won the reputation as the cruelest of tyrants for roasting enemies alive inside a hollow bronze bull under which his servants stoked fires (Pindar, *Pythian* 1, 95–96).[16] Other "bad" tyrants were Kypselos and Periandros of Corinth and Hippias of Athens.

Yet, the appraisal of Archaic tyrannies, even by later Greeks, remained ambiguous through the Classical period. Though Periandros and Pittakos were considered evil by some, they were numbered by others among the Seven Sages of Archaic Greece. Phalaris, the worst of all tyrants, was nevertheless remembered for constructing temples, walls, and a water supply for

Akragas – and even for his wisdom! The ambiguity seems to have arisen from conflicting sentiments. On the one hand, Archaic Greeks genuinely admired tyrants for their good fortune, power, and wealth. On the other hand, they observed that power and wealth could corrupt them and make them, in the worst cases, despotic and monstrously cruel.

The word "tyrant" acquired its decisively negative connotations at Athens really only after Hippias, the last Peisistratid, leagued with the Persians in the early fifth century and led them ashore at Marathon. The surviving Peisistratids were officially demonized by the Athenians, and "tyranny" was indelibly designated as democracy's arch-foe thereafter. Harmodios and Aristogeiton, assassins of Hipparchos, Hippias' brother, became democracy's institutionalized symbols. Statues of them were set up in Athens' *agora*, freezing them forever in the very act of assassination – and, the Athenians thought, liberation. Though Sicily remained a fertile ground for tyrants through the Classical period, the great age of tyranny on the Greek mainland, the islands and Ionia ended around the time of the Persian War.

3.3.3 Lawgivers and Law Codes

From the seventh century BCE, laws were written and displayed for the first time in many places in Greece: the earliest we know of is the Law of Dreros.[17] While that law's author is unknown, the philosopher Aristotle names several lawgivers from the Archaic period (*Politics* 1265b, 1273b–1274a). The biographies of Archaic Greek lawgivers were much embellished in antiquity, but their names, the timing of their law-giving, and their sheer number further support the impression of sea-change in Archaic Greek political life.

Aristotle cites Zaleukos of Lokris in Italy (*c.* 650 BCE) and Kharondas of Katana in Sicily (perhaps *c.* 525 BCE), both of whom were notable for setting precise penalties for offenses. Like the laws of Drakon, those of Zaleukos were famous for their severity. Another lawgiver, Philolaos of Corinth, journeyed to Thebes to write down laws for the Thebans, possibly at the end of the eighth century BCE. Aristotle says that Philolaos was concerned about adopted children and the number of estates in Theban territory, reacting apparently to multiple claims to the same land-holdings (*Politics* 1274b, 3–6). These lawgivers were empowered by their *poleis* to solve crises involving justice.

The two most renowned Archaic lawgivers to subsequent generations of Greeks were Lykourgos and Solon. Lykourgos is an elusive figure who is variously dated from the end of the eighth to the middle of the seventh century BCE. He reputedly delivered the so-called "Great *Rhetra*" to Sparta from Delphi after it was spoken to him by the oracle there (Box 3.4). Of course, much of the information we have about Lykourgos and Solon comes from much later in antiquity.

As we see, the original *Rhetra* explicitly favored the *damos* by affirming that it had "authority and power." Presumably, this affirmation was included to bolster the sagging morale of Spartan warriors after defeats in battles during the Second Messenian War. Yet, according to Plutarch, the assembly's "authority and power" were qualified by its inability to initiate proposals (Plutarch, *Lykourgos* 6.3), as well as by the Rider which gave the power to regulate assembly-meetings to kings and council. The gravity of King Theopompos, the victor in the First Messenian War, bolstered the Rider's authority, even if it was falsely ascribed to him later. Why the *damos* allowed the limitations remains unclear, but it may be that proposals were always made in assembly by the kings and elders and that the Rider simply spelled out what was implied by the

---

Box 3.4 The Great *Rhetra*

So enthusiastic was Lykourgos for this government that he brought back an oracle from Delphi concerning it which they call the "rhetra." It holds thusly:

"When a temple to Zeus Syllanios and Athena Syllania has been built, and you have designated the tribes and the villages [of Sparta] and have established the council of elders of thirty with the leaders [here "kings"], then from time to time hold an assembly between Babyka and Knakion and introduce and repeal. The *damos* has authority and power ...."

(Plutarch, Lykourgos *6.1–2)*[18]

"Rider" to the Great *Rhetra*

Later after the many had twisted and done violence to proposals with subtractions and additions, Kings Polydoros and Theopompos wrote this into the *Rhetra*:

"But if the *damos* chooses crookedness, then let the council of elders and the leaders (i.e., kings) dissolve the assembly ...."

(Plutarch, Lykourgos *6.4)*

---

oracle or tradition. As paraphrased by Tyrtaios (F 4), the original *Rhetra* seems to have bestowed assembly-primacy on the kings first, then the council of elders. (But why then would Plutarch have dated the qualifying Rider later?) Notwithstanding, **ephors** ("overseers"), established by the seventh century BCE in Sparta, began to monitor the kings and their actions, particularly from the mid-sixth century BCE. Yet, while the powers of the kings were diminished, they remained the most potent political leaders at Sparta.

The Spartan *agoge* was also attributed to Lykourgos. For this training, boys were taken from their mothers at age seven and assigned to bands led by older boys; at 14, they trained continuously and underwent extreme hardship, hardening them for war. Given only one cloak for the year and made to steal their food, they bathed in the frigid Eurotas River every day and slept outdoors every night until they reached 20 years. They then became full-fledged warriors, eligible for the common mess of Spartan soldiers, binding them to an adult male group. Personal desires were abandoned for the greater good of the army and the *polis*: Spartan warriors became units in Sparta's defense, shedding their individuality for the benefit of the collective. The Spartan army became the dominant institution of the *polis* from the mid-seventh century BCE; Sparta, the strongest military power in Greece from the mid-sixth century BCE. The *agoge* transformed Spartans into the finest warriors in ancient Greece, but the military system also suppressed freedoms and bases of political, social, and cultural change and evolution. Could the *agoge* and the Rider, both of which took freedoms away, be somehow linked? Lykourgos remains a shadowy figure whose very existence is open to doubt. Indeed, after promulgating his reforms, Lykourgos was said to have vanished. Whatever he may have actually done as lawgiver or even whether he existed are not as important though as the measures credited to him which re-made Sparta.

Things were quite different at Athens. As we have seen, the Athenian institution of the *thesmothetai* and term-limitations on offices are in the same spirit as the Law of Dreros. In 622/621

BCE, Drakon was chosen to formulate a law code for Athens, spelling out crimes and punishments. *Stasis* had ensued after Kylon failed to establish a tyranny, and action was needed to restore order. Drakon's remedies were very harsh: in his code, it was said that death was decreed for almost every offense. While only Drakon's homicide laws are now considered authentically his own, that he imposed a kind of martial law on the Athenians at the time is reasonable enough to imagine. *Stasis* and crises continued nonetheless and further measures were needed.

Solon was elected archon for 594/593 BCE, then designated lawgiver for 593/592 BCE. He immediately revised Drakon's code. He abolished debt obligations in what was called the "shaking off of burdens." Solon then freed the land for the so-called "sixth-parters," tenant-farmers who surrendered one-sixth of what they produced as an annual tithe to wealthy landlords. Solon also provided for the repatriation of Athenians sold as slaves who had made their own bodies sureties for debts they had incurred. Such enslavement was banned thereafter.

Solon then reorganized the Athenian *politai* into property classes, making the top two classes eligible for the highest offices. Now any Athenian included in the wealth-categories of "five hundred bushel men" or "horsemen" could hold office. The "yoke men" might hold minor offices, but not major ones; **thetes** ("landless, impoverished citizens") could not stand for office at all, but presumably could vote and speak in the assembly, even as Thersites had done centuries before. Solon's abolition of the property-qualifications for office formally ended the aristocratic monopoly of Athenian government. It was fundamentally a democratic reform.

Solon was said to have authored a very detailed set of laws, to have established a council of four hundred and a court of law – all democratic in nature. In fact, both of the latter measures have been doubted as inauthentic. Solon's sumptuary laws and other social legislation, detailed in Plutarch's *Life of Solon*, have also been called into question.[19]

Solon's reforms, although dramatic and far-reaching, apparently satisfied no one at Athens. The *aristoi* concluded that he had gone too far, while the *demos* decided that he had not gone far enough. Solon refused to grant the *demos* the wealth it desired by redistributing the land, asserting that what he had given it was quite enough. Solon then quit Athens to get away from pestering, recrimination, and squabbling on both sides. He was in any case no longer viable as a politician because he now had really no base of support among either the *aristoi* or the *demos*.

3.4 *Demokratia*

3.4.1 Background

Stasis followed Solon's departure. Conditions were worsened by a renewal of the war with Megara which went badly for Athens. Damasias, otherwise unknown, attempted to take and hold tyrannical power in 582 BCE, but failed. According to Herodotos (1.59.3), two political parties then dominated Athenian politics: the "men of the plain," presumably the *aristoi*, and the "men of the shore," apparently the *demos*. Neither faction could win out over the other.

Peisistratos, an unknown from eastern Attika, made a name for himself, first, as a warrior in the Megarian War. At length, becoming **strategos** ("war-leader"), he ended the conflict victoriously for Athens by capturing Megara's main port of Nisaia. The victory earned Peisistratos great popularity among the Athenians. Unlike Solon, who refused to be a tyrant,

Peisistratos took power with the *demos'* consent in 561/560 BCE, shortly after the Megarian War ended. According to Herodotos, he had established his own faction, "the men of the beyond-the-hills." Notwithstanding, the other faction-leaders were potent enough to oust Peisistratos once and once again from the tyranny. After nearly a decade in exile, Peisistratos returned to Athens in 547/546 BCE. With money in hand and allied warriors at his back, he easily overcame the Athenians arrayed against him and then "rooted" his tyranny. The tyranny lasted through his sons until 511/510 BCE.

Peisistratos established a monarchy in fact, but he and his sons attempted to cloak their actual power by maintaining the traditional offices and government. Officials like the *thesmothetai* and archons eponymous continued to be elected, though the old offices were now inconsequential. The Peisistratids manipulated the elections, making sure that their partisans were the ones elected into the offices. The formula worked well enough for most of the tyranny: some of the *aristoi* apparently wanted to hold office more than oppose the tyranny.

What really undergirded the tyranny at Athens were opportunities presented by Peisistratos and his heirs to the Athenians for acquiring wealth – what the *demos* most wanted, according to Solon. Schooled by the failures of Solon and other Athenian politicians before him, Peisistratos grasped the fact that continuous rule required the continuous consent of the *demos.* For that, a steady stream of enrichment possibilities was required. Whether through works-projects like temple- or monument-construction, colonies in the region of the Thracian Chersonesos, or other patronage, including bribery, the Peisistratids offered the Athenians what Solon and others could not or would not. Peisistratos' model for controlling the *demos* worked and became an example for other Athenian politicians, even after the tyranny was abolished. One of these, Kleisthenes, an aristocratic collaborator with the Peisistratids, also understood that political leadership at Athens required the *demos'* support and so endowed it formally with more political power than it had ever had before.

3.4.2 Kleisthenes and His Reforms

Kleisthenes' forebears, the Alkmeonids, held the offices at Athens when Kylon attempted his coup. Whether as archons or *prytaneis ton naukraron*, the Alkmeonids thwarted the plot, slaughtering some of Kylon's followers in the process. They were subsequently "accursed" because of that slaughter. Though expelled from Athens "forever," the Alkmeonids returned and re-established themselves so successfully that Megakles, Kleisthenes' father, became the leader of the "party of the shore," apparently, the *demos.* The Alkmeonids assumed this leadership quite possibly because, as the "accursed," they were no longer welcome among the *aristoi* and the *demos* was somehow more tolerant. At all events, the Alkmeonids well understood that the *demos* was key to political power, that it was led by promises, and that leadership was kept by making good on those promises. Peisistratos actually seems to have learned from them.

While Peisistratos may have exiled some of the Alkmeonids after his return, resilient as ever, they returned yet again. Kleisthenes insinuated himself so ably into the good graces of Peisistratos' sons that he was designated archon eponymous for 525/524 BCE. By then, he had become one of the tyrants' "own men." Kleisthenes witnessed the success of the Peisistratids, who in turn informed his own ideas of politics. When later the Alkmeonids fell out with Hippias and Hipparchos and were exiled yet again, they managed to ally with the Spartans. Returning to Athens with the Spartans, they ousted the last of the Peisistratids in 510 BCE. Though Kleisthenes was not strong enough to overcome his new rival Isagoras immediately, he trumped his opponent at length by taking the *demos* into partnership in government (Box 3.5).

Kleisthenes' democratic reforms were unprecedented. He bypassed traditional institutions by inventing new ones. His ten new artificial tribes disconnected *politai* from the original tribes and from the geography of Attika associated with them. Tribes were associations of *gene* which were themselves made up of **oikoi** ("households"). Each Kleisthenic tribe consisted of "thirds," one from each of the new Attic geographic divisions of "coast," "inland," and "*polis*." The tribes became the military divisions of the new Athenian army, each one having its own *strategos*. Elected by tribes annually, the *strategoi* were in some ways reminiscent of the old *basileis*, but also of the councils of *aristoi*, since altogether they formed a new college of elected associates. Kleisthenes also constituted a new **boule** ("council") of five hundred members to supersede the aristocratic Areopagos Council. Fifty from each of the ten new tribes were selected by lot to serve every year. The *boule*'s main function was to consider legislation and to set the agendas for the assemblies. Kleisthenes made the *ekklesia* sovereign in all political matters affecting Athens – the most democratic of all his reforms. Every adult male citizen of Athens could speak out in the assembly and could vote, and those of a certain age could be elected *strategoi*.

Political power was now directly in the hands of the adult male *politai* of Athens: birth and wealth were, technically, of no consequence. Kleisthenes was surely attempting to attach the politically potent *demos* to himself as its patron, but he strangely vanishes from Athenian history not long after his reforms. It could be argued that the Archaic period really ends with Kleisthenes' reforms, since these represent a very distinct break from what had existed before.

Box 3.5 Kleisthenes and *Demokratia*

… Worsted [by Isagoras], Kleisthenes made the *demos* his political companions. Afterwards, he made the existing four tribes, named for the sons of Ion, Geleon, Aigikores, Argades and Hoples, into ten. He invented names for them from other local heroes, except for Aias. Him, he added, though a foreigner because he was a neighbor and ally.

(Herodotos 5.66.2)

So when he had added to his own portion the *demos* of the Athenians, which before had been pushed away, he changed the tribes' names and made more than before. He made ten tribe-leaders in place of four and apportioned *demes* by ten to the tribes. And so arranging the *demos*, he was much superior to his opponents.

(Herodotos 5.69.2)

According to Herodotos, Kleisthenes empowered the *demos* politically for his own purposes, and we need not doubt it. What he created was something transcendent of his intentions, however. Once established, Athenian democracy took root and continued uninterrupted for a century.

What Kleisthenes created – direct democracy – whatever his motivations and howsoever it might be viewed as the result of Athens' political evolution, changed everything in Athens and in Greece.

3.5 The Evolution of Politics and Government in Archaic Greece: A Summary

The *polis* was a place, but, as a locale informing identity through political discussion and interaction between leaders and communities, it was also an idea. The roots of the *polis* extend to the Bronze Age and Mykenaian citadel-palaces, but the interdependency of leaders and followers through the Dark Ages is far more consequential for the development of the Archaic *polis*. Homer is a valuable source for the later Geometric and early Archaic periods. Leaders generally summoned the community to political assembly in the *agora* where they would listen to and speak about issues that affected all in common. Adult males seemed to have attended the assembly. Anyone could speak, provided he did so constructively and sensibly in the view of others assembled.

Archaeological evidence indicates significant changes in Archaic Greece in the eighth century. As populations grew, new lands were settled in Greece and colonies dispatched overseas. At the same time, smaller communities coalesced into larger ones and their *basileis* – or the leaders who had arisen in the smaller communities in the Dark Ages – and their descendants now associated with others in the amalgamated *poleis* to become governing *aristoi*. It is these who seem best identified with the "judge-elders" of Homer and the "bribe-eating *basileis*" of Hesiod. Assemblies of the *politai* voted on candidates, presumably ratifying without much discussion or questioning the candidates nominated by these colleges of *aristoi*.

From what Hesiod tells us in the *Works and Days*, however, by the beginning of the seventh century BCE, discontent with aristocratic governance was already present. Greed leading to the perversion of justice, arrogance in the face of community outcry about such abuses, and general disregard for the welfare of the community led to regulation in the form of term limits on offices, written laws published for all to see, read, and understand, and new offices to "guard the laws." The publication of laws was aimed primarily at removing the possibility of "crooked" interpretations by the privileged few and to prevent injustice by specifying exactly what crimes merited what punishments. Such curbs on the powers of the *aristoi* favored the *demos* and prove its political weight even in the early Archaic period. During the seventh and sixth centuries BCE, the Athenian *demos* was made increasingly aware of its power by *aristoi* willing to break ranks with others to further their own ambitions. Presumably, similar conditions obtained in other *poleis*.

Some Archaic Greek communities did not undergo such fundamental political change. Though the prerogatives of the Spartan kings were curbed by the council of the elders and the *ephors*, the dyarchy retained primary political power through the Classical period. Thought by the ancient Greeks to be the most conservative – but also the most stable and best governed – of Greek *poleis*, Sparta did not change its government after the Lykourgan reforms most likely because of its constricting military system and narrowed political aims. Other Greek communities kept their traditional polities into the Classical period and even beyond. *Polis*, *polis* governments, and politics in Archaic Greece were by no means uniform.

Yet, whatever the nature of *polis* governments in the Archaic period, Greeks assembled in *poleis* for political, religious, and social occasions.

Tyrannies first appear in Archaic Greece in the early seventh century BCE in Argos, then subsequently in Corinth and Megara, Miletos, Lesbos, Sikyon, Samos, and Athens, as well as in many Greek colonies in Sicily and on the Italian mainland. Tyrants or would-be tyrants were often aristocratic in background. The crises that encouraged their ambitions were frequently military or political in nature. Tyrants won popularity for their abilities to solve crises and so the consent of the *demos* to govern. Not a few tyrants drew attention to their good fortune, some even invoking connections to the Homeric heroes. Tyrants were of course nothing like such heroes and lost their popularity when, in the eyes of the populace, the crises had passed, the sheen of success wore off, and tyrants or their offspring were no longer needed. When tyrants fell into disfavor, tyrannies were dissolved and new governance sought or old ways revived. Though a transitory phenomenon in Archaic Greece, tyrannies weakened the influence and authority of the *aristoi* in politics.

In crisis at the end of the seventh century BCE and riven by *stasis*, Athens only temporarily averted tyranny when Solon was chosen leader of the *polis*. Solon had to gain approval from the Athenians before he could implement reforms. When he completed his commission to re-write the laws, even though his reforms were drastic in some ways, he satisfied neither the *aristoi* nor the *demos*. What the Athenian *demos* really wanted was wealth, but it was left to Peisistratos to discover ways to obtain it for them.

By all accounts, Peisistratos was an accomplished speaker and employed his skills as others had before him to persuade the *demos* to his purposes. His persuasion necessarily included promises of enrichment. Ancient sources agree that Peisistratos and his successors did not upset the existing polity of Athens, but rather manipulated it. Peisistratid tyranny provided a formula for politicians thereafter to follow: cultivate and capture the demos, and political power will follow. Stiff-necked *aristoi* at Athens, who continued to stand on ancient prerogatives and resist adaptation, were effectively sidelined.

Kleisthenes, seeking after his own ends, fully empowered the *demos* and so took the ultimate step in the evolution of politics at Athens. As we have seen, since the time of Homer and perhaps well before that, leaders required the consent of the *demos*. When Kleisthenes "took the *demos* into partnership" and made the assembly sovereign in all political matters, he completed the process, so establishing the first real democracy in history.

3.6   Politics and the Archaic Greek Farmer

The Archaic Greek *polites* was an adult male. He typically worked a small plot of land in the countryside outside of the *polis*, struggling perpetually as Hesiod says, against "wretched poverty." Summoned to the *agora* for an *ekklesia*, he traveled most likely by foot to his region's political, religious, and economic center. In some cases, it took perhaps most of the day to get there. Arriving at the *agora* at the appointed time, he might hear one or a number of speakers on various subjects affecting his community and himself. These could be noble or base, rich or poor, but in general, the Archaic assembly belonged to the *aristoi*, whom he and other commoners probably considered their "betters" – at least earlier on. He would speak with other *politai* like himself, neighbors and even those who lived more distantly. If there was an emergency such as war, the assembly would be brief: the questions were, shall we go to war and how shall we wage it? If yes, the *polites* went home to prepare, fetching weapons and armor (if he had it) and returning with speed to take his place with his *gene* and tribe. If he knew that war was already in the offing, he might come already prepared. If there were elections or discussions of domestic issues, he would listen and then assent or dissent when decisions were needed. He or his descendants realized at some point – and for a variety of obvious reasons – that the *aristoi* who had dominated the assembly were really not their "betters." They may then have clamored for change. At Athens, at Dreros, at Chios, and elsewhere, *politai* got change; in other places in Greece, they did not. Unless the issues were of considerable importance, the farmer would probably return home as quickly as he could to renew his struggle with the soil. The growing resident populations of *poleis* with their expanding mixtures of traders, artisans, craftsmen, and the landless would be increasingly responsible for changes that occurred there during the Archaic and Classical periods. For the Archaic Greek farmer, only exceptional issues like war or what affected him directly were of concern. The rest were probably of little interest and anyway were time-consuming. Let the townsfolk waste their time talking. An Archaic Greek farmer's most important relationship was with the land.

Notes

1. Shelmerdine and Bennet (2008, p. 291).
2. Hammer (2002, pp. 146–147 and 155 ff.) applies the term "plebiscitary politics."
3. The evolution toward democracy in Greece, which seems to have begun in the Dark Ages if not in the Bronze Age, does not lend itself to the notion that Greek democracy was excessively or predominantly influenced by the Near East: cf. Stockwell (Chapter 2, note 1) 123–135. Then again, Archaic Greeks were not unaware of governments and institutions of non-Greeks (e.g., tyranny).
4. M.H. Hansen, "The Copenhagen Inventory of Poleis," in Mitchell and Rhodes, pp. 9–10.
5. Thucydides 2.15.6.
6. Ten years: *CA* 3.1; Paus. 4.5.10; one year: Paus. 4.15.1.
7. M&L 8; Dillon & Garland, 32; and L.H. Jeffery, "The Courts of Justice in Archaic Chios," *ABSA* 51 (1956) pp. 157–167.
8. C. Thomas and C. Conant, *Citadel to City-State: The Transformation of Greece, 1200–700 B.C.E.* (Bloomington, 1999) pp. 38–41.
9. See also *Odyssey* 8.390–391.
10. F. Cairns, "The 'Laws of Eretria' (IG XII. 9 1273 and 1274): Epigraphic, Legal, Historical, and Political Aspects," *Phoenix* 45 (1991) p. 313.
11. Theognis' poems seem to mention Theagenes, the seventh-century BCE Megarian tyrant, but ancient writers date the poet to the mid-sixth century BCE.
12. A.J. Podlecki, *The Early Greek Poets and their Times* (Vancouver, 1984), pp. 64 ff.
13. Kennell, (Chapter 2, bibliography) p. 36, doubts the "Maidens' Sons" story.
14. Plutarch *Moralia* 298c (= *Quaestiones Graecae* 32). Gorman, (Chapter 2, bibliography) p. 108 ff.
15. Herodotos 6.103.2–3.
16. Diodoros Sikulos 9.19.1.
17. The Pythion laws of Gortyn dating to the Archaic period are fragmentary: cf. P. Perlman, "Gortyn: The First Seven Hundred Years. Part II: The Laws from the Temple of Apollo Pythios,"

in T. H. Neilsen, ed. *Even More Studies in the Ancient Greek Polis* (Stuttgart, 2002), pp. 187–188.

18 B. Perrin, *Plutarch. Lycurgus*. See http://www.perseus.tufts.edu/hopper/text?doc=Perseus:text:2008.01.0131.

19 The Solonian "sumptuary laws" may have been invented or greatly embellished by a later writer or politician, perhaps Demetrios of Phaleron in the fourth century BCE, and falsely ascribed to Solon to endue them with his authority.

Further Reading

Archaic *Polis*

L. Mitchell and P. Rhodes, eds. *The Development of the* Polis *in Archaic Greece* (London, 1997).

Archaic Political Thought

R. Balot, "Archaic Greece and the Centrality of Justice," in *Greek Political Thought* (Oxford, 2006), pp. 16–47.

Polis Origins

C. Shelmerdine and J. Bennet, "Mycenaean States: Economy and Administration," in C. Shelmerdine, ed. *The Cambridge Companion to the Aegean Bronze Age* (Cambridge, 2008), pp. 289–309.

Polis Evolution

W. Donlan, "The Relations of Power in the pre-State and early State Polities," in L. Mitchell and P.J. Rhodes, eds. *The Development of the* Polis *in Archaic Greece* (London, 1997), pp. 39–48.

K. Raaflaub, "Homer to Solon: The Rise of the Polis," in M.H. Hansen, ed. *The Ancient Greek City-State* (Copenhagen, 1993), pp. 41–105.

Homeric Politics

D. Hammer, *The Iliad as Politics: The Performance of Political Thought* (Norman, OK, 2002), pp. 144–169.

K. Raaflaub, "Homer and the Beginning of Political Thought in Greece," *Proceedings of the Boston Area Colloquium of Ancient Philosophy* 4 (1988), pp. 1–25.

Eighth Century BCE:

I. Morris, (Chapter 2, bibliography).

D. Tandy, *Warriors into Traders: The Power of the Market in Early Greece* (Berkeley, CA, 1997).

Tyrants

Stein-Hölkeskamp, (Chapter 2, bibliography) pp. 100–116.

Leaders and Lawmakers

K.-J. Hölkeskamp, "Arbitrators, Lawgivers and the 'Codification of Law' in Archaic Greece. Problems and Perspectives," *Metis* 7 (1992), pp. 49–81.

R. Wallace, "Charismatic Leaders," in K. Raaflaub and H. van Wees, eds. *A Companion to Archaic Greece* (Oxford, 2009), pp. 411–426.

Solon

J. Blok and A. Lardinois, eds. *Solon of Athens: New Historical and Philological Approaches* (Leiden, 2006).

Law

K.-J. Hölkeskamp, "Written Law in Archaic Greece," *PCPhS* 38 (1992): 87–117.

Democracy

K. Raaflaub, J. Ober, and R. Wallace, (Chapter 2, bibliography).

E. Robinson, *The First Democracies: Early Popular Government Outside Athens (Historia Einzelschrift 107)* (Stuttgart, 1997).

4

War and Violence in Archaic Greece

4.1 Introduction

Herakleitos of Ephesos, an Ionian philosopher-scientist of the late sixth century BCE, said that "war is the father of all and king of all; it designated some as gods and some as men, it made some slaves, some free" (D-K 22 B53). Herakleitos was not actually not making a statement about the human condition, but rather attempting to explain his conclusion that forces exist in nature that violently oppose one another. He adopted the metaphor because it was fitting, but also because he knew that his audience would grasp what he was communicating. Yet the metaphor is also fitting for Archaic Greece, for war was a deadly constant in the lives of the Archaic Greeks.

4.1.1 "Homeric" Warfare

Homer's descriptions of war in the *Iliad* are vivid and memorable; his depiction of the hero-mentality is essential for comprehending that of Archaic and Classical Greek warriors. Arms and tactics changed markedly in the eighth and seventh centuries BCE, but the warrior-ethos of the Greeks endured. Homer's heroes provided benchmarks for Greek warriors from Archilochos to Alexander the Great.

  In the *Iliad*, Homer's focus is upon dueling individuals, not armies, strategies, or set battles. The duels generally feature a hero and a "barbarian," most times, a Trojan. Warriors square off in the midst of battle, throwing spears at one another and then drawing swords. Archaic Greeks esteemed close-in fighting, wherein *arete* was proven and *kleos* earned. But Homeric warfare was not as neat or honorable as might seem the case at first. Archers actually shoot from far away, and spears find the backs of many warriors. Homer portrays war's grim realities as counterpoints to *kleos* and *arete*. For all of the glory earned for winning a duel, there is an awful price to pay which the poet intensifies with his sometimes lengthy descriptions of wounding, death, and dying. Many times these are horrendously graphic, many times poignant and quite distressing. For Simoesios (*Iliad* 4. 473 ff.) and Gorgythion (*Iliad* 8.302–308), Trojan boys really, Homer emphasizes their youth, innocence, and the utter waste of their lives in battle. It is as if mere children are slaughtered by the grizzled Greek warriors. The poet clearly aims to evoke great pity and regret for their deaths.

Archaic Greece: The Age of New Reckonings, First Edition. Brian M. Lavelle.
© 2020 Brian M. Lavelle. Published 2020 by John Wiley & Sons Ltd.

Homer also portrays the lot of Trojan non-combatants – wives, mothers, elderly fathers – especially in the suffering of Hektor's family. He reminds his audience of the terrible fate of Troy and the atrocious murders of the elderly Priam, all his sons, including Hektor, and Hektor's own infant son Astyanax. In Book 6, when Hektor bids farewell to Andromache, his wife, Homer's Greek audience would know that the parting is for the last time, that Hektor will be killed, and that Andromache, Hekabe, Hektor's mother, and Kassandra, his sister, will all be taken and enslaved by the Greeks. We can be sure that Greeks felt keenly for the suffering of war casualties, even among their enemies, and that Homer's treatment of war actually reflects the conflicted feelings the Greeks had about war. Pindar explains the ambiguity to some extent when he says that "war is a sweet thing to him who does not know it, but to him who has made trial of it, it is a thing of fear" (F 110).

There are several contrasting categories of warriors in the *Iliad*: noble and ignoble, famous and nearly anonymous, dutiful and self-centered, etc. We hear much about the likes of Achilles, Aias, and Diomedes – and, for that matter, Hektor and Sarpedon. These are hereditary chief-tains, possessing rights and privileges in succession from their chieftain-fathers. Yet, it is what they do – or rather are seen to do by others – that makes them heroes. Sarpedon, a Lykian ally of the Trojans, sets forth the rules that govern the hero's obligations. Fighters like himself *must* fight in the forefront and lead by example, if their communities are to continue to regard them highly (*Iliad* 12.310 ff.). Men honored as the best *must* act the part, he says.

Heroes in the *Iliad* seem to correspond to the Geometric period *basileis* near in time to Homer. They take counsel together and offer each other mutual, if sometimes grudging respect. Although Agamemnon seems the more authoritative of Greek commanders at Troy, it is because he commands the largest contingent of warriors and so has the most power, not because he is superior in fighting. Each hero, when he speaks in council, takes up the sacred scepter – just as the judge-elders do on the "Shield of Achilles" – and is heard as he speaks.

While these *aristoi* seem to live and fight in close proximity to common warriors, they are distinctly set apart from them. Common warriors are almost all anonymous in the *Iliad* because they conspicuously lack the fighting skills and the bravery to step out in front of other warriors to do battle and so gain the reputations of heroes. The real despite of the Archaic *aristoi* for commoners – the *demos* in Homer – is shown in the episode involving Thersites, but also very distinctly in the so-called "Song of Hybrias the Cretan," dated to the seventh century BCE (Box 4.1). Its rather harsh sentiments are throwbacks to times perhaps even before Homer's.

Despite their disdain, however, Greek heroes must play to the common warriors, needing them to recognize and validate their heroism – and of course to follow where they lead. Such recognition is indispensable for warriors whose heroism can never be self-declared or even left to the opinions of peers who relentlessly compete among themselves for glory and honor.

Some scholars have gone as far as to declare common warriors to be the decisive element in Homeric warfare, not the heroic fighters in the forefront. They point to descriptions of mass fighting in Homer implying organization and grouping. These they take to be precursors of the phalanx, the characteristic formation of hoplites going into battle. The Achaians at Troy do come to battle in divisions marshaled up by leaders and are described as fighting *en masse* in at least one place in the *Iliad* (17.365). But references to massed fighting in the *Iliad* are not proof of actual organized mass fighting at Troy, and what Archilochos describes in his time and can be seen in vase paintings from the late eighth through the earlier seventh centuries BCE suggest

---

Box 4.1 The Song of Hybrias the Cretan

> My great wealth is my spear and sword
> and beautiful rawhide shield, the protector of my skin.
> With this, I plow; with this, I reap;
> with this, I tread the sweet wine from the grapes;
> with this, I am called "master of slaves."
> Those who do not dare to hold a spear and sword
> and the beautiful rawhide shield, the protector of life,
> all these fall at my knees …
> … and grovel dog-like to their master and call me "great *basileus*."
>
> (Athenaios 15.50.24)[1]

These haughty verses supplement Sarpedon's declaration to Glaukos (*Iliad* 12.310 ff.) and underscore the fact that honor and status – even meaning in life to a Homeric hero – derive from proficiency in war. Hybrias' tone is almost despotic; the *persona* lords it over others who do not fight and so have no rights.

---

that phalanx formations were not necessarily widely employed even then. Heroes in the *Iliad* fight in a killing ground between massed common warriors whose fortunes seem to depend on these "fighters-in-the-forefront." There is only rather vague evidence in the *Iliad* for the precision of hoplite warfare, even as it is depicted on the Chigi Vase (see Box 4.7).

4.2 Land Warfare in the Early Archaic Period

4.2.1 "Servant of the War-God"

Although Archilochos' verses offer an insider's view of early Archaic Greek warfare, many of his poems are fragmentary and incomplete. These fragments range from a few words in a line to what might possibly be whole poems; his descriptions, from battle-action to anticipation of it, and from equipment used by warriors to behavior in combat and "off duty." He tells of warriors' common concerns and interests and offers information about what every soldier wants to know: how to survive.

Archilochos' portrayals of war and warriors resemble Homer's in some ways, and both provide information that is sometimes strikingly similar to what we know about the common experiences of soldiers throughout history. Yet, in Archilochos' poems, there is a conspicuous absence of the heroic or ideal. His soldier's world is very real and his words reflect that reality. Archilochos references Homer often but alters his references sometimes subtly to create his own, very different meanings (Box 4.2).

Archilochos' weapons were the ***dory*** ("spear"), the ***aspis*** ("round shield"), and the ***xiphos*** ("sword") – generally the same as for other Archaic warriors. The *dory* usually had an ashwood shaft, around *c.* 2.5 m in length, topped by an iron or bronze leaf-shaped head. Some had metal spikes on the butt-end of the shaft. The *aspis*, sometimes called the "Argive shield," was

---

Box 4.2 The War-God and the Muses

I am a servant of the lord Enyalios
and of the Muses, knowing their lovely gift.

(Archilochos F 1)

The poet's assertion of identity, placing his warrior-occupation on a par with that of poet, uniquely distinguishes him from Homer and Hesiod. It affirms his authority on war, but also his poetic skill and veracity.

Enyalios may be an epithet of the war-god Ares, but is also the name of a much older war-god, still worshipped in Archilochos' time.

---

around a meter in diameter. Its wooden core was sheathed with beaten metal. Archaic warriors also used the cheaper-to-make "Boiotian shield," more oblong than the *aspis* with concave notches on either side of the shield's center. These allowed thrusting with spear or sword through the shield rather than around or over it. The *xiphos* was a short double-edged sword, *c.* 0.6 m with a bronze or iron blade tapered to a point, like an elongated tree-leaf. While Archaic warriors like Archilochos may have possessed helmet, breastplate, and greaves, others did not. Archilochos mentions the use of slings, bows, and arrows in battle, though not in reference to himself. The Parian admires the "lords of Euboia" who favor the sword and so adhere to the Homeric ideal of close-in fighting (F 3). His preferred weapon seems to have been the spear which, like Hybrias, gave him his livelihood (F 2). Whatever heroism he might have displayed was jarringly upset by Archilochos' own admission of flight after combat of some sort (Box 4.3).

Shield-abandonment seems to have been fairly common among Greek soldiers, so Archilochos was by no means alone among Archaic Greek warriors in dropping his shield and running. While the act was considered cowardly, it was also practical for a soldier wanting to survive to lighten himself by discarding what was heavy. By contrast, the Spartans absolutely

---

Box 4.3 A Warrior Abandons His Shield

Some Saian is dancing for joy with my shield, which beside a bush,
faultless though it was, I left behind – I didn't want to.
But I saved myself. Why should that shield be any care to me?
To hell with it! I'll get another one right away that's just as good!

(Archilochos F 5)

Archilochos tries to mitigate the shame of flight by explaining that the shield does not have the same value as his own life. The fragment has usually been interpreted as a kind of breakthrough for its seemingly fearless assertion of unheroic humanity and repudiation of Homeric heroic idealism. Of course, it's also an admission of guilt.

We know from Herodotos that the Thracian Saians were among the fiercest fighters the Greeks had encountered to his time.

---

forbade shield-abandonment. Their ideology is summed up in the Spartan dictum never to relinquish one's shield, but to die before doing so.

Spartan sentiments seem to be rooted in the world of Homeric heroes, where shields are much more than weapons. A warrior *is* his shield. When armor is stripped from a corpse by a victor, it signifies his total triumph and the complete loss of the warrior-self by the dead man. Archilochos clearly felt shame for what he had done although he knew that other warriors had done it, too. Even a hard-bitten veteran could be affected by the idealized "code" for Greek warriors howsoever unrealistic it might be. Archilochos' proclamation nevertheless signals consciousness of the clash between ideal and real in war.

Archilochos uses the words **stratos** ("army"), **lochos** ("division"), and *strategos*. These indicate that warriors came together in some numbers and had commanders who led them into battle. Archilochos mentions sailing frequently in his poems, and warriors like him were also seamen and rowers as well as spear- and sword-fighters. From what he says, land fighting occurred in open spaces and around strong points like *poleis*. Battles could begin suddenly with no warning, as well as with advanced and formal notice. Archilochos mentions the singing of a war-song, a formation tune that kept warriors in order as they moved into battle – a hallmark of hoplite warfare. Whether Archilochos and his comrades were organized into any kind of orderly formation before battle, they did not preserve it for long it seems when fighting started.

In fact, battles in the earlier seventh century BCE seem to have been more like melees from the start than organized. Archilochos says that, as battle began, the air became "thick" with missiles of all types: stones, arrows, and spears (F 3, 1–2). These were probably launched all at once as an opening volley to soften up the enemy before the actual encounter. Then opposing warriors closed with each other, perhaps at a run, second spear or sword at the ready. Fighting then broke down into individual pairs or clusters, continuing until one or more of the warriors was killed, wounded, gave ground, or left the field altogether. Like brawls, these melees seem to have been chaotic – truly the work of Ares, Enyalios, and Enyo, his female counterpart (*Iliad* 18. 520ff.) (Box 4.4). The well-armed and well-trained did most of the heavy work of lengthier battles, fighting longer and harder than the lighter-armed, less well-trained warriors. Although the Archaic Greeks may already have been aware of the advantages of formation or cluster fighting, the evidence suggests that warfare was not yet as organized as it would be even in the mid-seventh century BCE.

Archilochos himself was not a particularly dutiful soldier. In fact, he seems more like a troublemaker. In F 4, traveling by ship apparently on watch-duty, he orders someone to bring the men wine from the casks that are aboard. No soldier is allowed to get drunk on duty, and Archilochos seems to flaunt this rule-breaking openly. No one will remain sober on the watch! Elsewhere Archilochos complains about aristocratic warrior-leaders, who, while they might look the part, don't act it (F 114). Archilochos' sentiments line up perfectly with those of other warriors from the beginning of time who despise officers who are more for show than actual leadership. Though a bastard son of an *aristos*, Archilochos aligns himself with the common warrior.

Archilochos seems to have hated his life in Thasos where he was sent to fight (Frs. 21 and 116). It involved dirty, inglorious warfare on the mainland, but apparently he had no choice. Things changed rather dramatically for Archilochos and others like him in 664/663 BCE when Ionian and Karian warriors landed in Egypt apparently on a marauding expedition. Psammetichos, a petty Egyptian king, offered them "great rewards" if they would serve him

---

Box 4.4 Melee-Fighting in the Later Geometric/Early Archaic Period

Figure 4.1 Melee fighting. Drawing from a Late Geometric amphora, Paros, *c.* 730–700 BCE.

In Figure 4.1, the helmeted warrior with a round shield on the left seems to be aiming his bow at the naked slinger on the right. The latter's drooping sling, along with the projectile near his head, might indicate not that he is throwing a spear, but that he has been hit by an arrow. Certainly arrows are flying thickly, all from the left, and a casualty – quite possibly another slinger from the look of him – lies between the warriors. Trailing the archer-warriors on the left, out of the frame, are mounted warriors. Behind the three slingers on the right is a helmeted warrior with shield and two spears, one perhaps for throwing, the other for jabbing. Could this have been a record of an actual battle on or near Paros?

---

instead of pillaging. They accepted and enrolled in his service as mercenaries. With these at his back, Psammetichos settled scores with his immediate enemies in the Nile Delta and, by 656 BCE, had made himself pharaoh of all Egypt, establishing permanent camps for Greek and Karian mercenaries in the Delta. The land of the Nile now presented itself as a possibility for Ionian fighters who could enrich themselves with regular pay and other "rewards" for relatively light duty. Egypt provided attractive prospects for Archaic Greek warriors (Box 4.5). Although he seems to have noticed the Egyptian expedition or its results in his poetry (F 216), it is not clear if Archilochos ever actually journeyed there.

Archilochos offers insight into the life of an Archaic warrior, but also into his own. It is not an "epic" life and he is no "hero." Rather by observing himself and others, reflecting on experiences and comparing them with idealized ones, and then concluding objectively about them, he grasped that there is rather a great difference between the ideal and the real. He strips the warrior's life of its sentimentality, romance, and fiction. He anticipates others of the Archaic period who will do the same but in different ways toward different ends.

4.2.2 Hoplites and the Phalanx

"Hoplite" seems to describe Greek warriors who carried the standard round shield, the *hoplon*. Hoplite equipment was essentially the same as that of Archilochos: spear, shield, sword, and, sometimes, a helmet (Box 4.6). The more well-to-do might own greaves and a breastplate.

Box 4.5 Greek Warriors in Egypt[2]

Inscription found on statue of Ramses II at Abu Simbel, 591 BCE:

> When King Psammetichos arrived at Elephantine, those sailing with Psammetichos, the son of Theokles, wrote these things. They came above Kerkis, as far as the River [Nile] allowed. The ***alloglossoi*** ["foreign-tongued," i.e., non-Egyptians] Potasimto commanded, the Egyptians Amasis. Archon, the son of Amoibichos wrote this and Pelekos, the son of Eudamos [or perhaps "Axe, the son of Nobody" – a typical soldier's joke[3]].

> Helesibios the Teian.
> Telephos wrote me, the Ialysian.
> Python, the son of Amoibichos.
> … and Krithis wrote me.
> Pabis the Kolophonian with Psammata [Psammetichos?].
> Anaxanor … the Ialysian when the king marched the army the first time [?]
> … Psammetichos.

These Greek mercenaries in Egypt, some of whom like Psammetichos, the son of Theokles, and perhaps the brothers Archon and Python, the sons of Amoibichos, might have been descendants of earlier mercenaries. They can't resist commemorating their service with Psammetichos II, a descendant of the pharaoh who made the original deal with the Greeks and Karians. On campaign up the Nile toward Ethiopia, they scratched graffiti into the left leg of a monumental statue of the ancient pharaoh. Some wrote their *poleis* as well as their names; some their fathers' names; one, Krithis, neither – just his own name.

Precisely when hoplite warfare began among the Greeks is not possible to say, but the archaeological record indicates that the round shield was in use in Greece no later than the end of the eighth century. More important, though, is when phalanx fighting became widespread. The best evidence so far for that is the Chigi Vase, dated *c.* 650 BCE, to which we shall return in Box 4.7.

Herodotos (1.171.4) says that the Greeks adopted the hoplite shield from the Karians, who in turn seem to have gotten it from the Assyrians. The latter used a round shield, short sword, and an iron-tipped spear a bit shorter than the Greek *dory* and went into battle in formation. Karians had a reputation for close-in fighting and were apparently the first in the Greek world to employ Assyrian weaponry and tactics. Whatever hoplite warfare may have owed to the Karians and other easterners, it was the Greeks who refined and mastered it.

The Chigi Vase is our first "text" on Greek hoplite phalanx fighting (Box 4.7).

Warriors march to battle in formation; behind the first line on the left, a piper plays to keep them in step. A second line follows on the left. The warriors are frozen by the artist just before "the moment of truth," as viewers are left to imagine the actual clash and its aftermath. While the equipment is the same on both sides, the shields are individually decorated.

Box 4.6 Fighting Over Patroklos' Body

Figure 4.2 Fighting over Patroklos' body. Attic Black-Figure *kalyx krater, c.* 530 BCE.

In Figure 4.2, the weapons, though incorrectly paired with ostensibly Bronze Age warriors, illustrate hoplite equipment in some detail. The warrior on the left holds his shield out by his left forearm, aided by a central band; his left hand grasps a leather thong on the rim of his Boiotian-type shield. Such control enabled the warrior to wield it better and to use it, if he chose, as a weapon in its own right. The warrior on the right has a *triskeles* emblem on his round shield and unusual leg armor that seems to cover his thigh. The opposing warriors are similarly engaged and have their spears poised for thrusts. All of the warriors depicted are outfitted in the full Archaic panoply.

The meaning of some of the shield-devices is clear enough. The Gorgon Medusa was renowned in myth for turning men to stone with her gaze: her visage on the shield was meant to strike terror into the enemy as he beheld it and so to provide both added aggressive power and protection to the bearer. The ox-head was a symbol of death; the lion's head, a heroic symbol that bespoke the courage and fearsomeness of the shield's bearer; the *triskeles* perhaps a substitute for the Gorgon. The iconographies of some of the other devices are unclear but must have been similarly intentioned. All would have been clearly recognized as wordless threats or boasts from one warrior to another just before they clashed.

The phalanx formation was rectangular in shape consisting of a front line of hoplites backed by rows of seven or more warriors and as broad across as warrior-numbers would allow. The marching phalanx was vexed by a problem that devolved upon the shield, according to Thucydides (5.71). Since shields overlapped and most warriors wielded their shields with their left arms and hands, each man in the line had to rely on the warrior to his right to share his

---

Box 4.7 Archaic Greek Hoplites about to Engage

Figure 4.3 Archaic Greek hoplites about to engage. The Chigi Vase: proto-Corinthian *olpe, c.* 650–640 BCE, detail.

In Figure 4.3, two lines of well-armed hoplites are about to meet in battle. As they march, they seem to be looking directly at the enemy opposite them. The warriors on the right all have different shield-emblems, emphasizing their individuality and identity in the otherwise homogenizing phalanx. All have the full panoply. The scene depicted may be fanciful – idealized or otherwise imagined – in order to create a pictorial prescription for what warriors *should do* in battle rather than a record of what they *actually did*. (As we shall see, Tyrtaios' poems are all about what Spartans *should do* in the battle-line.) The emphasis here might be on maintaining cohesion through the engagement – something not at all easy to do.

---

shield – and so to resist the natural instinct to cover himself more fully with his own shield. The formation's weakness was that each warrior tended to move more to the right to compensate for the instinct, causing the line to skew right as it moved or fought in formation. Such instinctive behavior could disrupt the formation and open fatal gaps in the line even before the battle was joined. The tendency had to be disciplined out of the hoplite by training.

Men behind the front ranks were not only reinforcements for those bearing the brunt. These also drove the front line forward into the enemy.[4] It was the *promachoi*, the men in the front ranks, who were most involved and most hard-pressed. Men shoved with shields, jabbed with spears over the shield-wall, or hacked at one another with swords until one side fragmented as men were lost to the ranks, whether dead, wounded, or fled. As gapping occurred, individual fights might break until one line or the other broke altogether. Hoplite battles usually ended in rout and pursuit.

As we have seen, until Archilochos' time, warriors fought in less-disciplined, less-organized ways. If *promachoi* were defeated or killed, the masses of common warriors lost their best fighters: battles might be decided on their fates alone. Now, let us imagine one of the old-style *lochoi* with *promachoi* encountering a disciplined marching hoplite phalanx. Such a phalanx, bristling with spears, would have plowed right through the *promachoi* killing them or pushing them back into the massed warriors. One warrior fighting alone, howsoever proficiently and heroically, simply could not withstand the onslaught of massed hoplite warriors. Even if the undisciplined mass behind did not break with the *promachoi* gone, it would encounter the phalanx, whose warriors would smash into them, shoving, jabbing, and hacking. If, as some scholars think, such encounters were actually not so one-sided – if hoplite arms and tactics were more gradually and generally adopted and employed – the more proficient side in such tactics would still have won the battles. Most Archaic Greek warriors were sometime soldiers anyway – farmer-militia rather than professionals. Those who could train more frequently, as the Spartans, were superior in battle, but were also quite exceptional.

The Chigi Vase seems to show that hoplite arms and close formation fighting were widespread in Greece by around 650 BCE. These had in fact become necessities, for *politai* could not defend themselves and their lands without adopting the same arms and tactics as their enemies. For such defense, more men had to be enlisted to fight. What mattered now were numbers and disciplined fighting. The individual virtuosities of *promachoi* were not only not needed, but undesirable because they undermined all-important phalanx cohesion entering battle. Some scholars have argued that the number of Greek males mustered into the phalanx would still have been relatively small because hoplite weaponry was expensive and few could acquire it. But basic equipment need not have always been purchased from the local smith by each hoplite: it could be acquired by stripping the dead, friend or foe, after battles; it could be gotten at cost from other warriors or pirates selling what they had picked up or stolen. Then again, wealthy *aristoi* had interests in arming others, since they could not defend their lands by themselves alone.

Thus, men who had been excluded from direct warfare before – the "stone-throwers" and others – were not only now eligible for service, but sorely needed. That need produced an irony, for they who seem to have monopolized warfare before were now leveled in the battle-line, becoming no better and no worse than the fellows next to them. Aristocratic *promachoi* were devalued, non-aristocrats saw their stock rise.

The ramifications appear to have gone well beyond war. New warriors meant new political prerogatives, especially when they realized how important they were to the community. A political stake in the *polis* was reserved for those who fought for it, heretofore *aristoi*, now non-aristocrats. The political changes discussed in the last chapter, datable to the seventh century BCE, the first law codes, limitations on terms of office, *stasis*, the rise of tyrants, all coincide with the spread of phalanx warfare.

Some scholars have seen the introduction of hoplite warfare as more sudden. The success of the *basileus*-turned-tyrant Pheidon of Argos, brief as it was, might be attributed to Argive employment of such warfare, which, at the time, the Spartans did not yet practice. The Argive victory at Hysiai in 669/668 BCE and the early defeats of the Spartans in the Second

Messenian War, implied in Tyrtaios' poems, compelled the Spartans to embrace hoplite warfare ardently. The Great *Rhetra*'s concession to the *damos* could reflect the political response to the sudden mustering into the army of numbers of formerly unenfranchised Spartan males.

Others, however, contend that the spread of hoplite arms and tactics throughout Greece was more gradual from the eighth century. As proof, proponents point to what they take to be references to formation fighting, if not the hoplite phalanx, in Homer, along with individual fighting. Furthermore, warriors are portrayed in vase-paintings from the later eighth and earlier seventh centuries carrying two spears into battle. Formations were only beginning to coalesce; of the two spears carried by warriors, one was for throwing, the other for jabbing.

The absence of clear and contemporary sources is at the root of the problem. Conflicting information makes it impossible to know precisely when the murky figure of Pheidon actually ruled and conquered; there is in fact no explicit connection of him to the Battle of Hysiai. What connection any of his successes had to hoplite warfare must be inferred. Proponents of the theory of gradual adoption, on the other hand, inflate the evidence for warrior-formations in Homer, while discounting the accounts of melee-type fighting described by Homer and Archilochos. These, taken together with the Chigi Vase, suggest a watershed some time before the mid-seventh century BCE.

Howsoever gradual the adoption of hoplite weapons and warfare by Archaic Greeks, the Chigi Vase implies that hoplite warfare was practiced widely in Greece by the date of its production, *c.* 650 BCE. The very nature of hoplite phalanx tactics required numbers of warriors to fill the ranks – the more the better. Such inclusion must have impacted communities in Archaic Greece, whether in short order or over time. Can it be simply coincidence that greater political power came to those who did not have it before, the *demos*, at the expense of those who did, the *aristoi*, beginning around the same time?

4.3 Land Warfare in the Later Archaic Period

4.3.1 Sparta, the *Polis* of War

The idea of "Sparta" captured the imaginations of the ancient Greeks, even as it does us today. It was Sparta's unique dedication to warfare that has fascinated and evoked admiration from many both ancient and modern. Sparta was alone among all other Greek *poleis* of the Archaic period in its very focused orientation to war.

After Sparta had subdued all of Lakonia by the end of the eighth century BCE, Spartans turned toward fertile Messenia, the region to the west of Mount Taygetos. The First Messenian War was long and hard fought, but, at length, the Spartans prevailed. The Messenians who did not flee were reduced to serfdom and worked the land for their Spartan masters, yielding up one-half of what they produced to them (Box 4.8).

When the Messenians rose up against the Spartans in the earlier seventh century BCE, the contest was to the death. Things did not go well for Sparta at the beginning: the Spartans were absentee landlords of the conquered land, and Messenia lay across formidable Mount Taygetos. Initially, the Messenians were successful, inflicting heavy defeats upon the Spartans. The Argive victory at Hysiai in 669/668 BCE may have demoralized the Spartans further and spurred on the Messenians.

Box 4.8 Messenians Reduced to Helotry

[The Messenians were:]
   …just like asses with great burdens weighted down
bringing to their masters under painful necessity
   half of all of as much as their land produces.

(Tyrtaios F 6)

Looking back from the mid-seventh century, Tyrtaios delights in Spartan victory in the First Messenian War. Embittered by the long war and the suffering that it caused, the Spartans may have treated the Messenians as harshly as they did because they feared them so much. Their oppression, however, spurred the Messenians to rebel and so substantiated Spartan fears in the next generation, that of Tyrtaios.

Tyrtaios gauges how badly things were with the Spartans in his poems of exhortation (Box 4.9). Spartan warriors were not holding their ground in battle, but were running away apparently, leaving their wounded and dying behind. It was a disgrace, and Sparta was in dire straits. Something had to be done. Things had become critical.

The Lykourgan reforms, which mark a political watershed at Sparta, fit well with its recovery from the mid-seventh century. Whether the *agoge* was introduced by Lykourgos or not, Spartan youths were turned into hardened warriors who could face any enemy, strictly obey their commanders, and do what was needed to be done in battle – exactly the opposite of the conditions implied by Tyrtaios. Renewed and invigorated, Sparta defeated the Messenians and preserved itself and its hold on Lakonia and Messenia. Something quite significant had to have brought about this sea-change.

Spartan youth divorced themselves from their parents and families at an early age and committed to living and fighting together with others just like them for the common good. Comrades-in-arms substituted for kinsmen, becoming the ultimate benchmarks for approval and status, just as warriors were in the *Iliad*. Needless to say, heroic values such as excellence in warfare, bravery, steadfastness, and duty amounted to the "gold standards" for Spartan warriors. As Tyrtaios illustrates, these values needed fine tuning to serve Sparta and the phalanx in the seventh century BCE.

Uniformity promoted cohesiveness and unit-effectiveness. Spartan soldiers of the Classical period looked alike, having long hair and beards; they carried shields and wore helmets that were all the same. Cemented by discipline, each warrior and *lochos* were aware that they were parts of the larger, far more significant whole. Individuals mattered, but the army – and Sparta – mattered more, and each soldier's conduct was integral to its success. There is no mystery why the Spartans became the best hoplites in Greece: their discipline was perfectly adapted to it. Such a peak of uniformity may not have existed in the Archaic period, but the foundations for it were certainly laid then.

The Spartans' re-dedication to warfare saved their country, but also transformed it. Messenian farmers, again reduced to serfdom and providing food for Spartan messes, freed the Spartans to become full-time soldiers and policemen of the helots. Spartans were allowed to drill and practice as no other Greeks could do. Because the phalanx relied on skill and discipline, especially

---

Box 4.9 Tyrtaios Exhorts Spartan Youth

Come on, you who are the race of unconquered Herakles,
    take heart! …
Do not fear a mass of men, do not be terrified,
    but let a man hold his shield straight toward the fore-battlers,
making his life an enemy and loving the black shades of death
    as he does the rays of the sun.
You know the annihilating work of Ares who makes many tears,
    and have learned well the madness of sorrowful battle,
you have been with those fleeing and those pursuing,
    O young men, you have had your fill of both.
Those who stand with one another and risk
    to go to the close-in fight and to the fore-fighters
they die in smaller numbers. And they save the mass behind them.
    But of the men who run away all *arete* is destroyed.
[…]
(It is a sad and shameful sight to be speared in the back.)
[…]
So let every man abide with both feet firmly planted,
    fixed on the ground, biting his lip with his teeth.
[…]
But going in close, hand to hand, let him pierce with long spear
    or sword and kill his enemy,
planting foot against foot, laying shield on shield,
    and with crest against crest, helmet to helmet,
and breast to breast, let him lay on and fight his man….
                    (Tyrtaios, F 11, 1–2, 3–14, 21–22, 29–33)

Tyrtaios repeats on purpose, as if he were a drill sergeant pounding in a lesson. After encouragement and dissuasion of cowardice, he gets down to the practicalities and basic indoctrination. This poem seems more like an address to conscripts, not veterans, and ancient sources tell us that, at various times, the Spartans resorted to such recruiting where they could as need forced them. Tyrtaios says that the warriors had run from battle, and his aim is to stop them from doing that again. So encouraging were his songs apparently that they were adopted thereafter as battle hymns to be sung by Spartan warriors as they marched into battle.

---

at the "moment of truth," individual Spartan toughness, rooted in the *agoge* and maintained by constant drilling, made the Spartan army irresistible. No other Greek *polis* that we know of rivaled Sparta through the fifth century BCE.

By the mid-sixth century BCE, Sparta dominated the Peloponnesos with the notable exception of Argos, its inveterate and bitter foe. Sparta's string of victories – and the intimidation that these permitted it – led to the formation of the Spartan-dominated Peloponnesian League.

It was Sparta's reputation for victory that made it the leader of Greek resistance to the Persians. It was Spartan proficiency in hoplite arms, discipline, and overall leadership that brought victory at Plataia and preserved Greek independence in the Persian War.

4.4 Epilogue: The Causes of War

Thucydides tells us that, until the Peloponnesian War of the fifth century, conflicts were small-scale affairs fought mostly between neighbors. Early on, these probably took the form of raids, just as the old warrior Nestor describes in the *Iliad* (Book 11. 670 ff.). Such attacks were aimed at taking land, property, or both and were answered by counter-attacks. Later, wars became more formal with war-declarations, designated battlefields, and times for battle. Yet war remained small-scale and, since most *poleis* could field only a citizen-militia, the campaign season was fitted in between reaping and ploughing, roughly, summer.

The largest-scale conflict during the Archaic period was the Lelantine War. It was waged by the people of Chalkis and Eretria on Euboia over the fertile Lelantine plain between the two *poleis*. Though local in nature, the war ultimately drew in most of the rest of the Greeks, according to Thucydides (1.15.3). Archilochos may be referring to this conflict in F 3, when he mentions the "spear-famed" warriors of Euboia who were renowned for fighting hand-to-hand. Strabo, a Greek geographer of *c.* first century BCE, notes that an inscription in the Euboian town of Amarynthos prohibited the use of missile-weapons in the Lelantine War (10.1.11−12).

The First Sacred War was said to be fought for control of the Delphic oracle, *c.* 590 BCE. The Delphic *Amphiktyonia* along with Kleisthenes, tyrant of Sikyon, punished the *polis* of Kirrha for abusing Apollo's land and pilgrims journeying to Delphi. The war ended with the siege, capture, and destruction of Kirrha by the coalition. Sources for the war are late, however, and somewhat confused, and the war's occurrence has been doubted.

War can be a powerful unifying force, providing a sense of common cause and community. It hardens nationalism by polemicizing "us" and "them." It is easy to imagine Archaic Greek leaders whipping up ardor among *politai* to aggressive war for their own purposes. Solon is said to have made his political debut at Athens by encouraging renewal of the war with Megara. Then again, every age provides a crop of naïve young men, who, hearing old soldiers' tales, fancy "seeing some action" themselves, until they, too, become "old soldiers" by experiencing the realities of war. As Pindar said: "War is a sweet thing to him who does not know it." Pride, standing among peers, self-esteem are all motives present in the *Iliad*: all contributed to a mentality among Archaic Greeks generally that was conducive to war.

4.5 Summary

4.5.1 The Land War Experience in the Archaic Period

An Archaic Greek warrior was an adult male, 18 years or older. Like his neighbors, he might be summoned to the *agora* of his *polis* to debate the question of war. Perhaps he was informed before the assembly that warriors from a neighboring *polis* or region were already marching or that his *polis*' leaders deemed it necessary to attack their neighbor. If so, he would have his spear, shield, and sword with him. Heralds would be sent to the enemy; enemy heralds would be formally received: both announced war and perhaps where and when the armies were to meet for battle. Heralds were sacrosanct and should move about untouched, even during hostilities. To harm them was sacrilegious – but harm came to them sometimes nonetheless. The assembly for war would be brief: if war was decreed, the mass of common warriors would array itself in divisions and go out to meet the enemy led by its *strategos*.

The Archaic citizen-hoplite trained regularly with others from his *gene* and tribe drilling in formation, but also running and wrestling. *Aristoi* generally remained *strategoi* in places like Athens for the most part even after seventh-century reforms limited their political prerogatives, for they were, by preoccupation, tradition, and training, still the best at war. Men without appreciable means could train less: farmers had much to do in all seasons but the growing one. Most Archaic Greek armies, made up mostly of hundreds rather than thousands of men, were populated by occasional soldiers, not professionals. Of course, the Spartans remained exceptional.

When armies came to the appointed place, the divisions arranged by tribe drew up in battle-formation, each man taking his place in the phalanx, usually next his kinsmen. Each division was led by a division commander, in early Athens, the tribe-*basileus*. Each army was led in turn by an overall commander, usually the most proficient, experienced, and successful warrior of the *polis*.

Before the advance, auspices were taken by a seer who accompanied the army to inform it of the will of the divine. Seers inspected the entrails of sacrificed animals before battle, looking for omens. If the signs were propitious, battle would be joined; if not, delay and more sacrificing until the signs were favorable. At Troy, the most notable seer was the Argive Kalkhas; at Thermopylai, Megistias of Akarnania.

The men then marched forward sometimes singing while a piper played. They endeavored to keep their line straight, their emotions in check as they neared "the moment of truth." As the enemy drew closer and closer, shield-devices – gorgons, lions, bulls, birds in flight – became clearer. The enemy, too, was singing, maybe beating his shield with his spear. Presumably the warriors quickened their pace, if only to keep their courage from flagging.

Phalanxes met with an almighty crash and shouting, the rear ranks pushing the front forward. After the initial impact, the battle began in earnest. Men jabbed furiously with spear and parried with shield. Confusion reigned along the line and a man's attention turned increasingly to his own life. Spears broke, but their butt-end spikes could be used as spares. Once those broke, a warrior had only his short sword – very inferior if the enemy retained his spear. The battle went on, sometimes for a short time, sometimes for hours, until one line or the other gapped, broke, or fled. Separations were inevitable: some men fought better than others, some could last longer; some died or were wounded and fell, creating gaps in the line. Gaps might be plugged by reserves from the rear ranks. However, at length, when reinforcements were exhausted or courage or strength ebbed, a line would waver. Bunches of warriors might then cluster around enemy-warriors isolated by the gapping. A warrior's chances fighting alone were very poor. With many in such straits and no more reinforcements, it would not be long before the whole faltering line gave way, its warriors retreating frequently pell-mell. Some – the braver – may have backed more slowly, but others dropped their shields and ran. The battle was over; the victory went to those who held the field when it was all over. Spartans would halt on the battlefield after victory, but others pursued the fleeing enemy, inflicting wounds or death as the vulnerable men exposed their backs. Pursuit could render a good deal of booty.

Casualty numbers varied depending upon circumstances. Thucydides says (4.101) that, in the big fight at Delion in 422 BCE between the Athenians and the Thebans much after the Archaic period, the Athenians lost nearly a thousand warriors, while the victorious Thebans lost nearly five hundred. But this was an uncharacteristically large action in the Peloponnesian War at the end of the fifth century BCE, and conflicts in the Archaic period were much smaller. While the greater number of casualties fell on the losing side in any battle and many of these died while being pursued, their numbers were limited by the size of the armies.

While hoplites were sometimes supported by cavalry and light troops, except in places like Thessaly, cavalrymen were few in number. The main use of cavalry was to protect the phalanx wings, to run down the enemy fleeing on foot, or to protect comrades fleeing. After the battle at Delion, Alkibiades, a horseman, saved Sokrates on foot by covering his retreat. Light troops consisted mostly of stone-throwers or slingers. Victorious warriors could plunder the dead, but armor might even be gotten during battle, as we find in the *Iliad*. Metal armor lying with the dead and wounded or discarded by those in flight was highly prized. After winning, the lightly armed could scavenge for hoplite armor and, acquiring it, might become hoplites.

Victors could go on to despoil their enemies' lands, taking goods, livestock, and human captives for slaves – whatever they could lay their hands on. During the Peloponnesian War, when the Athenians were locked within Athens' walls, their Theban enemies are said to have made off with everything they could take, including whole houses which they dismantled and carted back to Boiotia! Plunder remained a prime incentive for war for Archaic Greeks.

The defeated warrior had only his life to hope for as he abandoned the battlefield, walking or running back to his home or within the walls of the *polis* for regrouping or protection. Victors set up a trophy of captured arms on the battlefield to mark their triumph and thank the gods for it. Truces were arranged by heralds so that both sides could take up the dead for burial and the wounded for treatment. In a few years or even the following year, during the growing season, the same belligerents might do it all over again.

4.6 Conflict at Sea

4.6.1 Early Sea Travel and Piracy

The Greeks seem to have engaged in piracy very early on. In fact, Thucydides implies (1.4–5) that those who lived on the coast and the Aegean islanders turned to piracy as soon they learned to travel by sea. Piracy required no hard work, especially when undertaken with others. Individuals in small boats would be easy pickings for many in larger craft or multiple ships. A penchant for violence was useful, however, even as Odysseus describes in his false story (Box 4.10).

4.6.2 Archaic Greek Ship-Guilds

Greeks who wanted to engage in steady overseas trade realized the benefits of leaguing together against pirates by the late Geometric period. The likeliest to organize such leagues early in the Archaic period were the colonizing *poleis* of Khalkis, Eretria, and Corinth. These established several settlements in Italy and Sicily by the mid-eighth century BCE which can only have been

---

Box 4.10 The Voyage of (the False) Pirate Odysseus to Egypt

> But then
> my spirit compelled me to sail to Egypt
> after I fitted out ships well with companions like to the gods.
> Nine ships I readied and a mass of warriors came together quickly.
> [...]
> On the seventh day we boarded our ships and sailed off
> from wide Krete with a fine fair North wind
> easily, as if we were sailing downstream.
> [...]
> On the fifth day we raised Egypt, the fair-flowing,
> and we moored our double-oared ships in the Egyptian river.
> Then I commanded my faithful companions to stay there
> and, remaining with the ships, to guard them,
> while I ordered scouts to go for a careful look.
> But they yielded to *hybris* and gave way to madness:
> straightaway they began to plunder the very beautiful fields of
> the Egyptian men, and they led off the women and infant-children,
> but they killed the men.
>
> *(Homer,* Odyssey *14.245–248, 252–254, 257–264)*

Odysseus' description is realistic and likely reflective of actual piratical raids. Egypt was a favored Greek target during the Dark Ages because it was exceptionally rich. The Egyptians endured many such raids, the last of which resulted in Psammetichos' purchase of the services of the raiders for his own purposes. Like Archilochos, Greek pirates were both sailors and land-fighters.

---

managed profitably with a large number of ships whose captains and crews worked together. All three *poleis* were renowned for naval power during the Archaic period.

At Athens, as we have seen, the *prytaneis ton naukraron* opposed Kylon's attempt to impose a tyranny at Athens *c.* 636 BCE. Apparently even then, the four Attic tribes were also divided into 12 **naukrariai** ("ship-guilds") (*CA* 8.3). There has been a great deal of scholarly speculation about the name and nature of these: what precisely are *naukrariai*? From the words' roots, *naukrariai* and *naukraroi* involved naval matters. If we can take the information of the *CA* as valid, governance at Athens in the mid-seventh century was implicated with the leaders of these ship-associations. Could similar "guilds" have already existed in places like Khalkis, Eretria, and Corinth?

Perhaps federations of ships, crews, and captains joined with others, and at length the federations became institutions. At Athens, these "guilders" were called *naukraroi*, their leaders *prytaneis*; at Miletos, they seem to have been called the "forever sailors"; at Khalkis, Eretria, and Corinth, they perhaps had other names. Overseas trade and colonization were of central importance to many Greek *poleis* even in the eighth century BCE, and such ship-collectives were required for sustained success. It may have been then that *basileis* and their followers on the islands and in coastal regions – ships' captains and their companies – became part of the political fabric in *poleis* with overseas interests. It seems that they did at Athens. Presumably, these not only protected their own shipping, but preyed upon others, especially their enemies. Unfortunately, there is little firm evidence about the nature of such institutions.

Naval combat in the Archaic period varied. Sources tell of amphibious landings by men who became land-fighters after jumping off their ships. In the long Athenian-Megarian War, begun *c.* 650 BCE, the island of Salamis changed hands several times. In a late phase of the war, Peisistratos ended it by taking Nisaia, Megara's port, apparently in some kind of amphibious attack. We also read of deck battles with ships drawing up alongside one another. In the Classical period, hoplites accompanied ships for just this kind of fighting and so engaged in "land battles" at sea. Thucydides (1.13.4) mentions that, in the early seventh century BCE, the Corinthians and the Kerkyrans, their colonists, fought the very first sea-battle apparently on the decks of their ships hand-to-hand (cf. 1.49.1–2). The more agile tactics of mass ramming and shearing off oars do not seem to have developed until the fifth century BCE.

The most dramatic development involving navies in the Archaic period came in 483 BCE when the Athenian Themistokles "turned the Athenians toward the sea." Arguing that the Persians, who had come to Greece once before at Marathon in 490 BCE, would come again with much larger land and naval forces, Themistokles convinced the Athenians to divert revenues from their public mines at Laurion to ship-building. Such a fleet would be a means of escape, should victory at sea elude them, but could also be employed for profit in the meantime. Two hundred state-of-the-art triremes, long ships with three banks of oars, were commissioned. These ships changed the course of Greek history thereafter.

Naval development during the Archaic period may be traced from the eighth century BCE. Overseas colonies and long-distance trade imply that ships' captains and crews banded together before 750 BCE in *poleis* like Khakis, Eretria, and Corinth. Testimonies about *naukraroi* and *prytaneis ton naukraron* support the conclusion that aggregations of ships' captains and crews had federated by the mid-seventh century BCE and were politically implicated in their *poleis*. While these federations may have constituted proto-navies, the first standing navy in Greece was that of the Delian League of the early fifth century BCE. It was organized and led by the Athenians after Persia's defeat and withdrawal from the Aegean and Ionia at the end of the Archaic period.

4.6.3 Archaic Greek Ships

It is possible today to see ships in use in the Aegean that do not differ greatly from those used by Archaic Greeks (Figure 4.4). Many are still wooden, hand-made, not very large – perhaps 5–10 m in length and 3 or 4 m amidships. They are of shallow draft, capable of being handled by one person, and good in the water. These ships are equipped with motors today, whereas, in the Archaic period, such boats moved under sail, oar, or both. These ubiquitous boats are used for fishing, for carrying light cargoes, and simply for moving about – the same as during the Archaic period.

Small ships like these, a bit rounder perhaps at bow and stern, seem to be what Hesiod describes in the *Works and Days* (618 ff.). Their cargoes were modest, presumably the excess produce of the land. Their routes were most likely short and direct, even as today. From the port of Kreousa, near Askra, an Archaic Greek might sail to Corinth or Isthmia in part of a day. There, in a large market, he could trade with other Greeks or foreigners, exchanging his grain

Figure 4.4 Modern Greek fishing boat, Agios Nikolaos, Crete, summer 2017.

for pottery from Corinth, olive oil or wine from Attika or Lesbos, flint from Melos for fire-making, or any number of other things from any number of places. He could sail back to Askra the same long day.

Bigger ships, too, plied the seas from before Homer's time. Cargo ships were broadened to carry more rowers and trade-goods: Odysseus knew of such a ship (*Odyssey* 5.249; 9.323). Larger ships had 30 and 50 rowers respectively. Used both as warship and merchantman, the 50-oared ship was *c.* 30 m long by *c.* 4 m in width, its bow and stern tapered for speed. Because of its design and since it could accommodate more rowers – 25 to a side – it was faster and a better fighting ship. Polykrates' fleet consisted mainly of these 50-oared ships.

Although built for greater speed, the 50-oared ship was not particularly seaworthy in adverse conditions, and the Aegean could provide those almost instantly. Ancient Greek ships were best in calmer seas. To avert evil and "see" their way clear to their destinations, ships' bows were painted with eyes on the bows. Greeks sailed coastwise or island to island when they could. Unless the voyages were long – such as that of false Odysseus to Egypt from Crete – ships seem to have beached overnight. Sailors could then camp, eating and sleeping on the more comfortable, more secure beach where they could build fires and sleep outstretched. The sailing season was essentially spring to fall and, when it was over, ships of all types and sizes would be dragged out of the water and dry-docked, even as they are today (see Hesiod, *Works and Days*, 624–629).

Although triremes were used by Greeks as early as the seventh century BCE, they did not become the dominant warship-type until the fifth century. Longer at *c.* 37 m faster and more maneuverable than any of its predecessors, it had three banks of oars to a side. According to Thucydides (1.13.3), the ship was invented in Corinth in the later eighth century BCE by the Samian Ameinokles. However, Phoenicians used the type much earlier and the Samians may well have "borrowed" it from them. It is ironic that Greece owed its salvation to a Phoenician ship-type, since Phoenicians made up perhaps the largest contingent in the Persian navy at Salamis. Once again, as with hoplite equipment and phalanx tactics, the Greeks improved upon and employed more proficiently what they had "borrowed" from the easterners.

4.6.4   The Archaic Greeks and the Sea: A Summary

Almost any Greek, undaunted by the perils of sea travel, could put to sea in a small ship to profit from trade. Even a farmer could sail in a *caïque* to trade for what he needed or wanted. Such small trade was very ancient in Greece and remained commonplace throughout antiquity. Along their way, lone or few sailors could be waylaid by pirates who might take part or all of the cargo. If a sailor was unlucky, the pirates would take him, too, to sell as a slave – or just cast him into the drink. Arion of Methymna in Lesbos, a professional poet and singer of the later seventh century BCE, was almost drowned when sailors aboard his ship turned pirate, seized all his belongings, and ordered him to jump into the sea. According to legend, he was only saved because a dolphin, charmed by the music he sang, rescued him and brought him to shore.[5] Apart from perils posed by others, the seas surrounding Greece were capricious. Aegean storms could come up suddenly and rage furiously. Odysseus was caught in one such and nearly drowned off Scheria (*Odyssey* 5. 291 ff.).[6] The sea was a cause for great fear, and countless Greek sailors lost their lives at sea. But it didn't hold them back from voyaging.

Sea travel offered many attractions even in the Dark Ages, profit the foremost. The expansion of populations, but also the desire for gain pointed the Greeks toward colonizing. Prospects for profit prompted Greeks to colonize Sicily and Italy, Thrace, and the Black Sea region; it was wealth that attracted Karians and Ionians to Egypt as pirates and kept them there afterwards as mercenaries. As sea travel, trade, and colonization increased, so did the importance of ships and their captains and crews. Cooperatives of private ship-owners seem to have come into being as merchant seamen realized the potentials of pooling resources and the wisdom of convoying. By the mid-seventh century, heads of ship-guilds like the *prytaneis ton naukraron* at Athens had gained significant leadership roles in *poleis*.

Life was never comfortable for Greek sailors, whose daily work was back-breaking. Each rower sat in a small space, hard up against other rowers. The rowers pulled to a rhythm produced by singing or a pipe – the same instrument accompanying hoplites into battle. For the pilot, moving the heavy rudders even to steady the ship was no light task. Each night, after an exhausting day, the ship was drawn onto shore. Sailors generally took their meals and slept on the beach. When morning came, they dragged their ship back into the water and rowed and piloted again quite possibly for another full day.

While ship's crewman might not earn much, he would gain something from a successful voyage, whether trading or pirating. The more sailors in the company, the smaller the share, but the safer the venture. Sailors followed a seasoned leader like the one Odysseus pretends to be on trade or piratical ventures.

Each day, a sailor might pray to the god Poseidon, lord of the sea, or any number of sea-deities – Nereus, Triton, or Proteus – who the Greeks thought inhabited the deep. The sea could be deadly or pleasant, and the pleasure or displeasure of the gods could spell the difference between life and death. A prayer and libation offered to a sea-divinity might just ensure a safe voyage and homecoming.

Notes

1 *PMG* 909 (pp. 478–479).
2 M&L 7a–g; Dillon and Garland, pp. 69–70.
3 Cf. M. Dillon, "A Homeric Pun from Abu Simbel (*M&L*, 7a)," *ZPE* 118 (1997), pp. 128–130.
4 The tactic of "shoving" is disputed: cf. L. Tritle, "Inside the Hoplite Agony," *AHB* 23 (2009), pp. 57–58.
5 Herodotos 1.23–24.
6 Scheria, a fabulous land in the *Odyssey*, is sometimes identified as Kerkyra (modern Corfu) and the sea as the Ionian.

Further Reading

Greek Warfare

H. van Wees, *Greek Warfare: Myths and Realities* (London, 2004).

Archilochos the Warrior

B. Lavelle, "The Servant of Enyalios," in D. Katsonopoulou, I. Petropoulous, and S. Katsarou, eds. *Paros II: Archilochus and His Age: Proceedings of the Second International Conference on the Archaeology of Paros and the Cyclades. Paroikia, Paros, 7–9 October 2005* (Athens, 2008), pp. 145–162.

Archaic Warriors and Warfare

J. Hall, *A History of the Archaic Greek World*[2] (Oxford, 2014) pp. 165–181.

Hoplites

F. Echeverria, "Hoplite and Phalanx in Archaic and Classical Greece: A Reassessment," *Classical Philology* 107 (2012) pp. 291–318.
K. Raaflaub, "Soldiers, Citizens, and the *Polis*," in L. Mitchell and P.J. Rhodes, eds. *The Development of the* Polis *in Archaic Greece* (London, 1997), pp. 49–59.

Pheidon of Argos

J. Hall, *A History of the Archaic Greek World*[2] (Oxford, 2014), pp. 154–164.

Spartan Warriors/Warfare

J. Lazenby, *The Spartan Army* (Warminster, UK, 1985).

The Lelantine War

W. Donlan, "Archilochus, Strabo and the Lelantine War," *Transactions of the American Philological Association* 101 (1970) pp. 131–142.

Greek Ships and Naval Warfare

L. Beresford, *The Ancient Sailing Season* (Leiden, 2012), especially Chapters 1–4, 6.
T. Figueira, "Archaic Naval Warfare," *Historika. Studi di storia greca e romana.* 5 (2016), pp. 499–515.
J. Morrison and R. Williams, *Greek Oared Ships, 900–322 BC* (Cambridge, 2008), especially Parts I and II.

Greek Piracy

P. de Souza, "The Origin of Piracy from the Bronze Age to Alexander the Great," in *Piracy in the Greco-Roman World* (Cambridge, 2008), pp. 15–42.

5

Archaic Greek Myth and Religion[1]

5.1 Introduction

Archaic Greeks believed that their world was full of gods. These ranged from the earth itself – what amounted to their "universe" – to trees, rivers, and even small pools of water. Myriad deities moved about the environment singly or, in pairs, triads, or whole bands. Archaic Greeks believed that they were never alone – at least as we understand being alone – even in remote places.

While gods and spirits symbolized portions of the Greeks' external environment, others represented the "inner landscape" of human motivations and behaviors. Among the latter, for example, were Contentiousness (Eris), Battle-rage (Ares), and Lust (Aphrodite and Eros). Skepticism stimulated by scientific enquiry, speculation about their natures, and discontentment with what they seemed to be lessened the gods' significance over time. Yet most Greeks continued to believe in the ancient gods, some well into the post-Roman Dark Ages.

Greek gods were human in appearance and motivation. Zeus, god of lightning and thunder, was imagined as a temporal lord, recognizable by his age, scepter, or sometimes a stylized thunderbolt. He ruled gods and men as their "father," was jealous of his prerogatives, and exceedingly fearful of usurpation, just as any Greek *basileus* or *tyrannos* might have been. Aphrodite, a goddess-type "borrowed" from the Phoenicians by way of Cyprus, personified sex or, rather, the human desire for sex. She was conceived of as an irresistibly beautiful maiden. While such anthropomorphic projections were by no means confined to the Greeks, no other ancient people that we know of were as severely humanizing of their gods as they. Not only were Greek gods defined by human shape and emotions, they were also enfeebled by human weaknesses. They were not really even "god-like," for they were not the absolute rulers of the world nor did they control their own fates. To the contrary, the powers of the gods were circumscribed by forces greater than they. This circumscription is one of the keys to understanding not only how the Greeks conceived of their gods, but more importantly how they thought of themselves in relation to the gods (see Box 5.1).

Greek gods were by no means identical to humans. They were far larger in size, enormously powerful, incredibly fast-moving, and able to materialize or de-materialize at will. They were immortal and eternally youthful, and they did anything they pleased. Not one of them was

---

Box 5.1 Olympian Gods, *c.* 540 BCE

Figure 5.1 Olympian gods. Partially restored fragments of Attic Black-Figure neck amphora, Princeton Painter (?), *c.* 540 BCE.

In Figure 5.1, Athena and Hermes are clearly visible in the middle and right of the broken Black-Figure vase, while the lower torso and legs of Herakles, a human-become-a-god, appear on the left. Could the two unnamed figures, in front of Herakles and behind Athena, be Zeus, the father of Herakles, and Ares or Apollo?

---

completely free, however. There are stories of revolts by the other Olympians against Zeus which he put down. The lesser gods must bend to the sky-god's power and will. But Zeus himself must bow to the Fates.

Humans the gods tolerated, demanding respect in ritual and reverence, but reciprocating with benefaction as they pleased – and only if they pleased. The gods might grant a prayer or petition or they might not. Hesiod (*Works and Days*, 42–44) says that the gods could have made man's lot so easy that he would have to work only one day to gain all that he and his family would need to live on for a year. But the gods withheld that. Greek gods could be capricious, cruel, dangerous, and even deadly. Lacking benign natures and morals, their acts and intentions were unpredictable. Hesiod's gods were like the natural world itself to the Greeks – beyond morality, capable of good or evil.

A prime reason that the gods treated mankind so poorly was that they feared human potential – or so the Greeks believed. The myths of Prometheus ("Foreknowledge") show just how threatened the Olympians felt themselves to be. That mankind just might be able to gain what the gods possessed was in fact an encouraging thread to which the downtrodden Greeks clung as they lived their hard lives. Courage in the face of death and perseverance through suffering – both of which were needed for the unending struggle with the forces opposed to them – were actually human potentials denied to the deathless gods. Craft and intelligence could actually level the field, even as Prometheus demonstrated in his myth. The hope that was left in Pandora's jar was really not a consoling, listless ember but a glowing possibility.

The Olympians were conceived of as super-humans by the Greeks – conceptions that actually depict the Greeks' beliefs in their own possibilities. An excellent example in art summarizing the Archaic Greek conception of the sky-god, which derives nevertheless from the early Classical period, is the Zeus (or Poseidon) of Artemision (Figure 5.2). The over-life-sized Severe Style bronze statue presents the Olympian as a powerful human poised to hurl a thunderbolt (or trident). The sheer human power of the figure is offset by the divine visage. The god is unperturbed in releasing the thunderbolt's massive destruction. Yet, for all that divine power, majesty, and detachment, this Zeus (or Poseidon) of Artemision is a human being – a near-perfect specimen to be sure, but a human being nonetheless. The artist has rendered the immortal's perfection in mortal form, erasing the gap between human and divine. Anthropomorphic gods are found in Greek art as early as the Bronze Age and, in some instances, only explicit labeling of the gods in, for example, later vase-painting differentiates them from being mere mortals.

Despite their resentment of the gods' relatively carefree existences and their own hard lives, Greeks were nevertheless grateful to Zeus for establishing and maintaining order in a world

Figure 5.2 Zeus or Poseidon of Artemision. Bronze statue, *c.* 470–460 BCE.

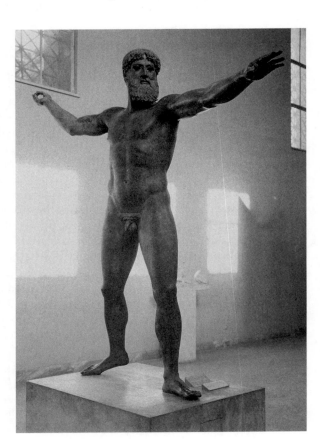

they thought was perpetually threatened with disorder. How the Greeks related to their gods was in fact complex – a mixture of gratitude, anger, envy, hope, and despair. The relationship was never a loving one, however. Rather we might call it "love-hate" – along the contradictory lines of that between "tyrannical" parents and "tyrannized" children. Needed, but resented by their "children," the gods, who seemed arbitrary, dictatorial, and confining, were also protective and assuring. The gods were really all the Archaic Greeks had to begin with to make sense of themselves in their environment.

Archaic Greeks worshipped their gods both individually and communally. Anyone might pray at any time during the day, from dawn to sundown, or spontaneously. Prayers might ask that a god be kind and grant a favor or avert an evil – or perhaps nothing more than that the day might pass without misfortune. Small sacrifices might be made on little altars outside dwellings, in the fields or on hilltops. These could range from the pouring of water or wine and grain-sprinkling to the killing of animals of various types and sizes upon sacral altars. Votives were of different types, shapes, and sizes, whether food or vegetation, durable clay, stone or metal statues, cups, or cauldrons. Men, women, and children could worship alone, in gender-segregated groups, or altogether with others. At Athens, the rituals of the *Thesmophoria*, a festival involving Demeter, Persephone, and the fertility of the soil, and the *Arrephoria*, rites for Athena, were performed by women and girls for the good of the *polis*. There were many other such communal rituals for individuals, communities, and religion, all of which were thoroughly implicated in Archaic and Classical Greece.

5.2   The Gods of Hesiod and Homer

5.2.1   Hesiod

Hesiod's *Theogony* describes how the gods came into being, how Zeus and the Olympians came to rule, and their relationships with each other and with human beings. A large part of the poem seems to be rooted in Near Eastern theogonic mythology. Elements in both the *Theogony* and the *Works and Days* seek also to account for the gap between human and divine.

The *Theogony* presents events leading to the triumph of the Olympians chronologically. First was *Chaos*, "void." From Chaos came *Gaia* ("Earth"), then *Tartaros* ("anti-Earth"), both gods and places, then others such as Eros. Gaia herself alone engendered *Ouranos* ("Sky") and, mating with him, produced the first of the Greek gods, the *Titans* ("Stretchers"). The youngest Titan, *Kronos*, was also the most powerful and, together with Gaia's help, conspired against his unrighteous father who feared usurpation and prevented his children from being born. Kronos violently attacked his father, castrating him with a sickle, so displacing him from power. With his Titan sister-wife, Rhea, Kronos then begat the Olympians. He, too, was frightened of his children and swallowed them down as soon as they were born. His youngest, Zeus, was also most powerful and, by Rhea's contrivance, escaped being swallowed. Although Hesiod does not say explicitly in the *Theogony* that Zeus displaced his father, it is clear that he did just that. Zeus' own sister-wife is *Hera*, the daughter of Kronos and Rhea.

Some scholars have posited that the Titans were the gods of the pre-Greek inhabitants of the Aegean. Zeus' displacement of Kronos might reflect the changes to religion and worship that the Greeks introduced after they arrived in Greece. Blending of religious beliefs certainly seems to be indicated: Kronos-worship persisted in Greece through the Classical period, and nostalgia for the "age of Kronos" surfaces in Classical Greek literature. Kronos may have been a consort of the all-powerful pre-Greek earth-goddess, one of whose names was Rhea, and so not at all like Zeus.

The displacement pattern in Hesiod's *Theogony* resembles the older Hurrian-Hittite myth of Anu, Kumarbi, and Teshub. Consequently some scholars accept it as the basis for Hesiod's account. Anu, the sky, is overthrown by Kumarbi, who begets Teshub, the Weather-God, and is in turn overthrown. Yet for its obvious similarities to the Kumarbi-myth, the *Theogony*'s narrative of divine displacement is different, emphasizing justice and injustice and right to rule. Zeus must legitimate his rule in a number of ways, not just take it.

According to Hesiod, after Zeus displaced Kronos, a long struggle ensued between the Olympians and the Titans. For ten years these fought until, on Gaia's advice, Zeus enlisted the "Hundred-Handed Ones." These, whose 50 bodies indexed their surpassing strength, had been confined beneath the earth by Ouranos who feared their power. Resurrected, the Hundred-Handed cast boulders that drove the Titans into Tartaros where they were imprisoned, thus ensuring the Olympians' victory and primacy. Evidently, a contingent of the old gods had to be co-opted to support the Olympians' ascendancy and so to validate the new regime. For their reward, they were made jailers of their brethren Titans in Tartaros!

For Zeus, however, there was one more struggle for him alone. Gaia and Tartaros begat *Typhoeos* ("Smoke-cloud"?) and, after a long and heated duel, Zeus dispatched the monster burning to Tartaros (Box 5.2). Zeus' lightning bolts also seared the earth, so punishing the unruly Gaia for unleashing disorder, but also demonstrating a mastery over that most formidable of potentially destructive environmental forces.

Zeus' duel with Typhoeos is a classic confrontation between good and evil, nature and culture, order and disorder. Zeus' triumph is thus also for mankind: he is in fact a kind of cultural hero. The Greeks needed order to prevail in nature to survive and prosper. Zeus' encounter with Typhoeos precedes those of the greatest Greek cultural hero, Herakles, Zeus' own son, several of whose labors eradicate monstrosities of nature afflicting human beings. By his triumph over Typhoeos, Zeus established world order once for all, identified himself as guarantor of that order, and so justified his right to rule.

Despite such benevolence, Zeus could also be quite malevolent. Prometheus, a Titan cousin of Zeus curiously sympathetic to mankind, conspired to trick Zeus before the first sacrifice. Prometheus advised humans to display two meat-bundles to Zeus to choose from, one lean, dull and unappealing, the other mostly bones, but covered with glistening fat. The one chosen would be offered to Zeus as sacrifice thereafter. Zeus chose the latter and so humans were allowed to keep the lean – the most nutritious portions of the animal. Although Hesiod says that Zeus saw through the trick, he also says that the god was very angry nonetheless. But how can a supremely intelligent god be tricked so easily?

More audaciously, Prometheus stole fire from heaven, concealing it in a hollowed fennel stalk to bring to mankind. Zeus' reprisal was swift and vicious. For Prometheus, he contrived a terrible punishment. The Titan was chained to a rock at the end of the earth, there to have an eagle tear out his liver every day. His agonizing punishment was near-eternal, for, as an immortal, he could not die: his liver grew back every night only to be torn out again the following day.

For mankind, Zeus conceived an everlasting bane. He ordered Hephaistos, the smith-god, to create woman, the first of her kind. Pandora ("All-gifts") was a "beautiful evil," according to Hesiod (*Theogony* 585). In the *Works and Days* (60–69), the poet says that Athena arrayed

---

Box 5.2 Hesiod on Zeus and Typhoeos

… from [Typhoeos'] shoulders
sprouted a hundred heads of a viper, an awful snake,
licking with dark tongues. From the eyes
on those fearful heads, beneath the brows, fire sparkled:
from all the heads fire burned as he glanced about.
And in all the heads voices came forth….
(god-speech, the roaring of a bull or lion, the barking of dogs, whistling)
[…]
And a thing would have happened on that day that could not have been undone
and indeed he would have ruled both gods and men,
if [Zeus] the father of gods and men had not keenly noticed it.
[…]
But when Zeus raised up his strength, and took his weapons,
flashing thunder-bolts and the blazing lightning,
he sprang from Olympos and struck,
and set fire to all the divine-sounding heads of that awful monster.
Then when he had overcome him, smiting him with blows,
he lamed and toppled him, and the great earth groaned.
And flame shot out of the lightning-struck lord …
[….]
And angry at heart, [Zeus] cast him into wide Tartaros.
From Typhoeos comes the wet force of winds blowing
[…]
… [some winds are] a great help to mortals.
But all the others blow rashly over the sea …
[…]
A great bane to mortal men, they rage as evil tempests,
they blow from this way and that and they scatter ships
and kill sailors …
Over the land which is without boundary and flowers they blow,
and they destroy the lovely works of earth-born men,
and overpower them with dust and grievous whirlwinds.

(Hesiod, Theogony *824–829, 836–838, 853–859, 868–869, 871–872,*
874–876, 878–880)

Pandora in fine clothes, Hermes, the trickster-god, endowed her with deceit and treachery, and Aphrodite made her irresistible. Pandora charmed all who saw her, but her charms were superficial, for she really brought endless pain to man. Given a jar from Zeus as a wedding gift, Pandora opened it and out poured all the world's evils. Only hope remained (*Works and Days*, 83 ff.). Hesiod implies that man cascaded from a much higher, perhaps even semi-divine state to squalor. It is important to note that Hesiod really does not blame Pandora for what happened to mankind. Rather, it is Zeus who is the author of mankind's ills. It was upon his order that Hephaistos constructed Pandora and the other gods made her what she was. It was Zeus who filled Pandora's jar with all the evils that beset mankind. Zeus conquered Typhoeos to save *his* power after all: his help to mankind was secondary to his own self-interest. (Hesiod steps very carefully with this, since he doesn't want to incur Zeus' wrath by griping too explicitly.)

Elsewhere in the *Works and Days* (109 ff.), the "Five Ages" myth explains the separation of gods and men differently. The present and near future are construed as the end-stages of a descent from a Golden Age and near-divinity to an Iron one where everything is base and broken. The "Five Ages" myth blames this squalid state of mankind on its unrighteous nature, not on the gods or Pandora. The myths of Pandora, Prometheus, and the "Five Ages" imply that humans were partly to blame for losing what could have been, when, of course, the fact of human and divine difference made the loss inevitable.

Pessimism about the gods and their own inclement environment was the result of the Greeks' fear and insecurity. Hesiod's humankind seems small indeed in comparison with the forces that surround them. Hindered mightily by their own flawed nature which simply added to their other difficulties, Archaic Greeks believed that the deck was stacked against them. No matter what they did, the gods or their own flaws would impede or undo them. The one real card humans had to play was their own intelligence. Human knowledge, craft, and potential Zeus feared. This was the "hope" left in Pandora's jar.

5.2.2 Homer

What is most outstanding about Homer's gods is their humanity. While they can be awe-inspiring and even truly godlike on occasion, they are also proud, vindictive, petty, cruel – and even despicable. Like Hesiod's gods, they are immensely powerful and their moods and actions can often have dreadful consequences for humans. Their flaws, however, make them more recognizable and comprehensible, but also less divine. Homer essentially defined the Olympians for the Greeks – and was roundly criticized for portraying them as he did by other Greeks. Notwithstanding the depictions of the gods, Homer and his audience care much more about the human beings in the *Iliad* and *Odyssey* than the Olympians, who are, after all, supporting characters to the human heroes.

The Olympians are introduced in the *Iliad* working evil for the Greeks. Angry with Agamemnon, Apollo strides down from Mount Olympos "like the night," raining death-arrows on humans and animals alike. Later in Book 1, Zeus agrees with Thetis, the sea goddess-mother of Achilles, to make the Greeks suffer for their ill-treatment of her son. Countless Greek warriors will die as a result. And this is just the beginning of the epic. The Olympians will work great misery and suffering on mortals.

Homer's gods can also be beneficial. In Book 1, Athena speeds down from Olympos to grab Achilles by the hair just as he is about to kill Agamemnon. In so doing, she averts disaster for him, Agamemnon, and the Greek army. Thetis, though a goddess, is compassionate as Achilles weeps near his ships: she comforts her son as a human mother would. In Book 3, Aphrodite intervenes to save her favorite, Paris, from death by wafting him away from the battlefield. Athena liberally aids this or that Greek hero throughout the *Iliad*, guiding a spear-throw to its mark or deflecting an arrow. She even fights with the hero Diomedes against her own god-brother Ares. She watches over Odysseus as he makes his way home in the *Odyssey*.

The appearances and activities of Homer's gods often explain extraordinary occurrences: they seem to be metaphors for what the Greeks witness but do not understand. The plague attributed to Apollo, Achilles' sudden cessation of blood-rage, a missile averted seem to the Greeks to be manifestations of divine presence and intervention. At the beginning of the epics, Homer invokes the Muses, asking them to come and tell the story of Achilles' wrath or Odysseus' suffering through him. Hesiod helps us to understand this "possession" when, at the *Theogony*'s beginning, he says that the Muses gave him the gift of song so that he might sing of the gods' origins. The epic poets were mediums through which divine knowledge flowed: the daughters of Zeus were directly responsible.

The nature and frequency of divine and human interaction in Homer's works are remarkable. The Olympians sometimes assume human form; other times, they reveal themselves as gods, materializing before humans quite suddenly. Sometimes the gods speak directly to humans; sometimes their presence is merely felt. Aphrodite appears to Helen as an old woman, leading her to Paris' bedchamber; Athena to Pandaros, a Trojan bowman, as a comrade-in-arms. She comes to Odysseus on the beach at Ithaka as a shepherd, but when he recognizes her, she reverts to divine form. Achilles feels her pulling his hair; Hektor only senses that Athena has deceived and deserted him, after she appeared as Deiphobos, his brother. There is no great divide between gods and men in Homer's *Iliad* or the *Odyssey*: they are together many times and, of course, the Greeks suspect their presence everywhere.

Yet, Homer is very clear that the gods are quite different from mortals. The greatest difference is not power or privilege, but death and suffering. The gods cannot die, and their suffering is mitigated by that fact. And they are very aware of the differences. Apollo sums it up neatly in the *Iliad* (21.461–467 ff.) when he says that wretched mortals are not worth fighting over for they are like the leaves of trees, coming and going, living and dying, unlike the gods. Or so the Greeks believed their gods thought.

Homer actually presents us with a double paradox about gods and humans. In the *Iliad* and *Odyssey*, the strengths of the gods are actually their weaknesses, whereas the seeming weaknesses of the Greeks are their strengths. The gods' powers and immortality cause them to be detached and unfeeling – and less human. Their untroubled existence actually degrades them, making them seem less consequential than human beings. Indeed, what humans must endure – suffering and death – are not only the bases of human nobility, but also hint at human superiority to the gods. Gods cannot display courage nor can they bear up under suffering as humans do: they cannot therefore be noble or heroic nor can they obtain *kleos*.

The *Iliad* is precisely about the suffering of many human beings; the *Odyssey*, primarily the suffering of one. Homer makes it clear at the outset that the *Iliad* will be about Achilles' rage and how it caused countless woes to the Achaeans at Troy. The *Odyssey*'s opening magnifies Odysseus' prolonged hardship:

> Tell me of the man, O Muse, the man of many ways, who was buffeted about so much … and endured so many afflictions upon the sea, all through his being, striving to preserve his life and the homecoming of his companions.
>
> (*Odyssey* 1–2, 4–5).

After the epic's brief prologue on Olympos where there is no suffering, Athena speeds down to Ithaka, Odysseus' home, where his son, Telemachos, and Penelope, his wife, are also suffering.

We encounter Odysseus on Kalypso's island, crying his eyes out because the goddess wants to detain him forever, making him immortal. Odysseus wants none of it. Kalypso's name, "I shall cover," reveals why: living with this goddess, even being an immortal, is not life as he knows it. It is in fact to be dead and "covered." When Hermes, the messenger-god, frees Odysseus to return home, the hero's suffering worsens. Poseidon stirs up a tremendous storm which destroys his raft, and Odysseus is saved only because the once-human "white goddess" Ino pities him because she has suffered, too. (She was transformed into divinity after being pursued into the sea by her Hera-maddened husband, Athamas.) Ashore, after making his way to the Phaiakian king, Odysseus recounts his "travels" before coming to Kalypso's island. The Phaiakians are moved to pity – as only humans can be – and agree to take him home forthwith. (For their kindness, Poseidon turns the Phaiakian ship of transport into stone.) On Ithaka, Odysseus finds no happy homecoming. Rather he must abide in the guise of a beggar – the lowest of the low as the Greeks thought it – as he watches Penelope's suitors despoil his possessions, press their suit for his own wife in front of him, and even abuse him physically. Only after great suffering is he restored as king and husband.

All heroes in the *Iliad* agonize. Greeks and Trojans alike know that they risk their lives whenever they enter battle, but still they do it. Achilles' struggle is greater than that of any other for he knows that he *must* die before the walls of Troy once he kills Hektor. When, after considering life and death, Achilles returns to battle to confront the Trojan, he sets the seal upon his own life. Why does he do it? For Homer, it is precisely because humans are not immortal that they must risk death. The Lykian hero Sarpedon declares (*Iliad* 12.310 ff.) that, if humans were like the gods and never died, there would be no reason to fight. As it is, humans *must* fight to obtain lasting glory, the only immortality that they may attain. Facing death bravely is the ultimate demonstration of heroism and earns undying fame.

Homer's gods are both more and less than the gods of Hesiod. They are more human, comprehensible, and familiar than Hesiod's gods, but capricious, cruel and, in some ways, quite foolish, they are also like base humans. Likened to the gods, Achilles, though mortal, seems to be a terrible divinity, isolated in his self-centered, widely destructive wrath. Yet, when he sees that Priam suffers as Achilles' own father will do when Achilles dies, he feels sympathy, relents of his anger, and returns to humanity – and nobility. With the exception of Athena's compassion for Odysseus in the opening of the *Odyssey*, Greek gods cannot sympathize because they know no real suffering and so lack humanity. Did the Greeks then actually think of their gods as inferior because they could not be human?

5.2.3 Xenophanes' Complaint

Xenophanes of Kolophon (*c.* 540 BCE) criticized Homer and Hesiod for their portrayals of the gods. Men, he says, imagine that the gods are just like they are (F 14 D–K) (Box 5.3). Why, look at the Thracians and the Ethiopians: the former make their gods pale and red-haired, and the Ethiopians black and with broad noses, characteristics that typify themselves (F 16 D–K). According to Xenophanes, there is no certain knowledge about the gods, only opinion. Of

---

Box 5.3 Xenophanes on Homer, Hesiod, and the Gods

Homer and Hesiod attribute all those things to the gods
that are among men reproachful and blameworthy:
stealing, adultery, and deceiving one another.

(Xenophanes F 11 [D–K])

If cattle and horses and lions had hands
or could draw with hands and do things just as men do,
horses would draw the images of gods like horses, and cattle like cattle,
and they would make their bodies just like the ones they have.

(Xenophanes F 15 [D–K])

But mortal men think that gods are born,
and have *their* clothes and *their* voice and *their* bodies.

(Xenophanes F 14 [D–K])

Xenophanes reacts against the humanization of the gods by the Greeks. For him, there is but one god or rather one divine entity that is intelligent beyond human abilities to comprehend it.

---

course, Xenophanes unconsciously undermines his own views on the gods with such a pronouncement (see also Chapter 7.4.1 in this volume).

While Xenophanes dismisses the poets' depictions of gods almost condescendingly, his notions of divinity are themselves murky. His desire to distance divinity from humanity reflects the abstraction of divinity originating lately – and very vaguely – with the Ionian philosopher-scientists. Xenophanes' objections are significant, but they gained little traction with Archaic Greeks. Rather, the epic poets' conceptions about the Olympians prevailed. Their gods were certainly more familiar and comfortable than abstractions posited by philosophers and scientists.

Xenophanes' complaints demonstrate that the discourse about the nature of the gods was ongoing and that Greek conceptions of the gods were never fixed unalterably. Speculations about the gods continued through the Classical period when astonishingly unflattering portrayals of the gods emerge in the works of the tragic poets. Even at that, skepticism and doubt about the gods remained confined to a relative few.

5.3 Sanctuaries and Seers

5.3.1 Sacred Space

Greek sacred spaces varied in size and were often remarkable for where they were located. The most renowned sanctuary of Zeus was at Olympia in the northwestern Peloponnesos. It consisted of a holy precinct within which were several cult-sites. Olympia may have been originally dedicated to an ages-old earth-goddess, but became Zeus' domain some time before 776 BCE, the date of the first recorded Olympic victory. The site today, at the base of the Kronion hill, is lush and serene. Ancient travelers approached Apollo's sanctuary at Delphi, high up on Mount Parnassos, from two directions. Both offered a stunning first-acquaintance with the precinct that must have added to their awe of the god and his presence on the mountain. Less well-known sanctuaries were still impressive in their own right. Artemis' precinct at Brauron in eastern Attika is much smaller than Delphi or Olympia, but is a numinous place nonetheless. On Naxos, Demeter's sanctuary rises from the surrounding fields like an island in the sea. While the ruinous state of most of these sites and their reputations and situations encourage romantic reactions today, the ancients located them where they perceived divine presences to be. Symbols of such perceptions could range from large, quite sumptuous buildings to simple heaps of piled up field stones.

While some sanctuaries were distant from *poleis*, others were closer or even within them. Perhaps the foremost of the latter is Athens' *akropolis* where the Athenians believed Athena was sometimes actually physically present (Solon F 4.4). The "high city" is a dramatic sight and, looking toward it, the Athenians believed that the goddess was there watching over them below. The Argive Heraion, however, is *c*. 8.5 km from Argos, while the sanctuary of Hera on Samos is *c*. 6 km from ancient Samos town (modern Pythagoreio). While many theories have arisen to account for differences in locations, the primary determining factor must have been the Greeks' sense of divine presence at the sites.

Within the ***temenoi*** ("precincts") oftentimes were ***naoi*** ("temples"). Geometric period temples appear to have been small and constructed of perishable materials, such as wood or mud brick. A late eighth-century BCE house or temple model in terracotta from the Argive Heraion (NM 15471) may represent what early Archaic temples looked like. The structure is unadorned: its pillar-supported porch protects a threshold leading into a small rectangular room covered by a pitched roof. The room is lit by an opening in the gable above the entrance and smaller triangular ones on its sides. Its basic plan is reminiscent of the throne room of a Mykenaian *megaron*. It, too, possessed an anterior space like a porch, possibly a transitional space separating the mundane from the sacred presence of king and god.

Greek temples became larger through the Archaic period. Among the earliest of the monumental temples in Greece is the first temple of Samian Hera, *c*. 750–700 BCE, the original of several temples dedicated to the goddess there. Its length (32.9 m), narrowness (6.5 m), and peripteral columns more resemble the *heroön* at Lefkandi on Euboia, *c*. 950 BCE, than the Mykenaian throne room. Notwithstanding, the unadorned rectangular plan became the canon for Archaic and Classical Greek temples.[2] Wood and mud bricks gave way to dressed local stone blocks, poros, limestone, and then marble, from about the mid-seventh century BCE, a sign of the new stone-working technology apparently derived from Egypt. The largest Archaic Greek temple was dedicated to Artemis of Ephesos *c*. 550 BCE, with significant donations from the Lydian king Kroisos. While worshippers hoped to curry divine favor by constructing such lavish abodes, extravagance was not an option for every *polis*.

Within temples were cult statues, some very old by the beginning of the Archaic period. The rough-hewn olive wood effigy of Athena *Polias* was said to have fallen from the sky, whereas the original statue of Samian Hera was a simple squared piece of wood. From the mid-seventh century, however, larger statues were made from stone, again owing to imported Egyptian stone-working technology. The Nikandre ***kore*** ("clothed maiden-statue") (see Figure 8.19 on p. 146) dedicated to Artemis on Delos *c*. 640 BCE, might be the goddess herself, while the monumental *kouros* (*c.* 590–580) dedicated to Poseidon at Sounion (NM 2720) might represent a male god. Windows somehow dropped from the Greek temple-canon, and cult-statues within were thereafter illuminated by braziers, torches, or whatever natural light might enter through doorways facing east.

Sacrifices were made to gods upon altars outside and usually east of temples; priests or priestesses conducted rituals as worshippers looked on. The ceremony was often followed by communal feasting. Priesthoods in the Archaic period were held mainly by *aristoi*, it appears, partly due to their pedigrees, but also because they could supply the requisite animal victims for sacrifice and feasting. Tyrants discovered the usefulness of cults and feasting for boosting their popularity. Peisistratos imported the cult of Artemis of Brauron from eastern Attika to the Athenian *akropolis*, while Kleisthenes of Sikyon re-established the cult of Dionysos. Polykrates and his forebears were especially attached to the cult of Hera on Samos.

Temenos and *naos* were inviolable. Markers or walls indicated the *temenos*-boundary and so the separation of the sacred from the profane. Water for purification was available just outside or just inside the precinct. Anything that could sully the *temenos* was prohibited. Birth, death, illness, intercourse, among other things, were forbidden. Of course, stealing anything from the god or the god's sanctuary meant death. By the same token, persons claiming the gods' protection were safeguarded by the right of sanctuary and no violence could be done them there – at least not righteously.

The *temenos* might be packed with offerings of all sizes. There were many such votives to Apollo at Delphi, many less and less costly ones at local cult-places as for that of Artemis at Brauron in eastern Attika. Small dedications included vases, jewelry, fibulae, and even pins; larger ones were tripods, helmets, shields, or spears, or even over-life-sized *korai* and *kouroi*. Votives, especially precious ones, would be stored in treasuries, small temple-like buildings within the *temenos*-boundaries or in the *naos* itself. Material evidence suggests that some sanctuaries were frequented more by women, others more by men, both of whom not only dedicated offerings to the gods but were also showing off their ability to dedicate to fellow-citizens. Votive numbers increased dramatically in the eighth century BCE at many sanctuaries corresponding apparently to new prosperity among the Greeks.

Sanctuaries were restricted and restricting spaces, but also gateways and so liminal places where individuals or communities could address a god or gods more directly. Crossing the boundary helped to convey a sense of transportation to an intermediary place, closer to the divinity; priests or priestesses were themselves interlocutors between the human and the divine. Cult worshippers were meant to feel the deity's actual presence in the *temenos*.

5.3.2 Seers, Prophets, and Sibyls

In an unpredictable world, knowing the future was more precious than owning gold – as Kroisos, the Lydian king, found out. Divination and prophecy originated among the Greeks many centuries before the Archaic period. The source of all knowledge, past, present, or future, was Gaia, but she was difficult to understand at best, while, at worst, she was completely incomprehensible. The power of prophecy remained Gaia's into the Archaic period, although Zeus and Apollo commandeered her oracular *temenoi* at Olympia and Delphi. Human intermediaries were nevertheless needed to translate divine communications. As poets were mediums for the Muses, seers, prophets, sibyls, dream- and bird-interpreters channeled Gaia.

There were many famous prophets in Greek mythology, both male and female. Kalchas of Argos, the renowned Greek seer at Troy, was an interpreter of birds and the entrails of sacrificed animals. At Aulis, where the Greeks assembled to sail to Troy, Kalchas observed two eagles rending a pregnant hare (Aischylos, *Agamemnon* 107 ff.). He proclaimed that Artemis was angered by that and that Agamemnon's daughter Iphigeneia must die if the Greeks were to sail to Troy. The sacrifice was duly performed: no Greek at Aulis could oppose Kalchas' authority or interpretation of the omen, not even Agamemnon. The famous Theban blind seer Teiresias lived before the Trojan War as a man, a woman, and then a man again, according to myth. Blinded by Hera for what she took to be an insult when he said that women enjoyed sex far more than men, Teiresias was granted the gift of prophecy as compensation by Zeus.[3] He was thus able to "see" the future. Such seers lived apart from their communities, isolated by their special gifts in the mid-space between human and divine. Away from human communities, those such as Teiresias were more in touch with nature and its signs which they interpreted.

Female prophets, sometimes called sibyls, were not "readers" as much as true mediums. Famous in Greek myth, the sybil Kassandra was the daughter of Priam, King of Troy. She requested and was granted the gift of prophecy by Apollo, her ardent paramour. But after she refused his advances, because he could not revoke his love-gift, the god gave it a rather bitter twist. Kassandra could continue to prophesy unerringly – but no one would ever believe her.[4] The most famous female prophet of all, however, was a real person. The Delphic Pythia was named after the serpent which guarded the holy ground that was originally Gaia's. Apollo slew the serpent, the Python, and took Delphi for his own. Gaia's channeler remained a female, however.

5.3.3 Dodona and Delphi

The oldest Greek oracle was that of Zeus at Dodona in northwest Greece. The site was known to the Mykenaians, but its ties to Gaia were much older. The prophetic source was a talking oak tree, whose rustling leaves were taken to be the god's whisperings. Or perhaps it was the whispering doves that perched in the tree. Or perhaps the three sibyls who were called "doves" who sat in the tree and sang their responses. The sanctuary's centerpiece, the oak tree, was in any case a conduit of prophetic information originating deep within the earth.

At Delphi, Gaia's prophetess originally sat or stood on the rocky outcrop called the Rock of the Sybil and channeled the earth's responses to those who questioned her. When Delphi became Apollo's, the Pythia's place changed to the temple of Apollo. There she perched upon a tripod over a fissure that may have exuded ethylene, a hydrocarbon gas, and from whose fumes she became intoxicated.[5] Alternatively, she may have ingested some kind of organic intoxicant, perhaps bay or laurel leaves. She then answered questions put to her.

Apollo established his oracle ostensibly to reveal Zeus' will and so to make it accessible to humans. Greeks asked specific questions about the future and sought clear answers from the god. However, no such gift from the gods seems to have come to the Greeks without strings attached. Questioning the Pythia was preceded by cleansing, the purchase and sacrifice of an animal, most often a goat – and the rendering of a fee to the guardian Delphic priesthood. The Pythia would accept questions only on certain days in the warmest months, not year round. Answers were direct, but voiced incoherently. Apollo's priests intervened in the process to interpret, writing down their interpretation in verse-form. Unfortunately for the questioner, even that response could be ambiguous. Apollo may have meant well in establishing the oracle, but he made it very difficult to know the future clearly.

The ambiguity of Delphic oracles was notorious in antiquity. Perhaps the most renowned oracle was that given to Kroisos, who had donated many costly gifts to Apollo to gain the god's favor. When Kroisos' representatives asked the Pythia what would happen if he crossed the boundary between his empire and the Persian one and attacked the Persians, he was told "a great empire would fall." Kroisos took that to mean that Apollo was on his side and he would be victorious. When he was defeated and captured by the Persians, he bitterly accused Apollo of perfidy. Apollo through the Pythia reminded Kroisos that, when he said that a great empire would fall if Kroisos crossed the border, he did not specify which empire. Instead of prudently asking *which empire* would fall, Kroisos jumped to his own faulty conclusion.

Notwithstanding such ambiguities, the wisdom and authority of the Pythian oracle were taken quite seriously by Archaic Greeks. Answers could be much more straightforward on occasion. Before colonists left their *poleis*, Apollo's will was ascertained: Should we Corinthians site our colony just here in Sicily? Should we Megarians site ours just there along the Bosporos? Who should lead it? What laws should it have and who should write them? Apollo was the guardian of order for new colonies.

Apollo's association with law and regulation sheds further light on this role. Apollo had bestowed the Great *Rhetra* on Lykourgos. When the people of Kyrene in eastern Libya came to Delphi to obtain laws for their *polis*, Apollo directed them to seek an Arkadian law-giver. The Kyrenaians duly appointed Demonax of Mantineia who then became the god's spokesman (Herodotos, 4.161). The Law of Dreros, which managed the office of *kosmos* in that *polis*, was written into Apollo's temple wall (see Figure 1.2 on p. 6).

Apollo also advised individuals how to regulate their lives with pithy sayings. The Delphic maxims, "nothing too much," "know thyself," and "respect the divine," were simple directives that really boiled down to "know and respect your limitations." More practical correctives than vague prescriptions, the maxims are concise reminders similar to more modern folk adages.

Apollo's oracle at Delphi remained a potent force through the Archaic period. Only when the reputation of the Pythian priests became sullied with accusations of bribery during the sixth century BCE and then with suspicions of Persian collaboration in the early fifth century did its influence begin to wane. Before that, Greeks accepted the oracle's pronouncements as veritable utterances of Apollo himself.

5.4 Gods and *Poleis*

5.4.1 Cult and Identity

In the *Iliad*, Hera states: "To me most dear are three *poleis*, Argos and Sparta and Mykenai of the wide ways" (4.51–53). The exclusivity of her Argive sanctuary to non-Argives is illustrated in Herodotos' story of a Spartan invasion of the Argolid (6.77 ff.). After Kleomenes had defeated the Argives at Sepeia in 494 BCE, he journeyed to Hera's temple to sacrifice to the goddess. The Argive priest there forbade him to do so since he was a "stranger" and it would be sacrilegious. It was only lawful for Argives to sacrifice, the king was told. After Kleomenes had the priest forcibly removed from his presence and whipped, he proceeded to offer sacrifice to Hera (6.81). Kleomenes had done something similar at Athens where, although as a Dorian he was forbidden entrance to Athena's temple on the *akropolis*, he entered anyway (Herodotos, 5.72.3). Perhaps Kleomenes wanted to drive home his victories and humiliate both Argives and the Athenians by degrading a central symbol of their nationalism.

The Samians outdid all others in Archaic Greece by furnishing Hera with increasingly more magnificent abodes. The grandest of them all was the temple associated with the tyrant Polykrates: built *c.* 530 BCE, its stylobate was 57.7 m × 117.6 m with columns 20 m high. Polykrates had amassed vast wealth as a pirate-lord and so envisioned a temple that would be the talk of the Greek world both then and for the future. The Heraion's implication with Samian pride is demonstrated by the later dedication of Mandrokles, chief engineer for Dareios' bridge-of-boats across the Bosporos in the late sixth century BCE. Mandrokles dedicated a picture of the bridging in the Hera temple for all to see, a commemoration, but a statement of pride in his work and his Samian identity (Herodotos, 4.88.1). (See also Chapter 6.4.2 in this volume.)

The Samians had followed the lead of the Ephesians who had built the immense Artemision, one of the Seven Wonders of the ancient Greek world. The Ephesians were fanatically possessive of Artemis and her cult: the goddess and her worship were part of the fabric of the *polis* and *polis* identity. Such a dwelling as the Artemision was a votive designed to win favor from the goddess, but also to display Ephesian wealth, ingenuity, and devotion for all the Greeks to see. Such temples as the Heraion and Artemision overshadowed the ostensible purpose for which they were intended: the edifices themselves and the *poleis* they represented upstaged the gods and their worship.

While countless ancient cults and cult-worships remained in every Greek community and throughout the countryside, others, like that of Artemis of Ephesos, emerged to bind *politai* together. At Athens, whose very name is derived from the goddess, *polis* and divinity were one and the same. That implication was spotlighted every year and then far more grandly every fourth year from 566 BCE during the festival called the **Panathenaia** ("the all-Athens festival") (see also Chapter 10.4.1 in this volume).

5.5 The Archaic Greeks and Their Gods: A Summary

5.5.1 Law, Order, and Justice in the *Kosmos*

Both Hesiod's farmer and Homer's hero moved uneasily through their worlds, contending with forces that were frequently capricious and often malevolent. As the gods could harm as much as help, there was really no telling which way their will – or fortune – might break at any time. Achilles sums this up (*Iliad* 24.527–533):

> There are two large jars standing on the floor of Zeus' house,//[holding] "gifts" that he gives to mortals: one is full of evils, the other blessings.//For the one to whom Zeus delighting in thunder mixes and gives,//that man sometimes gets evil, sometimes good.// But to him [Zeus] gives [only] from the jar of evils, he makes him wretched,//and evil grinding poverty drives him over the goodly land//and he wanders, being honored neither by gods nor humans.

For Homer, it seems that the best the Greeks could hope for was a life of mixed good and evil.

The basic, indispensable benefit that Archaic Greeks derived from their gods was order, for which Hesiod extols Zeus. While Zeus did no favors to mankind by withholding fire, he maintained order that was necessary for survival and prosperity. While he might suffer by comparison with Prometheus, who brought the gift of fire to man, a rebel like Prometheus could, in the long run, be much more dangerous than beneficial. Initially, in Aischylos' *Prometheus Bound*, the Titan seems right to have stolen fire for man and Zeus wrong for withholding it. As the play goes on, however, we realize that Prometheus is more consumed by seething hatred and rebelliousness than he is benefaction. Like Achilles, he is so blinded by self-centered anger that he cannot envision where his rashness might lead. As foresightful as he is, he fails to see that dethroning Zeus could possibly open the door to another Typhoeos – or worse, he does see.

Greek fear of disorder is ubiquitously depicted in myth and art. The battles of the gods and Titans, the gods and Giants, Lapiths and Centaurs, Herakles and the monsters, all retold many times and portrayed in sculpture and painting, depict the need of the ancient Greeks for reassurance that order will prevail. It was not necessarily the order that they might want – regulation can chafe after all – but it was far better than lawlessness and chaos. In a world where catastrophes could occur suddenly, the gods and their presence, oppressive as they might otherwise seem, were also comforting. How the Greeks conceived of Zeus' rule explains to some extent their ambiguousness toward tyranny and vice versa: order is maintained, but freedom sacrificed. Could there ever be a felicitous balance?

Hesiod's *Theogony* establishes the indispensability of Zeus; his *Works and Days* shows just how important Olympian order was for the farmer. Zeus ensures the cycle of seasons and, by extension, the orderliness of society. What helps society function smoothly is *dike*, and Zeus guards that, too. He observes and guarantees oaths between people; he sees all and punishes oath- and law-breakers. It was he who sanctioned punishment for Troy after Paris broke the law of hospitality. Justice between humans must obtain just as natural order must obtain. But an Archaic Greek might well ponder, why, then, are the gods sometimes so unjust and at times so disorderly?

Prometheus remained perpetually attractive to the Greeks because he acted out the Greeks' own discontentment with the gods' oppressiveness. There is much more than a hint of the latter in the portrayal of the gods' inhumanity in the epics. When Prometheus stole fire, he weakened the Olympians by making mankind stronger. The gods withhold the "stuff of life," because, Hesiod implies, mankind would challenge the gods even as Prometheus challenged Zeus.

By the gods' reckoning, humans in the *Iliad* are like the leaves of trees. But by human reckoning, they themselves might just be superior to their gods precisely because of their mortality. Homer foregrounds, indeed, glorifies the deadly risks that human heroes face. They can display bravery when faced with death; the gods cannot. Homer highlights what heroes at Troy must undergo, but also how, as they do, they become more impressive than the gods. In the *Iliad*, the gods are much less impressive than the heroes.

By the time of Homer, at the very beginning of the Archaic period, the gods are more defined – and so deflated – because they are likened to humans. Archaic Greeks cherished and resented their gods, needed and did not want to need them. Their ambiguous feelings and their expressions of those feelings might seem childish – more part of a "family dynamic." Ancient Greeks apparently never realized that the gods were really projections of themselves and what they knew – and didn't know – into their environments.

5.6 The Olympians

- *Zeus*, the greatest Olympian, was the son of the Titans Kronos and Rhea. He evaded the fate of his siblings whom Kronos swallowed up as they were born. Secreted in a Cretan cave, Zeus grew strong enough to challenge his father, whom he made to disgorge the Olympians, his sisters and brothers. These together overthrew the Titans. Zeus' domain was the sky, but he predominated on earth because of his powerful weapons: thunder and lightning; he guarded terrestrial order. For all his power, however, Zeus remained fearful of displacement – a fear which depicts his vulnerability and limitations and helps to construe his seeming oppressiveness to humans. Although his "legitimate" consort was Hera, Zeus was amorous and sired countless offspring with many partners, human and divine. His most renowned sanctuary was Olympia. He is depicted in art as an older male, usually bearded, holding a scepter or wielding a lightning bolt.
- *Hera*, Zeus' sister, reigned as queen of the gods. Though Hera's divinity was rooted in ancient fertility worship, her children with Zeus were few. Jealous of her prerogatives, Hera was extremely hostile to Zeus' many divine and human paramours and offspring by them. She was especially inimical to the hero Herakles, whom Zeus sired with the mortal Alkmene. Hera was nevertheless regarded as a benign goddess and patroness, especially by married women. Her most famous sanctuaries were in Argos and on Samos. She is depicted in art as a mature female.
- *Demeter*, another sister of Zeus, was also a very ancient fertility goddess. By the Archaic period, she was the goddess of grain. Her child by Zeus, Persephone, became the consort of Hades, god of the Underworld. Hades abducted the girl to be his bride with Zeus' consent. When Demeter left Mount Olympos to seek Persephone, she wandered over the earth, bringing nature to a standstill. Nothing grew until she subsequently agreed with Zeus and Hades about Persephone's presence with her. This agreement restored natural order, but also explained the cycle of seasons for the Greeks. Demeter's most renowned sanctuary was at Eleusis in Attika. Greeks initiated into her "mysteries" there were promised "something more" in the afterlife, for associated with her was the belief that what dies can be reborn, including human life, just as the earth returns to life in spring. Demeter is depicted as a mature female.
- *Poseidon* was Zeus' brother and god of the sea. Possibly the original male consort of the earth-mother of the pre-Greeks, after the Greeks arrived, Poseidon seems to have been "demoted" to sea-god. This is explained in Homer (*Iliad* 15.190–191) as the result of Poseidon's drawing the "lot" of the sea as his portion. Poseidon remained a powerful god nonetheless, especially reverenced by the Athenians among others. His consort was the minor sea-goddess Amphitrite. Important sanctuaries were at Isthmia near Corinth and Sounion in south-eastern Attika. Poseidon is depicted as a mature male, sometimes difficult to distinguish from his brother Zeus.
- *Hades* was Zeus' other brother and god of the Underworld. When "lots" were drawn after the Titans' defeat, Hades drew the worst domain of all (*Iliad* 15.191). He presided over the dead along with Persephone. A grim presence, Hades was neither a recruiter of souls nor a sponsor of evil, but simply proprietor of the gloomy realm of death. One of his few sanctuaries was in Elis near Olympia. He is depicted as a mature male.
- *Athena*, daughter of Zeus and Metis ("Intelligence"), was brought to term inside Zeus, who had swallowed her pregnant mother. Athena emerged fully armed from Zeus' head when

Hephaistos struck it open with an ax. She was a god of warfare, but unlike Ares, represented strategy and tactics in war. She was also patroness of crafts, particularly weaving. By the Archaic period, she was also explicitly the goddess of wisdom. Athena helped heroes whom she favored, such as Herakles, Achilles, and Odysseus, endowing them with war-craft and cunning. She could also be quite destructive to those whom she disfavored, such as Aias. Her major sanctuary was on Athens' *akropolis*, but others were at Tegea in the Peloponnesos; at Marmaria, near Delphi; and at Sparta. A virgin goddess, she is depicted in art as a maiden.

- *Apollo*, son of Zeus and Leto, probably originated in Anatolia. He was apparently fully an Olympian by the end of the Bronze Age, however. Apollo was, like Zeus, a god of order and civilization – benefactions to mankind. He was also god of healing, music, and prophecy, the latter, a domain which he shared with Zeus. Apollo, like Zeus, was amorous and pursued, among others, the Trojan seer, Kassandra. His major sanctuaries were at Delphi and on Delos, which he shared with his twin, Artemis. He is depicted in art as a male youth.

- *Artemis*, the daughter of Zeus and Leto, is to be associated with *Britomartis*, the Minoan goddess of the mountains, and Mykenaian *Potnia Theron*, the "Lady of the Animals." Her haunts were mountains, woods, and nature in general. She was goddess of hunting, but also of the untamed wild, which endued her with a certain savagery and need for blood. Her major sanctuaries were at Ephesos and on Delos, which she shared with her brother Apollo. A virgin goddess, she is depicted as a maiden.

- *Aphrodite* was the daughter of Zeus and Dione (Homer) or generated from Ouranos' severed genitals cast into the sea by Kronos (Hesiod). Aphrodite was "borrowed" by the Greeks from the Phoenicians. She symbolized lust, not "love." She prompted Helen to leave with Paris and so began the Trojan War. Her consort was Hephaistos, but she had relations with Ares and Anchises, the father of the Trojan hero, Aeneas. Other goddesses despised her (*Iliad*), but Sappho made her a confidant in her poetry. As Pandora, a "lovely evil," Aphrodite brought both desire and destruction. Major sanctuaries were at Paphos on Cyprus, Kythera near Sparta, and Corinth. She is depicted as a very beautiful young maiden.

- *Ares*, son of Zeus and Hera, god of savage warfare, may have originated in Thrace, but was Olympian by the Bronze Age. Loathsome to the Greeks, Ares symbolized the blood-rage of war. He was caught *in flagrante* with Aphrodite by Hephaistos, her husband, and so became with her a laughing stock to the other gods (*Odyssey* Book 8, 266 ff.). He is depicted as a male youth, although sometimes bearded.

- *Hephaistos*, either the son of Zeus and Hera (Homer) or of Hera alone, sometimes called the "Limping God," was the husband of Aphrodite. Hephaistos was associated with molten metal and volcanoes (the word derives from his Roman name, Vulcan). He was also the "smith-god" and could create fabulous things, such as the "Shield of Achilles" (*Iliad* Book 18, 478 ff.). He is depicted as a male older than a youth, often bearded.

- *Hermes*, son of Zeus and Maia, was famed as messenger-god, but may have begun as a male counter-force to unruly nature, protecting humans in the uncontrolled spaces between settlements. He was the god of travelers, as well as the conveyor of the dead to the Underworld, of cleverness, deceit, and theft. He helped Odysseus endure Kirke's witchcraft by supplying him with an herbal antidote to her magic. Hermes is depicted as a male youth.

- *Dionysos*, son of Zeus and Semele, was a god of wine, ecstasy, and inspiration. As Apollo, he was assimilated into the Greek pantheon from outside of Greece. He was born from Zeus' thigh after being rescued to it from the womb of his dead human mother. Although Dionysos might seem to have encouraged excessiveness, in fact, he promoted distance from the mundane in order to achieve insight and enlightenment. Dionysos presided at *symposia*, as well as dramatic performances which were educative. He was attended by satyrs, goat-men like Pan, and by ecstatic women called *maenads* or *bacchai*. He is usually depicted as a male youth, though is sometimes bearded.

Notes

1 Cf. T. Palaima ("Mycenaean Religion," in C. Shelmerdine, ed. *The Cambridge Companion to the Aegean Bronze Age* [Cambridge, 2008], p. 344):

> At its most basic, religion "is a system of thought founded upon belief in an unseen and non-material world interacting with the visible world around us." Religion serves as a significant cultural marker, "a unified set of beliefs and practices relative to sacred things" that unites a community. Historical Greek religion had an overall ritual framework and belief structure, but it was uncanonical, undogmatic, and improvisatory.

2 Cf. Neer, pp. 83–84.
3 Apollodoros, *Library* 3.6.7.
4 Apollodoros, *Library* 3.12.5.
5 J. Zeilinga de Boer and J. Hale "The Oracle of Delphi – Was She Really Stoned?" *Archaeology Odyssey*, November/December 5 (2002) pp. 46–53, 58–59.

Further Reading

Greek Religion

W. Burkert, *Greek Religion, Archaic and Classical* (London, 2004).
D. Ogden, ed. *A Companion to Greek Religion* (London, 2010).

Hesiod and Eastern Religion

M. West, *The East Face of Helicon: West Asiatic Elements in Greek Poetry and Myth* (Oxford, 1999), esp. pp. 276–335.

Homer and the Gods

E. Kearns, "The Gods in the Homeric Epics," in R. Fowler, ed. *The Cambridge Companion to Homer* (Cambridge, 2004), pp. 59–73.

Sanctuaries

J. Pedley, *Sanctuaries and the Sacred in the Ancient Greek World* (Cambridge, 2006).

Prophecy and Divination

M. Flower, *The Seer in Ancient Greece* (Berkeley, CA, 2008).
S. Johnson, *Ancient Greek Divination* (London, 2008).

Delphi

J. Fontenrose, *The Delphic Oracle: Its Responses and Operations, with a Catalogue of Responses* (Berkeley, CA, 1981).

Religion in the *Polis*

L. Zaidman and P. Schmitt Pantel, *Religion in the Ancient Greek City* (Cambridge, 1992).

6

Early Greek Science

6.1 Darkness and Lumination

For most Archaic Greeks, the gods and their powers provided answers enough to questions about the natural world. The sun rose and set as Helios drove his fiery chariot through the vaulted sky from east to west; lightning strikes were caused by Zeus throwing thunderbolts; storms at sea were stirred up by Poseidon (or Zeus). A sudden death was the result of an arrow shot by Artemis or Apollo; a dearth of grain could be attributed to the displeasure of Demeter, while someone roused to desire for another might simply have been touched by Aphrodite or Eros. Such myths helped to explain the unknown and diminish its fearfulness.

Not all Greeks were content with such answers, however, and changes in the ways Archaic Greeks addressed questions about their world are evident by the end of the eighth century BCE. It is then that they began to observe their world more closely and objectively and record their observations, even as the Babylonians and the Egyptians had done centuries before them. One signpost is Hesiod's *Works and Days*, a portion of which is a kind of farmer's almanac. In it, Hesiod urges his brother Perses – and other Greek farmers less directly – to heed his advice, signaling that doing what he says will lead to success in farming. Hesiod implies that his authority for this instruction is observation and experience and that these have led to a clearer understanding of the conditions affecting Greek farming. *Works and Days* stands at the very beginnings of Archaic Greek science.

A more distinct watershed in Greek science may be dated to 664/663 BCE when Egypt was permanently opened to Greeks. Egyptian science and technology suddenly became available to the Greeks and contributed to the "great leap forward" of the later seventh century BCE, stimulating, among other things, what has come to be called the Ionian Enlightenment. Miletos, apparently the main port for Ionian Greeks going to and coming from Egypt, became the Enlightenment's epicenter: Thales, Anaximandros, and Anaximenes, the first Greek scientists, were its citizens. The more immediate effects of Egyptian technology may be observed in the first large Greek stone sculptures and temples dating from 650 BCE.

Ionian scientists were interested primarily in practical ends, but also answers to broader, more abstract questions. What is the essential ingredient of all things? Where did all things come from and go to? What is the nature of nature? Contacts with other cultures and peoples also prompted questions about ethics, morality, and shared or contrasting laws and cultural

Archaic Greece: The Age of New Reckonings, First Edition. Brian M. Lavelle.
© 2020 Brian M. Lavelle. Published 2020 by John Wiley & Sons Ltd.

values. The establishment of scientific enquiry was arguably the most significant occurrence of the Archaic Greek period.

6.2   A Farmer's Handbook: Hesiod's *Works and Days*

Science may be defined as the systematic study of nature. Its methodology consists of observation and data collection, rational data assessment, and conclusion based on that assessment. Technology is the application of science to practical ends. In Archaic Greece, applied science and the practical advantages that it could provide mattered much more to Greeks in general than pure science, certainly earlier on.

Hesiod's farming advice in the *Works and Days* is not at all theoretical. His instruction devolves upon the cycle of seasons. Charting them and what occurs in them establishes a responsive agenda for plowing, planting, and reaping, among other tasks. It is reasonable then that astronomy became the first interest of Archaic Greek scientists inasmuch as its results could produce a more precise calendar and so an agenda for farming and a better forecast for sailing. Ancient calendars, set by the sun and the moon, were all-important for specifying religious occasions, sacrifices, festivals, etc., but Hesiod's seasonal one was primarily concerned with farming practicalities.

The poet begins his advice with harvesting and plowing (383 ff.). He pegs it to the Pleiades, a cluster of stars in the constellation of Taurus, thought by the ancient Greeks to be the daughters of the Titan Atlas. When in spring the Pleiades are rising, he says, the harvest should begin, but plowing when the Pleiades set in fall. Long before Hesiod, the Pleiades' movements had been recognized as markers for reaping and sowing by Near Eastern astronomers. In fact, the more precise information that the Pleiades disappeared altogether for 40 nights in March and then reappeared to rise in May seems to have come to the Greeks from Phoenicians.[1] Hesiod implies that what he says about farming and the seasons derives from observing repeating seasonal signs and responding correctly and in a timely fashion to them. He has confirmed the synchronisms and their results.

All the necessaries for plowing must be stored up, Hesiod says, including a woman for work – not for marrying! The plowing must be done speedily in any conditions (Box 6.1). A middle-aged man is best with the plow: a younger man will just be distracted. The plow has to be made of oak, and the wood for it is to be cut in September, well before plowing. Plowing and reaping must be done in the nude – a vestige of ancient superstition and magic. All of this, Hesiod says, so that a man might have an abundance at harvest and not have to go begging at someone else's door – a disgraceful thing.

Hesiod's tone seems confident, strongly implying that any farmer will benefit as he has benefitted. His advice was apparently widely accepted by Greek farmers who were grateful for any practical help they could get. According to a disdainful Herakleitos in the early fifth century BCE, Hesiod was the **didaskalos** ("teacher") of the many because they thought him to have possessed the greatest knowledge.[2]

Hesiod's key advice for farming success is grounded in neither superstition, magic, nor god-signs. It is true that the Pleiades are taken to be divinities, wind-personifications like Boreas can blow down crops – and, of course, one should plow in the nude. Yet most of Hesiod's advice is devoid of direct connection to divinity or superstition. The Pleiades are

---

Box 6.1 Working the Soil

> Right away when plowing season appears to men,
> then get a move on, your servants and you alike,
> plowing through wet and dry at the plowing time of year,
> speed the work early so that your fields will be full.
> In spring, go over the soil; in summer, furrowing
>   won't play you false either.
> Sow the plowed up earth while the soil's still dry and light.
> [...]
> So will the corn-tassels nod to earth in their ripeness,
> that is, if the Olympian himself sends a good end to things –
> and you will free your pantry-bins from spider-webs.
> I expect that you will be pleased, taking from your stores within,
> and you will come to bright springtime, relieved of stress,
> and not look out to others, but another will be in need of you.
> *(Hesiod,* Works and Days *458–463, 473–478)*

While there is no guarantee that something unexpected might not happen – Zeus' goodwill was indispensable, but variable in the lives of the Archaic Greeks – the farmer's best chance is to follow Hesiod's general prescription: "Good order is best for mortal men, disorder worst." For Hesiod, order depends upon the cycle of seasons and the farmer's response to seasonal signs is absolutely critical for well-being.

---

star signs, not goddesses, whose appearance and disappearance amount to the numerals of a cosmic clock. The cry of the crane tells when planting is to begin, not the god who makes it cry. He cautions that the man who waits until the solstice, another celestial sign, will only reap bitterly when the time comes. Management of farm tasks based on observing and reacting to the seasons is all-important. Disaster will result from ignoring that cycle and leaving things to chance.

The "science" of *Works and Days* is based on environmental and celestial observations and so anticipates Ionian astronomy. What knowledge actual observation had produced provides not just an improved method of farming, but the superior way to farm to Hesiod's time. While the gods are never absent in Hesiod's world, recognizing and reacting to signs in nature offer the best possibilities of success to farmers.

6.3   The Near East, Miletos, and Science

For the Archaic Greeks, Egypt was a paradise. Its soil was cultivated without great effort, its yield marvelously bountiful. The wealth of the Egyptians was in fact incalculable. Bronze Age Greeks were in regular contact with Egypt, and that did not cease when the Mykenaian civilization ended. Egypt's riches – which Dark Age Greeks thought were shared in every household (*Iliad* 9.382) – were perpetually alluring to them. The type of pirate-raid Odysseus lies about to Eumaios was small-scale compared to the Karian-Ionian expedition of 664/663 BCE, but suggests regular marauding before it. However, when the Karians and Ionians came ashore in the Nile Delta and were offered "great rewards" if they would serve Psammetichos instead of pillaging, they agreed and settled in Egypt. Their settlement changed everything for the Archaic Greeks.

With Psammetichos' special permission, Ionian Greeks built an *emporion* at Naukratis on the Nile not far from his original Nile Delta capital of Sais. Although Milesians were prominent in the founding of Naukratis (or its predecessor), Ionians from different *poleis* came to populate what became the main Archaic Greek settlement and trading post in Egypt. A steady stream of mercenaries arrived in Egypt from Ionia, who, between campaigns, became merchants conveying cargoes to and from Egypt. Egyptian grain, linen, and papyrus were among other commodities exchanged at Naukratis for such things as Greek olive oil, wine, and silver. More importantly, new ideas were also traded there, as they are at all such places, and it may well have been at Naukratis where Greeks learned most about Egyptian science and technology.

What the Egyptians had done and could do must have overwhelmed the arriving Greeks. Monumental temples and sculptures in stone and, of course, the massive pyramids astound even today. The Greeks discovered that such wonders were produced by a superior technology grounded in science, especially geometry. Buildings and sculptures were conceived beforehand, plotted on the land or the stone, and then constructed or chiseled out. Egyptians had already worked out an elaborate solar calendar tied to agriculture; their knowledge of medicine far outstripped that of the Greeks; they could write on a kind of paper made from papyrus plants. While it may be that Greeks themselves imported technologies such as stone-working, it is very possible that at least some Egyptians came to Greece bringing technologies with them. One famous potter of sixth-century BCE Athens was "Amasis," whose name was Egyptian.

The Egyptians and their technology were by no means the only stimuli for Archaic Greek science. Babylonian astronomers had, for some time, fixed solstice dates and predicted eclipses. They had invented the synodic or lunar month which figured as the basis of many ancient calendars. Phoenician star navigation was more precise than Greek reckoning;[3] the Phoenicians possessed advanced ship types which the Greeks "borrowed." Indeed, Phoenicians were sailing in triremes years before the Greeks made them their standard. The Phoenician alphabet was adapted for Greek writing and reading, a key development in the acquisition and spread of technology, all before the mid-eighth century BCE. Despite the rivalry between Greeks and Phoenicians, they frequently traded and even settled together: Greeks were at Al Mina in Syria and Phoenicians were settled in Crete during the Archaic period.

Miletos was the fortunate recipient of the streams of scientific and technical information arriving from Egypt in the seventh century BCE. This was due to several factors: Miletos' role in the original settlement of Egypt, its trading ties to the eastern Mediterranean, and its felicitous location on the southwestern Anatolian coast. Its citizens also seemed to have been uniquely receptive to new knowledge and ideas. Miletos was the largest *polis* in Ionia, its population diverse. Its inhabitants were Greeks, Karians, and Phoenicians among others – not infrequently intermarried. Miletos also possessed many colonies especially toward and around the Black Sea. Milesians were accustomed to diversities of people, ideas, beliefs, and practices, all of which in turn will have stimulated observation, comparison, and reflection. As Athens became in the fifth century BCE by its wealth, position, and openness to innovation the foremost *polis* in Greece, so did Miletos provide the best environment in Archaic Greece for the reception of new knowledge from Egypt.

What blended together particularly well in Miletos were Greek desires for more practical, beneficial information and the astronomical and mathematical knowledge of the Phoenicians and the Egyptians. Ionian scientists were keen to know about the seasons, the sun and stars, and, more broadly, the *kosmos*, its nature and how it functioned. Thales and his successors sought to name the ***arche***, the "first principle" and primal source of all things, and to comprehend how things worked in nature. Of course, what they conceived and declared about the *kosmos* was confined by their own observational and intellectual limitations. They were quite unaware of these constraints, however, supremely confident in their rationality, and rarely circumspect about them. Yet, howsoever natural it might seem to them to move from observable phenomena to speculations about their nature and origins, Archaic Greeks did not inherit from Egyptians or the Babylonians the compelling desires to know the ultimate source of the natural world and its forces or to understand and explain them logically to others. Rather, those and where they led seem to have been uniquely Greek.

6.3.1 Thales, *Physikos kai Astronomikos*[4]

Thales was a Milesian of mixed Karian, Phoenician, and Greek ancestry; his family, the distinguished Thelidai, were descendants of the Phoenicians Kadmos and Agenor. Active in the political affairs of Miletos and Ionia during his lifetime, *c.* 625–*c.* 545 BCE, Thales was famous for urging the Ionians to unite and establish a pan-Ionian capital at Teos – political ideas well ahead of their time.[5] Herodotos (1.75.4–6) says that Thales was also an engineering adviser to Kroisos. Most of what we know about Thales and other Archaic scientists and philosophers derives from sources much later than his lifetime.

Thales is said to have visited Egypt specifically to learn about geometry and astronomy and to observe the land and the River Nile. While in Egypt, he measured a pyramid's height by the shadow it cast in relation to his own, a calculation based on the measurement of angles. If Thales actually did that, he borrowed from the Egyptians who were already highly proficient in mathematics.[6] Whether he traveled to Egypt at all, Thales was credited with introducing geometry to the Greeks, and Egyptian science was certainly a potential source for him.

Thales' primary interest seems to have been solar phenomena, which he observed and charted. Two works ascribed to him, "On the Turning" and "On the Equal Day," composed in verse, focus on solstices and equinoxes. Thales achieved renown for predicting the solar eclipse of 585 BCE (Herodotos 1.74.2), information about which he might have obtained from the Babylonians, perhaps directly or filtered through Phoenician intermediaries.[7] The Babylonians, like the Egyptians, recorded eclipses and were apparently able to predict them by means of the saros cycle, a period of synodic or moon-cycle months between eclipses. Some scholars, however, doubt eclipse prediction in antiquity, suggesting that Thales' astronomical interests and his contemporaneity with the famous eclipse of 585 inspired the false ascription.

For Archaic Greeks, a solar eclipse was a terrifying occurrence, as Archilochos implies (Box 6.2). To them, the eclipse threatened to blot out the sun's light forever – a fear that persists in some places in the world even today. Thales could know from Babylonian eclipse recordings

---

Box 6.2 Archilochos and the Eclipse

> ... there is nothing unhoped for nor impossible
> nor to be wondered at, since Zeus, the father of the Olympians,
> made night out of midday, hiding away the light
> of the shining sun, and grievous fear came upon mankind.
> From this, all things are to be believed and expected
> by men ...
>
> *(F 122, 1–6)*

Archilochos may be referring to the eclipse of 648 BCE, which was a total eclipse on Paros, his home island. Another in 660 BCE, though nearer in time to Archilochos' floruit, 664/663 BCE, was only partial.

The eclipse of 585 BCE is said to have so terrified Lydian and Median warriors battling each other that they stopped fighting, ended their war, and concluded a peace on the spot (Herodotos 1.74.3) – a further index of the fear triggered by eclipses in the Archaic period.

---

that solar eclipses were not "out of the blue," but regular occurrences, and that the light of the darkened sun would appear again. Predicting eclipses even if only approximately correctly reduced the terror of the event which to the undereducated might seem catastrophic.

Thales' interests in the sun's movements and solar events were obviously spurred by a desire to better understand the solar year. Perhaps he had realized that the sun's movements offered a far more reliable predictor of seasons and seasonal change than did flights of birds, weather, or even the rising and setting of stars like the Pleiades. The Roman Pliny observed that Hesiod said that the Pleiades set with the autumn equinox, whereas Thales stated much more precisely that the stars set on the 25th day after the autumnal equinox (*Natural History* 18.213).

Thales reputedly introduced navigation by the stars to the Greeks and distance-reckoning at sea, both of immense practical value. Although Thales may not have been author of the "Nautical Star Charts," a work in hexameters about sailing by the stars, Kallimachos, an Alexandrian poet of the third century BCE, implies that Thales introduced the Phoenician method of navigating by Ursa Minor. Thales was also credited with *triangulation*, the determination of otherwise unknown distances by the use of fixed points and angles. If so, Thales was transmitting to the Greeks what had been well known to the Phoenicians and Egyptians for centuries before his time.

Thales' reputation for applying knowledge practically is found in a famous anecdote in Aristotle's *Politics* (1259a, 5–21). The philosopher says that Thales was roundly criticized for useless pursuits – these apparently having to do with his speculation about the origins of all things. But Thales ascertained that there would be a particularly good olive harvest one season in the area around Miletos. Anticipating that harvest and wanting to profit from his knowledge, Thales put down deposits on all the available olive presses in Miletos and Chios for himself. He speculated that, when the olive harvest came in, every olive grower in the area would be looking to press the harvested olives into oil and the presses he controlled would be in high demand. When the harvest came in, all went according to plan. The olive harvesters had to pay Thales' price in order to process their olives, and he made a handy profit. Thus, Thales worked the "law of supply and demand" to perfection, proving that science, such as it was, could serve practical interests. The story seems apocryphal, but nevertheless demonstrates how Greeks thought that scientific knowledge could be practical and used to profit, as well as how they connected such profiting with Thales. Such material gain mitigated to some extent the disturbing effects of scientific enquiry and the erosion of conventional wisdom it generated.

Thales' more abstract pronouncements were less practical – and somewhat unsettling for his contemporaries. According to Aristotle (*Metaphysics* 983b, 6–12, 17–27), Thales speculated that "water was the first principle of all things" – a concept he surely "borrowed" from the Babylonians possibly by way of the Phoenicians.[8] Although Thales did not deny the divine its existence – he said that "gods" were in everything – he diminished it by reducing the primal source to water and stimulated others to go even farther than he did. (We take up Milesian philosophy in Chapter 7.)

The pronouncements of Thales and other scientists and philosophers did not go down easily for some Greeks, it seems. They were perturbed by such new thinking and turned to derision to block out their unease, especially when they could not grasp the importance of scientific and philosophic enquiry and speculation. One anecdote ridiculed Thales as overly absorbed with star-gazing and detached from the world (Box 6.3).

His perceived eccentricities, "silly" enquiries, and disturbing pronouncements notwithstanding, Thales' voice and opinions carried considerable weight with contemporary Ionians, according to Herodotos. He was the first to have revealed ***physis*** ("nature") to the Greeks and was considered one of the wisest men of his time. His wisdom and reputation among contemporaries and later generations of Greeks established him as one of the Seven Sages of Archaic Greece.

Box 6.3 Thales, Not Well-Grounded

> As Thales was charting the stars … and, looking upward, fell into a well, a certain Thracian slave-woman, witty and sharp, is said to have jeered down at him [saying] that, while he was very eager to know about the things in the sky, he was oblivious to things right in front of him and at his feet.
>
> (Plato, Theaitetos *174a4–7)*[9]

His "head in the clouds," Thales is derided as an "absent-minded professor" would be today. Such derision is based upon a popular conception that scientists are involved in ridiculous pursuits. Actually, such ridicule is a way of defusing some of the disturbance caused to "civilians" by those who challenge accepted beliefs and practices: the latter and their more disturbing investigations are disarmed as silly and of no consequence.

There are other barbs in the story. Although, according to Diogenes Laertios (1.33), Thales reportedly prayed thankfully every day to the gods that he was born a man and not a beast, a man and not a woman, and Greek and not a barbarian, he is ridiculed here by a barbarian slave-woman. The anecdote may have been invented much after Thales' lifetime.

6.3.2 Anaximandros, Hekataios, and the World Imagined

Anaximandros (*c.* 610–546 BCE) was a younger contemporary and perhaps a student of Thales. One testimony implies that he was the leader of Miletos' colony to Apollonia (Sozopol in Bulgaria), but that is highly suspect, since the Milesians had founded Apollonia many years before Anaximandros' reputed birthdate. It may nevertheless be taken as a testimonial to Anaximandros' political activity and status among the Milesians.

Anaximandros' practical focuses were the heavens, time, and space. He was said by the Greeks to have "discovered" the *gnomon* ("sundial"), an instrument known to the Babylonians and Egyptians centuries earlier. The basic sundial is most commonly created by standing a right-angled blade –modernly called the *gnomon* – upright upon a plane surface in unshaded outdoor space. The shadow that it creates not only moves during the day, but lengthens or shortens depending upon the season of the year due to solar declination. Anaximandros' *gnomon* could mark summer and winter solstices and vernal and autumnal equinoxes, as well as indicate more precise times during the day. The instrument fine-tuned time-telling for Archaic Greeks.

Sundials are simple and cheap to construct: every Greek could possess one. Although the *gnomon* is never completely efficient, especially on cloudy days, Greeks could count on more days of sunshine every year than cloud. The times of the day and year would be visible to anyone who could read shadows and where they fell on the sundial face. Anaximandros is said to have traveled to Sparta and set up a *gnomon* there – a further testimony to his association with the instrument, howsoever dubious the story of his sojourn to Lakonia might be.

The first map of the world known to the Greeks was also attributed to Anaximandros, who adapted the concept apparently most directly from the Babylonians. His primary reason for the map may have been visually to relate Miletos to the rest of the world, including its colonies. Such a map was an important supplement to nautical star-charts for sailors since it marked fixed and observable geographical features in relation to others.

Anaximandros' map depicted land and sea, the Ocean stream encircling all, and the continents separated into Europe and Asia. While his original rendering may have been a simple drawing on a wooden tablet, it apparently generated more elaborate copies. Aristagoras, tyrant of Miletos in the later sixth century BCE, presented a bronze map of the world to Kleomenes of Sparta (Herodotos 5.49.1), which must have been based on Anaximandros' map. While his model may have been Babylonian, Anaximandros added Greek ports, *poleis*, settlements, and known landmarks based upon his own investigations and testimonies from travelers who visited Miletos.

Hekataios (*c.* 560/550–*c.* 490 BCE) improved upon Anaximandros. A Milesian *aristos* and political advisor like Thales and perhaps Anaximandros, Hekataios is said to have counseled the Ionians not to rebel against their Persian overlords in 499 BCE. He asserted that Persian forces were too numerous and the Ionians would be overwhelmed in any war with them (Herodotos 5.36). The Ionians should gain mastery of the sea, he urged. The pronouncements are suspiciously predictive of Miletos' failure in the rebellion and of Athens' naval power in the fifth century BCE. Such was Hekataios' reputation for practical wisdom, whether or not he actually gave such advice.

Hekataios' discouragement of rebellion against the Persians because of its empire's vastness was perhaps attributed to him because of his renowned knowledge of barbarian peoples. In the

"Circuit of the Earth," Hekataios described a voyage in the Mediterranean beginning at Gibraltar, proceeding along its north coast and then into the Black Sea. Re-emerging into the Mediterranean, the progress continued on its south side and finished on the north shore of Morocco, just opposite Gibraltar. Excursuses from the direct route included islands like Sardinia, but also countries like Skythia, Egypt, and Persia. The work was divided into two books, the first encompassing Europe, and the second Asia and North Africa. Hekataios also included what he took to be facts about particular places and local history as well as myth.

Hekataios' revisions were apparently prompted by his judgment that Anaximandros' map was not good enough. That sense must have derived from a comparison of what he knew and thought he knew with Anaximandros' data. Hekataios was called "much-traveled" and he is said to have journeyed to Egypt among other places. If, as it seems, he consciously sought to verify at least some of his data by personal observation, Hekataios represents a new standard of objectivity. Such verification, which the Greeks called **autopsia** ("seeing, verifying with one's own eyes"), is a keystone of scientific methodology and became a basic principle in Greek historiography and geography.[10]

The same discontentment with received knowledge appears to be evident in Hekataios' "Stories about Ancestors," also called *Histories*. In it, Hekataios sought to separate myth and fact, famously declaring at the beginning of the work: "I write these things as they seem to me to be true. For the stories of the Greeks are both many and laughable, as they appear to me."[11] Hekataios believed that myths contained facts but that these had become clouded by misunderstanding: his purpose was to clarify. The standard for much of the clarification, however, was himself and his own sensibilities – what some scholars have called "rational probability." Like other Milesian scientists, Hekataios employed his own confident reasoning, interpreting **logoi** ("stories, accounts") and what impressed him as rational.

Hekataios could certainly lose touch with objectivity. He explained Kerberos, the hound of hell, as a mere snake and Geryon, the famous three-bodied man-monster whom Herakles bested in a famous fight, as a human being and king.[12] He etymologizes "Mykenai" as derived from *mukes*, the "cap" or "scabbard" of Perseus, the mythical ancestor of the Mykenaians.[13] Hekataios' rationalisms are frequently quite subjective and he accepts some myths outright, just as Herodotos will do 50 years hence. Yet, in spite of that subjectivity, Hekataios laid the foundation for objective historiography.

The maps of Anaximandros and Hekataios helped to illuminate what was dim or unknown. By drawing the world, Anaximandros compassed and reduced it to a comprehensible image; Hekataios' annotations endued it with humanity. "Gaia" was no longer Hesiod's murky monstrosity, but rather a more comfortable partner for civilization. The earth was masses of land, but now dotted with settlements of human beings, named features and landmarks, with stories about them. It was a knowable, more benign, less threatening, and less fearful environment. The maps of the Milesians, though ridiculed later, were significant steps in the progress of the Greeks toward comprehension of their world.

Hekataios was called a "story-maker" by Herodotos (5.36.2), but was rather a reviser of stories. He is a link between Thales and Anaximandros and the Greek skeptics of the fifth century BCE. His attempts to separate fact from fiction, howsoever imperfect, anticipate Herodotos and the "scientific" history of Thucydides. Herodotos knew well Hekataios' "Circuit of the Earth" and "Stories about Ancestors," and, according to one ancient author, actually borrowed freely from them for his own work.

6.3.3 Milesian Science: A Summary

The appearance of Milesian science marks a distinct watershed. Thales and Anaximandros were not simply "star-gazers" fascinated by the lights and paths of the sun, the moon, or the other bodies as they moved in the night skies. Their interests were oriented in the first place toward practical advantage. Both sought to establish better, more accurate ways of telling seasonal time. With Anaximandros' introduction of the *gnomon*, the Greeks possessed a serviceable, roughly accurate solar clock. Their celestial observations benefitted Greek farmers, but also seafarers who could navigate more precisely by the stars.

At the heart of their practical endeavors was measurement. Thales showed how to plot distances by triangulation; Anaximandros, however, scaled distances to make them visual and so more comprehensible. Hekataios improved upon Anaximandros by adding "facts" about the places and peoples of the world map. Herodotos surpassed Hekataios by including ethnographic information in his *Histories*. Measurement of time and space, but also, less directly, of themselves in comparison with others were the primary aims of these Ionian Greeks.

Ionian scientists exceeded the merely practical, however, by speculating about the nature of everything. Their interest in theoretical science was connected to the primary philosophical question, who are we ? Each of the Milesians had his own answer, each bequeathed to his successors the bases for criticism, extrapolation, and further speculation and conclusion. Most significantly, the Milesians stimulated the study of nature *as* nature and not divinity. Although, as we have seen, Hesiod was the first to distance the gods from natural phenomena, it was the Milesians who detached them. Moving decisively away from blind belief in the gods as forces in nature, these set the table for Herakleitos, Xenophanes, and, in the Classical period, Parmenides.

6.4 "Wonders"

As mentioned, the design of early Greek temples has been linked to Mykenaian *megarons*, the throne rooms of high kings who may have been deemed intermediaries between gods and humans in the Bronze Age. Certainly simple construction predominates in early Greek temple design. Before the seventh century BCE, Greek temples were small and built of impermanent materials such as wood and mud brick. The structure of the earliest Archaic temple of Apollo at Delphi was made of laurel, it was said, and covered with branches or thatch. The best example of a very early Archaic Greek temple may be the terracotta house or shrine model from the Argive Heraion. Larger buildings were more expensive to construct, requiring capital to build them proportional to their size, architectural expertise and planning, community cooperation, and laborers possessing building skills. Nevertheless, by the mid-sixth century BCE, Greeks were constructing such wonders as the colossal Artemision, a temple that required surpassing building skill, enormous capital, and a massive number of laborers. How did this dramatic change occur?

6.4.1 The Evolution of Archaic Greek Temples

Three examples of ancient Greek temples from the Archaic period will be useful in demonstrating the development of Greek building technology from *c.* 750–*c.* 550 BCE. The very simple temple of Apollo *Delphinios* at Dreros in Crete is dated to the mid-to later eighth century

BCE; that of Poseidon at Isthmia near Corinth dates to perhaps the second quarter of the seventh century BCE; and finally, the Artemision at Ephesos, *c.* 550 BCE. In each case, their builders sought to exceed those temples that had gone before.

The Delphinion of Dreros was a simple rectangular stone structure, about 10.9 m by 7.2 m. Two footings supported wooden posts which held up the main beam of its pitched roof. A sacrificial hearth where goats were offered to the deity was constructed between the posts, and a bench stood against the wall in the southwest corner upon which cult figures were discovered. The roof was steeply pitched above the altar, the gables open to let smoke from the hearth escape. A small prostyle porch stood in front of the single north-northeast-facing entrance. The plan of this modest building with its internal altar and benches for idols is reminiscent of both the post-Mykenaian cult rooms at Karphi in Crete and the "chieftain's house" at Nichoria in Messenia. Nonetheless, some type of planning preceded the building of the temple walls, whose construction is fairly precise. That the temple was an important religious and secular building for Dreros is proven not only by the sacral objects found within it and its location at the *polis* center, but also by the Law of Dreros inscribed into its wall.

The far richer *polis* of Corinth undertook the impressive, innovative temple of Poseidon at the Isthmus *c.* 50 years later. It is a much larger edifice, *c.* 39 m × 14 m, and so nearly four times as long and twice as broad as the Apollo-temple at Dreros. Local limestone blocks were used for the structure and plaster applied to smooth the limestone's pocked surface. The temple roof, which sat partially upon the walls, was made of terracotta tiles, an innovation perhaps of the Corinthians themselves. The *cella*, the main room of the temple, contained five columns arranged down its center to support the pitched roof, and around it was a 7 × 18 column peristyle. The temple was regular in plan, symmetrical in fact, and monumental in design: it was meant to impress and surely did just that. It was built more systematically and precisely than any Greek temple before it. "Standard-sized ashlar blocks were laid in isodomic courses to the roof line, and the mold-made tiles were designed with respect to the spacing of columns and timber framing. The building thus embodies a unified system using standardized parts."[14] The Poseidon-temple at Isthmia and the later temple of Apollo at Corinth represent prototypes, further informing the canon for Greek temples.

Finally, the Ionic order Artemision, whose monumental size, 115 m × 46 m, was nearly three times as long and four times as wide as the temple of Poseidon at Isthmia. The interior, hypethral and so open to the air, was surrounded by a doubled peristyle with columns *c.* 18.5 m in height. A triple row of columns flanked front and back, some of which were decorated with life-sized relief sculptures. The inspiration for this enormous votive for Artemis was almost certainly Egypt, where there were many such hypethral temples.

The expertise for building this vast edifice was attributed to Khersiphron of Knossos, along with his son Metagenes. The first problem Khersiphron – or perhaps another architect, Theodoros of Samos – had to solve was the marshy ground of the temple's site, chosen so that the building could survive earthquakes. To stabilize the foundation, the architect put down packed charcoal overlaid with sheepskins (Pliny, *Natural History* 36.21) – something he must have learned from what had actually worked elsewhere, most likely Egypt. According to Vitruvius (10.2.11–12), Khersiphron also constructed special rolling devices to transport columns and architraves from the quarry to the temple-site, a technique that surely derived from the Egyptians. Finally, according to Pliny, to drop the monolithic architrave blocks into place atop the columns, Khersiphron utilized bags of sand which were piled up beyond the level of the column capitals and apparently around them. When the architrave blocks were dragged up and moved onto the sandbags surrounding the columns, the lowest bags were punctured and sand was let out and then hauled away. Gradually the architrave lowered itself into place. Of course, the use of sand points again to Egyptian models. Whether or not Khersiphron and Metagenes were real, extremely sophisticated technology was employed in the temple's building, from surveying to laying the foundation to constructing each piece of the temple.[15] The Artemision was one of many sixth-century BCE monumental Archaic Greek temples.

The differences between the temples at Dreros, Isthmia, and Ephesos are plain enough. Progressively stronger, more durable materials were used for each; temple construction became more precise from conception to completion; structures evolved from humbler to grandiose because Archaic Greeks, having been inspired by the monumentality of Egyptian architecture and learning about stonework from the Egyptians, continued to expand upon what they had learned, experimenting and innovating. Whatever the fictions involving Archaic Greek temple master-builders, later Archaic Ionian temples were built by architects who could conceive of them from foundations to finials and who possessed the technological skills in applied geometry and engineering to bring them off. They were abetted in their conceptions and constructions by *politai* who took great pride in these symbols of their *poleis*.

6.4.2 Tunnels, Moles, and Bridges

The most renowned engineering feat of the Archaic period was the tunnel of Eupalinos on the island of Samos. Herodotos (3.60) says that the tunnel was 7 **stades** long (1 *stade* = 185 m) and 2.5 m square. In fact, the actual tunnel is *c.* 1.8 m × 1.8 m and just over 1 km in length. Its purpose was to provide ancient Samos (modern Pythagorio) with fresh water and, to do that, the tunnel had to be cut through Kastro hill from northwest to southeast. Polykrates sponsored the project, which was both strategically important and politically advantageous. The thick walls of Polykratean Samos suggest the tyrant expected attack, and a safe, steady water supply was needed to withstand it. In the meantime, the populace of Samos could enjoy the water brought into the *polis* and credit the tyrant.

We know next to nothing about Eupalinos of Megara, the engineer of the tunnel, except that, like contemporary Greek temple-architects, he knew geometry very well and how to apply it practically and successfully. Eupalinos was in fact a remarkable engineer. He proved that his tunnelers, who had only picks, shovels, hammers, and metal chisels to break the stone of the tunnel, could start from opposite sides of Kastro hill, follow his reckonings, and actually meet beneath it. Though the passages were by no means arrow-straight, the tunnelers did come together underground and fairly precisely – an astonishing accomplishment for the time.

How could Eupalinos with just crude surveying instruments bring off such a project? How did his crew know in precisely which direction to tunnel to be able to meet in the middle, maintaining the slight inclination of the tunnel's floor to enable water to flow down through it to Samos? To dig a straight tunnel through rock and soil for 1 kilometer with such rudimentary tools and knowledge of surveying seems impossible.

Most modern scholars now agree that Eupalinos first established a guideline that tunnelers could follow through Kastro, but disagree about how he did it. Perhaps Eupalinos employed the method described by Heron of Alexandria, a renowned mathematician and engineer of the first century CE who wrote about the Samian tunnel. Moving westward around Kastro at a fixed elevation from the north tunnel start-point to a south one, Eupalinos could determine the legs of a large right triangle by means of measurements east-west and north-south. The large triangle's hypotenuse would be the actual line of the tunnel. Smaller right triangles extending from the hypotenuse-line at both ends of the tunnel would provide internal guidelines for the tunnelers as they worked toward the middle from both ends. The slight deviations in the tunnel's path may have been caused by adjustments to softer rock- or soil-types or seepage that the tunnelers encountered.

But how did Eupalinos determine the elevation that enabled the tunnel's floor to drop slightly to allow water to flow through it from the north to south end? One suggestion is that Eupalinos may have used a long leveling bow made of saplings of equal length joined in the middle. Lifted in the middle, the two ends should clear the ground at the same time, if the ends are at the same elevation. Again working westward around the mountain, Eupalinos could determine the northwest's elevation relative to that of the southwest: stone piles set up around the flank of Kastro whose heights were measured and set relative to one another would allow calculation of elevations with only small error.[16]

Eupalinos will have acquired his expertise in Egypt, in Ionia, or perhaps even on Samos. He must have employed Egyptian technology in any case since Egyptians knew very well about surveying, establishing elevations, and how to tunnel in rock. Presumably Eupalinos also used their surveying tools. Two renowned architect-engineers resided in Samos around the time of the tunnel's construction, Rhoikos and Theodoros, both of whom seem to have visited Egypt. Rhoikos was the "first" architect of the Heraion on Samos (Herodotos 3.60.4) and was credited by Pausanias (8.14.8), along with Theodoros, with the Greek invention of metal casting. An associate or successor to Rhoikos in the construction of the Samian Heraion, Theodoros reportedly wrote a book about the temple. He was said to have learned statue-carving in Egypt (Diodoros Sikulos 1.98.5–9). Rhoikos' visitation to Egypt might be confirmed by the dedication of an early sixth-century BCE East Greek cup to Aphrodite of Naukratis by one "Rhoikos." Late Archaic Samos, whose connections to Naukratis were quite strong through the Archaic period, seems thus to have been a center for applied science.

Polykrates financed other impressive constructions as well. A harbor mole or breakwater, attributed to Eupalinos, was made of rubble and over 360 m in length. It was created to protect the harbor of Samos town: atop it was a wall that fortified the harbor. Polykrates' largest project – one that certainly impressed Herodotos – was the reconstruction of the "Rhoikos" temple of Hera, meant to outdo the Artemision.

Mandrokles of Samos may have been a student of Eupalinos. He built a pontoon bridge for Dareios, the Persian king, across the Bosporos in 513/512 BCE, whereby Dareios' army could cross from Asia into Europe (Herodotos 4.87–88). It was a mighty accomplishment, since, in addition to seemingly ceaseless winds blowing down from the Black Sea, Mandrokles had to cope with currents that moved in opposite directions in the narrows, just as they do in the Hellespont. Mandrokles had to know how to construct a temporary bridge that could span the strait successfully, that would be strong enough to carry Dareios' army, its animals, and its baggage into Europe, and that would resist those forces of nature for an extended period of time to enable Dareios' army to march back across it in due course. Mandrokles constructed that bridge successfully (and perhaps another one over the Danube River). So proud was he of his accomplishment that he commissioned a painting of the bridging and dedicated it to Samian

Hera. Though the Persians were enemies, the Greeks could appreciate the "wonder" of Samian engineering accomplished even for a foe.

6.5 Medicine

Healing is practiced in the *Iliad*. Machaon and Podaleiros, Thessalian sons of Asklepios, are "physicians" for the Greeks at Troy. When Menelaos is injured by an arrow, Machaon sucks the blood from the wound and applies ***pharmaka*** ("healing drugs") to it (*Iliad*, 4.204–219). These drugs Machaon obtained from Asklepios who learned them from the centaur-teacher Cheiron, a medium between nature and culture. Asklepios, the son of Apollo, seems to have been grafted onto the family tree of every famous early Greek physician as ancestor.

Although Machaon and Podaleiros are gifted physicians in the *Iliad*, warriors also treat each other. Patroklos applies *pharmaka* to the wound of his comrade Eurypylos (*Iliad* 11.842–848). Patroklos had learned such healing from Achilles who in turn had learned it from Cheiron. There is of course no real science here: the "physicians" all seem to be practitioners of folk-type medicine. When Odysseus was gored by a boar, Autolykos' sons bound his wound and sang an incantation (*Odyssey* 19.455–458). Machaon and Podaleiros, who are also warrior-leaders,

Figure 6.1 Achilles bandages Patroklos' upper arm. Rendering of Attic R-F *kylix tondo*, Sosias, *c.* 500 BCE.

seem to be only occasional physicians, not professionals. Nonetheless, according to Nestor, a battlefield-healer was worth "many men" (*Iliad* 11.514).

There is evidence for actual medical science during the Archaic period, although it is sketchy. The most famous physician of antiquity was Hippokrates of Kos, who lived during the fifth century BCE. His father, Herakleides, reportedly taught him medicine, while Herakleides' father, another Hippokrates, seems to have instructed him in turn. This Hippokrates lived in the sixth century BCE and was reputed to have composed works on human bones, "About Fractures" and "About Joints." The ascription is highly suspect, but Egyptian physicians, from whom the Greeks must have learned, were knowledgeable of human anatomy from *c.* 3000 BCE. The grandfather of this earlier Hippokrates, Nebros and his son Chrysos, were also said to be physicians. They were summoned from Kos by the Delphic *Amphiktyonia* during the First Sacred War (*c.* 590 BCE) presumably because a plague was ravaging the allied army as it laid siege to Kirrha.[17] Nebros especially became more famous for employing his skill to harm rather than heal. He introduced hellebore into the Kirrhan water supply to incapacitate the Kirrhans and allow the Amphiktyons to take the *polis*. The story, while intriguing, is quite dubious, however.[18]

The tradition of medical practice extending back in time from Hippokrates suggests that professional physicians were in fact operating in Archaic Greece. Egyptian medical science and practice were ancient by the time of Nebros, and the acquaintance of the Greeks in Egypt with that science and practice must have had a considerable impact on the formation and evolution of Greek medical science, especially in the neighborhood of Ionia. As it happens, Kos of all places became most famous as a center of healing in the Greek world: it was the home of Hippokrates and his physician forebears.

The most famous Greek physician of the Archaic period was Demokedes of Kroton, whose father, Kalliphon, also a physician and priest of Asklepios, moved the family from Knidos, not far from Kos, to southern Italy. Becoming physician to Dareios of Persia after leaving the court of Polykrates of Samos, Demokedes outdid the resident Egyptian physicians at the Great King's court, applying gentler, more effective methods of healing upon Darieos and Atossa, his wife.[19] Once more, it seems, Greeks altered what they "borrowed" and would in due course surpass the Egyptians in medical science and practice in the persons of Hippokrates and his successors.

6.6   "Civilians," Science, and Technology

How did Archaic Greek science and technology impact the unscientific farmer, sailor, or artisan? Practically, for a farmer who heeded even Hesiod's homespun pre-scientific instruction might do better. Any Archaic Greek could tell time better with Anaximandros' *gnomon*, but a farmer could produce more – and so sell more – if he knew the time of the year more precisely. When a sailor, who might also be a farmer, navigated by the stars or remembered or referred to versions of Anaximandros' or Hekataios' maps, he could arrive at his destination more surely and easily. An artisan who learned how to carve stone or throw a pot and paint it better could produce a much more appealing, better-selling product for patrons. Larger and more durable and impressive stone temples could be built by communities. It simply paid the Archaic Greeks to learn and apply new technology which derived from science.

Information about technology and science must have been available to any Greek who wanted to hear about it in the *agora*, just as he could hear about politics, religion, philosophy, or just about anything else there. Stories about Thales' "killing" in the olive oil market, for example, would be big news, perhaps "the great capitalist" himself recounting his triumph as a "teaching moment" for audiences at Miletos and elsewhere. Many returning merchants and mercenaries from Egypt disembarking in Miletos, Ephesos, or Halikarnassos would have much to share then and there or fanning out to other parts of Ionia, the Anatolian shore, or the Greek mainland with information about new technology and skills or new implements to do things better with. Like Hesiod's father, Ionians might relocate to the Greek mainland and bring new knowledge – or news of it – to their new homes. The first *kouroi* appear on the Greek mainland near the end of the seventh century BCE, the result apparently of stone-working technology making its way across the Aegean by way of Paros and Naxos.

The less direct results of this new knowledge were assurances even for common Greeks that they could do better where they lived and worked or sailed. But there was surely also some disquiet. Things were not as they had been before Thales and the Milesians: science by its nature diminished the Greek gods and increased confidence in man's own intellect. Notwithstanding, sincere religious belief persisted among most Greeks through the Classical period, the great temples of the fifth century proving the potency then of belief in the Olympian gods. Yet, even in the *Works and Days*, the direct influences of the Olympians in a farmer's life already seem to be rather less than they were in those of the *Iliad*'s heroes.

Notes

1 Cf. M. West, ed. and comm. *Hesiod. Works and Days* (Oxford, 1978), pp. 254–256.
2 Hippolytos *Refutation* 9.10.2 (Graham 19, pp. 144–145).
3 Archaic Greek sailors reckoned by stars from the time of Homer (*Odyssey* 5.270–277), but certainly not as well as the Phoenicians at the time.
4 "Enquirer into nature and skilled in astronomy."
5 Herodotos 1.170.3.
6 Plutarch (*Moralia* 147a [Graham 33, pp. 34–35]) says that Thales used a staff to measure the pyramid's shadow (cf. L. Redlin and N. Watson, "Thales' Shadow," *Mathematics Magazine* 73 [2000], pp. 347–353).
7 Thales may actually have visited Babylonia: cf. R. McKirahan, *Philosophy Before Socrates* (Indianapolis, 1994), p. 25.
8 Graham 15, pp. 28–29.
9 Cf. H. Blumenberg, *The Laughter of the Thracian Woman: A Protohistory of Theory*, translated by S. Hawkins (London, 2015), esp. 1–21.
10 Other travel writers of the Archaic period include Euthymenes of Massilia (Marseille), earlier sixth century BCE (?), and Skylax of Karyanda, later sixth century BCE.
11 *FrGrHist* 1, F 1.
12 Kerberos: *FrGrHist* 1, F 27; Geryon: *FrGrHist* 1, F 26.
13 *FrGrHist* 1, F 22.
14 E. Gebhard, "The Archaic Temple at Isthmia: Techniques of Construction," in M. Bietak, ed. *Archaische griechischen Temple und Altägypten* (Vienna, 2001), p. 41.

15 On Khersiphron: A. Sparavigna, "Chersiphron & Son Engineers," https://arxiv.org/abs/1110.5849.

16 Apostol, pp. 35 ff.

17 Thessalus, *Oratio in Hippocr. Opera*, vol. iii, p. 836.

18 A. Mayor, *Greek Fire, Poison Arrows, and Scorpion Bombs: Biological and Chemical Warfare in the Ancient World* (Woodstock, New York, 2003), pp. 102–103.

19 Herodotos 3.130.3. On Demokedes, see Herodotos 3.125, 129–137; cf. A. Griffith, "Democedes of Croton: A Greek Doctor at the Court of Darius," in H. Sancisi-Weerdenburg and A. Kuhrt, eds. *Achaemenid History II: The Greek Sources* (Leiden, 1987), pp. 37–51.

Further Reading

Greek Science

B. Farrington, *Greek Science* (Nottingham, 1980).

G. Lloyd, *Early Greek Science* (New York, 1974).

Hesiod and Farming

A. Edwards, *Hesiod's Ascra* (Berkeley, CA, 2004), esp. pp. 127–158.

M. West, comm. Hesiod. *Works and Days* (Oxford, 1978).

Milesians and Early Greek Science

D. Graham, *Explaining the Cosmos: The Ionian Tradition of Scientific Philosophy* (Princeton, NJ, 2006).

Thales

P. O'Grady, *Thales of Miletus: The Beginnings of Western Science and Philosophy* (Aldershot, UK, 2002).

Anaximandros

R. Hahn, *Anaximander and the Architects* (Albany, NY, 2001).

Hekataios

S. West, "Herodotus' Portrait of Hecataeus," *JHS* 111 (1991) pp. 144–160.

Greek Temples

W. Biers, *The Archaeology of Greece*[2] (Ithaca, NY, 1996), esp. pp. 112–118, 133–143, 156–164.

Tunnels, Moles, and Bridges

T. Apostol, "The Tunnel of Samos," *Engineering and Science* 67 (2004) pp. 30–40.

N. Hammond, "The Construction of Xerxes' Bridge over the Hellespont," *Journal of Hellenic Studies* (1996) pp. 88–107.

Greek Medicine

J. Longrigg, ed. *Greek Medicine: From the Heroic to the Hellenistic Age: A Source Book* (London, 1998), pp. 18–30.

7

Archaic Greek Philosophy

7.1   Introduction

Greek philosophers contemplated the nature of the physical world, but also questioned standards of morality and ethics. Philosophical enquiry is conceptual and intellectual in nature rather than scientific or empirical; like science, however, its language is logic and reason. While Greek philosophers pursued their own paths of enquiry and achieved notoriety individually doing so, they nevertheless engaged in dialogue and were strongly influenced by the views of their predecessors and contemporaries. Some became identified with "schools" of philosophy associated with Miletos, Elea in southern Italy, and, later, Athens. Philosophy as we know it was invented by the ancient Greeks: it was in fact their gift to the world. No other society produced as many significant philosophers, as many giants in the intellectual history of the world, as the ancient Greeks and several of these lived during the Archaic period.

Greek philosophers have been popularly conceived of as detached, bearded, white-haired old men meandering about in shoulder-draped robes, pontificating to others about trivial and even foolish things. Such caricatures actually derive from the ancient Greeks themselves. As we have seen, Thales, considered the very first philosopher and scientist, was ridiculed for falling into a hole while contemplating the stars. Sokrates was later more famously derided in Aristophanes' *Clouds* for communing with the clouds in a basket suspended in air and for being interested in such trivial exercises as determining how many "flea feet" a flea could jump. Portraits of philosophers mostly imagined by Greek artists reinforced the image of the bearded, balding seniors. Such ridicule devolved mainly upon the failure of most other Greeks to comprehend what philosophers were pursuing or saying about their pursuits or why they bothered with philosophy at all. To the majority of Archaic and Classical Greeks, philosophy offered no real practical advantage and so was essentially pointless.

Such caricatures are obviously quite misleading. What Greek philosophers were trying to ascertain was the nature of being – the very essence of humanistic pursuits. Concomitant questions were, what is the nature of the environment we live in? Is it real or conditioned by what we think it is? Where did we actually come from and where do we go at death? An ultimate question of course is, what is it to be human? Such questions may overlap with scientific enquiry, and several of the earliest Greek philosophers were also scientists.

Thales, Anaximandros, Anaximenes, Herakleitos, and Xenophanes were not detached, aloof, or even single-minded about their scientific or philosophical pursuits. Except for Pythagoras perhaps, they did not conceive of themselves as "philosophers" in any modern sense of the word and, apart from their intellectual pursuits, they did not conduct their lives in ways vastly different from other Archaic Greeks who were not "philosophers." Herakleitos apart, they did not live alone, detached from or oblivious to their communities. As we have seen, the Milesians, beginning with Thales, pursued knowledge for practical ends. As later Greek philosophers, the Milesians sought to win reputations for wisdom among their fellow Greeks as well as the influence – and prestige – that such reputations could bring them. Thales and the other early "philosophers" became important politically because their wisdom was widely acknowledged by their fellow-*politai* as beneficial.

Archaic Greek "philosophers" did not employ the rigorous standards that are expected of modern philosophers today. They asserted their beliefs without what would be considered solid proof provided by compelling argumentation today. What seemed plausible and could win approval if only from a small group was apt for publication. Depth of enquiry is what separated Archaic Greek "philosophers" from others who merely had ideas to proclaim. Their concepts and conclusions were more profoundly considered, discussed, and reasoned than others were. Yet, although they laid the foundations for Greek philosophy by employing logic, reason, and rational debate, the Milesians and their Archaic Greek successors might best be thought of as "pioneers of philosophy."

The investigations and speculations of Archaic philosophers mark significant changes in what at least some Greeks thought and believed. In the proems to their epics, Homer and Hesiod cite the Muses as the sources for what they sing to their audiences: there is a distinct gap between the human and the divine. By the time of Pythagoras, however, Greek philosophy had come to include the belief that the human soul was immortal and thus that humans were somehow divine in nature, if not actually god-like. Early Archaic philosophers like Thales, who blended the practical and concrete with the theoretical and abstract, were considered "wise men" because, like the epic poets, they were thought to convey wisdom derived from a divine source. Indeed, the Seven Sages, in whose number Thales was always included, were especially linked to the god Apollo. Later Greek philosophers who were more given to abstractions and less to practicalities were more distanced from and so somewhat less well regarded by their fellow Greeks.

7.2   Hesiod and Zeus

Any study of Archaic Greek philosophy must begin with the poet Hesiod. There are three philosophical topics prominent in his *Theogony* and *Works and Days*: cosmogony, world order and human order, and *dike*, all of which are implicated with that most important of divinities, Zeus. The poet's depiction of Zeus in the *Theogony* differs from that in the *Works and Days* and not just because of the different content of the poems.

Hesiod's primary aim in the *Theogony* was to account for how things came to be arranged in the ***kosmos*** ("universe") as they were in his time. The progression moves in episodes away from the primordial murkiness of Gaia and Ouranos to the relative brilliance of Zeus. For Hesiod, there is no creator or prime mover to begin with, no *arche*, only space or "gap." From Chaos emerges Gaia and, from her, almost everything else that is tangible or meaningful. Before Zeus' final triumph, the world is beset by violence and disorder. Ouranos is displaced for preventing the births of his children by his son Kronos, who is in turn displaced by his son, Zeus, for the same reason. Zeus is, however, sanctioned and abetted by Gaia, Ouranos, Rhea, his Titan mother, and other Titans to stop Kronos' unrighteousness and, implicitly, to establish order and the rule of justice.

The Olympian proves himself capable of maintaining cosmic order on his own in his final encounter with Typhoeos. The unholy mating of Gaia and Tartaros that produced Typhoeos underscores the capriciousness of nature and its threat to world order, the necessity of controlling it, and so the indispensability of Zeus. Zeus overcomes and imprisons Typhoeos, but also chastises Gaia and so seeks to prevent further threats to world order. His guardianship accounts for why the world does not relapse into disorder and assures that nature will not destroy mankind.

Natural order in the *Theogony* is based upon what seems right to Hesiod, but also upon what is beneficial for mankind. It was therefore quite unjust for Ouranos or Kronos to war with nature by preventing the births of their offspring and for the wind-demon Typhoeos to seek to destroy natural order. Natural order and justice are inextricably linked: justice begets order, disorder arises from injustice and must be corrected. Moral order is part of natural order, and its guardianship also falls to Zeus. As Typhoeos was punished for disrupting order, so, too, does Zeus punish humans who disrupt order by behaving unjustly. While Hesiod is also concerned with natural order in the *Works and Days*, Zeus' role in the poem is more focused on human justice. The whole community, he says, suffers if there is but one man doing or even plotting to do evil. Disorder results and must be corrected (Box 7.1).

Box 7.1 Crime and Punishment

> O Perses, you pay heed to *dike* and do not compound your *hybris*
> […]
>   … The other road to travel
> is better, the one leading to justice. *Dike* is stronger than *hybris*
> when it comes out in the end. Once he's suffered even the fool knows this.
> […]
> For those who are minded to evil *hybris* and wicked acts,
> upon them, the son of Kronos, Zeus of the wide brows, decrees justice.
> Very often a whole *polis* is despoiled by an evil man
> who sins and plots recklessness.
> To them from heaven, the son of Kronos brings down great suffering
> famine and plague both, and the masses waste away.
> Nor do women bear children, houses wither
> by the plan of Olympian Zeus. Another time
> he destroys their broad army or their wall
> or on their ships at sea does the son of Kronos take his vengeance.
> […]
> The eye of Zeus sees all things, knows all things
> […]
>   nor does it escape him
> such justice as the *polis* keeps within it.
>   (Hesiod, Works and Days, *213, 216–218, 238–247, 267–269*)

Every individual is obliged to act justly because the whole community is affected. Zeus applies suffering to the evil man and community alike because both are destructively out of sync with the *kosmos*. Individuals, society, and *kosmos* must be in harmony.

Order extends from the outer limits of the *kosmos* to the inner recesses of the *polis* and the very thoughts of individuals. *Dike*, the divine daughter of Zeus in the *Works and Days*, who harmonizes human interaction, is the most important of the social deities and the link to cosmic harmony.

For all of his concern for justice and order, Zeus himself can be quite capricious and even unjust. As forces of nature themselves, the Olympian gods frequently behave badly, leaving it to humans to wrestle with the contradictions. The fact that the gods themselves act unjustly and unreasonably sparks the chorus' famous lament in Aischylos' *Agamemnon* (160–182). There is only "Zeus" to answer the complaint of the chorus of elderly Argives about the human suffering wrought by the gods that they cannot fathom. The gods' apparent injustice and destructiveness remained distressing to the Greeks because they wanted their gods to be all-just and ever-benign. The too-human imperfections of the gods of Homer and Hesiod were criticized and rejected by later philosophers like Xenophanes.

That cosmogony and the cosmic order can be described by Hesiod is significant in itself. Human beings *can* know about the gods and the origin of the universe and Hesiod *can* communicate about them. It is true that the poet says at the beginning of both the *Theogony* and *Works and Days* that he is a conduit for the Muses. Yet *his* song and *his* words are necessary to make the "gifts of the Muses" intelligible to his fellow Greeks. His message to them is that cosmic order and harmony are fragile and dependent in the first instance upon Zeus, but finally upon human beings who must act justly, doing their part to help maintain that order.

7.3   Ionian Philosophy

7.3.1   The Milesians and the *Kosmos*

The nature of the *kosmos* and its harmony also fixed the interests of early Archaic Greek philosophers. Thales speculated that the first principle was water – a concept derived ultimately from Babylonian mythology. For the Babylonians, Apsu and Tiamat covered everything on the Earth until Marduk slew Tiamat and overlaid the fresh water with half of Tiamat's body, thus making dry land. The ocean remained to surround the land. Unlike the Babylonians, however, Thales did not seem to believe that water was divine like Apsu nor that it emerged from Chaos or Gaia. Rather, for Thales, water is a mundane element, while "God," the ***nous*** ("mind") of the *kosmos*, fashions everything from water and moves it about.

Thales' speculation about water was supported by observation. Water is ubiquitous, it exists in different states at different times in different places, and is necessary for all living things. It was therefore not unreasonable to conclude that it was the source of all things. For Thales, the nature of the Earth itself was explained as a logical extension of the *arche*: it was "like a piece of wood which floats upon [the water]."[1] By the same token, it was not "Earthshaker" Poseidon who caused earthquakes, but rather the action of surrounding water tossing about the wood-like Earth. Thales did not deny the Olympians their divinity, but qualified their power by specifying what was really significant in nature. For him, "everything is alive and full of ***daimones***," animate forces rather than Olympian divinities.[2] Thus, although Thales did not repudiate the gods or their existence – far from it – his assertions about the *arche* served to diminish them and stimulate others to proceed farther than he did.

Box 7.2 Anaximandros on "Coming-Into-Being" and "Passing Away"

> From which living things have their origin, into the same destruction it occurs by neces-
> sity. For they give *dike* [i.e., pay the penalty] and render recompense to one another for
> their *adikia* ("wrongdoing, injustice") according to time's order.
>
> *(Simplicius,* Physics *24.18–21; Graham 8, p. 50)*

The passage is difficult and controversial. What is Anaximandros saying? One interpretation is
that Anaximandros' *kosmos* is anthropocentric, like Hesiod's. When disorder is created, "justice"
must be served to restore harmony. As has been pointed out, this is no metaphor: rather, imbal-
ance is redressed in the "society" of the *kosmos* in the same way as it is in the *polis*.[3] The idea
might well derive from ideas about human justice current in Anaximandros' time.

Anaximandros, Thales' pupil, also posited a "first principle," but one that differed markedly
from his teacher's. The ***apeiron*** ("the boundless") is the source of all. It is in motion apparently swirling around a motionless center. It is ageless and undying; material and immaterial; around, but yet in everything. It is, in essence, undefinable. Primary genesis occurred
when a portion of "the boundless" separated and became a fire-shell that enclosed an enormous cool mist.

The Earth, composed of condensed mist, sits at the center of this *kosmos*: a cylinder, like a
column drum, one-third as deep as it is wide. It is suspended, fixed and unmoving, equidistant
from everything else – an astonishing, purely theoretical concept – and all around it is the fire-
shell. The sun, the moon, and the stars, fires enclosed in circles separated off from the fire-shell,
move around the Earth, shining as if through tubes. (Eclipses occur when the moon- or sun-
tubes are blocked.) The Earth, which began as mist, was dried hard in some places by the heat
around it, hence rock; in others less dried, hence liquid.

Anaximandros' conception of the *kosmos* is an astounding advance in abstract and speculative reasoning, though it relies on mundane objects like column drums and tubes to explain it.
The *apeiron* might seem at first glance to be Hesiod's Chaos by another name, a container in
which "coming-into-being" and "passing away" take place (Box 7.2). It is, however, far removed
from that, for it also stores the material from which all things come and go. Unlike Chaos, it
is active and moving, not static; it is not a backdrop or a mere container, but the constant
source of all things. Most significantly, it is *not* divine in the same sense that Hesiod's gods are
divine, since it is not at all linked to them nor is it defined. Its essence really is the philosopher's
own original, unself-conscious conceptualization of it. Anaximandros declares the *kosmos* to
be as he *thinks* it to be. That, in turn, depends both upon what he perceives and what seems
to explain his perceptions to him. The similes of tubes and column drums and Anaximandros'
theory of geocentric symmetry will have helped the Greeks of his time to comprehend his
thought.

The last of the great Milesian philosophers was Anaximenes (*c.* 546 BCE). We know little
about him other than that he was younger than Anaximandros and said to be his pupil.
While he seems to have believed in an *apeiron*, unlike Anaximandros, he considered the
arche to be air or rather vapor and responsible for all things by "thinning" or "thickening."
Anaximenes' "Rarefaction" and "Condensation" made the *kosmos* less abstract than

---

Box 7.3 Anaximenes on Rarefaction and Condensation

When air is thinned, it becomes fire; becoming thicker, wind, then cloud; still more, water, then earth, then rock.

(Simplicius, Physics *25.1; Graham 3, p. 74)*

Anaximenes' reversible processes explain how the forces in the *kosmos* are dynamic, while what contains the *kosmos* is at rest – and really no longer consequential. While his model might be considered a more sophisticated articulation of Anaximandros' one, his specification of a tangible *arche* suggests Anaximenes' regard for Thales. Could he have been attempting to reconcile the views of those great philosopher-forebears?

Anaximandros' conception of it and so more comprehensible and communicable, since his explanation relied for proof upon observable phenomena (Box 7.3). "Coming into being" and "passing away" originate and end similarly, and his proposal of harmonious opposition seems to have influenced Herakleitos' concept of unified oppositions.

While Anaximenes did not disbelieve in divinity, air for him was neither an Olympian god nor an Olympian's creation. In this, Anaximenes aligns with Thales and Anaximandros in that the known gods are not responsible for the genesis of the *kosmos*, nor are they absolutely essential in its working. The drift of such thinking will result in the conclusion, first articulated in Greek philosophy by Parmenides of Elea, that human perception is actually more significant than nature itself. That "man is the measure of all things" is finally proclaimed in the mid-fifth century BCE by Protagoras of Abdera.

The explanations of the Milesian material *monists*, believers in a singular primary element for all things, follow one after the other with important differences. Thales explains the source of all as water. Anaximandros, who noticed problems in Thales' explanation – namely, that all things do not appear to have water in them – posited an entity that was undefined as the source for all things and so could better account for differences. Material things "separated off" from "the boundless" and became differentiated. Later they were absorbed back into it. So he explained coming into being and passing away. Anaximenes accepted that the underlying principle was one and "boundless," but defined it as "air." He thus tried to account for sameness and difference: things were essentially the same, but differed depending upon their states of "thinness" or "thickness." By the time of Anaximenes, Greek philosophy had evolved away from Hesiod and his views on cosmogony, world order and, of course, divinity.

7.4 Skeptics, Critics, and Epistemology

7.4.1 Xenophanes

Xenophanes fled Ionia in 546 BCE, eventually settling in Elea in southern Italy. There he is said to have established an "Eleatic school" of philosophy. Xenophanes was certainly the first in a line of notable Elean philosophers that included Parmenides and Zeno. He was well aware of the views of other earlier and contemporary philosophers and poets and not only skeptical but

---

Box 7.4 Xenophanes' "God"

> There is one God, among gods and mortals the greatest,
> Neither in body like mortals is he nor in mind.
> *(Clement,* Miscellanies *5.109; Graham 35, pp. 110–111)*

> But always in the same place he abides moving himself in no way,
> and to change his place is not right for him, first one place and then another.
> [...]
> But, without labor by the thought of his mind, all he sets in motion.
> *(Simplicius,* Physics *23.11–12, 20; Graham 38 and 37, pp. 110–111)*

Xenophanes' conceptions might seem to have affinity especially to Anaximandros' immortal, boundless, and unmoving *apeiron*. But Xenophanes' "God" is really an omnipotent sentience, quite unlike the *apeiron* or any Homeric or Hesiodic divinity.

---

disparaging of them – and Greeks, in general – for their arrogance. Xenophanes was in turn roundly censured by Herakleitos.

As we have seen, Xenophanes criticized the Greeks and humans in general for wrongly fashioning the gods in their own likenesses and after their own thoughts. His own conception of divinity, which he obviously took to be superior to all others, is abstract and incorporeal. For Xenophanes, "God" is one alone and infinite – ageless, changeless, and deathless (Box 7.4).

Although Xenophanes condemns the epic poets especially for making the gods too human, the philosopher nevertheless describes divinity in human terms: "God" thinks, sees, and hears. Xenophanes seems to want to combine Milesian philosophical speculation about the *kosmos* with more traditional religious conceptions, thus arriving at a reconditioned version of divinity. He had his own view on the *arche* – he considered it to be both earth and water – but perhaps his most important philosophical contribution was epistemology.

What could anyone actually "know"? How could they "know"? What separates "truth" from "opinion"? Such questioning depicts a deeper self-consciousness among Archaic Greek philosophers about philosophy – it certainly influenced Parmenides, who was said to be Xenophanes' pupil. It led to more profound consideration about what human knowledge is or can be (Box 7.5).

Of course, Xenophanes undermines his own pronouncement by saying that everything is really ***dokos*** ("opinion, belief"), but offering nothing explicit for believing that what he himself says is better than "opinion." Vagueness and such contradictions in Xenophanes' assertions weakened them for later Greek philosophers. Aristotle complains that Xenophanes "did not clarify anything" and denigrates him, calling him "rather primitive."[4] Theophrastos cited the unresolved contradiction in Xenophanes about whether "God" was both bounded and unbounded, and Galen stated that Xenophanes was "unsure about everything."[5] There is some unfairness here, since Xenophanes, like the other Archaic philosophers, was breaking new ground and was constrained especially by language: later philosophers like Aristotle did not really take into account the context of Archaic Greek philosophy, but judged it rather anachronistically.

Box 7.5 Truth and Opinion

Neither does any man know the real truth nor will there be anyone
who will know about the gods and all that I say.
For even if he happened to speak about the things that occurred,
still he does not know: *dokos* – (and here he must mean "opinion") – fashions all.
(Sextus Empiricus, Against the Professors *7.49.110; Graham*
74, pp. 126–127)

Does this mean that all efforts toward knowing are automatically rendered invalid? Apparently not, for, in another fragment (Graham 77, ibid.), Xenophanes states that "in time, through experience, those who seek will discover what is better."

Notwithstanding, Xenophanes' tone does seem magisterial and rather condescending. In his poem criticizing Panhellenic athlete-victors (F 2) – considered the *crème de la crème* of Archaic Greek *poleis* by their fellow *politai* – Xenophanes says that they really do nothing for the common interests or good of any community. While good fortune may be thought to attend the *polis* whose athlete takes an Olympic, Pythian, or other crown in victory, the reactions of *politai* are out of proportion to the real benefits produced. Rather **sophoi** ("wise men") like Thales, Anaximandros, and, of course, Xenophanes himself are far more precious and beneficial, since their presence, good counsel, and advice bring much greater and far more certain return to the *polis*.

7.4.2 Herakleitos

Herakleitos, the scion of a very ancient family, was born at Ephesos *c*. 540 BCE. He inherited a ceremonial kingship, preparation for which during his younger years may have strongly informed his philosophy and personality. Then again, Herakleitos was called a child-prodigy and noted for his intellectual precocity. Although as a youth he claimed he knew nothing, grown up, he asserted that he knew everything. And that from being self-taught!

   Herakleitos' precocity, along with his august aristocratic and lofty social status, might explain his utter disdain for his fellow-Ephesians and general misanthropy. His haughty criticisms of Hesiod and Homer, philosophers like Xenophanes, his fellow-citizens of Ephesos, Greeks in general, and apparently the entire human race, point both to remarkable knowledge as well as remarkable disagreeability. When the Ephesian *politai* approached Herakleitos to re-write the law code for the *polis*, he refused and withdrew to the hill country surrounding Ephesos, eating what he could find, living where he might. However, when he was overcome with edema, he returned to Ephesos where he died *c*. 480 BCE.

   Herakleitos produced only one major work in his lifetime, a book called *Concerning Nature*. It was divided into three parts: the "all," politics and ethics, and theology. The subject of the first was the *arche* and was obviously inspired by the Milesians. The second seems to have focused on **sophia** ("wisdom"), very topical at the end of the sixth century BCE.[6] The third seems to have been a corrective, perhaps inspired by Xenophanes, aimed particularly at Hesiod and Homer and their view of the gods. Several fragments of Herakleitos' work survive, mostly as short quotations embedded in other, later works.

Herakleitos' book was no easy read, even when it was complete. When asked by Euripides about it, Sokrates is said to have replied that the part he understood was very good – and the part that he didn't understand was probably excellent too![7] The view that Herakleitos deliberately made it obscure may stem more from the inability of ancient Greek readers to comprehend it than from his intention. The language of the fragments is intricate and allusive, however, and Herakleitos made no effort to clarify his meanings for his readers: indeed, he says that most won't understand what he says.

An explanation might be found in Herakleitos' ceremonial kingship and the fact that he deposited his finished book in the great temple of Ephesian Artemis. Greek temples served as depositories for sacred writings in the Archaic period, and Herakleitos may have considered his book oracular and himself a kind of prophet. According to Herakleitos: "The lord-king, whose oracle is at Delphi, neither says nor hides, but signifies."[8] Like Apollo's oracle at Delphi, Herakleitos spoke as he spoke, and it was up to his readers to discern his meanings.

For Herakleitos, *logos* is the essence of the *kosmos*. Its Herakleitan meaning is difficult to pin down precisely: "word," "story," "reason," or "governing principle," among other things, have been proposed. It is up to the listener or, in this case, the reader to discern his precise meaning. The *logos* is present and available to all but most do not comprehend it, even from experience, Herakleitos says, although they believe they do. There are certain similarities to Xenophanes' thinking which may have given rise to the notion of his teaching Herakleitos.[9] Unlike Xenophanes, who concedes that knowledge is "opinion," however, Herakleitos believes that the truth of the *logos is* knowable – but very, very difficult to apprehend (Box 7.6).

The *logos* regulates the *kosmos* which is itself made up of and harmonized by unified oppositions which cannot be without each other. An example is sea water, which Herakleitos says "is the purest and the most foul. For fish, it is drinkable and safe, but for men, undrinkable and destructive."[10] Opposite properties thus exist in the same entities: "cold things warm, hot things cool, wet things dry, and dry things moisten."[11] Such entities thus have only *seemingly* different natures; they have actually one in different states. Such oppositions actually unify the things that must possess these properties. The *logos* comprehends all things: "out of all things, one, and out of one thing all."

Box 7.6 Herakleitos on *Logos*

That this *logos* is without end, men are imperceptive, both before they have heard of it and having heard it for the first time. For although all things come about in accordance with this *logos*, they seem without experience encountering such words and actions as I explain to them, defining each according to its nature, and saying to them how things are. Other men are unconscious of what they do when they are awake, just as they are when they sleep.

(Sextus Empiricus, Against the Professors *7.132–133; Graham 8, pp. 140–143)*

Herakleitos endeavors to make available what he considers to be the way toward the deepest level of understanding. Although his words imply that it is possible for all who read to know and attain the wisdom that he has, Herakleitos is really speaking to a very rarefied audience: his "account" is not for "the many," but "the few."

Herakleitos' *kosmos* is in constant flux, like a river flowing, and so we might conceive of it as never steady. But again that is only apparent. Similarly, it only *seems* to be paradoxical that "war" orders the *kosmos*, for rather than static and brittle or random and chaotic, the *kosmos* is steady because it is animate with change. Material and immaterial things unceasingly come into one state or pass into another. Such movement and change result in **eris** ("strife") but also – and by the same token – order. This seems to be a direct correction of Anaximandros' view, for whom change seems intermittent and disorderly, correcting the *adikia* of one act with another. For Herakleitos, strife and justice are unified opposites.

Fire is the primary substance of all things for Herakleitos. Fire can become air, air water, and water hardened becomes earth. The symbol of the *arche*, which "would and would not be called Zeus," is the thunderbolt "which guides all."[12] Of course, the thunderbolt is also the symbol and bearer of celestial fire. Like the Ionians before him, Herakleitos does not reject or eliminate the Olympians altogether from his explanations of the world and the forces in it, but he does alter perception of them. Zeus is – and is not – "God."

Herakleitos looks backwards to the Milesians, forward to later Greek philosophers, but also, ostensibly, away from philosophy as it had evolved to his time. He offers his view of the *kosmos* as a corrective, most especially to the "childlike" conceptions of the influential epic poets, Homer and Hesiod, and their followers, as well as other Archaic Greek philosophers. Herakleitos considers Xenophanes, Pythagoras, and Hekataios of no real account, but, significantly, seems to take no pernicious aim at the Milesian School. Indeed, Herakleitos does not name Anaximandros specifically or his conception of movement and equilibrium, but he must have known of it. His criticisms of those who accept appearances as realities are part of the epistemological discourse begun by Xenophanes and taken up by Parmenides and the fifth- and fourth-century BCE Greek philosophers. The possibilities imagined in that discourse and Herakleitos' allusion to "conservation of matter," that is, that matter may change, but not perish, will lend themselves to later Greek philosophers' notions of immortality.

7.5 Mathematics and the Mystical

7.5.1 Pythagoras

The facts about Pythagoras are much harder to discover, since, as a legend even in his own time, a great deal of fable grew up about him and his life. Additionally, nothing has survived that can be directly attributed to Pythagoras, information that others wrote about him is of uncertain value, and all of it come to us in fragmentary form. As a result, a kind of fog surrounds the life of Pythagoras and what he actually thought, said, or wrote down. Some ancient sources even go so far as to portray him as a miracle-performing demi-god with a golden thigh!

Some information about Pythagoras seems plausible enough. He was born on Samos *c.* 570 BCE, the son of a gem-engraver. Like Herakleitos, Pythagoras was eager for knowledge even as a child and traveled widely to learn, most notably to Babylonia and Egypt, where he is said to have mastered geometry. The "Pythagorean theorem," a fundamental law of geometry well known to mathematicians beginning with the Babylonians, was attributed to him erroneously by the Greeks.[13] Pythagoras is called "polymathic" rather disdainfully by Herakleitos, although from "The Things Heard," sayings attributed to Pythagoras, he possessed rather wide-ranging interests.

About the age of 40, Pythagoras left Samos for southern Italy, either because he opposed the tyranny of Polykrates or felt himself overburdened by obligations toward his fellow Samians. It may be, too, that southern Italy offered him and his followers more freedom than they enjoyed in Samos. Pythagoras settled at Kroton on the Gulf of Taranto, which then became the center of "Pythagoreanism" in the Greek world. He and his disciples seem to have quickly taken charge of the *polis*, living lives that incorporated philosophy, mathematics, mysticism, and a self-disciplining physical regime. One of Pythagoras' more famous followers was Milon of Kroton, a six-time Olympic wrestling champion and legendary figure in his own right. (Demokedes, the renowned physician, seems also to have been a Pythagorean.)

The Pythagoreans who abided with the master in Kroton, however, appear to have rubbed up the native Krotoniates quite the wrong way, perhaps because of their rigid lifestyle, secrecy, and a galling self-importance enhanced by their own exclusivity. One stated reason was that the Pythagoreans would not apportion the land taken from the conquered *polis* of Sybaris. After a violent revolution perhaps in 504 BCE, the Pythagoreans were expelled from Kroton and Pythagoras was nearly killed. He fled to Metapontion where he resided until his death. Pythagoreans nevertheless endured in southern Italy well after the master's demise.

In fact, what Greeks knew as Pythagoreanism appears to have been more informed by Pythagoras' disciples than by Pythagoras himself, although it may have been based to some degree upon his own words, beliefs, and actual practices. Certainly by the end of the sixth century BCE, Pythagoras and his philosophy were famous enough among the Greeks to be derided by Xenophanes and dismissed by Herakleitos, who called Pythagoras the "headman of liars." In fact, the cranky Ephesian vilified him, suggesting that, for all his fame, Pythagoras was a charlatan. Such criticisms notwithstanding, Pythagoreanism acquired many followers.

Disciples of Pythagoras were designated ***mathematikoi*** ("the learned") and ***akousmatikoi*** ("the listeners"). While both seemed to have practiced a living that centered on a kind of asceticism involving ritual, the *akousmatikoi* were perhaps a lower-level group, simply memorizing Pythagoras' doctrines, directives, and statements verbatim and without question, and practicing what he had allegedly preached. So when Pythagoras said: "Do not urinate or stand upon your nail and hair (clippings)" or "abstain from beans" or "from animal flesh," "the listeners" followed the instructions apparently without question. Just exactly what "The Things Heard" of Pythagoras were and what they required of disciples are not completely clear, but what is preserved seems largely superstitious. The *mathematikoi*, as their name implies, were concerned with numbers, theorems, and formula and so with the more profound core-beliefs of Pythagoreanism. Their mathematical enquiries and discoveries, which placed "the learned" in the upper levels of the Pythagorean hierarchy, seem to account for Pythagoras' renowned association with mathematics. These designations may have come into being after Pythagoras' lifetime, but in any case help to account for the odd division between rational and irrational Pythagoreanism.

Pythagoras or, more probably, later Pythagorean *mathematikoi* like Hippasos of Metapontion, Archytas of Taras, and Philolaos of Kroton, construed the *kosmos* quite differently from other philosophers or scientists. They believed that "all is number" and that mathematics could explain everything. Their efforts to render number-relations and mathematical functions into universal principles resulted in "laws" governing mathematics and so, they believed, the *kosmos*. One example was of course the "Pythagorean theorem." The theorem states that, in a right triangle, the square of the hypotenuse is equal to the sum of the squares of the other

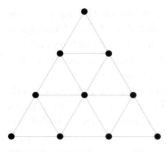

Figure 7.1 Tetractys.

two sides or $a^2 + b^2 = c^2$ with c being the hypotenuse. The theorem can be applied to measure distances between points, perimeters, and surface areas from very small to extremely large and so help to comprehend even theoretical space. The classification of numbers as even and odd and prime and composite, and the determination of the "golden ratio" or "section" (*a* + *b* is to *a* as *a* is to *b*) were all attributed to Pythagoras by the Greeks. The ratio (1.618) was in fact already long known to the Egyptians.

Pythagoreans also observed that music was subject to number-ratios. As the story goes, Pythagoras was passing a blacksmith's shop when he noticed that different-sized hammers made different tones when they struck an anvil. Simple ratios could account for different sounds, he concluded. It's a good story, simplifying a formula that can really only be applied to strings. But it is valid for strings and tuning them, and actually making music devolving upon musical intervals with pitch frequency ratios like that of the "perfect fifth" (3:2).[14] This "discovery" was again "borrowed" from the Near East, but attributed by the Greeks to Pythagoras.

Pythagoreans interpreted the *kosmos* through the implications of numbers, ratios, music, and harmonies. According to Pliny the Elder, Pythagoras specified the distance between the earth and the moon as a complete tone, while that between the moon and Mercury was a half-tone.[15] The planets and other celestial bodies were thus "harmonized throughout." The basis of all harmony in the *kosmos* was the *tetractys*, a graphic representation of the perfect number in perfect arrangement – an equilateral triangle (Figure 7.1). It was a sacred symbol for Pythagoreans, representing simultaneously the natural world, cosmic harmony, and divinity.

Notably, Pythagoreans did not consider the earth the center of the *kosmos*, but outside it. At the center they believed was fire and around the fire the sphere of stars, the five planets, the sun, the moon, the earth itself, and counter-earth – ten in all – moving in harmony. Understanding the harmonies of the *kosmos*, comprehending the relationships between numbers, music, and life, and adhering to Pythagorean dicta would in turn, they believed, harmonize one's thoughts and being.

The soul's immortality seems to have been at the heart of Pythagoras' own philosophy. While he was undoubtedly aware of the ideas of "coming-into-being" and "passing away" of the Ionian philosophers and these may have influenced his thought about immortality, Pythagoras declared that at the death of the body, the soul migrated into the body of other creatures, human or not. Xenophanes ridiculed him in verse (F 7a):

> Once while he was passing a little dog being abused// they say that he took pity upon it and said the following word:// "Stop! Do not beat him, for that is the soul of a dear friend// which I knew when I heard it yowling!"[16]

For Pythagoras to have asserted to the Greeks that anything animal or human could be immortal is astonishing, since that was tantamount to saying it was divine. Such an idea was altogether foreign to Homer and Hesiod, for whom the gap between human and divine was unbridgeable. For Pythagoreans, the kind of life a person led – pure, righteous, contemplative, and comprehending – would help to purify the soul and result in a better afterlife. Scholars have drawn links between Pythagoras' belief in the transmigration of the soul at death, the Eastern idea of reincarnation, and Orphism which perhaps came to the Greeks in its earliest form from Thrace.

The curious philosophy of Pythagoras might be considered by some an eccentric detour in the evolution of Greek thought. While cosmogony, order in the *kosmos*, and harmony were the same foci as Pythagoras' philosophical predecessors and peers, Pythagoreanism combined rational and logical investigations and conclusions, most notably involving mathematics, with mystical beliefs and practices which by their nature were irrational. Pythagoreanism and its emphasis on immortality – in particular, refining one's life thoughtfully to purify it – nonetheless markedly influenced Socratic philosophy in the later fifth century BCE.

7.6 Summary

7.6.1 Early Philosophers and the Archaic Greeks

What impact did these Archaic philosophers have on the average Greek farmer, sailor, or craftsman? Herakleitos complained that "Hesiod is the teacher of the many: they believe that he knows the most."[17] Like those of the Classical period, Archaic Greek philosophers apparently held forth in public places where they and their ideas could be heard by as many as cared to listen. While most listeners were undoubtedly more interested in learning practical wisdom, Pythagoras for one seems to have acquired disciples who accepted his teachings and the lifestyle he espoused. For the most part, Archaic Greeks seem to have permitted the new ideas of the philosophers, howsoever unorthodox they may have been.

Those who offered up less abstract messages seem to have drawn somewhat greater attention and adherence. Hesiod's advice to his brother about work and justice applied to anyone who heard the *Works and Days* and might account for the popularity of Hesiod about which Herakleitos complains. Apparently most popular and renowned were the Seven Sages who offered pithier, easily digested and remembered messages to live by than the complexities of the Ionians, Herakleitos, or Pythagoras. In fact, the Sages were really not philosophers at all. (We return to the Seven Sages in Chapter 11.)

Philosophers and wise men were considered different and apart and yet were integral to Archaic Greek society. We have seen how caricatures were made of Thales and later Sokrates and how their pursuit of knowledge was derided as eccentric. Yet, the fact is that Archaic Greek philosophers, as Greek scientists and sages, lived and functioned within their communities, not on the peripheries. They were not stifled by censure, utter contempt, or neglect, but rather were permitted and perhaps even encouraged to think freely and to publish their views. As with speakers in the assembly, farmers, sailors, and craftsmen of the Archaic period were willing to listen to anyone about anything who could improve their lot – until, as in political assemblies, they determined what they heard was blasphemous, upsetting, or just not worth their time. Ancient Greeks always seemed ready to hear about something new, rewarding, or just stimulating about themselves, others, and the world in which they lived. Archaic Greeks were no different from their descendants.

Notes

1 Aristotle, *On the Heavens* 294a, 28–33 (Graham 18, pp. 30–31).
2 Aristotle, *On the Soul* 411a, 7–8 (Graham 35, pp. 34–35).
3 Cf. McKirahan, p. 45.
4 Aristotle, *Metaphysics* 986b, 18–27 (Graham 40, pp. 112–113).
5 Cf. Simplicius, *Physics* 22.22–24 (Graham, 42, pp. 114–115) and Graham, p. 131; Galen, *On Philosophical History* 7 (Graham 80, pp. 126–127).
6 Plutarch, *Life of Themistokles* 2.4.
7 Diogenes Laertios 2.22 (Graham 163, pp. 180–181).
8 Plutarch, *Moralia* 404e (Graham 152, pp. 176–177).
9 Xenophanes had departed Anatolia many years before Herakleitos' approximate birth-date.
10 Hippolytos, *Refutation* 9.10.5 (Graham 79, pp. 162–163).
11 Tzetzes, *On the Iliad* 126 (Graham 86, pp. 162–163).
12 Clement, *Miscellanies* 5.115.1 (Graham 147, pp. 176–177); Hippolytus, *Refutation* 9.10.7 (Graham 56, pp. 156–157).
13 Cf. D. Mansfield and N. Wildberger, "Plimpton 322 is Babylonian exact sexagesimal trigonometry," *Historia Mathematica* 44 (2017) pp. 395–419, on Babylonian trigonometry *c*. nineteenth–sixteenth century BCE (with a very good bibliography on Pythagorean and Babylonian mathematics).
14 A "perfect fifth" spans seven "half-steps" or semi-tones on the musical scale.
15 Pliny, *Natural History* 2.20.
16 Diogenes Laertios 8.36 (Graham 18, pp. 106–107).
17 Hippolytos, *Refutation* 9.10.2 (Graham 19, pp. 144–145).

Further Reading

Archaic Greek Philosophy

W. Guthrie, *A History of Greek Philosophy:* Vol. 1, *The Earlier Presocratics and the Pythagoreans* (Cambridge, 2010).
R. McKirahan, *Philosophy Before Socrates* (Indianapolis, 1994).

Hesiod and Philosophy

C. Rowe, "'Archaic Thought' in Hesiod," *Journal of Hellenic Studies* 103 (1983) pp. 124–135.

Thales

P. O'Grady, *Thales of Miletus* (London, 2002).

Anaximandros and Anaximenes

D. Graham, *Explaining the Cosmos: The Ionian Tradition of Scientific Philosophy* (Princeton, NJ, 2006), pp. 1–85.

Xenophanes

H. Fränkel, "Xenophanes' Empiricism and His Critique of Knowledge," in A. Mourelatos, ed. *The Presocratics: A Collection of Critical Essays* (Princeton, NJ, 1974), pp. 118–132.

J. H. Lesher, *Xenophanes of Colophon: Fragments: A Text and Translation with Commentary* (Toronto, 1992).

Herakleitos

C. Kahn, ed. *The Art and Thought of Heraclitus* (Cambridge, 1981).

Pythagoras

C. Riedweg, *Pythagoras: His Life, Teaching, and Influence*[2] (Ithaca, NY, 2008).

L. Zhmud, *Pythagoras and the Early Pythagoreans* (Oxford, 2012).

8

The Art of the Archaic Greeks

8.1   Introduction

Although Bronze Age and Dark Age traditions are discernible in Archaic Greek art, it was most heavily influenced by new and contemporary trends, styles, and techniques, both local and foreign, during the seventh and sixth centuries BCE. The desire to represent the human form and human drama to engage the viewer and elicit emotional response is already present in late Mykenaian art: it is found, for example, in the painted plaster head of a goddess or sphinx (NM 4575) and the "Warrior Vase" (NM 1426), both from the thirteenth century BCE. Conversely, symmetry and precision in mostly linear design and decoration dominate Greek Geometric vase-painting. In the seventh century BCE, however, Near Eastern influences are prominent in Proto-Corinthian and Proto-Attic vase painting, whereas the prototypes for Greek *kouroi* were very obviously Egyptian. Archaic Greek art is in fact a distinctive fusion of native tradition and innovation, informed through the period by changing Greek style and taste affected by foreign aesthetics, techniques, and expressions.

Archaic Greek artists seem most determined to portray the human form realistically. These endeavors may be charted especially in the evolution of *kouroi* and *korai*. Early *kouroi* are humanoid in appearance, but distorted, unnatural-looking, and in some ways abstract. By the end of the sixth century BCE, however, Greek sculptors are able to render believable human figures in bronze and marble. The best of these are nevertheless imperfect, for Archaic Greek artists had already learned that an ideal human lacks perfection and that strict symmetry is to be avoided. Closer observations of what a human being actually looks like dispelled mistaken or malformed impressions of the body and clarified realities. Sculptors were able progressively to fashion stone and bronze into more convincing representations of humans and the human form. These perceptible changes in Archaic art were grounded in evolving Greek science and technology, but also in the artists' expanding awareness of the human body, how it functioned, and how to render it more convincingly.

Greek artists were creating their art as *politai* and members of their societies, stimulated by poetry, philosophy, new trends in science and learning, and new thinking in general about human experience. Rhoikos and Theodoros of Samos, both associated with the Heraion as its builders, were also renowned for their work in bronze casting and sculpting. Both had gone to Egypt to learn, and Theodoros was credited with inventing the lathe, the level, and the carpenter's square.[1] Khersiphron, the architect of the Artemision, was also an inventor, whereas

Gitiadas of Sparta, the builder of Athena's Brazen House there, composed lyric poetry and a hymn to the goddess.[2] This tradition continued into the Classical period: Sokrates, a stone-worker probably like his father, may have helped fashion the Parthenon sculptures and the metopes upon the building. Plato, his pupil, was a painter, then a dithyrambic, lyric, and tragic poet before he devoted himself entirely to philosophy. The tragedian Euripides studied both painting and philosophy. The interests of Archaic and Classical Greek artists and intellectuals were broadly stimulated and what they produced was informed by a wide range of observations and experiences in among their contemporaries.

8.2   Archaic Pottery-Painting

8.2.1   Later Geometric Pottery

The Geometric **Dipylon Amphora** (Figure 8.1) from Athens, dated *c.* 750 BCE,[3] provides a good beginning for a survey of Archaic Greek art. It is called "Dipylon" because it was discovered near Athens' "Double Gate" in the burial place for Athenians of the Archaic and Classical periods. At 1.55 m in height, the amphora is a monumental commemoration of an unknown, but obviously notable person. The surface of the vase is covered with monochrome decoration including geometric meanders, triangles, dotted diamond boxes, and geometrically stylized goats and deer on the vase's neck.

Its shoulder register (Figure 8.1a), however, contains a narrative composition using impressionistic geometric figures. The deceased is laid out upon a bier under a stylized shroud. Left and right of the bier are seven bereaved figures – 14 in all – while beneath the bier are four more. All have hands to heads in the traditional ancient Greek attitude of mourning. One of the mourners on the right appears to be a child, smaller than the other six – perhaps an afterthought by the artist added to achieve symmetry of number. Beneath the bier, two mourners are kneeling and two are seated. The numbers of mourners are thus balanced, but the depictions vary to avoid rigid balance: indeed, though all arms are raised in mourning, they are not all raised similarly. The artist thus "fractures" the symmetry of the narrative making it more reflective of what humans actually do.

While the scene is a commemorative "snapshot" of an occasion, as a funeral scene, it was intended to evoke sympathy, perhaps even sadness, from the viewer. The mourning depicted makes the death seem recent, the mourners' grief fresh. Their number implies the importance of the dead person who will be missed by many. The artist apparently wanted to impress the passer-by, to create interest in the narrative, and to elicit a somber, if

Figure 8.1 Dipylon Amphora. Dipylon Master, *c.* 750 BCE.

Figure 8.1a Dipylon Amphora: detail: *Prothesis*.

not sympathetic, response to the scene. The composition was surely informed by the artist's calculation of audience-response based upon observation or experience.

8.2.2 Early Archaic Pottery: Orientalizing, Proto-Corinthian, and Proto-Attic

The Proto-Corinthian style of pottery-painting replaced vase surfaces congested with geometric designs with stylized animals, floral motifs, and sometimes human figures in separate registers around the vases. Yet, while Proto-Corinthian pottery painting displayed great promise, offering sometimes some very lively human scenes, Ripe Corinthian style (*c.* 600 BCE) seems mired in repetitions of walking or grazing animals, birds, or sphinxes, crowded in upon by stifling floral designs (Figure 8.2).

The Proto-Corinthian **Chigi Vase**, *c.* 650 BCE, is only 26 cm but an exceptional piece. In the lowest register, scenes of hunting are portrayed, while, in the second register, the artist has painted the Judgment of Paris and a procession. In the topmost register, hoplites are about to engage (see Figure 4.3 on p. 59). The latter is a "snapshot" whose implied movement compels the viewer to supply the complementing "frames" of the "moving picture." The Chigi Vase painter understood how to draw the viewer into the painting by freezing the warriors in mid-movement just before the moment of collision.

Why did Corinthian potters abandon such lively and promising possibilities to adhere to merely pretty, far less interesting Orientalizing formulae? The answer might be artistic conservatism, lack of foresight, or the decay of the pottery industry at Corinth. In fact, the best, most innovative Corinthian painters may have moved to Athens, where the pottery industry continued to evolve and thrive through the sixth century BCE.

Figure 8.2 Corinthian *olpe,* Sphinx Painter, 630–610 BCE.

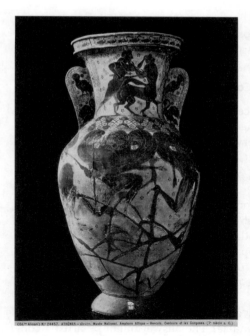

Figure 8.3 Nessos Amphora. Proto-Attic Black-Figure amphora. Nessos Painter, *c.* 620 BCE.

Decoration of the Late Proto-Attic **Nessos Amphora**, 1.22 m in height, dates to *c.* 620 BCE (Figure 8.3). It includes vestigial filler-decoration but is dominated by two scenes drawn from Greek myth. On the belly and shoulder of the vase, Perseus is being pursued by the sisters of the Gorgon Medousa, whose head Perseus had just lopped off. The trunk of Medousa falls to the ground behind her sisters. The artist attempts to show both the hideousness of the gorgons, who face fully outwardly, and their pursuit. He captures the moment of triumph for Perseus, but really not the harrowing nature of the hero's deed and his narrow escape. The Gorgons are more peculiar looking than petrifying as they run quite unnaturally to the right of the viewer. Every Greek knew that Perseus escaped them anyway. Where is the drama?

The neck of the vase, a "snapshot" of the story involving Herakles and the centaur Nessos, offers something quite different, however (Figure 8.3a). Nessos had agreed to carry Herakles' wife, Deianeira, on his back across the River Evenos. Reaching the other side, however, Nessos tried to assault her while Herakles struggled through the river behind them. Herakles came to the rescue,

Figure 8.3a Nessos Amphora: detail: Herakles and Nessos.

however, killing the centaur and saving his wife. Here the painter freezes the precise moment preceding the centaur's death. Nessos moves to the right in the frame, his arms twisted round and his right hand touching the chin of Herakles in supplication. Herakles leans into Nessos with his left leg up and foot planted on the centaur's lower human back. He has Nessos by the hair and his death-strike is imminent.

The artist uses verticals and horizontals to guide the viewer to the complexity of the conflict. Nessos' horse-body provides the main horizontal, with Herakles' leg highlighted above it. The upper bodies of Herakles and the centaur frame the arms of the two crossing: the one offers supplication, the other grasps Nessos' hair by one hand, ready to deliver death with the other. Further intensity is created by the overlapping bodies and isolation of Herakles' foregrounded sword and leg in the reserve between the two figures. Our eyes are drawn to Nessos' supplication and Herakles' impending violence.

But whose side are we on? Any Archaic Greek might say Herakles, for he is a human champion of law and order. Centaurs in myth are generally unpredictable, most often violent and even murderous: Nessos had just attempted rape after all. But that's not what the artist presents. In the painting, Nessos is depicted as helpless, his death is imminent, and he is begging for mercy. Herakles is the overpowering murderous force in the scene: the actions of beasts and humans seem to be reversed. The viewer may be conflicted. Why would the artist confuse things in this way? Why would this decoration be fitting for a funerary vase like this one?

8.2.3 Later Archaic Pottery: Black-Figure and Red-Figure Ware

The **François Vase**, 66 cm in height, a volute krater which probably functioned as a wine-bowl, dates from *c.* 570 BCE (Figure 8.4). The painter Kleitias, who signed it, has in some ways reverted to Geometric style by filling every space of the vase's surface. However, most of the

Figure 8.4 François Vase, Attic B-F volute krater. Kleitias, *c.* 570 BCE.

decorations are of human figures in episodes from several different Greek myths, all of them dramatic or emotional in one way or another.

Kleitias invites the viewer's involvement literally everywhere on the vase. The top register of the vase depicts the "Kalydonian Boar Hunt" on one side and "The arrival by Theseus and the Athenians" on the other. One of the sailors in the ship exults in their arrival throwing his arms up in the air – an attempt at depicting elation. The second register shows the "Funeral Games for Patroklos" with chariots in full charge on one side and battles between Lapiths and centaurs on the other. The third register displays the "Marriage of Peleus and Thetis" – a scene of discord between the goddesses Hera, Athena, and Aphrodite which brought about the Trojan War. The last register of human figures shows the "Return of Hephaistos to Olympos" on one side and the "Ambush of Troilos by Achilles" on the other. Achilles is just about to pounce on the Trojan youth as his team of horses gallops off. The deadly leap of Achilles spells his end and so the end of Troy.

Even this little scene elicits sadness, sympathy, and perhaps even outrage: a mere boy is about to be slaughtered by the supreme slaughterer of Troy. Yet again, the viewer's emotions are conflicted. On the one hand, Achilles is *the* great hero of the Greeks; on the other, Troilos is a young innocent about to be murdered. Elation for the Greek hero's glory is deflated by dismay for the child-victim. An ambiguity of feeling results – very akin to that prompted by verses in Homer's *Iliad*. The painting is reminiscent of, among other scenes in the *Iliad*, the death of the innocent Simoesios at the hands of the Greek hero Aias (*Iliad* 4.473 ff.).

Less troubling, but perhaps more immediately sorrowful, is the miniature handle painting of Aias carrying the dead body of Achilles from the battlefield (Figure 8.4a). The great hero is draped across the shoulders of Aias, his hair and right-hand fingers extending far downward from the limp body form. The sheer weight of the arcing figure burdening Aias increases the

Figure 8.4a François Vase: detail: Aias and Achilles.

sense of grief and loss weighing upon the bearer. It is a moving depiction of lifelessness – and of warrior camaraderie – executed in a very small field.

Among the earliest of Athenian Black-Figure vase-painting examples, the François Vase was also signed by the potter Ergotimos. The vase is a fine ware piece, the craftsmanship at a higher level than that of the Nessos Vase which is much bigger. The signatures imply competition already among Athenian pottery-makers and -painters. Black-Figure vase-painting uses silhouettes set against a buff or reddish background with details picked out with a burin. Kleitias attempts to show humans in action and so endues his paintings with animation and a sense of reality. He seems to elicit excitement from the viewer from his depiction of the "Kalydonian Boar Hunt," joy from "The Arrival of the Athenians," apprehension from the "Marriage of Peleus and Thetis," pity from the imminent death of Troilos, and sorrow from Aias and Achilles.

Exekias' **Suicide of Aias** (0.69 m), dating *c.* 530 BCE, is simultaneously powerful and subtle, tumultuous and serene (Figure 8.5). The great hero is pictured alone. He crouches fixing a sword into a small mound of dirt as he readies himself for his suicide. Aias was maddened by an angry Athena to slaughter sheep he thought were his human enemies. Coming to his senses and recognizing what he had done, Aias lapsed into despair and committed suicide.

The composition is stark and evocative of Aias' isolation just before his suicide. Two verticals, a palm tree on the left and a helmet poised atop a shield on the right, frame the highlighted portion of the composition – the upright sword dead center. Spears from the right and the lines of the hero's arms from the left lead to that center, as the hero's body leaning in anticipates his

Figure 8.5 Suicide of Aias, Attic B-F amphora, Exekias, *c.* 530 BCE.

falling upon his sword. The composition captures Aias' extreme loneliness – and despair – the moment before the hero's death: we seem to be there with him on the verge of his final fatal act. The scene is one of intense drama, for once more, the viewer supplies the "before" and the "after" to what is depicted in the "snapshot."

It is a terribly sad scene, but there are conflicts implicit in it. Aias offended Athena and so invited her vengeance, but his madness, humiliation, and suicide really came about because of the injustice of Athena's favorite, Odysseus. The wily Odysseus cheated Aias out of the dead Achilles' armor which was his by right to inherit. Victimized by the schemer, Aias sought vengeance on Odysseus, Agamemnon, and Menelaos, but Athena stopped him with madness. Athena is a god and no man should cross her, it is true, but does the noble Aias, the second best Greek at Troy, really deserve what he gets, especially after Odysseus' cheating? Conflicting emotional responses are elicited by the painting which stimulates memory of Aias' tragic story.

Rather more intense is Exekias' famous version of the **Duel between Achilles and Penthesilea** (0.41 m), *c.* 530 BCE (Figure 8.6). Achilles and the Amazon queen are in the ultimate stage of their duel. Penthesilea inclines toward the right of the frame, low and away from Achilles, as her head looks backward to him, torso twisted. She has been mortally wounded: the hero's spear-point has penetrated her white neck. Achilles striding toward her leans forward as he looks down upon her. The bodies of each comprise the composition's slanted verticals, which are countered by Penthesilea's very noticeable white upper arm, but also by the spears each is wielding. The crossing of the spears leads the viewer's sight down to the death-strike of Achilles. There is yet another line that crosses, invisible but very powerful – that of the gaze between Achilles and Penthesilea. The subject of the "snapshot" is the exact moment of death.

Achilles might seem simply to be vanquishing another "marquee" Trojan opponent. Penthesilea, a warrior-queen, was certainly a worthy adversary. Yet he is also overcoming a human being and a female. Exekias wanted to evoke much more than sympathy in this composition, especially with the locked-in gaze of the combatants. According to the myth, just as Achilles was delivering death to Penthesilea, they gazed at each other – and fell in love, a supreme irony. What then was Exekias really trying to communicate here? Why would his Archaic Greek patrons find any charm in this depiction of a particularly ironic, indeed very cruel, twist of fate?

Red-Figure vase-painting appears in Athens *c.* 530 BCE. Whereas in Black-Figure, subjects were painted in silhouette and details scratched out within the silhouette, Red-Figure images are reserved against an all-black background and details are rendered with deft, slender brush

Figure 8.6 Achilles and Penthesilea, Attic B-F amphora, Exekias, *c.* 530 BCE.

strokes in black. Red-Figure style allowed for the human figure and its painted details to be highlighted against the black background.

Euthymides, who proudly signed his vases, produced a famous rendition of **Three Old Revelers**, *c.* 510–500 BCE (Figure 8.7). The vase is 0.605 m in height. On it, two figures, both facing inward and lifting left and right leg respectively, frame the central figure. His rather large body moves toward the right side of the frame, while his upper torso twists backwards looking at the dancing figure behind him as he holds his walking stick above him. Euthymides has managed to unite the three figures by means of the central figure's counter-movements, animating all in a dancing unison. The painter foreshortens the central figure, that is, distorts the rendering of a figure, to create an illusion of depth as well as torsion. This is one of the first examples of foreshortening in Greek vase-painting.

As with renderings of other sympotic or celebratory scenes, there is no drama here, no intellectual challenge – at least none that is obvious. Rather, the all-too-humanly overweight males

Figure 8.7 Three Old Revelers, Attic R-F amphora. Euthymides, *c.* 510–500 BCE.

Figure 8.8 Youthful Revelers, Attic R-F *skyphos*. Brygos Painter, *c.* 490–480 BCE.

create rather a comic scene. The mood is joyous, the appeal to lighter emotions and the senses rather than the intellect. The "snapshot" invites the viewer to supply the music and next steps in the dance and so to become a participant in it. Euthymides was very proud of his accomplishment, portraying the foreshortened figure as he did, so much so that he inscribed the vase to pique a rival pottery-painter: "As Euphronios never [could]!"

The Louvre's **Youthful Revelers** on a cup by the Brygos Painter (19.5 cm) dated *c.* 490–480 BCE evokes a rather different response (Figure 8.8). Pictured are two pairs of young revelers, two males and apparently two *hetairai* ("courtesans"). By the look of them, the youths are inebriated. The pair on the right gaze at each other erotically as they move to the right of the frame, the *hetaira* turned backward as she walks. The pair on the left drift to the right in a kind of slow-motion dance step. The youth is behind the girl in the frame, moving with her, but turned round and gazing too intensely into her eyes. She appears to shrink back from the look, she doesn't smile. Why seems to be made clear by his right arm around her shoulder, his right hand grasping a stick, and the very forceful grip of his left hand on her left wrist. It looks as if she is being coerced.

The young man might remind the Greek viewer of some god whose suborning of women was a commonplace in myth. The young man's grip might also resemble a bridegroom's as he leads the girl to wedded bliss. There is, however, a sinister sense in the engulfing of the girl by the drunken, naked youth and of misgiving if not full-on fear implied in the maiden's shrinking backward. The "fun" of this drunken revel is countered by the apparent loutishness of the inebriated youth, its erotic sense undercut by the girl's palpable discomfort. What does the painter want his audience to make of this? The disquieting scene provokes a response that is not the same at all as that of Euthymides' "Three Old Revelers."

Even such a brief chronological survey of Archaic Greek pottery-painting as this allows us to see the increasing proficiency in design and composition of vase-painters and in rendering the human form more accurately even in action. Archaic artists engage and challenge viewers visually and intellectually. To the end of the Archaic period, Greeks were invited to consider what they saw, to be transported into the "moving picture" implied by the "snapshot" vase-paintings. The "messages" become increasingly challenging because scenes provoke conflicting feelings. But this sort of challenge was apparently precisely what the paying audience wanted from their vase-paintings. From the broad distribution of Archaic Greek pottery throughout the Mediterranean, it is what many non-Greeks wanted as well.

8.3 Archaic Greek Sculpture

8.3.1 Introduction

Several types of sculptures were produced during the period, the earliest of which were carved from softer materials such as ivory or wood. Greeks traveling to Egypt seem to have learned rather quickly how to carve hard stone into recognizable shapes. This survey focuses on three types of Archaic Greek sculpture: (1) architectural relief sculpture; (2) *kouroi*; and (3) *korai*. The *kouros*-type is grounded in Egyptian models, but far exceeded imitation, especially as Archaic Greek sculpture evolved. Greater technical skill resulted in progressively more convincing sculptures of males and females through the Archaic period.

8.3.2 Later Geometric Sculpture

Late Geometric sculptures in bronze, ivory, or terracotta that have survived are for the most part small, highly stylized, and rather unnatural in appearance. The **Ivory figure of a woman** (24 cm), *c.* 730 BCE, was discovered in a grave in Athens (Figure 8.9). It betokens wealth, but also taste that ran to the imported, the expensive, and the exotic. While the artist may have been attempting to represent an eastern goddess, perhaps Astarte, the Phoenician equivalent of Aphrodite, the figure's stiff legs, frontal gaze, and the geometric designs on her headpiece suggest that the object may have been produced locally. Though the statuette might be plausibly linked to *kore*-figures, she is notably nude – something *korai* are not.

Similar is **Mantiklos**, a small bronze figure of a male from Thebes (20 cm), dated *c.* 700 BCE (Figure 8.10). The Geometric tradition is fully present in the triangles of the torso, elongated neck, and head. Yet signs of softening and naturalism are visible in the curved mouth, cleft chin, and suggestions of musculature. The small statue anticipates the marble *kouroi* of the seventh and sixth centuries, demonstrating the Greek preference for sculptural renderings of nude males well before Egypt

Figure 8.9 Figure of a woman, ivory carving, Athens, *c.* 730 BCE.

Figure 8.10 Mantiklos, bronze figure, Thebes, *c.* 700 BCE.

was open to the Greeks. It shows how the Archaic Greek *kouros* resulted from a blend of Egyptian models and Greek tradition. An inscription on its leg says that it was dedicated to Apollo and names its dedicator:

> Mantiklos offers me to the far-shooting silver-archer as a tenth-part. You, Phoibos, give back a favor in return.

8.3.3 Archaic Architectural Sculpture

The metope of the **Cattle Raid of the *Dioskouroi* and Idas** from the Treasury of Sikyonians at Delphi is made of limestone, 0.58 m in height, and dated *c.* 560 BCE (Figure 8.11). The arrangement of the three figures and the cattle stolen from Arkadia is almost completely symmetrical. The three men march looking straight ahead, their right arms rigidly to their sides, their spears in their left hands, resting on their left shoulders. In front of each are cattle, the heads of the nearest at 90 degrees to their bodies as they walk, looking directly at the viewer. Men and cattle are nevertheless in lock-step. While the detailing of the figures, especially the clothing, hair, and faces of the cattle, is impressive, the composition might seem tedious because of its rigidity and unnaturalness. In fact, the artist's attempt to render depth-perspective by sculpting the figures at different levels, men and four rows of cattle, is an important advance in Greek art.

Once more, the composition invites the viewer to supplement what is actually to be seen. Idas and his brother Lynkeos were cousins, but also rivals of the *Dioskouroi* and it was after this cattle raid that the kinsmen fell out. A quarrel developed initially over the division of the very herd the men are here leading and it would result in their deaths. The artist here presents a contradiction to the violence that will occur, but also an anticipation – the "calm before the storm" as it were, when all *seems* to be harmonious among the cattle-thieves. What message is the artist really trying to convey? What would the viewer think?

The Treasury of the Siphnians also at Delphi is dated *c.* 530 BCE. Dedicated by the then very wealthy islanders of Siphnos, the treasury was embellished lavishly. It was constructed of costly marble and featured two very impressive *karyatides* ("column-statues of maidens") to hold up the shallow porch before its entrance. The importance of the edifice is summed up concisely by Richard Neer:

> It is the earliest known building on the Greek mainland to be constructed entirely of marble (i.e., Siphnian, Naxian and Parian); it bears one of the earliest carved Ionic

Figure 8.11 Cattle Raid of the *Dioskouroi*, metope, Sikyonian Treasury, Delphi, *c.* 560 BCE.

friezes; it is the linchpin of late Archaic chronology; and its sculptural decoration ranks among the great masterpieces of ancient art.[4]

The **North Frieze of the SiphnianTreasury** is 8.6 m in length and 0.64 m in height. Its subject is the combat between the Olympian Gods and Giants (Figure 8.12). On the left, out of the frame, the figure of Hephaistos is named and near him are two goddesses, perhaps Demeter and Persephone. Two Giants are charging at the gods. Behind Themis' lion-drawn chariot and facing away from them, Dionysos moves to the attack. In the frame, the lion of Themis, no Olympian herself but a divine presence signifying order, has caught a Giant with his claws and teeth. The Giant's legs move in one direction, but his torso is turned back into the lion. In front of him the Divine Twins, Apollo and Artemis, seem to chase another Giant (Kantharos?), who flees before them with his tunic flaring as he runs. In fact, he is behind them. Ephialtes, a Giant whose leg is visible in the frame, lies dead before them. A further line of named Giants in hoplite formation is moving to attack the Twins.

The artist uses single figures and engaged pairs, connecting the strong verticals of the figures with horizontal lines visible or implied. Themis (out the frame) is joined to the turning Giant by the horizontal of her chariot and the lion's massive body. Apollo and Artemis seem to lean into the figure of the fleeing Giant, but are really facing the phalanx of Giants charging at them. Torsion in the bodies of the two fleeing Giants, foreshortening of the lion and lion-mauled Giant, and depth perspective of the frieze contrast distinctly with the "Cattle Raid of the *Dioskouroi*," carved around thirty years earlier. Observation has led to greater understanding of

Figure 8.12 Gigantomachy, relief sculpture, Siphnian Treasury, Delphi, North Ionic frieze, *c.* 530 BCE.

what human movements actually look like. Even the depiction of the slight force of air against the fleeing Giant's clothing, which flairs out slightly from it, conveys the sense of movement better. The North Frieze is actually a *tour de force* of motion, confusion, and carnage: it resembles an actual battle between human beings. The artist, whose name was inscribed in the work but is now lost, obviously took great pride in what he had done. He was also advertising his skills for other customers, just as vase-painters continued to do.

Why would the artist sculpt such a tumultuous, unsettling scene of battle, death, and dying along the north side of the treasury facing the Sacred Way of Delphi, where it could be seen by so many pilgrims as they made their way up to Apollo's temple? In fact, the "Gigantomachy" is a recurrent sculptural subject especially on Greek temples. It displays the eternal struggle between the forces of order and chaos – really "good" and "evil" – and encourages gratitude toward the Olympian gods and Themis, the goddess of "divine law." Appropriately, the forces of good are winning – as win they always must.

Gods and Giants are nevertheless portrayed as human beings. The former are quite recognizable and distinguished from the Giants, whose faces are obscured by helmets as they battle. This obscurity increases their anonymity and inhumanity. The contrast between the two contingents would have been made even more distinct by the bright colors painted on the frieze, now vanished. There is no ambiguity here, no sympathy for the Giants who are more on the verge of being punished forever than merely defeated in battle.

Finally, the metopes of the Treasury of the Athenians at Delphi, *c.* 490–480 BCE, built as a thank-offering to Apollo for the victory over the Persians at Marathon. Although constructed of Parian marble, the Treasury is a very simple building by comparison with the Siphnian one. It is adorned with Doric order metopes rather than the continuous frieze of the Ionic order, its

Figure 8.13 Herakles leaping on the Keryneian Hind, metope, Treasury of the Athenians, Delphi, *c.* 490 BCE.

columns are plain. The metopes depict the exploits of Herakles, a Doric hero, and Theseus, an Athenian/Ionian one, in some ways very much like Herakles. The metopes are, most of them, in bad shape today. One that is better preserved portrays **Herakles and the Keryneian Hind**, one of the hero's famous Twelve Labors (Figure 8.13).

Herakles is just on the verge of capturing the Hind which was notorious for leading hunters on an endless track and so to their doom. In the metope (0.67 × 0.6 m), Herakles is frozen in air leaping upon the deer which seems to be standing still. Best preserved is the hero's muscular body which arcs over the beast, visually implying the imminent subjugation of the animal. His body's anatomy reflects his effort: his right ribs are exposed as the skin is drawn tightly around them, and his calf muscle bulges as his knee and thigh gain purchase on the Hind's back. The artist has rendered Herakles' torso muscles, his hair and beard, and his cloak draped over his quiver in great detail. The paused leap freezes the moment of greatest drama, anticipating immediate triumph. Yet the artist has missed endowing Herakles with the kind of concern a human being would show amidst such exertions. His impassive face is actually characteristic of the late Archaic and Severe Styles of Greek sculpture, which sometimes combine vigorous bodily action with lack of facial emotion, as for example, the Zeus (or Poseidon) of Artemision (see Figure 5.2 on p. 75).

Metopes allowed sculptors the same opportunity to "snapshot" a moment and so to infuse the composition with drama as vases did vase-painters. The Siphnian Treasury's frieze sculptor seems to have employed a series of "snapshots" to make a kind of episodic "movie." "The Cattle Raid of the *Dioskouroi*," only three decades older than the Siphnian Treasury "Gigantomachy," actually seems light-years from it artistically. "Herakles and the Keryneian Hind," which freezes athletic action in mid-air enduing the composition with both grace and animation, displays further advancement.

8.3.4 *Kouroi*

Kouroi begin appearing in mainland Greece toward the end of the seventh century BCE, ranging in magnitude from monumental to under life-sized. According to the canon, an Archaic Greek *kouros* is a nude male youth standing stiffly with face to the front, left leg in front of the right as if to suggest movement forward; his arms are fixed rigidly to his sides. The *kouros*' hair is long, but highly stylized to begin with; it becomes shorter and more natural-looking by *c.* 500 BCE. The "archaic smile," a mouth drawn up tightly as if smiling, is present in both *kouroi* and *korai* early on, but disappears by the end of the period.

Whether the *kouroi* represented actual persons, gods, idealized or heroized human beings is still debated. In fact, while a *kouros* might be any of these, the sculptures were certainly meant to represent human beings. *Kouroi* could function as grave-markers or votives and are sometimes inscribed linking the statue to particular individuals or gods. Egyptian statues provided prototypes for Greek *kouroi*, but they also differed from them significantly. While their arms are to their sides, one foot is in front of the other, and the statue is forward-facing, Egyptian figures are clothed and frequently still engaged with the stone rather than free-standing. Nudity was an element of Greek athletic games, and the *kouroi* seem to have been meant to represent idealized youthful Greek athletes. Direct descendants of *kouroi* in the Classical period are the *Diadumenos* and the *Doryphoros* of Polykleitos.

The **New York *kouros*** (Figure 8.14) is among the earliest examples extant and provides a good baseline from which to measure the evolution of the *kouros*-type.[5] Discovered in Attika, the monumental statue (*c.* 610–580 BCE) is made of Naxian marble and stands 1.93 m in height. Large almond-shaped eyes stare out from an elongated face on an overlarge head (0.3 m in length); around the head is a fillet suggesting that the youth is an athlete. There is another fillet around the rather long neck. Impressionistic ears are pinned too far back and too high up on either side of the face. The hair is highly stylized and wig-like, further implying Egyptian inspiration. The torso narrows unnaturally to the hips, making the figure quite long-waisted; muscular legs nevertheless spring from the narrowed torso. Arms are clasped tightly to either side, and the left leg is advanced in accordance with Egyptian prototypes. Though the head is much too big for the body and the torso undersized for the length of the figure, the statue's proportions and details are accurate enough to suggest humanity. The sculptor seems to have

Figure 8.14 New York *kouros,* marble statue, Attica, *c.* 610–580 BCE.

paid rather more attention to some parts of the anatomy than others. Thus, while the musculature of the overly large legs, especially around the knees, is fairly detailed, the abdominal muscles are merely suggested. The rendering of the statue implies that, although the sculptor may have studied other statues and perhaps even human bodies, he was still some ways from being capable of portraying a nude human male realistically.

Kleobis and Biton (1.97 m) were offered to Apollo at Delphi not much later *c.* 580–570 BCE (Figure 8.15). The pair were local Argive heroes, who, because they died in the prime of youth after a conspicuous act of filial piety, were immortalized by their fellow-Argives.[6] As exemplars of extraordinary humility, the Argives thought them worthy to be memorialized and appreciated by other Greeks visiting Apollo's shrine. The pair of nearly matching statues was produced by an Argive sculptor who rendered the bodies and limbs more proportionately than did the sculptor of the New York *kouros*. Their heads and faces, however, were not well observed. The pair have almost no forehead, and their facial features are scaled for much larger heads; their hair seems a matted cap with cylinder-

Figure 8.15 Kleobis and Biton, *kouroi*, marble statues. Delphi, *c.* 580–570 BCE.

like tapering braids down front and back. Moreover, their torso musculature is mostly incised lines. Since Kleobis and Biton represented the best of the Argives, these statues must also depict the best efforts of the Argives at the time of their dedication.

The **Anavysos** *kouros* was dedicated in southwestern Attika, not far from Sounion, *c.* 530 BCE (Figure 8.16), about fifty years after Kleobis and Biton. It is a monumental grave-marker for one "Kroisos," who is named in an inscription on the statue's base. Standing about life-size, this *kouros* is significantly different from earlier examples. Kroisos' body is more rounded and proportional, head to torso and limbs. The face in particular is believably human, while the articulation of legs, arms, and torso displays a greater understanding of human anatomy. The figure is still very rigid, the "archaic smile" is present, but the rest of the statue conveys a sense of individualism, dignity – and even heroism – more than of canonical rigidity and sameness. The sculptor has been able to depict a humanity freed from the stone.

The statue's inscription states that Kroisos was "slain by Ares" and so a casualty of warfare. The passer-by is asked to stop and pity the youth, since he died in battle heroically fighting in the forefront. Though the memorial's design was informed by the same need to capture the attention of onlookers and impress them as the Dipylon Amphora, the statue obviously far exceeds the Geometric memorial in impressiveness. The figure's believability intensifies the relationship between the deceased youth the sculpture represents and the viewer/passer-by and makes pondering Kroisos the person and his sad fate more compelling and emotional.

Figure 8.16 Kroisos, *kouros,* marble statue. Anavysos, Attica, *c.* 530 BCE.

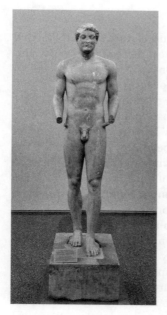

Figure 8.17 Aristodikos, *kouros*, marble statue, Athens, *c.* 500 BCE.

In fact, Kroisos is essentially apotheosized by the statue and inscription. The words, "slain by Ares," imply that Kroisos was not killed ordinarily, but rather in combat involving the war-god. The reference conjures the great hero Diomedes and his titanic fight with Ares in the *Iliad* (5.846 ff.) The statue's massive frame and musculature further emphasize Kroisos' impressiveness and formability in life, but also, with the inscription, suggest legendary heroism and so perhaps transportation to the Islands of the Blessed rather than the joyless Underworld. The statue and inscription have made the youth Kroisos, named after the fabled Lydian king, much larger than life and elevated him to the level of the heroes of old.

The **Aristodikos** *kouros* is 1.95 m in height and dates *c.* 500 BCE (Figure 8.17); it is so-called because it was Aristodikos' grave-marker. It shows that the artist has learned to round the stone to fit the contours of a human body far more realistically. From the crown of the head with its proportional facial features and softened hair peeking out from under a cap (or helmet?), to the neck with its articulated ligaments, the shoulders with its subtly carved clavicles, the well-executed torso muscles, and the detailed legs, the Aristodikos *kouros* seems almost real. The artist has broken the *kouros* canon by inclining the head of the subject slightly downward and he has detached the arms from the torso to increase the impression of realism. The *kouros* has lost the "archaic smile."

While successful in other ways, Aristodikos is inferior as a *kouros* to the heroic Kroisos. His slender body is fleshier than it is muscled: he is not the warrior-hero Kroisos is. Susan Woodford observes the problem confronting the *kouros*-sculptor: "The dilemma [stiffness] must have seemed insoluble as artists came to realise that each new, improved naturalistic detail only served to reinforce the apparently unnatural rigidity of the (sc. *kouros*) pose."[7] The *kouros*-style was essentially finished by the end of the sixth century BCE because the demands of its canon could not be reconciled with the aim of the sculptors to present greater naturalism in the figures.

The **Kritios Boy** (Figure 8.18) breaks completely with the *kouros* canon. Named after the sculptor, the statue, dated *c.* 490–475 BCE, is only a little over 1 meter in height. Its size belies its importance, however. The statue's head is turned down and perceptibly to his right; his gaze is impassive, with no "archaic smile." The statue's facial features are convincingly proportional. The torso and limbs are now well-rounded over implied muscle, although the body is itself fleshier than muscular. The sculptor has softened the *kouros* stance as well as the body, so that the figure weights most of his body on his left leg, with his right one relaxed. The softened stance

Figure 8.18 Kritios Boy, marble statue, Athens, *c.* 490–475 BCE.

infuses the statue with a realism that had defied sculptors heretofore; its other better observed and executed features add to the impression. The Kritios Boy looks backward – partaking of the *kouros* canon as a nude youth – but also anticipates the athlete-statues of the High Classical period like the *Doryphoros* and these the fleshier male sculptures of the fourth century BCE such as the Antikythera youth.

Although the *kouros*-type was inspired by Egyptian prototypes, it is a distinctively Archaic Greek sculptural form. Sculptors seem to have been working early on from imperfect observations or mere impressions of their subjects; their skills were not well developed. The Anavysos *kouros* of *c.* 530 BCE, however, represents the acme of the *kouros*-type among the examples that are extant, uniting the canon to which it adheres, with a far more realistic rendering of a male youth. The Aristodikos *kouros* and Kritios Boy break the canon – and so the constrictions of the *kouros*-type. Both stand as forerunners of the Severe and Classical sculptural styles.

8.3.5 *Korai*

Korai also appear on mainland Greece after the mid-seventh century BCE. They, too, vary in size from slightly under to more than life-sized; their canon possesses three essential elements. Each statue depicts a young female looking forward. One hand is usually extended in offering, the other pulling at the lower part of her clothing; a *kore*'s feet are firmly together. There is

Figure 8.19 Nikandre, *kore*, marble statue, Delos, *c.* 640 BCE.

generally no implied movement as with *kouroi*. The "archaic smile" is usually present; the hair, clothing, and adornments are sometimes elaborate and, like architectural sculpture, brightly painted. (Traces of original pigment survive on several *korai*.) The form seems to wane about the same time as *kouroi*, although the canon survives in *karyatides* and statues like the monumental Athena *Parthenos* of Pheidias of the mid-fifth century BCE.

The Daedalic **Nikandre *kore***, *c.* 640 BCE, is the earliest extant and provides a good baseline for measuring change (Figure 8.19). Discovered on the island of Delos, the statue is 1.9 m tall and was a votive to Artemis. The sculpture itself is made from a thin, indeed plank-like, piece of marble, the thickness never exceeding 17 cm. The stone itself seems to have dictated the statue's two-dimensionality: the sculptor's skills were obviously quite limited. A rather large head surmounts a torso that tapers to the waist which is belted; the arms are tight to the sides. The hair is wig-like, suggesting Egyptian influence. Some take Nikandre to be a marble version of a ***xoanon***, a crude type of wooden statue that preceded stone ones in Greece.

The inscription on the statue announces that it is a dedication of Nikandre, who is called "outstanding"; it also names her male relatives. The statue was meant to advertise her and her family in an enduring way to the multitudes who visited Delos as pilgrims or concelebrants at the Delian festivals. If the statue is a memorial, it stands in a tradition which included the Dipylon Amphora and the Anavysos and Aristodikos *kouroi* (see also Chapter 12.2.2).

The **Berlin Goddess** or ***Kore*** dates *c.* 570–560 BCE and is *c.* 1.9 m in height (Figure 8.20). The provenience of the statue at Keratea in the Attic *mesogaia* implies local manufacture. The statue stands very rigidly. The neck is very long and surmounted by a head that is too small for its very large, bulging eyes and misplaced and oversized ears. A side-view of the head shows that the features are all pulled forward to the front of the face, leaving an unnatural expanse of cheek. The subject's mouth is drawn up into a tight "archaic smile," while atop her head sits a *polos*, decorated with maeanders and lotus buds. Beneath the *polos* is very stylized, wig-like hair. Her body is quite disproportionate: while she has very large shoulders, accentuated by her heavy clothing, she has extremely narrow hips proportionately. Her feet, poking out from her gown, seem after-thoughts. She wears a necklace and earrings that appear to be vegetal, and a bracelet on her left wrist. With her left hand, reaching across her body, she grasps the fold of her over-garment, while in her lower right hand, she holds what is taken by some to be a pomegranate. Traces of pigment remain on the statue which was brightly painted in its original state.

Iconography suggests that the Berlin *Kore* is to be associated with death and fertility and in particular with the queen-goddess of the dead, Persephone. The pomegranate signifies

Persephone's permanent passage into Hades; the *polos* is depicted with goddesses. Persephone appears from the Underworld every spring to be together with her mother Demeter, goddess of grain. Great care was taken to preserve the statue: she was discovered wrapped in lead. Scholars have assumed that the statue was carefully hidden before the Persian invasion in 480 BCE to prevent the invaders from looting or destroying it.

Whether or not the statue portrays a goddess, it fits the *kore*-type. Even though the rendering is unrealistic and even strange-looking, it is more three-dimensional than Nikandre. Excepting the eyes, the features of the face, though squarish, are more proportional; the rounded hips, catenations of the shawl, and detail of the hair – best seen viewing the statue from the back – are better observed and rendered than in Nikandre's case.

Phrasikleia, named after an inscription on the statue, is yet another product of the Attic *mesogaia* (Figure 8.21). The statue was discovered in a pit along with a *kouros* in Myrrhinous (modern Merenda), not far from Keratea, apparently again to keep it from the Persian invaders who were on orders to destroy everything in Attika. She is 1.86 m in height and dates *c.* 540 BCE, or about 100 years after Nikandre. Phrasikleia stares forward, holding out a lotus in her left hand. With her right hand, she gathers her lower garment. Her face, while certainly not divinely attractive, is

Figure 8.20 Berlin *Kore*, marble statue, Attika, *c.* 570–560 BCE.

realistic: the proportions of wide eyes to nose to mouth to ears are well observed, her "smile" is less severe. Her hair remains unnatural-looking in back, but wavy and more convincing in the front. The gown of the statue is elaborately decorated with rosettes and meander patterns, and a good deal of the original red pigment upon the statue survives. She is adorned with jewelry, and a wreath crowns her head. Phrasikleia stood upon a base inscribed with words that were designed to evoke emotional response (see Chapter 12.2.2). The girl died before she was married – a particularly tragic consequence as ancient Greeks saw it. The emotion elicited is somber: Phrasikleia herself is detached, serene, and regal. Like Kroisos of Anavysos, she seems almost divine.

The inscription also bears the name of the sculptor, Aristion of Paros. Parian sculptors had worked island stone for centuries: the tradition of marble sculpting in the Aegean stretches to the Cycladic figurines of the third millennium BCE. Parian marble was the gold standard for Archaic Greek sculpture. While Aristion surely took great pride in his work, he, too, was advertising himself in the inscription, and Athenians of the Archaic period proved to be a very receptive audience for sculptors of *kouroi* and *korai*.

Finally, there is the Athenian statue today called simply ***Kore* 674** (Figure 8.22).[8] The statue dates to *c.* 510–500 BCE; the fragment, just under 1 m in height, was discovered on the Athenian *akropolis* in 1888. While her neck is somewhat elongated, her well-observed and well-sculpted facial features are proportional to her head size. Her shoulders are narrower than other *korai* and sloping. Her delicate gown falls from her right shoulder in an arc just over her left breast,

Figure 8.21 Phrasikleia, *kore*, marble statue, Merenda, Attika *c.* 540 BCE.

Figure 8.22 *Kore* 674, marble statue, Akropolis, Athens, *c.* 510–500 BCE.

which is covered by her undergarment. She holds out her right hand, while her left gathers her undergarment at mid-thigh. The detailing of *Kore* 674 from her headpiece and cabled hair to the meticulously carved over-garment, anticipates the near obsession with female drapery of Classical Greek sculptors.

Most significant, however, is the rendering of her face. The sculptor has learned how to convey the illusion of a beautiful, sentient being. The effect is achieved through the expression of her sensitive mouth, the slightly downcast look, and the slight narrowing of her almond-shaped eyes. She is, of course, roughly contemporary with the Kritios Boy. With *Kore* 674 and her contemporaries, the *kore*-type reaches its zenith – and, as with the Kritios Boy, its limit. The static tradition has little room for further evolution, and sculptors had already discovered that even slight variation from the canon could help to animate the statue.

Sculptors of *kouroi* and *korai* were by no means solely intent on realism. From the beginning, they sought to portray an ideal beauty. Classical sculptors were aware that idealized statues of human beings could be created by means of basic geometry applied in proportional progressions. The "canon" was expounded in the fifth century BCE by Polykleitos and very likely derived from the Pythagoreans, who in turn "borrowed" from the Egyptians. As we have seen, the Pythagoreans were preoccupied with mathematical harmonies.[9] Greek artists came to understand how proportions, harmonies, and asymmetries worked to produce the humanizing effects they sought.

Archaic sculptors were much more constrained than their successors of the Classical period. *Kouroi* and *korai* were dedications to gods or commemorations of deceased individuals, whether they portrayed divinity or not. While details could be altered, canons did not change fundamentally until, at the beginning of the fifth century BCE, real people, such as the Athenian tyrant-slayers, Harmodios and Aristogeiton, could be portrayed as themselves in action and displayed in the *agora*.[10] Pottery-painters were allowed far freer rein to explore the humanity of subjects. Portraying actual human beings in sculpture may have entailed social sanctions, especially early on in places like Athens. These sanctions had apparently waned by the end of the Archaic period and would be all but vanished by the end of the fifth century BCE.

8.4 Summary

8.4.1 Archaic Greek Art and Archaic Greeks

Archaic Greek artists created to please and impress their paying customers. The Dipylon Amphora was produced for a specific patron whose desires were high in the minds of the potter and painter: the narrative portion reflected directly upon the deceased and indirectly upon the patron. Though the Nessos amphora was also a grave-marker, its painted scenes referred only obliquely to the deceased person. We assume that that obliquity pleased the patron. Finely painted pottery was interred with the dead, especially in Etruria, outside of Greece, and scenes from mythology, such as Exekias' "Achilles and Penthesilea," commonly appear on Athenian vases buried with Etruscan dead. By the later sixth century BCE, scenes involving real people doing mundane things, as, for example, the "Three Old Revelers" of Euthymides and the Brygos Painter's "Youthful Revelers" seem to increase in number. These changes in artists' subjects should reflect changes in patrons' tastes and their endorsement of the trend toward greater realism in the portrayals of human beings. Archaic potters and pottery-painters competed with each other to please their customers, while artists like Kritios and the unknown Siphnian treasury frieze master may have created to more exact specifications. Archaic Greek patrons and consumers of art partnered with artists in its development, moving Archaic art toward renderings that were both increasingly more realistic and aesthetically pleasing. The refinement of Archaic Greek art must also reflect refinement in the tastes of the Archaic Greek audiences.

Notes

1 Pliny *Nat. Hist.* 7.57.
2 Pausanias 3.17.2.
3 Most art objects from the ancient world are dated approximately because they cannot be dated precisely. By far, most from the Archaic period are dated stylistically and, where possible, in relation to others similar in style that can be dated more precisely.
4 R. Neer, "Framing the Gift: The Politics of the Siphnian Treasury at Delphi," *Classical Antiquity* 20 (2001) p. 288.
5 *Kouroi* appear first in the Cyclades, but the earliest *kouroi* are likely to have been sculpted in Ionia whether by Greeks or non-Greeks.
6 Herodotos 1.31.
7 Woodford, p. 46.
8 The Italian epithet, "La Delicata," which was obviously artificially and arbitrarily imposed on *Kore* 674, is as misleading and so barren a designation as "The Lily Prince" or "La Parisienne" are for those Minoan frescoes.
9 Tobin (1975), pp. 307 ff.
10 On these statues, see most recently V. Azoulay, *Les Tyrannicides d'Athènes: vie et mort de deux statues.* (Paris, 2014).

Further Reading

Archaic Greek Art

J. Hurwit, *Art and Culture of Early Greece, 1100–480 B.C.* (Ithaca, NY, 1987).
R. Osborne, *Archaic and Classical Greek Art* (Oxford, 1998).

Dipylon Amphora

B. Bohen, "The Dipylon Amphora: Its Role in the Development of Greek Art," *Journal of Aesthetic Education* 25 (1991) pp. 59–65.

Black-Figure Vase-Painting

J. Boardman, *Athenian Black Figure Vases* (London, 1985).

Red-Figure Vase-Painting

J. Boardman, *Athenian Red Figure Vases: The Archaic Period: A Handbook* (London, 1985).

Archaic Greek Sculpture

J. Boardman, *Greek Sculpture: The Archaic Period* (London, 1985).

Kouroi

G. Richter, *Kouroi: Archaic Greek Youths. A Study of the Development of the Kouros Type in Greek Sculpture*[3] (New York, 1988).
S. Woodford, *An Introduction to Greek Art* (Ithaca, NY, 1986), pp. 38–46.

Egypt and *Kouroi*

J. Carter and L. Steinberg, "*Kouroi* and Statistics," *American Journal of Archaeology* 114 (2010) pp. 103–128.

Korai

K. Karakasi, *Archaic Korai* (Los Angeles, 2004).
M. Steiber, *The Poetics of Appearance in Attic Korai* (Austin, TX, 2004).

Canon of Polykleitos

R. Tobin, "The Canon of Polykleitos," *American Journal of Archaeology* 79 (1975) pp. 307–321.

Archaic and Classical Greek Sculpture

R. Neer, *The Emergence of the Classical Style in Greek Sculpture* (Chicago, 2010).

9

Archaic Greek Literature

9.1 Introduction

Although epic poetry seems to have dominated early Greek pre-literature, it gives way to lighter, more personal lyric and elegiac poetry early in the Archaic period. The *Iliad*'s "stars" are heroic *aristoi*; its messages are about life, death, and human suffering. Homer's heroes want to achieve and maintain *kleos* and so standing among other heroes: they risk death routinely to do just that. The poet sang of these ancestors of the Archaic Greeks before entire communities which were both entertained and inspired by what they heard. Not much later than Homer, however, Archilochos criticized aristocratic pretensions, contrasting them with real-life experiences. Reality mattered more to him it seems than anything ideal or imagined. Lyric and elegiac poetry covered all manner of subjects from fighting and dying to friendship and the joys of living and loving, from losing badly in battle to winning gloriously at Olympia, and from abject suffering to ecstatic abandon. Above all, human beings, their experiences and their emotions, were its focus. Some poems are about the gods, but many of these are about divinities acting like humans.

Archaic Greek poetry is an indispensable source for the period, but presents considerable problems, for while it provides the possibility for understanding Archaic Greeks better, it also works against that possibility. Poetry by its very nature is indirect in the way that it communicates, its precise meanings and its messages are often difficult to know. Moreover, a great deal was nuanced for and so well understood by Archaic Greek audiences, but is quite unclear to us.

9.2 Homer

Homer's epics were rooted in the Bronze Age. His lengthy poems were composed of lays which were preserved orally by generations of *aoidoi* apparently from the time of the Mykenaian migration to Anatolia in the later twelfth century BCE. During that preservation, parts of the originals were lost, while other parts were added. By the mid-eighth century BCE, the earliest possible date for the *Iliad*'s composition, what had come to Homer was markedly different from that which post-Mykenaian bards had sung five centuries before. The *Iliad* and *Odyssey* were "sewn together" by Homer – or perhaps another just before him – from parts

Archaic Greece: The Age of New Reckonings, First Edition. Brian M. Lavelle.

transmitted through the oral epic tradition. Though he did not originate the epics, Homer was accepted by later Greeks as undisputed author of both. Among the last of his kind, Homer composed his poetry without writing.

To be able to recall so many lines of epic poetry for performance, *aoidoi* were trained in a unique poetic language that consisted of music, diction, and meter. Each one of the lines had to conform to a metrical pattern called dactylic hexameter. Accordingly, each line was divided into six measures and to each syllable in the verse was attached a sound value, long or short. The words in each line had to amount to five dactyls (ˉ ˘ ˘) or combinations of dactyls and spondees (ˉ ˉ) and end with a spondee (Box 9.1).

Like other *aoidoi*, Homer sang his verses as he played the lyre, a small harp-like instrument whose strings were stretched over a wooden frame and a tortoise-shell sounding-box (Figure 9.1). The sounds made by plucking or strumming accentuated the words, lines, or sound value stressed as the poet sang. The *aoidos* may have modulated his voice, prolonging words or sounds between notes, increasing or decreasing emphasis or volume to color what he sang as he wished.

Epic diction was both economical and expansive. It consisted of words apt for meter, but also for metrical phrases, whole lines, sets of lines, and even extensive portions that could be repeated. Such repetitions were called *formulae*. *Aoidoi* could reuse familiar combinations and invent new ones as they sang – even as musicians make music from memory but also spontaneously today. Greek *aoidoi* must also have had truly exceptional memories and were undoubtedly enthusiastic about the songs and stories they sang and the part they played in preserving poetic traditions. They were thought of in their day as mediums, transmitting song inspired by the Muses rather than originating it themselves.

While epic performances were entertaining, they were also important social and cultural events especially during the Dark Ages and Archaic period. The lays were not simply tales of long-dead heroes, but reconnections of communities to the memories of powerful ancestors who lived in far better times. The stories evoked nostalgia, but also solidified identity and

---

Box 9.1 Homeric Epic

From *Iliad* 1, lines 1–2:

ˉ ˘ ˘/ ˉ ˘ ˘/ ˉ// ˉ ˉ/ ˉ ˘ ˘/ ˉ ˘ ˘/ ˉ ˉ

μῆνιν ἄ/ειδε, θε/ὰ, Πη/ληϊά / δεω Ἀχι/λῆος
(mēnin a/ eide t'e/ ā Pē/ lē-i-a/ dyō Ak'i/ lēos)

ˉ ˘ ˘/ ˉ// ˉ/ ˉ ˘ ˘/ ˉ ˉ/ ˉ ˘ ˘/ ˉ ˉ

οὐλομέ/νην, ἣ/ μυρί᾿ Ἀ/χαιοῖ ς/ ἄλγε᾿ ἔ/θηκεν
(oulome/ nēn, hē/myri'///A /k'aiois/ alge' e/ t'ēken)

The *menis* sing it, goddess, of Peleus' son, Achilles,
ruinous, which numberless sufferings on the Achaians set…

In the opening of the *Iliad*, there are four dactyls in the first line and three in the second; there are two and three spondees respectively. A pause within a line //, usually at the middle of the verse, is called a *caesura*.

Figure 9.1 Woman playing a lyre. Attic R-F squat *lekythos. c.* 470 BCE.

renewed idealism and optimism, all the while offering temporary respite from hard-led lives. Epic performances were vital reinvigorations of common Greek culture, identity, and pride.

Homer's epics were not written down until well after his lifetime. *Aoidoi* seem to have given way to ***rhapsodoi*** ("song-stitchers"), who may have recited rather than sung the epics, reproducing them as faithfully as they could.[1] Although the Homeric poems were reportedly written down in Athens *c.* 525 BCE, the 24 books of each that we have today are the products of the great Alexandrian librarian-editors of the Hellenistic period. The Greek text of the *Iliad* was finally printed in Florence in the late fifteenth century CE, and what we have of the epics is mostly what the later ancient Greeks and Romans had. However, that may be quite different from what the Archaic Greeks heard in performance.

Homer's poems became the bases for ancient Greek pedagogy, especially for Greek males, almost from the time of their composition. Every Greek youth knew the stories of Achilles' anger and the suffering of Odysseus as he struggled homeward. Archilochos seems to have known Homer inside out, and references appear abundantly in Archaic and Classical poetry and tragedy. Alexander the Great carried a copy of the pre-Alexandrian *Iliad* wherever he went.

9.2.1 *Iliad*

The *Iliad* is a poem about heroism and honor, mortality and immortality. It centers on the great warrior Achilles in the tenth year of the siege of Troy. A quarrel develops in Book 1 between Achilles and Agamemnon, the Greek expedition's leader, coming down to who will retain an honor-prize awarded by the army. Because Agamemnon is forced to surrender his prize for the army's sake, he seizes Achilles' prize as compensation. The seizure ignites Achilles' ***menis*** ("furious anger"). He unleashes a torrent of anger first at Agamemnon, then at his warrior-comrades. His sea goddess-mother, Thetis, begs Zeus for vengeance on his behalf, and the god allows the Trojans to triumph over the Greeks temporarily.

From Books 2 through 8 of the *Iliad*, we see no more of Achilles, who has withdrawn from battle. Instead, many other heroes are introduced, both Greek and Trojan. A brief, single combat ensues between Paris, who had stolen the beautiful Helen away to Troy and so caused the war, and Menelaos, Helen's very angry husband. Helen is physically enthralled by Paris though he is a foppish coward. Hektor, Paris' blameless brother, is by far the greatest Trojan hero, and his devotion to duty and his people throws both Paris' and Achilles' selfishness into unflatteringly high relief. Hektor's final conversation with and parting from his wife, Andromache, and their doomed child, Astyanax, in Book 6 are poignant and evoke pity.

When Achilles reappears in Book 9, the Trojans have the Greeks on their heels and are facing doom. Agamemnon finally accepts blame for the quarrel and promises enormous compensation to Achilles if he will rejoin the fight. But Achilles refuses so extravagantly that the great Greek soldier-hero Aias criticizes him for his savage nature. The Greeks need Achilles, but, like a malevolent god, he remains aloof from battle.

Arrogance alone does not spur Achilles' refusal. He knows from prophecy that, should he remain at Troy, he will inevitably encounter Hektor in battle, kill him, and, soon after killing him, die. Thus, Achilles' ultimate path to the greatest *kleos* is also the path to certain death. His respite from war has allowed him to consider his destiny: he weighs *kleos* and death against long life without glory. Which is better? We learn later from the Lykian hero Sarpedon that a hero may achieve *kleos* and immortality *only* by fighting (Box 9.2). There is no other way.

Things go so badly for the Greeks in Achilles' absence that Patroklos, his close companion, can bear it no longer. Could he not at least lead Achilles' Myrmidons into the fight, if the hero won't? Achilles softens, lending Patroklos his armor and followers, but warning him not to go too far. In the heat of battle, however, Patroklos disobeys and, running afoul of Apollo who protects Troy, is finally slain by Hektor with Apollo's help. Hektor strips Patroklos of Achilles' armor. Hearing the news, Achilles is rendered utterly disconsolate, yet his *menis*, which he now re-directs at Hektor, burns even hotter. Achilles will re-enter the fight – and he will die. He accepts his fate nonetheless because love and honor demand vengeance for Patroklos.

Box 9.2 Sarpedon to Glaukos on Why Homeric Heroes Risk Death

> O my good friend, if we together could flee this war
> and live always, ageless and undying,
> neither would I myself fight in the forefront
> nor would I send you into battle which brings men glory.
> As it is, the dooms of death stand beside us,
> numberless, and no man can flee or ward them off.
> So let us go and yield glory to another or he to us.
>
> *(Iliad 12, 322–328)*

Though a Lykian, Sarpedon, the son of Zeus, is perhaps the noblest of fighters in the war at Troy. He states precisely why heroes risk all in deadly combat.

When Hektor and Achilles finally meet in the ultimate battle of the *Iliad*, Homer positions us with Hektor, not Achilles. We run with Hektor from the pursuing Achilles, know his thoughts as he ponders what to do, and stand beside him when he turns finally to confront the "best of the Achaians." Hektor's death is inevitable, but his final display of heroism is memorable. "Wanting to do something big for later generations of men to talk of," Hektor launches himself at Achilles with only a sword. Achilles spears the oncoming Hektor and then, savage to the end, vaunts over the corpse of the far nobler man. What do we make of Homer's treatment of these two heroes?

While Hektor is morally superior, the two heroes are fundamentally indistinct. Both strive for *kleos* and need each other as benchmarks of their *arete*, their fighting excellence. The supreme irony in their final meeting underscores the interwoven identities of the pair. When Achilles confronts Hektor, the Trojan hero is wearing Achilles' armor which he had stripped from Patroklos. Killing Hektor, Achilles actually slays himself because his death is now imminent. Achilles and Hektor are really one and the same hero: death and glory are achieved almost simultaneously for both.

Homer abandons facile polemic in the *Iliad* for a much deeper message. By alienating the Greek hero and making the "enemy" sympathetic for the audience, the poet forces it to think more deeply about war and humanity. For Homer, war, triumph in battles, and glory inextricably entail defeat, destruction, and mortality. The cost of *kleos* is death. In fact, the *Iliad* is a poem celebrating neither war nor peace, but one observing the persistence and consequences of both – the reality of life as the Greeks knew it. The quandary that war and Greek values present is summed up in what Achilles ponders alone on the Trojan shore: is a short, glorious life actually better than a long one without glory? In the *Iliad*, the lines between "friend" and "enemy" are blurred in order to convey the totality of war and the shared humanity of the belligerents.

Homer's tale does not end with Hektor's death. Achilles rages on, treating the body of Hektor atrociously until even the gods can bear it no longer. With their help, Priam arrives before Achilles to plead for his son's body. When Achilles recognizes his own father in Priam and shares with him the grief of war, his rage finally dissolves. Achilles realizes for the first time that others suffer, too, and so feels sympathy for Priam's misery. This realization and the surrendering of Hektor's body to Priam signal Achilles' coming-of-age and reinstatement to humanity: it is a reassuring demonstration that human beings can feel for other human beings, even great enemies in the midst of unending war, sorrow, and tribulation.

9.2.2 *Odyssey*

The *Odyssey* is very different from the *Iliad*: it is about one man's struggle to get home after many years away; its governing value is survival, not honor. Because of Odysseus' prolonged absence from Ithaka, evil men have assumed him dead and taken over his home. These are pressing his wife, Penelope, to marry one of them so that the chosen one may occupy the vacant throne. But Odysseus is very much alive. There is a constant undertone of urgency in the epic: Odysseus must get home before Penelope's choice is made. The *Odyssey* is a vivid, dynamic folktale, while the *Iliad* is a profound, somewhat static tragedy.

The *Odyssey*'s first four books are really about Telemachos, Odysseus' son, and his coming-of-age. Taking human form, the goddess Athena arrives in Ithaka to goad the boy into leaving home to seek news of his father. The boy is frightened, but complies, arriving first in Pylos, governed by the excellent Nestor, aged adviser to the *Iliad*'s heroes. From Pylos, Telemachos journeys to Sparta where he encounters the very strange domesticity of Menelaos and Helen, now returned from Troy. (Relations between men and women are a central theme in the *Odyssey*.) Menelaos offers the welcome news to Telemachos that Odysseus is alive.

Book 5 abruptly switches to Kalypso's island, where Hermes has come to liberate Odysseus held captive by the goddess. With Kalypso's reluctant help, Odysseus builds a raft and departs Ogygia, the goddess' island. Surviving a tempest stirred up by a wrathful Poseidon, he comes to land on the island of the Phaiakians. After meeting the plucky princess, Nausikaa, Odysseus is offered hospitality by Alkinoös, Nausikaa's father.

It is among the Phaiakians that Odysseus recounts his famous travels. In the land of the Lotus-Eaters, Odysseus must forcibly re-embark some of his crew who by eating the lotus have lost all desire to return home. In a horrifying episode for ancient Greeks, Odysseus confronts the one-eyed giant Polyphemos who has locked the Greeks in his cave. The monster cannibalizes some of Odysseus' crew before the hero can devise a way to blind and escape him. Before getting clear, however, Odysseus errs terribly – but all too humanly – shouting his name in triumph, earning thereby the implacable hostility of the Cyclops' father, Poseidon. On Aiaia, he overcomes Kirke, an enchantress who had turned some of his men into swine. The most harrowing of episodes is Odysseus' journey to the Underworld where he encounters many ghosts. In a famous renunciation of Iliadic values, Achilles' ghost avers to Odysseus that he would rather be alive as a slave than dead in the Underworld. Achilles thus underscores the message of the *Odyssey*, that living is far better than dying, even with great honor.

Reaching Ithaka, Odysseus must disguise himself as a beggar before he can move to reclaim his home. In such disguise, he must endure physical abuse even in his own home to learn self-discipline. At length, at precisely the right time – and at a supremely dramatic moment – Odysseus throws off his disguise before the startled suitors and then sets about killing them all, while Telemachos and other faithful servants join in. Odysseus cleanses his home of blood-stain – but he is not yet "home."

The long-suffering Penelope cannot be sure that her husband has actually returned and, when Odysseus presents himself to her, she slyly orders the marriage-bed within her chamber to be brought out for him to sleep on. Odysseus fumes because he had made that bed immovable, anchoring it to an olive tree stump. It is in fact *still* anchored. His outburst proves his identity to Penelope, for no man but he could know the intimacies of their marriage-chamber. The bed's pristine state emphasizes Penelope's chasteness and the solidity of their marriage, but also shows that Penelope is herself of "many wiles" and more than a match for her husband. She has tricked the truth out of the trickster. Odysseus is finally home in the epic. In myth, however, his travels are far from over.

Odysseus' interactions with females, both human and divine, are frequent and foregrounded in the *Odyssey*. Athena appears often in the epic, significantly helping Odysseus and Telemachos on their journeys. Like Athena, Nausikaa, her mother, Arete, and the human-turned-sea goddess Ino are all "helpers," whereas Kalypso and Kirke are, at first, "hinderers." Odysseus' most significant relationship is with Penelope who is in fact "home" to him. Superhumanly faithful through the nearly 20 years of Odysseus' absence, she fends off the suitors with cleverness and subterfuge, keeping "home" and marriage intact. Penelope is a hero in her own right. Homer's counterpoint to Penelope is Klytemnestra, a constant reminder of the worst of marriages. Helen, however, is a more ambiguous character and suggests that Homer wanted his audience to consider male-female relationships more deeply.

Unlike Achilles, Odysseus provides a model for the common Greek. His wit, intensity, and discipline, the keys to his success, are imitable: he is no out-of-reach superhero. In the *Odyssey*, attainment and safety of home and hearth are paramount aims. This message is supported by Odysseus' refusal of the immortality offered him by Kalypso and implied by Kirke in the epic. Such messages reinforce common folk values: there is in fact "no place like home."

While the *Iliad* is really a tragedy played out by aristocrat-warriors, the *Odyssey* concerns the struggles of, essentially, a common man who overcomes obstacles by wit and word. Yet both epics are similar. Both focus on principals who face the threat of death to attain their goals; both emphatically stress that isolation from others is destructive and that connection to others is an absolute necessity.

9.3   Hesiod

Hesiod's epics are very different from Homer's. Whereas the *Iliad* and the *Odyssey* are dramatic fictions, educating obliquely, Hesiod's *Theogony* and *Works and Days* are (what he took to be) factual, didactic, and involve much less emotion. Hesiod's purpose is to convey profitable information to his contemporary audience. His gods are rather different from Homer's: those of the *Theogony* are more remote from human beings than they are in the *Iliad* or *Odyssey*. *Works and Days* is really about human beings, not gods.

As we have seen, Hesiod's *Theogony* explains how the *kosmos* came into being and how the gods came to rule within it; in the *Works and Days*, Hesiod informs Perses, but really all Greek farmers about justice, work, and how to harmonize their farming efforts with the order of the physical world. In both epics, beyond their theological and philosophical elements, is important evidence about how Archaic Greeks thought about themselves and their relations to divinity. These are stated somewhat obliquely in the myths involving Metis, Prometheus, Pandora, and the Five Ages of Man.

9.4   Early Greek Lyric and Elegaic Poets

Poetry following Homer and Hesiod is quite different. Poems are shorter and, though influenced by the Greek epic tradition, more immediate, emotional, and even intimate. Lyric and elegiac poetry could reflect the mood of the poet, how she or he wanted to express her sentiments or engage and affect the audience on the moment; it was also apparently what the audience wanted. Lyric poetry was accompanied by the lyre, the same instrument used by epic poets; elegiac poetry was accompanied by the flute. Archaic Greek poetry could be performed in many settings, from small group *symposia* to weddings to rituals and other public occasions including political ones.

9.4.1 Archilochos

The warrior-poet of Paros led a very eventful life in the early seventh century BCE as we have already seen. His poems suggest that he traveled far and wide: he knew about southern Italy and the Thracian shores; he may have enlisted as a mercenary in Egypt. His life was also a violent one and he was finally killed by one Kalondas. The latter was condemned by the Delphic oracle for slaying "the Muses' own servant."

Greeks seem to have regarded Archilochos ambivalently, both as god-favored and vulgar. An apocryphal anecdote explained his genius as coming directly from an encounter with the daughters of Zeus when he was very young. The Hellenistic poet Theokritos and the Roman critic Quintilian praise him,[2] but Pindar says that he was "the lover of blame grown fat on invective" and Kallimachos that he spewed venomous verses.[3]

Archilochos' reputation for bitterness derived especially from his attacks on Lykambes and his daughter Neoboule. Apparently Lykambes had promised Neoboule in marriage to Archilochos, but then reneged. The change of heart wounded Archilochos' pride so much that he unleashed a torrent of abuse against father and daughter in reprisal. So withering were the attacks that father and daughter are said to have committed suicide. Because of the mostly fragmentary nature of Archilochos' poetry, we have only traces of that invective.

Archilochos mainly employed iambic dimeters or trimeters in his attack-poetry. This type of verse, which was used in ritual vilification linked to Demeter and Dionysos, was designed to cut haughty persons down to size. Such poetry might seem more playful than hateful inasmuch as the nature of the abuse was conditioned – and limited – by its ritual association. Archilochos, however, repurposed iambic with apparently deadly effect and applied it relentlessly (Box 9.3). Others like Semonides, Hipponax, and even Kallimachos attacked others using such verse, but none, it seems, so viciously as Archilochos.

What fascinates us most about Archilochos' poetry, however, is his focus on himself. An intelligent, thoughtful person, he strives to make sense of his existence and place in the world. He is not afraid to note his imperfections, admitting to drunkenness, lust, fear, and cowardice in battle. He is no hero. Archilochos' frankness is unexpected, but quite compelling, for he seems to see the world and himself in it in a clearer way, setting down the truth of it for himself and others. He communicates in "snapshots": an episode here, a feeling there, an encounter, an impression. While he sometimes gives words to figments like "Charon the Carpenter" in his poems, these characters nevertheless portray Archilochos' own thoughts and emotions.

As a warrior, Archilochos was bound to a system of martial values partially described in Homer. When he discarded his shield to save himself, he undoubtedly felt shame: it was an act of cowardice, after all. However, rather than abiding with that shame, Archilochos proclaimed the shield's relative worthlessness counted against his own survival. Why should I die for a mere piece of metal?, he asks. His defiant words defined what was important and what was not in his real world. Like Odysseus, survival is more important than honor for Archilochos. But by the same token, his unheroic world is uninspiring and lacks the luster of heroes and heroics.

Archilochos can sometimes be quite profound (Box 9.4). He confesses to fear as he witnesses a storm gathering over the heights of Gyrai, a tiny island opposite Tinos in the Aegean (F 105). As we have seen, when an eclipse darkens the sky, the poet's persona seems dumbstruck (F 122). His self-awareness is most apparent in a parody on Odysseus' famous rumination from the *Odyssey* (20.18 ff.).

Box 9.3 Archilochos, Lykambes, and Neoboule

> Would that I could touch my hand to Neoboule
> [...]
> and drop the worker on the wineskin, and throw
> belly against belly and thigh against thigh,
> [...]
> just as I know how to start up the beautiful song of lord Dionysos,
> the dithyramb, even when my wit has been shattered by wine.
>
> *(Frs. 118–120)*

Archilochos parodies Homer in line 3, likening sex to combat. His tone is giddy – or drunken. He proudly notes his connection to the dithyramb, the choral song of Dionysian festivals.

> Father Lykambes, what's this you say?
> Who's taken you away from your wits,
> which before were so battened down? Now
> you are for certain a great joke to the whole town.
>
> *(F 172)*

Archilochos inveighs relatively mildly here, but his disappointment is palpable and his expression already verging on the extravagant. Things will only get worse:

> No longer does your tender skin bloom like it did. Rather
> it withers with wrinkles, and is ruined by evil old age.
>
> *(F 188)*

> Many a blind eel you have entertained.
>
> *(F 189)*

Archilochos goes for the jugular by imputing two "crimes" to Neoboule: age and promiscuity. One ridicules her, the other is meant to obliterate her reputation, her marriageability, her standing in the community, her future, and so any chance at happiness. While Archilochos' society would have expected a reaction from him for the slight he endured, the degree of reprisal seems to have shocked Greeks generally.

Archilochos was a keen observer of his world, others in it, and himself moving in and among them both. His perspective is informed by observation and contemplation, but also hardened by war experience. Archilochos knew from first-hand what war was really like. Honor existed for warriors like him, but did not govern them or their actions as it *seemed* to have done in Homer's *Iliad*. In the real world, warriors do not want to die. What was said of Sophokles in comparison with Euripides by Aristotle might be applied to Homer in comparison with Archilochos: the one portrayed men as they should be, the other, as they are.[4]

Box 9.4 Archilochos Talks to His Soul

Spirit, my spirit, confounded by troubles unyielding:
rise up and drive off your enemies, throwing your chest
forward; amidst the ambushes of the enemy stand up close
and sure. And if you are victorious, don't rejoice too much,
nor being beaten, fall down at home and cry about it.
But take pleasure in pleasures and amidst evils grieve –
but not too much. Know that such ups and downs are the lot of men.

(F 128)

Archilochos encourages himself and others, as if in battle. Life's fortunes fluctuate, and reacting appropriately – rather than adhering statically to Apollo's "middle way," we note – is the best course. There is just the glimmer of stoicism here and harmonizing with the world as it is.

9.4.2 Semonides

We know little of Semonides of Amorgos, a near-contemporary of Archilochos, apart from his poetry. Like Archilochos, he employed iambics and his poetry was sometimes abusive. What has survived of Semonides' poetry is little, but we may just perceive in his iambics the roots of later Greek comic poetry.

In his notorious F 7, Semonides launches what seems to be a very mean-spirited attack on women, by equating them with certain types of animals or elements, and on their habits and behaviors. So, for example, the "mare-woman" (ll. 57–70) is like the horse in the field. She avoids work, washing herself all the time, reveling in her looks, and doing nothing to help the household. A husband who has her has expense. The "changeable woman" is of the sea (ll. 27–42). She is by turns good-natured and intolerable: like the sea, her moods can alter instantly. There is only one good one, Semonides says, the "bee-woman" (ll. 83–93). She works hard with her husband, is blameless, chaste even among other married women, and obviously industrious. All the rest, according to Semonides, are disastrous by the gods' will.

Semonides' equations resemble Hesiod's portrayal of Pandora to some extent (*Works and Days*, 90–95; *Theogony*, 590–612). Women, according to Hesiod, were the greatest evil fashioned by Zeus for man. There are two primary grounds where "bad" women go wrong: they work too little and sexually misbehave too much. Is this poem just an exercise in meanness by Semonides? Semonides' generalizations are absurd and seem well over the top, so could the poem be an attempt at humor?[5] Ridicule, sarcasm, exaggeration, even teasing are elements of comedy and satire, both of which are designed to air, but also to ameliorate by airing, concerns and anxieties. What would Archaic Greeks have made of Semonides F 7?

9.4.3 Tyrtaios

We know next to nothing about Tyrtaios except that he composed elegies for the Spartans around the mid-seventh century BCE (Box 9.5). (Elegiac couplets consist of two lines, a

---

Box 9.5 Tyrtaios Urges the Spartans to Fight

To die is a beautiful thing for him who falls in the forefront of the battle,
    that great good man, struggling on behalf of his fatherland,
but to leave one's *polis* and rich fields
    to become a beggar is the most grievous thing of all things,
wandering with his dear mother and aged father,
    with his small children and lawful wife.
Hated will he be to those he might encounter,
    yielding to need and hateful poverty.
His *genos* ["clan"] is disgraced, his shining appearance concealed,
    All dishonor and distress follow him.
[…]
    So let us fight for this our land and for our children,
and let us die, no longer sparing our lives.
    O young men, fight standing beside one another,
do not start disgraceful flight or panic-fear.
    Make your spirit strong and great within your breast,
do not cling to life as to a lover, fighting with men.

(F 10, lines 1–10, 13–18)

---

dactylic hexameter followed by a dactylic pentameter.) Tyrtaios was almost certainly a Spartan.[6] Many poems appear to be efforts to shore up the morale of Spartan warriors during the Second Messenian War. As we have seen, Sparta's very survival seems to have been on the razor's edge.

Tyrtaios combines the loftiness of epic and its themes of honor, glory, and personal accomplishment, with the realities of war and practical need for both *polis* and family. If the Spartans are defeated, they will lose not only glory and honor, but everything and will become, with their families, beggars. Hesiod says that nothing worse can befall a man than poverty since he must go begging door-to-door. When Odysseus adopts the beggar's guise in the *Odyssey*, he becomes a man without roots and so is mistreated as an abused animal. He may only eat the scraps granted to him by others, must sleep in the courtyard like his poor old out-of-favor dog Argos, and has a stool and a cow's hoof thrown at him. Tyrtaios hearkens to Homer in his exhortation, but blends in frighteningly real possibilities to drive home the urgency of not losing the war.

We do not know how much Tyrtaios' songs helped initially, but the Spartans did win the war. Thereafter, Tyrtaios' songs became the songs the Spartans sang as they marched into battle. The elegiac verses supplied the marching cadence, but also encouraged the Spartan ranks as they moved toward the moment of truth in battle. Generations of Spartans after Tyrtaios were reminded of the stakes of war and the immediate battle, but also of their ancestors and the hard fight that they had won against odds, heeding the poet's words. Everything the Spartans had been and could and should be was in the songs of Tyrtaios.

9.4.4 Mimnermos

Mimnermos of Smyrna (*c.* 632/629 BCE) was most famous for the *Smyrneis* and the *Nanno*. *Smyrneis* was a lengthy account of his *polis* in elegiacs. Included apparently was an account of the defense of Smyrna against Gyges, the Lydian king. Like all Ionian *poleis*, Smyrna was on the frontline facing an incessantly aggressive Lydia. It finally succumbed to Alyattes, the father of Kroisos.

Although other Greeks seemed ambivalent about the Lydians, Mimnermos was not. In F 14, he points with pride to a powerful ancestor whose exploits on the battlefield kept the Lydians at bay (Box 9.6). Like Tyrtaios and Kallinos of Ephesos, Mimnermos might be exhorting the young men of Smyrna to do battle by comparing them with heroic forebears. Rather than directly addressing the youth of Smyrna, however, Mimnermos chooses narrative. Perhaps direct exhortation came elsewhere in the poem, although there is more nostalgia in the fragment we do possess than urgency.

Mimnermos was more renowned for his love-poetry, particularly those verses included in a collection called *Nanno*. According to ancient Greek sources, Mimnermos was smitten by the flute-girl named Nanno and devoted elegiac lines to her, enough to fill a book. At least one of the fragments of the poem does not seem particularly ardent, however. When Mimnermos speaks of *eros*, he does so with a sense of its very fleeting nature – and that of life itself (Box 9.7). He seems obsessed with youth and aging and how the latter destroys the sweetness of *eros*. Would a real Nanno have been impressed with such "love-poetry"?

Like his predecessors, Mimnermos borrowed from Homer (F 2), but created something new that was highly esteemed later in antiquity. Propertius, a Roman lyric poet, even proclaimed that Mimnermos' love-poetry counted for more than Homer's verse (1.9.11). Just the few lines

---

Box 9.6 Mimnermos on the Hero of Smyrna

> Not at least was the strength of him and strong-hearted spirit
>   which I learned of from those elder to me who saw him
> driving through the thick columns of Lydian horsemen
>   up through the Hermos' plain, this man, this wielder of the ashen spear.
> Pallas Athena never found fault of any kind
>   with his hardened strength of heart, whenever up through the fore-fighters
> he would rush in the combat of bloody war,
>   forcing himself against the biting arrows of the enemy.
> For no man among the hosts was better than he
>   for going to the work of the piercing battle-cry
> while he bore himself in the rays of the swift sun.
>
>   *(F 14)*

There seems to be something missing before the first line of the existing fragment which may have read something like "There may be strength in you, young men, but not the strength of your ancestors." If this were an encouragement, it was to no avail, since Smyrna fell to the Lydians, possibly during Mimnermos' lifetime.

Box 9.7 Mimnermos on "Golden Aphrodite" Come and Gone

> What is there to life, what to delight in, without golden Aphrodite?
>   Let me die when these things don't matter anymore:
> secret embraces, pleasing gifts, and the bed of love.
>   Such are the lovely blooms of youth
> for men and women. But whenever hated old age
>   comes upon us, which makes a man disgusting and vile,
> always around his heart, evil cares dance
>   nor does he even take delight looking on the rays of the sun,
> He is hateful to boys, and laughed at by women.
>   So did god make age to be full of pain.
>
> *(F 1)*

Mimnermos glides past the better parts of love: we must imagine what he means by "secret embraces" and "pleasing gifts." (Compare this with Sappho 31 in Box 9.8.) Rather he moves swiftly into a rather dismal reflection about what love *won't* be anymore. His poem contrasts with the much more playful treatment of *eros* and aging by Anakreon.

---

extant display notable sophistication and gracefulness. Although there is very little with which to compare Mimnermos, signs of literary self-consciousness and formality imply that his poetry might have been ahead of his time. Indeed, *Nanno* may have been more an exercise in poetic virtuosity than of passion.

9.5 Later Lyric and Elegaic Poets

9.5.1 Sappho

Sappho of Lesbos (*c.* 600 BCE) achieved a level of excellence in her poetry quite unmatched by any other Archaic Greek poet. A master of meter, from the complex Aeolic (i.e., "Sapphic") to elegiac, iambic, and others, a creator sometimes of exquisite imagery and capable of remarkable felicity in word-choice, Sappho combined poetic talent with genuine passion and notable craftsmanship to produce verses that can only be described as sublime. Although she composed for formal occasions like weddings, her poetry is often personal and emotional. In fact, Sappho seems rather fearless in revealing her own emotions, even more so than Archilochos. She was renowned for professing ardent attachments to other women in her poems.

According to the biographical tradition, Sappho was an important personage and prominent politically in Mytilene. Recognized as divinely-inspired by her community, she was not only a poet for significant community occasions, but also a teacher. She was the leader of a ***thiasos*** or circle of women who were her companions and pupils. Although Sappho's poems were recognized at once for their brilliance by her fellow Mytilenaians, she had detractors elsewhere in Greece. She was disparaged as ugly by jealous and resentful competitors and others who had never seen her, but were unsettled by her talents, her accomplishments, and her power.[7]

Box 9.8 A Lover Reacts to a Rival

He's like the gods,
that man who sits before you, face to face,
and beside you as you speak so sweetly
listens

as you laugh in such a lovely way.
All of this makes my heart fly in my chest.
When I see you even for a second,
I cannot speak, not even a word.

I cannot move my tongue,
my skin burns like fire,
I cannot see, and there is only pounding
in my ears.

Cold sweat runs down me, and I shiver
all over, green as grass
I turn, and I think
I am dying.

But all must be risked …
(*Sappho 31, 1–15* S&A)

Sappho creates an amusing, yet touching scene in which a jealous lover regards her beloved in company with another. The poet's audience is right there with her in the scene and feels as the persona feels the agony of jealousy. It is in her words that everything unfolds at once before us; it is through her eyes we witness the scene. Sappho provides us with the bittersweet paradox of love and pain in just a few brief lines. It is certainly a pity that we do not have the rest of the poem.

The checklist of physiological responses, piled one upon the other, would be more apt for an observer to describe than one so afflicted. It is surprisingly intense self-observation – almost clinical in fact. Was such unnatural self-consciousness meant to be humorous? The sentiments could be real, but Sappho seems to be leaving judgment up to us.

Much of Sappho's extant poetry depicts an environment very different from Hesiod's or Archilochos'. There is no struggle here with gods, nature, or in war. Rather, poetry is of the interior and intimate, of emotional reflection and a desire to communicate that reflection. Each line is well-crafted, each word seems thoughtfully chosen. Sappho's poetry became renowned during her lifetime and not just among a leisured class. Appreciation of urbanity, refinement, grace, and beauty, as well as emotional – and erotic – intimacy were not reserved merely for the elite of Archaic Greece (Box 9.9).

F 2 is much more than an invocation of the goddess Aphrodite. It describes a sensory Eden, appropriate to the goddess of sex. David Campbell sums it up very well: "The imagery of apples, flowers, gardens, and horses is strongly erotic, and all the senses are involved, sight, smell, touch, hearing, even taste in the mention of nectar."[8] Sappho creates a dreamy mid-space

---

Box 9.9 The Sacred Grove of Aphrodite

Come here to me from Crete, to this temple-place,
holy, where is your charming grove
of apple trees, and the altars burn fragrantly
with frankincense.

Here, cold water-sounds stream through branches
of apple trees, the place is all shaded
with roses, and down the leaves all-shimmering
a dream-sleep pours.

Here a meadow good for horses grazing blooms
with springtime flowers, breezes
blow softly …

"Here you … Kypris, take
and in golden wine cups gently pour
nectar to be mingled with our feast."
                                    (Sappho 2 S&A)

The fragment's text was preserved in odd pieces until the discovery of a potsherd dating to the third century BCE – apparently the product of a student practicing Sapphic meter!

---

hovering cloudlike in between heaven and earth. The fragment captures the sublimity of Sappho's poetry especially because of her ability to transport her listener to the paradise she has conceived.

In the extraordinary F 1 (*S&A*), Sappho summons Aphrodite as though she were an intimate, asking her to help her win a girl's heart. Sappho even imagines Aphrodite answering in playful exasperation, as though Sappho, too, were the goddess' familiar. "Who wrongs you now, Sappho? Whom must I persuade?" (18–20). Aphrodite alludes to helping Sappho before with *eros* and implies that she will do so again; the two seem to be the best of friends.

Regrettably, we possess so little of Sappho's poetry. Perhaps much did not survive because the poems were deemed too personal, inappropriate, and risqué in Late Antiquity and the early Middle Ages to be recopied. Time to time, new bits of Sappho's poems emerge from Egypt's sands written on papyrus or by other means, but not nearly as much as we would like.

9.5.2 Solon

Solon is most famous for his role in Athens' economic and political crisis *c.* 600 BCE. His political poems were often directly addressed to the Athenians, as he attempted to bring order out of *stasis* by introducing new laws into the *polis*. He also composed erotic, sympotic, and other types of poems, but most of what survives appears to be oriented to the political crisis.

Box 9.10 *Eunomia*

Our *polis* will never be destroyed by the decree
   of Zeus and the wills of the blessed deathless gods:
for the great-hearted guardian, whose father is mighty,
   Pallas Athena holds her hands out from above.
Rather they themselves are wanting to destroy this great *polis* from folly,
   the townsmen, persuaded by material riches.
The mind of the *demos'* leaders is unrighteous, who are ready
   from great *hybris* to endure many ills,
for they do not know how to control wealth-insolence or
   to harmonize the present good times of feasting peacefully.
[…]
Thus the common evil comes to each one in his home,
   the doors of the yard are unwilling to hold it out still,
but it leaps over the highest fence, and finds him anyway,
   even if he flees into the inner recess of the house.
The spirit within compels me to teach these things to the Athenians:
   Disorder brings many evils to the *polis*,
but *Eunomia* sets out all things in harmony and straightly
   and quickly claps fetters round the unrighteous.
She soothes the rough, stops wealth-insolence, eclipses *hybris*,
   she withers the growing bud of folly.
She sets straight crooked laws, and arrogant acts
   she tames: she stops the acts of factional disagreement,
and the bile of grievous strife, and by her
   all things that are man's are right and reasoned.

(Solon 4, 1–10, 26–39)

Solon's famous poem on **Eunomia** ("Good Order") (Box 9.10) specifies unrighteous behavior, and warns against it, personifying the divine abstract that corrects disorder. He is like Hesiod in his interest in justice and order and similarly emphasizes that all are affected by disorder. But he is unlike him in that his concerns are focused specifically on Athens. Solon speaks directly to a *polis*-centered populace, which included artisans, craftsmen, and traders, as well as to aristocrats and farmers.[9] Other near-contemporaries like the aristocrat-poet Theognis of Megara also address *politai* about the ills affecting them and the *polis*.

Solon's tone in F 4 is confident and authoritative: the repetitions of *Eunomia*'s benefits are driven home and again for the Athenians. He employs the word "to teach" in the poem, designating himself master among his Athenian pupils. Unlike Hesiod, whose wisdom is informed by the Muses, Solon seems to believe that, while poetic craft comes from the Muses, wisdom derives from himself – with Zeus' help. Because he is saying what is reasonable and constructive, the Athenians should heed him, not because he has been chosen by the gods. In verses that remind us of Hesiod and his concern for *dike*, harmony, and the

---

Box 9.11 Prayer to the Muses

Wealth I long to have, but unjustly to possess it
   I do not want: justice later surely comes to call.
The riches the gods give come to a man
   secure from bottom to top,
but those which men get from *hybris*, and come without order
   and brought along by unjust acts,
these do not come of their own and soon are all mixed up with folly.
[…]
But Zeus sees the end of all …
[…]
… Nor in every case
   just as a mortal man is he sharp with anger,
but always, without let he sees him, the man who holds
   a sinful heart, it always shows forth at the end.
One pays right away, another later on. Those who flee
   and the coming fate of the gods does not find them,
it comes out later: the innocent pay for such work
   either their children or the clan thereafter.
(Solon 13, 7–14, 17, 25–32)

Solon hammers away at the theme of wealth tied to justice for the Athenians, qualifying how much one should have and how one should get it. Solon's point in this and other poems is that either extremity is bad. Moderation is best in all things. Solon reminds the unrighteous that, one way or the other, Zeus will exact retribution for their unrighteousness, immediately or upon later generations.

---

polites' responsibility to the *polis*, however, Solon notes that the evil of the community and the individual are thoroughly implicated (Box 9.11).

Like Thales, Solon was ranked among the Seven Sages. Again, these were not merely aristocrats, but rather new men of sound thought for a new age who could persuade their fellow citizens through action, reputation, and reasoning. By Solon's time, *sophia*, the stock-in-trade of the Seven Sages, was assessed in terms of politically, socially, and morally beneficial practical advice for *polis* and *politai* inclusively. This standard reflects the new realities of the Archaic period, for which a new type of wise man was needed for leadership. (We return to the Seven Sages in Chapter 11.3.1.)

9.5.3 Anakreon

When the Persians advanced to the Ionian coastline in 546 BCE, Anakreon fled his native Teos for Abdera in Thrace. From there, after making his reputation as a poet, he was summoned to Samos by Polykrates, where he remained as a court-poet until the tyrant was slain in 523 BCE. Anakreon was then conveyed to Athens on a warship sent by Hipparchos, the son of the tyrant

---

Box 9.12 The Girl and Eros' Purple Ball

A ball, again, a purple one,
Eros of the golden hair has thrown at me,
And, with a dapple-sandled girl,
he calls me out to play.

But she, well, she's from "well-founded
Lesbos," and my hair,
– it's white, you know – she scoffs at it
and goes off gaping at another girl.
(Anakreon 358 PMG)

The term "well-founded" in line 5 is a Homeric echo. Anakreon wanted to demonstrate his facility with the *Iliad*, a way of nuancing a poem for his sophisticated audience, who knew the Homeric epics very well.

Peisistratos. There he resided as one of a number of poets attached to the Peisistratids apparently until Hipparchos was slain in 514 BCE. Anakreon moved on to the court of the Thessalian Skopadai, but returned to Athens at length to live out his life. Notwithstanding his affiliation to tyrants, the Athenians erected a statue of him on the *akropolis*.

Anakreon's verses are markedly different from those before him. They are highly self-conscious and crafted to delight sophisticated patrons. These were entertained by Anakreon's shorter, lighter poems on urbane topics, which were cleverly worded and arranged in charming ways. His poems are about laughter, drinking, and of course *eros* – all very apt for *symposia*, the place most fitted for his poetry to be sung and heard (Box 9.12). Of course Anakreon also produced flattering verses for his moneyed patrons.

Anakreon references Sappho in poem 358, most directly by his mention of Lesbos and the girl's attraction to another girl. Anakreon's familiarity with Eros, the personification of sexual desire, recollects Sappho's intimacy with Aphrodite. The poet's notice of – and feeling for – the girl are charmingly portrayed in the ball-throwing of the goldilocks boy, who, as Desire itself, blends together with the girl. Anakreon doubles down on this blending with the remarkable coinage "dapple-sandled," an epithet that conjures Sappho's Aphrodite on her "dappled-throne" (F 1, 1). The girl and the goddess seem to become one and the same. Anakreon has deftly layered the girl and her effect on him for his audience, but has also left it to the audience – as good poets do – to take ownership of the image of the girl by leaving out details.

For all that hope and possibility, however, the growing fire becomes cold ash in an instant – all because the girl is from Lesbos. She is completely turned off by the aged poet, whose washed-out white hair contrasts with the color words that further imply the girl's own youth and erotic attractiveness. Bitterness about "grievous eld" and what it does to erotic possibility, reminiscent of Mimnermos, about the girl's preferences, and about Eros himself who has tricked and humiliated the poet give way to good humor. Unlike the gloomy

---

Box 9.13 Thracian Filly

Thracian filly, why do you look at me
with those eyes sidelong
and then run away without a look back? Do you think
me a complete amateur?
Know this: prettily on you
could I fit the bridle and bit,
and holding the reins, take
you to the course's limits.
Right now, you graze in the meadow,
skip lightly and play:
you don't have that experienced rider
who knows fillies so well.

(Anakreon 417 PMG)

Mimnermos, Anakreon seems to be laughing at himself, since, as an old man, his pursuit of a young girl is absurd anyway. That's a lot in eight lines!

The allegory of horse and rider interplay mutes the poem's overt eroticism to some extent (Box 9.13). The girl is a "filly" who runs and jumps in a meadow; the poet, a breaker of horses who will tame her with bit and bridle. The thinly veiled implication is that he will have his way erotically with her in the end. The tone is one of mastery and conquest: it comes across as boastful – something Anakreon's male *symposion* companions might have found amusing. Horse-and-rider erotic imagery is recurrent in Greek and Latin literature.

While Anakreon's verses represent a new, higher level of sophistication, poetic craftsmanship, and greater self-consciousness, they lack the intimacy, spontaneity, and engagement of earlier Greek poetry. It was perhaps the next logical step in the evolution of Archaic Greek literature, like Baroque after Renaissance art. Poets like Anakreon, Ibykos, and Simonides, all retainers of tyrants, were sometimes in direct competition with each other for recognition, fame, and wealth – and so for the continuing attention of their wealthy patrons who were themselves competing with other patrons.

9.5.4 Simonides

Simonides of Keos, born *c.* 556 BCE, came to Athens in the time of the younger tyrants as a court-poet. Like Anakreon, he subsequently joined the Skopadai in Thessaly, but returned to Athens thereafter, possibly during the Persian War. Though he commemorated Greek victories over the Persians many times in his poetry, Simonides composed a funerary epigram for the exiled Peisistratids, allies of the Persians and enemies of the Athenians, shortly before his death in 468 BCE. Again like Anakreon, he earned no ill-will among the Athenians for his past or even his continuing affiliation with the tyrants. He ended his life in Sicily in the company of Hieron, tyrant of Syrakusa.

Box 9.14 On Reality and the "Good Man"

Pittakos' saying doesn't sound right to me,
though it was spoken by a wise man indeed:
"Hard it is to be excellent," he said.
A god alone can take such a prize, for a man
it's impossible not to be bad,
a man who's brought down by unexpected disaster.
Every man while he's doing well is an excellent man,
bad if badly he fares.
For the most part the best of men are those
whom the gods love.
[…]
I'm no fault-finder and fine for me
is the man who is not worthless nor overly lazy
who knows *polis*-profiting justice,
the man of sound character. No indeed, I will not
find fault [with him]. For the race of complete fools
knows no end.
All things are good which
aren't mixed up with what is shameful.
                    (*Simonides 542, 11–20, 33–40* PMG)

Simonides composed many types of poems, including hymns, choral odes, elegiacs, dirges, and victory odes. The latter were performed by choruses praising Olympic, Pythian, or other Panhellenic festival victors for their triumphs. Although Pindar became most famous for such victory odes, Simonides is the first important author to compose this type of poem. Simonides also produced many epigrams. He possessed a prodigious memory – he said so himself! – and was famously avaricious. Yet, although he was not esteemed by some of his fellow poets and even sometimes ridiculed, Simonides was renowned among Greeks in his lifetime.

Simonides' poetry is sometimes celebratory, many times reflective. He was considered a wise man, but, unlike Solon or even Thales, without political focus. Indeed, he seems to have reckoned himself a cosmopolite rather than a citizen of any single *polis*: his philosophical poems are addressed broadly to Greek audiences, and his messages transcend *polis* boundaries. In fact, Simonides has been labeled a forerunner of the sophists, the itinerant teachers who traveled from *polis* to *polis* in Classical Greece, teaching wisdom and rhetoric – for a price.

Simonides softens the pessimistic challenge of Pittakos by emphasizing that humans are not divine and simply cannot be as "excellent" as the gods (Box 9.14). Mortals suffer vicissitudes in life that gods do not and must not be held to the same standards. For Simonides, the man, knowing what is right and who *tries* to live righteously is good enough. His bar for human achievement is set more realistically, albeit lower than it was by Pittakos about a century before him.

Simonides' standard for "goodness" is again inclusive without apparent social or economic boundary. He had dwelt in Athens for many eventful years, witnessing first Athens' prosperity

---

Box 9.15 Perseus and Danae Adrift

When in a wondrously wrought chest, the blowing wind
and the sea heaving
flooded her with fear,
with her cheeks streaming tears,
she put her dear hand around Perseus
and spoke to him: "O child, I have such pain.
You sleep so well, in your infant way
slumbering so peacefully
on hard planks riveted with bronze nails
lit by the night-sky,
stretched out in deep sea darkness.
The cresting water above your head
brought on by every coming wave you pay no mind, nor
the shrill of the wind, lying in
your blanket of purple, your face so beautiful.
If to you this danger was danger,
you would incline your little ear to my words.
But I say to you: sleep my newborn.
And sleep, you sea, and sleep, too, our measureless trouble."
                    (Simonides 543, 1–22 PMG)

---

under the tyrants, then the dissolution of the tyranny, the establishment of Athenian democracy, and then its triumph against Persia. Was his heart democratic? Was he criticizing obsolete aristocratic standards of "goodness" as he does in F 579 (see Box 9.17)? Whether his outlook was in fact "democratic" – he was happy to take money from tyrants to the end of his life, it seems – his words stimulated the thoughts of such as the sophist Protagoras who believed that *arete* could be learned. Simonides anticipates the famous philosophical debates in Athens in the fifth century BCE about the nature of ethics, morality, justice, and divinity.

The beautiful fragment is part of a much longer poem on the myth of Danae, who, along with her baby son, Perseus, was cast adrift by her wicked father, Akrisios, the king of Argos (Box 9.15). He had learned that Danae would bear a son who would kill him some day and so wanted to avoid his fate. When Akrisios failed to prevent Danae's pregnancy, he constructed a buoyant wooden box, put mother and son in it, and sent them out to sea to die. His hands would thus be clean of the pollution of murder.

Simonides' verses take us inside the watertight coffin-box where we overhear Danae's loving address to her sleeping son. Simonides uses color-words in an admirable economy of composition to paint a vivid picture. The roaring sea and gale outside the box portray the peril of Perseus and Danae, but the young mother's tender address to her baby seems serene amidst such danger. Simonides juxtaposes tumult with tranquility, the howling storm with a mother's soft whispers. It is a contrast between death all around outside and life within. Images of infant and mother are of course universally appealing, and the poet evokes profound sympathy for the unfortunate Danae and Perseus, who will nonetheless be preserved by divine will and fate. His words, so vivid and absorbing, suspend our memory of that salvation by placing us together with mother and child in their current parlous circumstance. Simonides treated many other myths in his poems.

In a celebrated grave-epigram, Simonides evokes pity and awe for Leonidas of Sparta and the famous "Three Hundred" who perished together at Thermopylai fighting against the Persian invaders in 480 BCE. The epitaph is rendered as if they are speaking out to passers-by from their heroes' grave at Thermopylai (92 D Campbell):

> O stranger, tell the Lakedaimonians that in this place
> we lie, obedient to their laws.

Rather than abandon the battlefield – and their honor – the Spartans died at their posts, earning undying glory, as Homeric heroes had done before them.

Simonides also composed an epigram for his friend, the seer Megistias, who had accompanied the "Three Hundred" to Thermopylai (Box 9.16). Megistias displayed the same bravery as the Spartans by remaining with them even though he was no Spartan and knew that death was certain. The epitaph magnifies Megistias' heroism, placing it beyond Spartan heroism – and on par with Achilles' – because of that foreknowledge. Simonides composed other lengthier works celebrating allied Greek victories during the Persian War, including poems on the battles of Artemision, Salamis, and Plataia.

Simonides personifies *Arete* who may not be "seen" without great exertion, in a way renovating Hesiod's advice to Perses about hard work with this allegory of high rocks, climbing and attaining the summit (Box 9.17). *Arete* is not attained simply by birth or wealth, the old aristocratic standards. Rather, she may be attained by any, rich or poor, base-born or *aristos*, who struggle to scale the rugged heights she occupies. The straining for excellence, however, becomes more than heroic for attainment of *arete* implies association with the immortal. While Simonides' lines mirror the recurrent theme of humanity's struggle in Greek art and literature, especially in the Classical period, his personification of *arete* shows that already the idea of divinity had begun to shift in the minds of Greeks away from the gods and more toward human beings, their aspirations, and their institutions. These, Classical Greeks would find, were what mattered to them most after all.

Although Archaic Greek lyric and elegiac really ends with Simonides, his poetry, though based in the poetic traditions from Homer to his own time, was wide-ranging, innovative, and highly influential of later Greek poets and other artists. As we have seen, Simonides accepted

---

Box 9.16 Epigram for the Seer Megistias

> This is the memorial of famous Megistias, whom the Medes
> slew when they crossed the River Spercheios,
> a seer who, although he saw death coming clearly,
> could not bring himself to abandon the leaders of Sparta.
>
> *(Simonides 83D Campbell)*

Box 9.17 *Arete*

> It is said
> that *Arete* lives high up on rocks, hard to climb,
> and keenly she protects that holy place,
> nor by the eyes of every mortal
> is she to be seen, but only of him who bleeds the spirit-biting sweat
> from within,
> and reaches the pinnacle of his courage.
>
> *(Simonides 579 PMG)*

---

the limitations of human beings, criticizing unreasonable Archaic standards and expectations from before his time, but he also encouraged a striving to ascend and break free from mere humanity – both of which topics would be pursued by Greek philosophers, poets, and artists from the fifth century BCE. One of Simonides' frequent objectives, to elicit emotion in his poetry, was a subject of great interest for Greek artists and tragedians of the later fifth century BCE. Steeped in the literary traditions of the Archaic period, but anticipating the explorations and advances of others after him in the Classical period, Simonides was truly a liminal figure in ancient Greek literature.

9.5.5 Pindar

Pindar, born *c.* 522–518 BCE, may have been a Theban aristocrat, but certainly esteemed aristocratic values. As a young man, he learned poetic craft at Athens apparently from Peisistratid court-poets, among them Simonides, Anakreon, and Lasos of Hermione. He is most famous for his Olympic and other Panhellenic games victory odes which he composed primarily for wealthy victors such as the Sicilian tyrants.

Although Pindar's poetry seems complex, the words allusive and the thought rambling and difficult to grasp, his odes are actually highly structured. The victory ode by rule must include praise for the victor, his virtues and good fortune, and his ancestors' deeds, and, of course, it must laud his victory. Pindar does this but also introduces myths or myth-excerpts that help to link the present victory with past glory, thus elevating his patron and his accomplishment to the realm of the fabled and legendary. He also employs diverse and variegated metaphors and similes throughout his odes.

The odes might perhaps best be thought of as lyrics in the modern sense of the word. The verses of a Pindaric victory ode are actually communicating on several levels simultaneously, as song lyrics sometimes do. Certainly the odes were sung in choruses in Doric Greek with Aeolic Greek elements. The consummate beauty of the victory ode is unfortunately lost to us because we do not have Pindar's musical accompaniment.

Pindar's poems were recognized in his day as masterpieces. Later Alexandrian poets were greatly influenced by him, but the Roman Horace offers perhaps the highest praise, saying that Pindar's poetry was irresistible "like a river rushing down from the mountain, that overflows its banks" (*Odes* 4.2). The Roman Quintilian (10.1.61) named him the greatest of all Greek lyric

---

Box 9.18 Hieron's Victory in Olympic Horse-Racing, 476 BCE

Best of all things is water, then gold which like sparkling fire in the night
stands out beyond any other wealth of hero-men.
But if you long to sing of contests,
dear heart,
look for no other shining star than the sun
that is more warming in the day
through the vacant air,
nor proclaim any contest better than Olympia
from where the renowned hymn takes wing
by poets' craft to sing
the son of Kronos, as they come to the wealthy,
blessed hearth of Hieron,
who manages the scepter of law in verdant
Sicily …
But the Dorian lyre,
take it down from the wall-peg, if by chance the delight
of Pisa and Pherenikos
puts you in mind of the sweetest thoughts,
when by the Alpheios he coursed,
straining his body ungoaded in the races,
and brought conquest to his master,
the Syrakusan rider-king.
His *kleos* shines forth
in the noble home of Lydian Pelops.

(Pindar, Olympian *1, 1–24)*

Pindar goes on to recount the myth of Pelops, the eponymous of the Peloponnesos and hero associated with the Olympic Games. Hieron was credited with the victory as the owner of the victorious chariot, not because he drove it himself (Box 9.18).

---

poets, outstanding in thought and eloquence. Pindar was in fact venerated as a national treasure by the Classical Greeks. When Thebes rebelled against Macedon in 335 BCE and was captured by Alexander the Great, the conqueror leveled every Theban structure to the ground excepting only one – the house of Pindar.

9.6   Summary

Archaic Greek poetry provides insights into the lives and interests of Archaic Greeks, as well as Archaic Greek poets. Poetry and performance in early Greece were interactive occasions for poets and communities from well before Homer and Hesiod. Poetry communicates viscerally and aesthetically: its words, sounds, thoughts, and meanings are like threads woven together into a variegated cloth to enfold the consciousness of the audience during the moments of performance. Archaic poets preserved tradition, but also subverted it by freely adapting it. Epic poetry, which most Greeks knew, is both background and foil to Archaic lyric poetry. The latter reflects the changing times and tastes of Archaic Greek poets and audiences.

The rebelliousness of Archilochos, measured in many ways against Homeric standards, had to have been abetted at least to some degree by his contemporaries. Sappho was surely supported by her fellow-citizens of Mytilene. Yet dissenting voices were not the only ones to speak and be heard. Tyrtaios adapted Homeric standards of honor and bravery in order to reinvigorate the sagging spirits of the Spartan army in the mid-seventh century BCE. Archilochos may ask, why should a person die where his shield is planted? Because he saves the *polis* and those behind in the battle-line, Tyrtaios answers. For Archilochos, a dead man is simply forgotten apparently no matter what he does, but for Tyrtaios the man who falls bravely in the forefront lives on in the memory of those he's sought to preserve. Archaic Greeks heard and could approve both sides.

For Homer's Odysseus, emotional restraint is all-important: it is in fact a matter of life and death for him. If he reveals himself to the Suitors through any kind of emotional display, he is as good as dead. Sappho, on the other hand, fearlessly describes a person who in an elaborately stated jealous reaction reveals to the smallest degree the extent of jealousy and emotion. Nothing seems to be hidden. Should one guard one's self at all times or be honest and unrestrained with emotion? Homer is certainly teaching through Odysseus, but is Sappho? When, if ever, should one exhibit true emotion and when not?

The Greeks came to Troy to fetch Helen back, but really to capture the city and take its wealth. What was spear-won was honorable, admirable in the *Iliad*. Odysseus, striving to survive, will do what he can as he must get home. But Solon wants nothing to do with wealth that is stolen or otherwise ill-gotten and cautions any person who thinks to acquire riches unjustly. Such unrighteousness will not escape Zeus' retribution. (Poseidon's retribution certainly dogged Odysseus.) What, then, and who is right?

Homeric standards, though weakened by obvious contrasts with real life, nevertheless retained their potencies. Pindar's victory odes, performed in the early fifth century BCE, involve contemporary choruses celebrating the old-style values of honor and glory achieved through victory in competition. Archaic poets reflect a general reconsideration of conventions in view of new realities sharpened by heightened consciousness. Simonides roundly criticizes the "wise" saying of the sage Pittakos for being unrealistic. Even Anakreon playfully confronts conventions in his little poem on the girl from Lesbos. Archaic Greek audiences, which supported the poets and their poetry, were apparently unafraid to have all kinds of thoughts and questions put to them by poets. Lyric poets and poetry reflect the appetite of Archaic Greek audiences to consider – and to reconsider – their own humanity.

Notes

1 This long-held idea of *rhapsodes* succeeding *aoidoi* is challenged by J. Gonzalez, *The Epic Rhapsode and his Craft: Homeric Performance in a Diachronic Perspective* (Washington, DC, 2013), p. 344 ff.

2 Theokritos, *Epigrammata 21* Gow (*Anth. Pal.* vii.664); Quintilian (*Instit. Orat.* 10.1.59–60) describes Archilochos as forceful, lively, and inferior only in terms of subjects.

3 Pindar, *Pythian Ode* 2.55; Kallimachos, F 380 Pf.
4 Aristotle, *Poetics* 1460b, 34–35.
5 Easterling, "Semonides," p. 113.
6 That Tyrtaios was an Athenian teacher, lame of foot, summoned to Sparta after an oracle directed the Spartans to do so, is almost certainly a fiction (Pausanias 4.15.6).
7 Two vase-paintings, one from the late sixth century BCE (Warsaw 142333) and one from *c.* 470 BCE by the Brygos Painter (Munich 2416), show very clearly that Archaic Greeks hardly considered Sappho "ugly."
8 Campbell, p. 167.
9 Although some scholars suggest that Solon's political poems were not delivered publicly, he certainly addressed the Athenian *demos* politically: cf. Frs. 4, 11.

Further Reading

Archaic Greek Literature

A. Lesky, *A History of Greek Literature*[3] (London, 1996), pp. 1–240.

Early Greek Poetry

P. Easterling and B. Knox, eds. *The Cambridge History of Classical Literature: Greek Literature, Vol. 1, Part 1: Early Greek Poetry* (Cambridge, 1989).
A. Podlecki, *The Early Greek Poets and Their Times* (Vancouver, BC, 1984).

Homer and Epic

G. Kirk, *The Songs of Homer* (Cambridge, 2005).
R. Fowler, ed. *The Cambridge Companion to Homer* (Cambridge, 2004).

Hesiod

F. Montanari, C. Tsagalis, and A. Rengakos, eds. *Brill's Companion to Hesiod* (Leiden, 2009).

Lyric/Elegaic/Choral Poetry

D. Gerber, ed. *A Companion to the Greek Lyric Poets* (Leiden, 1997).
L. Kurke, "Archaic Greek Poetry," in H. Shapiro, ed. *The Cambridge Companion to Archaic Greece* (Cambridge, 2007), pp. 141–168.

Archilochos

D. Katsonopoulou, I. Petropoulos, and S. Katsarou, eds. *Archilochos and His Age: Proceedings of the Second International Conference on the Archaeology of Paros and the Cyclades* (Paroikia, Paros, October 7–9, 2005) (Athens, 2008).

Semonides

P. Easterling, "Semonides," in P. Easterling and B. Knox, eds. *The Cambridge History of Classical Literature: Greek Literature, Vol. 1, Part 1: Early Greek Poetry* (Cambridge, 1989), pp. 112–115.

Tyrtaios

D. Gerber, "Tyrtaeus," in D. Gerber, ed. *A Companion to the Greek Lyric Poets* (Leiden, 1997), pp. 102–107.

Mimnermos

D. Gerber, "Mimnermos," in D. Gerber, ed. *A Companion to the Greek Lyric Poets* (Leiden, 1997), pp. 108–112.

Sappho

D. Campbell, "Sappho," in P. Easterling and B. Knox, eds. *The Cambridge History of Classical Literature: Greek Literature, Vol. 1, Part 1: Early Greek Poetry* (Cambridge, 1989), pp. 162–168.
E. Greene, ed. *Reading Sappho: Contemporary Approaches* (Berkeley, CA, 1999).

Solon

B. Knox, "Solon," in P. Easterling and B. Knox, eds. *The Cambridge History of Classical Literature: Greek Literature, Vol. 1, Part 1: Early Greek Poetry* (Cambridge, 1989), pp. 105–112.

Anakreon

B. MacLachlan, "Anacreon," in D. Gerber, ed. *A Companion to the Greek Lyric Poets* (Leiden, 1997), pp. 198–212.

Simonides

E. Robbins, "Simonides," in D. Gerber, ed. *A Companion to the Greek Lyric Poets* (Leiden, 1997), pp. 243–252.

Pindar

B. Currie, *Pindar and the Cult of Heroes* (Oxford, 2005).

10

Festivals and Games of the Archaic Greeks

10.1 Introduction

10.1.1 Pre-Olympic Festivals and Games

Athletic contests and spectacles occurred in Greece as early as the Bronze Age. Frescoes from Minoan Crete show young men and women leaping over bulls before large crowds, *c.* 1600–1450 BCE. According to one interpretation, the youths seized the horns of the charging animal and, grasping them, somersaulted onto its back as it was running at them at full speed. Though some scholars have taken this exhibition to be part of a fertility ritual, it may also have been, as modern Spanish bullfighting, a demonstration of human heroics and skill.

The Minoan "Boxer fresco" from Akrotiri on Thera, *c.* 1600–1550 BCE, depicts two adolescent males boxing each other with single gloves on their right hands (NM 1974.26β). The two seem quite seriously intent upon their match, suggesting this is not mere "horse play." The fresco itself is proof that such bouts were entertaining and drew spectators.

Some evidence for Mykenaian athletic contests might be found in the "Funeral Games of Patroklos" in Homer's *Iliad* Book 23. Achilles proclaims them in honor of his slain companion whose death had only just occurred; he also presides over the games as judge and awarder of prizes. Homer wants his audience to believe that the games were authentic, although there are elements in them that are closer in time to Homer's own age.

Premier in Achilles' games for Patroklos is the chariot contest, which became the "glamor" event of the Olympics. Horse competitions were monopolized by wealthy *aristoi* inasmuch as horses were very expensive to keep in Greece and the Greek world. Other events honoring Patroklos included boxing, wrestling, foot racing, mock combat, lump iron-throwing, archery, and spear throwing, all of which were obviously oriented toward warfare, just as the Olympic contests were. (The games at the court of Alkinoös of Phaiakia include the long jump and *diskos* throwing [*Odyssey* 8.100 ff.].)

Events in the *Iliad*'s "Funeral Games" occur sequentially beginning with the chariot-race. The old "horse-breaker" Nestor instructs his son Antilochos, telling him that skill is more important than speed in such a contest (*Iliad* 23.306–348). Watch for openings, he says, and drive close to the turning post – but not too close, since it can destroy the chariot altogether. The track seems to be an oval: the horses drive away from the Greek camp on the beach, loop

Archaic Greece: The Age of New Reckonings, First Edition. Brian M. Lavelle.
© 2020 Brian M. Lavelle. Published 2020 by John Wiley & Sons Ltd.

around the turning-post in the plain, and then return. Phoinix, an old guardian of Achilles, stands as judge at the post to report after.

Eumelos, the son of Admetos, is in the lead as they break for home, followed by Diomedes. Apollo tries to intervene on behalf of Eumelos, but Athena favors Diomedes and breaks up Eumelos' chariot. Far behind are Antilochos and Menelaos. After Diomedes wins, Menelaos claims that Antilochos had fouled him. The young man acknowledges his rashness and apologizes to Menelaos, ceding to him his second-place prize. Fairness and honor preserved, Menelaos returns the prize to Antilochos. (See also Section 10.2.2.)

Boxing and wrestling follow the chariot-race. Boxers belt up and then wrap their fists in leather. A very large man named Epeios uses his brute strength to overcome his undersized opponent Euryalos with one blow to the head. Despite his small size, Odysseus excels as a wrestler, relying on his wit to match up to the hulking Aias. Odysseus is descended from the famous wrestler Autolykos, who was himself the teacher of Herakles: Odysseus is thus "many-wiled" and "knowing of tricks" (*Iliad* 23.709). He manages a draw with Aias and then goes on to come first in the foot race. Diomedes triumphs in the mock duel and, after weight-throwing and archery, Agamemnon wins the spear-throwing ***akoniti*** ("uncontested"), since Achilles names him best of the spear-throwers.

Achilles bestows lavish prizes upon not only victors, but contestants who place as low as fifth. Achilles' prizes for the chariot-race winner are a slave woman, "good at crafts," and a deep two-handled tripod. Second prize is an unbroken mare pregnant with a mule foal; third, a brand new metal cauldron; fourth, two measures of gold; and fifth, a large new amphora. No competitor leaves the assembly of *aristoi* prize-less and so dishonored. Even the aged non-contestant, Nestor, receives a large amphora as a prize-gift. This is all very different from the Olympics whose later first-place prizes were intrinsically valueless, but symbolically priceless.

Although some scholars have drawn connections between the "Funeral Games of Patroklos" and the Olympic ***agones*** ("athletic contests"), the former seem quite unique. All the contestants are *basileis* or *aristoi* whose competitions commemorate Patroklos; the contests are seemingly impromptu and occur on the Trojan plain. (In the *Odyssey*, the Phaiakian games occur in the *agora* [8.109].) At Olympia, the games ostensibly honored the living Zeus more than the very dead hero Pelops. Specialist heroes excel in their competitions in the *Iliad*, even as they are expected to do, and events turn out neatly, just as expected. At Olympia, the first recorded victor was a commoner, *not* a *basileus*, and subsequent victors were non-nobles. Then again, Achilles seems to be able to pull an amazing array of gifts out of his "prize closet," apparently never wanting for something costly to bestow.[1]

While the "Funeral Games" are similar to the eventual roster of Olympic competitions, from the information we have, they cannot be directly linked to the Olympics of the early eighth century BCE, let alone Bronze Age games. Traditionally, there was only one contest at Olympia, the ***stadion*** ("one *stade* race"), until 720 BCE and only three more added by 700, about the time of Homer.[2] Notwithstanding, Homer's model for the "Funeral Games" must have been more contemporary than remote, for, among other things, the prizes awarded in them – lumps of iron, cauldrons, and tripods, the latter very much in evidence at Olympia in the Geometric period – are objects more appropriate to the eighth century BCE than the Bronze Age.

10.2 The Olympic Festival and Games

10.2.1 Origins and Arrangements

Olympia is in the western Peloponnesos at the confluence of the Alpheios and Kladeos Rivers beneath a wooded hill called the Kronion. It was purely a religious site in the Archaic period, never a *polis*: the sacred precinct, called the **Altis** ("Grove"), contained several cults of great age (Figure 10.1). The oldest, most significant sites in the Archaic period were the temple of Hera, the Pelopion, and the altar of Zeus, all clustered at the base of the Kronion. Hera's cult, the most ancient, may have been the vestige of pre-historic mother-goddess worship there. Women served as custodians of Hera's cult during the Classical period, and Pausanias, a Greek author of the second century CE, says that young women still ran in foot races honoring Hera that had been established in Pelops' time (5.16.2,4). It is ironic that women were barred from the witnessing the Olympic Games under penalty of death in the Archaic and Classical periods. The Pelopion was dedicated to the Bronze Age hero, and some have ventured that, like the games for Patroklos, the Olympic ones might have originated as commemorative of him. Close by stood the altar of Zeus, the site of great sacrifices of cattle, the premier ritual of the festival. Ash from the sacrifices mixed with water was shaped and hardened so that, by the mid-second century CE, Zeus' altar had grown to a height of nearly 7 m. By 776 BCE, the traditional date of the first

Figure 10.1 The *Altis* at Olympia: the Philippeion and Temple of Hera.

Olympics, Olympia was Zeus' sanctuary. Olympic athletes took oaths to Zeus at the beginning of the games; they worshipped him during them; they propitiated him afterward.

The establishment of the festival and games is variously accounted for in Greek myth. In perhaps the most famous version, the wicked Oinomaos of nearby Pisa in Elis challenged all comers to a chariot race from Olympia to the Isthmus of Corinth, the prizes being his daughter Hippodameia and rule of Elis. All had failed – and were killed by Oinomaos – until the young Pelops succeeded by trickery, besting the king, who was himself killed, and winning both the kingdom and the "Lady of Horses." Pelops celebrated with games at Olympia. In another myth, it was Pelops' descendant, Herakles, who marked off the *Altis* and planted it with olive trees sacred to his father, Zeus, before reviving the games. In yet another myth, Iphitos, another king of Elis, revived the games at the direction of Apollo through the Delphic oracle to bring peace among warring states.

Hippias of Elis records the first Olympic victor in 776 BCE, although Pausanias implies that the ancient games were revived by agreement between Elis and Sparta in the ninth century BCE (5.4.5). Though the information is garbled, at least one event is likely to have preceded 776 BCE, itself an arbitrarily set date. The earliest Olympic festivals were probably regional affairs and pretty simple at that. Yearly ritual worship at the site may have provided a neutral ground for local chiefs to meet, negotiate, sacrifice, feast together, and consult the oracle of Zeus. The earliest Olympic *agon*, the *stadion*, may have originated with the ritual connected with Zeus' altar. Presumably, racers sprinted to the altar of Zeus running into the *Altis* rather than outside and away from it. The victorious runner was he who first touched sacred fire to the altar's tinder. The festival remained a one-day affair through the Archaic period, centering on sacrifice and feasting, but was lengthened in the fifth century BCE to five days, two before and two after the sacrifice-day (Pausanias 5.9.3). Additions of athletic competitions, which became very popular and came to outshine the religious significance of Olympia decisively in the later Classical period, compelled the festival's lengthening.

While later Greeks believed that the Olympic festival was Panhellenic from the start, victor-list entries indicate that early victors hailed from Elis, Messenia, or Achaia, regions neighboring Elis. The games seem to have become extra-regional only late in the eighth century BCE. Oxythemis of Koroneia in Boiotia and Orsippos of Megara were victors of record in the *stadion* in 732 and 720 BCE respectively, their *poleis* some ways from Olympia. The contests ultimately attracted hundreds of athletes and thousands of spectators – all apparently male – from all parts of the Greek world.

The usual time for the Olympic festival seems to have been during the second full moon after the summer solstice, that is, in August. It occurred quadrennially in conformance with an 8-year lunar-solar cycle. Messengers were sent out to Greek *poleis* announcing the impending games, inviting participation, and proclaiming the Olympic truce. During the truce, which lasted one month, athletes traveled without hindrance, molestation, or injury to and from Olympia. No weapons or warfare were allowed within the borders of Elis, and no death penalties were to be carried out.

10.2.2   *Agones*

10.2.2.1   Running Competitions

For the *stadion*, the original event of the Olympics (Figure 10.2), runners poised themselves at the starting line in a standing position with arms extended. At a signal, they ran for *c.* 185 m

Figure 10.2 The *stadion* at Olympia.

as fast as they could (see Box 10.1). According to tradition, Koroibos of Elis, a cook, was the first recorded *stade* race victor in 776 BCE. Before 720 BCE, runners wore clothing when they raced, perhaps a loincloth. Orsippos of Megara changed that by losing his loincloth during the race of 720 BCE, either purposefully or by accident (Pausanias 1.44.1). The story is probably apocryphal, but nudity was the rule for Olympic athletes later. By the mid-sixth century BCE, runners ran in a *stadion* east of the *Altis* which subsequently became the site for all foot races and several other competitions. Each Olympiad was commemorated with the name of the victor in the *stade* race, and the list was kept orally until the fifth century BCE when it was written down by Hippias.

Other running competitions added over time were variants of the *stade*-race. For the **diaulos**, the two-*stade* race, added in 724 BCE, athletes ran up and back, ending up where they started (Figure 10.3). The most significant, dramatic – and entertaining – portion of the race, the finish, would unfold in front of the spectators grouped nearer the start. The third running competition, added in 720 BCE, was the **dolichos** ("long course"), amounting to *c.* 12 *stadion* laps or *c.* 4.5 kms.[3] As the two-stade race, the *dolichos* seems to have been designed to lengthen the engagement of the spectators and so their entertainment. On appearances, those attending the festivals were demanding more drama and more excitement, and those who controlled the festival were apparently willing to give them what they wanted – more *agones*.

Figure 10.3 Runners in a foot race. Attic B-F Panathenaic amphora, attributed to the Euphiletos Painter, *c.* 530 BCE.

The last running competition added during the Archaic period was the ***hoplitodromos***, the full-armor sprint. For this, the runner was required to wear helmet and greaves and carry a shield. The total weight added was *c.* 20–25 kilos. The race's distance was two *stades*. The early version was not as grueling or tricky as other and later hoplite-races: in the Panathenaic Games at Athens and later at the Olympics, fully armed hoplite-runners ran and jumped on and off a moving chariot!

The grueling ***pentathlon*** ("five contests") was established in 708 BCE, incorporating a *stade* race, but the original race kept its luster and not just because of its seniority (see also "Field" below). The sprint is the simplest of competitions, unencumbered by elaborate strategies, tricks, or guile: it is the purest of the Olympic competitions even today. Its ancient connection to the ritual torch race, from which it seems to have evolved, conveyed a sacral character which enhanced it. Short distance sprints are among the most popular events of the modern Olympics.

10.2.2.2 Other Sporting Competitions

Wrestling was also introduced in 708 BCE. Wrestlers began by standing up and leaning into each other. A wrestler's aim was to throw his adversary to the ground.[4] Victory went to the wrestler who threw his opponent three times without being thrown himself. Greek wrestling was a competition of agility and cunning as the myths involving Autolykos and Odysseus show, but it was also one of sheer strength and could be rather dirty. Though no hitting or gouging was allowed, picking up an opponent bodily to slam him to the ground, chokeholds, and even bending back (but not breaking) the fingers of one's opponent were permitted. A competitor under duress could signal that he'd had enough by raising his index finger to the judge.

Box 10.1 The Foot Race at Troy: Odysseus and Aias, the Son of Oïleus

> They stood in a line, Achilles showed the end of the track.
> From the starting post, the racing track stretched out before them. Then swiftly
> the son of Oïleos broke forth; godlike Odysseus launched himself
> right behind …
>   … so Odysseus ran near him, still from behind
> his footfalls hitting Aias' prints before the dust could settle about them.
> And he breathed down upon his head, godlike Odysseus did,
> always swiftly running. And all the Achaians cheered
> him on as he strove for the victory, and called to him as he was straining.
> But when they were about to reach the end of the race, right then Odysseus
> prayed to Athena of the grey eyes from his heart:
> 'Hear me, goddess most excellent, bring aid to my feet!'
> So he spoke praying. And the goddess Pallas Athena heard him.
> She made his knees nimble, and his feet and hands from above.
> But just when they were rushing at the prize,
> then Aias slipped while running – for Athena harmed him –
> (and he fell into muck)
> … much-enduring Odysseus took the prize cup,
> having finished ahead, and radiant Aias took the cow.
>   *(Homer, Iliad 23.757–760, 763–775, 778–779)*

Homer's description of the race during the "Funeral Games" gives some sense of Olympic foot-racing during the Archaic period and the drama that spectators seemed to have relished most. Odysseus gains his victory over Little Aias really only at the finish line, some might say, because of Athena's foul. Little Aias complained, but to no avail, since Odysseus did nothing wrong.

The most famous Greek wrestler of all time was Milon of Kroton in southern Italy, who won six times at Olympia, beginning in boyhood (perhaps 540 BCE). Over the course of his career, he also earned seven Pythian victories, ten at the Isthmian Games, and nine at the Nemean ones. Legends about Milon and his strength abounded. His hands and indeed his fingers were immensely strong, and it was said that he carried a bull around the *stadion*, then killed and ate it (Athenaios 10.4). Even his veins were strong. He could tie a cord around his head and then expand his veins until they broke the cord! (Pausanias 6.14.7). Milon won one wrestling crown at Olympia *akoniti* – others were too afraid to wrestle him, the highest compliment an athlete could receive from other athletes. He must have been a very daunting opponent indeed!

Boxing was introduced in 688 BCE. Boxers wrapped both of their fists in leather, allowing their fingers to protrude (Box 10.2). Blows were aimed mostly at the head, rather than the body – blows "below the belt" were strictly forbidden – and the leather wraps did their work. (Boxers were not supposed to gouge with fingers, though some did.) Later portraits of Olympic and other boxers show them with broken noses, cauliflower ears, and facial scars. There were no rounds, and blows would be exchanged until one man was knocked out or gave up, so

---

Box 10.2 The Boxing Match of Polydeukes of Sparta and Amykos of the Bebrykians

When the two had strengthened their hands with the oxhide straps
and around their limbs they had wound the long leather strips,
they came to the middle breathing death upon one another.
There was much hard jockeying for them both eager to fight
as to which would have the sun at his back.
Polydeukes skillfully got past the big man
and the [sun's] rays hit Amykos full in the face.
Straightway, angry in his heart, he launched forth,
aiming with his hands. But on the end of his chin,
the child of Tyndareus struck him as he came on.
But [Amykos] was roused up more than before
and made the fight all confused
and pressed in upon him, head
bent to the earth. And the Bebrykians shouted at him, and heroes from
the opposite side shouted encouragement to strong Polydeukes,
fearing lest, having pressed heavily upon him, he would conquer
him in the narrow space, this man resembling Tityos.[5]
But the son of Zeus stood up here and here
and he stung him on both sides in turn,
and he held the son of Poseidon from his attack
even though the man was mighty overbearing.
He stood drunk from the blows and spit out blood
all crimson. And all the best men roared out,
when they saw the grievous wounds about the mouth and jaws,
his eyes closed off in his swollen face.
The lord king confounded him showing him false threats with his fists
from all sides. But when he noticed that he'd been rendered defenseless
high on the nose at the brow, he struck him with all his force,
and he tore away all the forehead down to the bone. Straightaway so stricken
falling back, he lay stretched out in the spring flowers.

(*Theokritos, Idyll* 22, 80–106)

Theokritos, a Hellenistic poet, give us some idea of Olympic boxing in his depiction of the famous mythical fight between Polydeukes and Amykos. Polydeukes is the most renowned boxer in Greek myth. His famous affiliation with Sparta, whose warriors were practiced at boxing as part of war-training, may have had something to do with that reputation. Tremendous punishment could be inflicted on boxers even as Theokritos shows: smashed teeth, spurting blood, and even mortality. Boxers must nevertheless use cunning as well as strength to win. The match-up of Amykos, very strong, but dull-witted, with the clever son of Zeus was really one-sided.

matches could go on for a very long time. If both boxers agreed, however, single punches could be exchanged until one either fell or gave in. (This seems akin to the modern "shoot-outs" of soccer and ice hockey.)

Matches for both wrestling and boxing occurred in the *stadion* in a small dirt- or sand-filled rectangle reserved there. Bouts were overseen by judges who watched closely for fouls and punished the boxer or wrestler who committed a foul by striking him smartly with a stick.

The *pentathlon* consisted of the *stade* race, a wrestling match, a long jump, *diskos* throws, and javelin throws. The popularity of the individual events would seem to have influenced the addition of the "five-contests," but the competitiveness of Greek athletes and the crowd's desire to witness one athlete emerge as superior after a grueling combined competition will also have figured.

For the long jump, competitors used weights that were thrown out in front of them just as they launched. They then pushed back in the air to help propel them further. The added weight apparently helped them jump farther than they could without them – or so they thought. The late Archaic *pentathlete* Phaÿllos of Kroton is said to have jumped *c.* 16.9 m (nearly 55 feet) using such weights![6]

The *diskos* was thrown by athletes in one movement of the body and so without the extraordinary spinning wind-up of modern discus-throwers. The famous *Diskobolos* of Myron of the fifth century BCE shows the athlete just as he is about to come forward with the throw. The same Phaÿllos was said to have thrown the *diskos* about 32 m. *Diskoi* were of varying sizes and weighed up to 6.5 kg; the average was *c.* 2.5 kg. When not in use, *diskoi* were stored in the Treasury of the Sikyonians dedicated *c.* 648 BCE according to Pausanias (6.19.1–4).

The javelin (**akon**) was a light spear conducive for throwing. (The hoplite's *dory* was a heavier jabbing spear.) Each javelin was *c.* 2 m long, had a wrapping around it which, when attached to the thrower's finger, would unwind and "rifle" the spear. The result was a much more accurate throw, even as it is for a bullet transiting a "rifled" gun-barrel. The thrower would run forward and throw – much the same way modern javelin-throwers do today.

There remains some controversy about how the *pentathlon* was won, since it involved so many contests. Presumably it was an elimination contest to begin with. If an athlete lost three of five events, he was out. If he won three, he was victor. That might mean that the last two competitions could have had only three competitors at most and that anyone who won the first three events was immediately declared the winner. Of course, if one athlete won two competitions and another two, then the final event, the *stadion*, would decide it all – and rather dramatically.

The most intriguing, unusually brutal, and, so to speak, un-Olympian contest was the ***pankration***, introduced in 648 BCE (Figure 10.4). Xenophanes (F 2, 5) called it "the terrible contest" because competitors could be severely injured, maimed, or even killed. Indeed, the *pankration* was a combination of boxing and wrestling but taken to extremes. Except for gouging of the eyes and biting, no holds were barred including kicks to the stomach, arm twisting, strangling, hair-pulling, tripping, etc. The object was the opponent's submission, and the contest could go on as long as neither contestant submitted.

As might be expected in such a competition, there were some bizarre matches. In one contest in 564 BCE, Arrachion of Phigaleia in Arkadia, a multiple victor in the *pankration*, was caught in a chokehold by his unnamed opponent who also controlled him in a leg-scissors (Pausanias 8.40.2). While being choked, Arrachion was able to get his hands either on his opponent's toe or

Figure 10.4 *Pankration*, Attic B-F *skyphos*, attributed to the Theseus Painter, *c.* 500 BCE.

ankle, which he then dislocated. The opponent in great pain held up his finger to break off the match, but, by then Arrachion had died from asphyxiation. Arrachion was awarded the victory posthumously.

Running, wrestling, boxing, and the *pentathlon* for boys were contests added in the later seventh century BCE. The boys' *pankration*, however, was not introduced until 200 BCE.

10.2.2.3 Equine Competitions

The most glamorous of Olympic competitions, the four-horse chariot race, was added in 680 BCE. This event was reserved for aristocrats and the wealthy because they were the only ones who could afford teams of horses, chariots, and chariot-drivers (Figure 10.5). The aristocrat-owner did not himself drive the chariot, but got all the credit if the chariot won when his name and not the charioteer's was announced as victor. The glory was great indeed for the owner, but the cost was immense and the danger to the chariot-drivers possibly lethal. The chariot-race certainly recollected the deadly mythical race between Oinomaos and Pelops.

The Olympic hippodrome was south of the *stadion*. The length of the oblong track is said to have been three *stades* or *c.* 555 m. A 12-lap race would have been *c.* 6.7 km. The track had two turning posts and no separator so the possibilities for bunching and crashing at either end or for collisions were great (see Box 10.3). Speed increased the risk. Sources tell us of the frequency of crashes and of horses running out of control. In the hippodrome was an altar of ***Taraxippos***, "Horse-Frightener," a *daimon* of the track perhaps, where the drivers prayed to avert crashing.

The horse-race was added in 648 BCE. Riders mounted horses bareback and raced for six laps around the hippodrome. Very late in the Archaic period, the mule-cart and mare race were added, but discontinued not long afterward.

10.2.3 *Nike* ("Victory")

Victory in the Olympic or other Panhellenic Games assured an Archaic Greek athlete lasting fame. The wild olive leaf crown of Olympia, woven from branches taken from Zeus' sacred trees, belies the great prestige and notoriety a victor earned. Triumphant athletes were honored

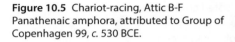

Figure 10.5 Chariot-racing, Attic B-F Panathenaic amphora, attributed to Group of Copenhagen 99, *c.* 530 BCE.

at the games, but idolized at home, where they were lavished with praise, gifts, and money, and even maintained at public expense for their lifetimes. A few of them, like Milon, became significant political figures or, like Phrynon of Athens, colony-founders. Kylon of Athens sought to parlay his Olympic victory (640 or 636 BCE) into a tyranny, whereas the Athenian Kimon, a three-time victor in the four-horse competition (536, 532 and 528 BCE), was assassinated, apparently because he seemed to be verging on taking power at Athens. Archaic Greeks believed that athletes' good fortune was god-given and would somehow rub off on them. The crowns of wild olive were, after all, the symbols of Zeus' extraordinary favor.

Xenophanes was very put out by the accolades bestowed on games victors (F 2). The victorious athlete wins way too much honor from his fellow *politai*, he says, and what does he really do for the *polis*? Xenophanes may have been correct from a practical point of view, but, as with his pronouncements about the gods, his sentiments about Olympic victors were not shared by other Archaic Greeks. Far from it: victors in Panhellenic Games were the talk of the Greek world. Whether Greeks had in fact gone to Olympia to witness the games themselves and heard the names of the victors proclaimed by heralds there or got it at second- or even third-hand, they made Olympic and other games victors the celebrities of their day.

Such laudation sometimes encouraged bad conduct in athletes. Victors could be bribed into renouncing citizenship in their own *polis* to take it up in another. Archaic and Classical Greeks wanted to promote their *poleis* through their identification with athlete-victors after all. (Is the modern proclivity for Olympic medal counting not inspired by similar feelings?) Such results upped the stakes for some who were not above cheating. While judges punished fouls observed during competitions, athletes caught cheating were fined and shamed. In the Archaic period,

Box 10.3 The Chariot Race at the Pythian Games

The next day, when, the sun finishing its swift-footed course,
there was a contest of horses,
[Orestes] entered along with many other chariot-driving men.
One was an Achaian, one from Sparta, two
Libyans, very knowledgeable of the yoked chariot.
[Orestes] was among them, having Thessalian
horses and was fifth in position …
[…]
Standing where the game-organizers put them
by shaking out the lots and placed the two-horse chariots,
at the sound of the bronze trumpet, they
yelled at the horses and shook the reins with their hands.
The whole track was filled with the crash of rattling chariots,
and dust flew up. At the same time, all bunched up,
they spared nothing of the goads so that one of them
could hurtle beyond the wheel box chariots and the horses' neighing.
There was foam about their backs and the wheels turning,
as the horses' breath fell about them.
and Orestes, holding tight against the far turning post
grazed the wheel box: freeing the right-hand
horse's rein, he held in the nearer one.
Till then all the chariots were upright,
but then the Ainian man's hard-mouthed colts became unmanageable
running violently. Ending the sixth lap and turning into
the seventh, his team crashed head-on with the team from Barkaia
and from there, one after the other, because of this one crash,
the chariots shattered and broke up. And
the whole plain of Krisa was filled with horse-and-chariot wreckage.
The skilled Athenian charioteer saw this
and drew to the outside and held back, letting by
the flood of chariots churning in the middle.
Orestes kept his horses last, holding back his fillies,
trusting to the end of the race.
But when he saw the Athenian was the only one remaining,
he shouted sharply in the horses' ears
and pursued [the Athenian] with his swift fillies, and, making their teams equal
they drove them on, first one, then the other
pushing forward the head of the chariot-horses.

(Sophokes, Elektra, *698–704, 709–740)*

Sophokles' passage describes a fictional two-horse chariot race at Delphi, but gives some idea of the danger involved in chariot-racing. The passage goes on to describe yet another accident, occurring because the driver, Orestes, gets too close to the turning post and rips his chariot apart. He falls over the front of it, becomes tangled in the reins, and is dragged to his death by his running horses. (So Orestes' tutor said.) Such accidents were sure to have occurred everywhere that such chariot races were held.

cheating seems to have occurred less frequently than later: the renowned statues erected from fines assessed from athlete-cheaters were only set up in the *Altis* from 388 BCE.

Olympic victors were allowed to set up statues of themselves in the *Altis*. One Timasitheos, a native of Delphi, was victor in the *pankration* two times at Olympia and three at Delphi, all of which had to have occurred before 510 BCE. His statue in the *Altis* was seen by Pausanias more than 600 years later. The artist was the famous Agimeladas of Argos, the teacher of Myron and Polykleitos. The *Altis* became a veritable forest of victors' statues from the fifth century BCE.

The proliferation of such statues in the *Altis* is symptomatic of how the idolatry of the victorious Olympic athlete grew to overshadow the cult-significance of the god and his festival. While Zeus bestowed favor on the victor, it was the victor's celebrity that increased, not reverence for Zeus. Such idolization of victor-athletes as Xenophanes notes along with the *Altis'* victor-statues and the addition of competitions may be taken to indicate that Archaic Greeks were more and more focused upon the athletes, their capacities and achievements, and less and less upon Zeus and the gods except as they figured into those capacities and achievements.

10.2.4   The Panhellenic Ideal

In the splendid settings of Olympia and Delphi, in Nemea or even Athens, the Greeks could assemble, enemy mingling with enemy, at peace with petty quarrels quieted for the moment. The sense of Greekness, reinforced by common language, worships, beliefs, institutions, and values, gave rise to the Panhellenic ideal. Coming together in such places cooperatively encouraged the notions that Greeks were actually one people who could unite and so that a united Greece was a real possibility. Though each *polis* was tied to region, local customs, divinities, and sometimes even the way they spoke Greek, and to ages-old contentions with neighbors about borderlands, Panhellenic festivals allowed Greeks to forget regional differences and the gloom of perpetual antagonism if only temporarily and, for the brief time, to conceive of the glorious potential of Greece as a nation. Although the Panhellenic ideal is most evident after the Persian War, it was alive in Greek consciousness at least from the time of Homer.

On the other hand, Panhellenic Games fueled competitiveness and distinction and could accentuate regional differences: war trophies set up at Olympia and Delphi by antagonistic *poleis* surely did little to assuage long-standing animosities. Greeks were in fact never able to settle their disputes for any appreciable length of time, and games spectators went home to re-engage with enemies with whom they had sat together in the *stadion*, dined in the *Altis*, and worshipped Zeus the peacemaker in his sanctuary. The strengths of *polis* ties and allegiances were in the end too strong to allow for a transcendent sense of "Greece." The one time many Greeks came together in common cause was the Persian War, and even then other Greeks favored Persia. The Panhellenic ideal was in fact a pleasing mirage revived from time to time in places like Olympia and Delphi, but never realized.

10.3   Other Games and Festivals

10.3.1   The Pythian, Nemean, and Isthmian Games

The heights of Mount Parnassos formed the dramatic backdrop for the Pythian Games at Delphi, so named after Apollo's oracle there (Figure 10.6). The earliest festival honored Apollo for his victory over the Python, the snake-guardian of Gaia's sanctuary. It was replaced by a

Figure 10.6 Delphi: Theatre and Temple of Apollo.

more elaborate festival in 582 BCE. The original events of the Games were musical contests featuring the **kithara**, a stringed instrument Apollo favored. Gymnic and equestrian *agones* were added to the reorganized Games, which reportedly came into being mainly because of Kleisthenes, tyrant of Sikyon, after the so-called First Sacred War.

In control of the route from the Gulf of Itea to Delphi – apparently, the preferred route in antiquity – the people of Kirrha were abusing pilgrims and using land dedicated to Apollo in the early sixth century BCE. An alliance of regional *poleis* and federated peoples self-proclaimed as the Delphic *Amphiktyonia*, along with Kleisthenes, besieged and captured Kirrha, and punished the Kirrhans severely. Reorganization of the Pythian Games and festival followed to hallmark their victory.

Like the Olympic festival, the renewed Pythia was quadrennial and held in summer, but meant to complement, not compete with the Olympic – at least as far as timing was concerned. Its celebrations fell in between each Olympiad. Yet it was surely meant to rival, if not outshine the Olympics in the number and nature of its competitions. The musical *agones* remained the centerpiece of the festival games: *kithara*-singing and playing competitions occurred on the festival's third day. The two days preceding the musical *agones* were for sacrifices and a reenact-ment of Apollo's slaying of the Python, and feasting; the two days after were for the newer competitions, ending with chariot-races in the plain of Kirrha below Delphi. Laurel wreath crowns from Apollo's sacred tree were the victor-prizes in the reorganized festival.

The Pythian festival became the second most important stephanitic or crown-awarding festival in Archaic Greece after Olympia. One index of its prestige is the number of Greek tyrants who were attracted from near and far to compete in the equine competitions. As at Olympia, Pythian chariot victories were frequently commemorated in victory odes by Pindar. Kleisthenes of Sikyon himself gained a victory in the first chariot-race in 582 BCE. In the early Classical period, Polyzalos, tyrant of Gela in Sicily, won the chariot-competition at Delphi in 474 BCE and, to memorialize his victory, set up a group of bronze statues there. The famous "Charioteer" is all that remains of the chariot, horses, charioteer, and two horse-grooms, dedicated at Delphi to remind visitors of Polyzalos' victory.

While apparently most festival attendees came up to Delphi from the Corinthian Gulf through Itea, others followed the famous track from Thebes and Daulis – the road taken by Oedipous on his fateful journey from Delphi. Greek pilgrims arriving would stop first at the Castalian spring outside Apollo's precinct to refresh and cleanse themselves after an arduous walk uphill. In the *temenos*, they would have seen the fabulous treasures of Delphi, most notably those donated by Lydian kings. As at Olympia, most of the Games' spectators would have eaten and slept under the sky, presumably wherever they could find space. Even in the Archaic period, as those who attended other Panhellenic Games elsewhere, they were prey to peddlers, guides, fortune-tellers, magicians, buskers, poets, pitchmen, forgers, and assorted other charlatans looking to separate the visitors from their money. Pilgrims earned goodwill from Apollo in whose name the Games were celebrated, but, as at Olympia, came increasingly for the spectacle and sheer enjoyment of the Games and the crowds.

The Isthmus of Corinth near the Saronic Gulf was the site of the Isthmian Games. The local deity worshipped was Melikertes-Palaimon, nephew of Sisyphus, who either died at sea or was transformed into a sea-divinity. (Melikertes, whose name derives from the Phoenician god, Melqaart, was the son of the woman-turned-sea goddess Ino and was, like her, an aid to sailors.) Pindar (F 5 [1].6) says that the daughters of Nereus, the old man of the sea, bid Sisyphus establish "the far-seen prize" for dead Melikertes. Another myth had Theseus, the great Athenian hero, instituting competitions for Poseidon, emulating Herakles who had established the Olympic Games for his father, Zeus. Poseidon, like Zeus at Olympia, became titular deity of the Isthmian Games, though the shrine of Melikertes-Palaimon remained a significant landmark at Isthmia.

Although the *agones* resembled those at Olympia and Delphi, horse-competitions were conspicuous – fittingly, since Poseidon was god of horses. The games were held biennially in late spring of the first and third Olympiad years. Isthmian victors received wreaths of pine through the sixth century BCE because it was said that the dead body of Melikertes had lain among pine trees near the sanctuary. Of course, the pine is an evergreen and a symbol of life even in the dead of winter.

The Isthmian festival was local to begin with, but reorganized in 582 BCE. It was supervised by the Corinthians, from which the impetus for reorganization is likely to have come. Kleisthenes' success at Delphi may have spurred a competitive spirit in neighboring Corinth. The re-establishment of the Isthmian festival – and its frequency – further signifies the growing Greek appetite for stephanitic games in the Archaic period. It was relatively easy for Greeks to reach Isthmia, since the precinct was situated at the most important land and sea crossroads on the mainland, and the Games occurred within the Olympic cycle. Victories in the Isthmian Games did not lack prestige, and Pindar composed several odes for victors in the early fifth century BCE.

Greeks believed that the Nemean Games, held just south of Corinth, were established to honor the infant Opheltes, the son of the Nemean king, who had been killed by a snake. The baby had been placed amidst wild celery by his neglectful nurse who had gone off to give water to passing Argive warriors on their way to Thebes to attack its famous seven gates. These warriors then decreed the earliest festival in honor of the dead child. As the origin-myths of Olympia and Isthmia, the story suggests the Nemean Games' connection to a dead hero and demi-god. Another version, however, derived from a later Greek source, made Herakles the founder of the festival and games after he had killed the Nemean Lion. This helped to explain how Zeus became the titular deity at Nemea.

The earlier, smaller-scale local festival was made over in 573 BCE; like the Isthmian Games, Nemea's were also biennial and occurred in summer and early fall of the second and fourth Olympiad years. The governors of the Nemean Games, the people of Kleonai, a *polis* between Corinth and Argos acting on behalf of the latter, ordained the same rules as those at Olympia, including a proclaimed truce and the dispatch of messengers announcing the festival. Crowns were of wild celery. Featured contests were equine and gymnic for boys, youths, and men. Though on a smaller scale than those at Olympia and Pythia, the Nemean Games held place as the last of the four premier stephanitic contests in Archaic and Classical Greece.

Nemea was the site of one of the most horrific endings to a Panhellenic boxing match ever recorded (Pausanias 8.40.3–5). Kreugas of Epidamnos and Damoxenos of Syrakuse fought a truly grueling bout. At length, with neither winning, they agreed to trade single blows. Kreugas threw his punch at Damoxenos to no avail. Damoxenos, however, directed his blow beneath the ribs with his fingers out and stiffened – a foul. His blow drove into Kreugas' mid-section and, with his hand, Damoxenos pulled out Kreugas' intestines. Kreugas expired immediately, but the judges disqualified Damoxenos then and there for multiple punches, counting each finger a blow! Kreugas was named victor posthumously. So keen was the competition to win even the celery-crown of Nemea![7]

Though the Olympics remained the premier games in ancient Greece – and really for all time – victories in the stephanitic games added in the early sixth century BCE brought prestige and celebrity to the victors. In the mid-sixth century BCE, one Aristis of Kleonai was commemorated in the Archaic period for winning the Nemean *pankration* four times.[8] As a representative of a *polis*, village, or nation group in a Panhellenic arena, a victor brought enormous pride to the community. The man, youth, or boy represented not only the aspirations of family, friends, and neighbors, but other Greeks as well. By the beginning of the sixth century BCE, the Olympic Games had become so famous and attractive that local festivals and *agones* were made over into Panhellenic ones.

10.4 Local and Regional Festivals

10.4.1 *Panathenaia*

The Athenians believed that their yearly *Panathenaia* was established by Erichthonios, the "child" of Athena and Hephaistos, deep in Athens' mythic prehistory. Its focus nonetheless was Athena *Polias*, the goddess of the "high city," very likely the Athenian version of the Mykenaian "citadel-goddess." The yearly festival marking Athena's birthday, known later as the *Lesser Panathenaia*, was ancient by the time of Homer. The main elements of cult-activity consisted of a sacrifice and feast, a procession to the *akropolis*, and the presentation of a sacred garment to Athena.

The *Greater Panathenaia* was inaugurated in 566 BCE under the auspices of Hippokleides, an Athenian *aristos*, near in time to the reorganizations of the other major Panhellenic festivals. Like the Pythian festival, the *Greater Panathenaia* was made quadrennial and *agones* were added to the original roster. The enhanced festival brought Athenians and the residents of Attika together in collective celebration, reminding them of their shared identities through their common worship of Athena, the centerpiece of their *polis*, political life, and Athenian religion. As a Panhellenic festival, the *Greater Panathenaia* advertised Athens and the Athenians to the larger Greek world. The reorganized *Panathenaia* was a kind of "coming-out party" for Archaic Athens.

The Panathenaic festival and games took place in late July/early August over a number of days before the civic rituals devoted to Athena. Men, boys, and "beardless" youths competed in running, field, and equestrian events. The *agones* began with musical competitions consisting of *kithara-* and flute-playing and singing. It may have been on the same day that *rhapsodoi* offered lays of Homeric poetry – a competition that may have been added by Peisistratos or his son Hipparchos. The three categories also competed in the pyrrhic dance, a "military ballet" evolved from a warrior's fighting movements in battle.[9] The following days were for the *stadion*, *pentathlon*, boxing, wrestling, and *pankration*, just as at Olympia and Delphi. Equestrian events included horse- and chariot-racing. Contestants in musical and singing competitions were awarded money prizes, while athletes obtained measures of Athena's sacred olive oil contained in special Panathenaic vases. Crowns were of olive, but prizes were given to those who placed as well, just as at the games for the dead Patroklos.

The last two days of the festival seem to have been for Athenians only. The night of the penultimate festival day witnessed a torch race from the grove of Hekademos to the *akropolis* by relay. The object was to bring fire kindled there to the altar of Athena, so that sacrifice could be made. All-night feasting, dancing, and singing ensued, leading up to the procession and presentation of Athena's robe the following day. All members of the community joined in with the procession, from archons and *aristoi* to common citizens. It began outside of Athens and then moved through the *agora* along the "sacred way" to the *akropolis*. Our only near-contemporary representation of what might be the Panathenaic procession comes from the Parthenon frieze of *c.* 438 BCE, which depicts the various participants including horsemen, libation-, basket- and tray-bearers, older men, and sacrificial victims. Selected Athenian females presented Athena *Polias* with the newly woven garment so that her ancient wooden statue could be clothed for the next year.

The Panhellenic aspects of the *Greater Panathenaia* seemed to have been fused onto the existing ones of the local *Lesser Panathenaia*. The exclusions of the last two days, unlike the other festivals and games, may well have been grounded in Athens' Dark Age experiences and fear of aliens, but also in the Athenians' sense of special relationship to their goddess. Dorians were prohibited from entering Athena's temple on the *akropolis*, and the Athenians considered themselves quite distinct – even from their Ionian "colonists." The Panathenaic festival was a celebration of Athens and Athena after all.

The primary tangible evidence of Athenian nationalism is to be found in the many Panathenaic **amphorai** ("two-handled jugs") awarded to victors from 566 BCE (Figure 10.7). The *amphorai*

Figure 10.7 Panathenaic amphora, Attic B-F vase attributed to the Princeton Painter, *c.* 550–540 BCE.

contained olive oil derived ultimately from Athena's sacred olive tree on the *akropolis*. The goddess had caused it to grow overnight in her own contest with Poseidon for Athens. This was a very special prize for Panathenaic Games victors. Pictured upon every Panathenaic *amphora* was Athena on one side usually accompanied by lettering saying "from the games of Athens." On the reverse was a depiction of the actual athletic contest, for example, boxing, running, or the two-horse chariot race, for which the victory was achieved.

Some scholars have suggested that such a prize hearkens to Geometric Age practice as found in the Funeral Games for Patroklos, and that is supported by the practice of awarding prizes to contestants as well as victors. *Amphorai* were trophies and objects of beauty, to be sure; the sacred olive oil added inestimable value to the mere "packages." Yet while the brimming Panathenaic vases were rewards in themselves, they were also advertisements for an Athens now seeking status and distinction among other Archaic Greek *poleis* in the early sixth century BCE. As Donald Kyle has pointed out, Panathenaic *amphorai* "emphasize origin (donor) rather than ownership (victor)."[10] These Panathenaic vases were a master stroke of publicity for the *polis*, its goddess, and Athens' pretensions to take its place among the premier *poleis* and festival-sites of Archaic Greece.

10.4.2 Other Local and Regional Festivals

Among the more renowned local and regional festivals of the Archaic period was the quadrennial *Delia*, said to be established by Theseus on the island of Delos. It was sacred to Apollo and Artemis and was celebrated by Cycladic islanders, Ionians, and Athenians with music, dance, and gymnic contests. The *Panionia* was a festival honoring Poseidon and shared by the 12 Ionian *poleis*. It took place on the Mykale promontory in western Anatolia, but was terminated by the Persians when the Ionian revolt failed. Finally, the Spartan *Karneia*, an expiatory festival in honor of Apollo. It was distinctly martial in nature and most famous because its celebration prohibited the Spartans from sending more than 300 men as a honor guard with Leonidas to Thermopylai 480 BCE. It also delayed the dispatching of a Spartan army to help the Athenians before the battle at Marathon in 490 BCE.

10.5   Festivals and Culture

10.5.1   *Dionysia* and Drama at Athens

Athens' other great festival was the *Dionysia*, an annual celebration of the god of wine, ecstasy, altered states, and the new consciousness that these produced. The so-called *City Dionysia* took place in later March by our calendar. It was based upon earlier rural celebrations centered on Dionysos in villages in Attika, one of which, Eleutherai, on the mountain border between Attika and Boiotia, was heavily implicated with the *City Dionysia* of Athens. The *Rural* or *Village Dionysia* occurred in December of each year at various dates in different Attic *demes*.

Processions in villages seem to have been pretty basic affairs. A celebrant carrying a jar of wine and a vine-branch led the way; another dragged a he-goat for sacrifice. Another celebrant followed carrying a basket of dried figs, trailed finally by a phallus-bearer.[11] All were symbols of Dionysos' fertility, and the procession reminded worshippers at the winter solstice of the god's power to reanimate the earth. The goat was sacrificed and feasting followed, bawdy songs were sung, and celebrants turned to drinking. Then perhaps villagers donned masks and satyr-costumes and sang in chorus stories of the god's exploits.

The much grander *City Dionysia* was either created by the Peisistratids or greatly enhanced by them. Scholars coordinate its establishment with the incorporation of Eleutherai into Attika in the second half of the sixth century BCE, at which time the ancient cult and statue of Dionysos *Eleuthereos* were transferred to Athens. The first "coming" of Dionysos to Athens was then re-enacted every year as Dionysos' statue was carried to the grove of Hekademos outside Athens where it reposed for some days until it was led back into Athens in torchlight procession for the festival. The statue signified the god's renewed presence and was restored to Dionysos' little temple south of the *akropolis*.

On the first day of the *City Dionysia*, after the statue was replaced in the temple, the Athenians, marched in procession solemnly round the east end of the *akropolis* to the god's *temenos*. After sacrifices of animals, the Athenians feasted, then devoted the evening to the *komos* – roistering, singing, and dancing by torchlight in worship of Dionysos. The following days of the early Archaic festival were given to the performances of songs by trained choruses. If the *Rural Dionysia* was meant to help relieve the tedium of winter for villagers, the *City Dionysia* was to punctuate the arrival of spring for the Athenians.

10.5.2   The Dithyramb, Thespis, and Attic Tragedy

The **dithyrambos** was a type of choral song for Dionysos. The chorus consisted of up to 50 costumed men or boys who sang and danced to the flute, relating stories in verse about the god, even as choruses seem to have done in Greek villages during the *Rural Dionysias*. Archilochos (F 120) knew of the dithyramb perhaps from its performances at the *Delia*: he was certainly not its inventor. According to Herodotos (1.23), Arion of Methymna on Lesbos, *c.* 600 BCE, was the first Greek to have composed, named, and taught the dithyramb. Forms of Greek poetry and performance evolved over time, and Arion may have influenced changes in the dithyramb rather than invented what was undoubtedly quite old by Archilochos' time. Lasos of Hermione, a noted musical innovator, is said to have introduced dithyrambic competitions to Athens in the later sixth century BCE. Lasos probably contributed to changes in dithyrambic performances at Athens, but the authority to add competitions to festivals then was really with the Peisistratid tyrants.

The dithyramb certainly seems to have evolved uniquely at Athens during the later sixth century BCE. According to Aristotle (*Poetics* 1449a), the **tragoidia** ("goat-song, tragedy") derived from the dithyramb, both of which were performed at the *City Dionysia*. Thespis of Ikaria, a village in Attika associated in myth with Dionysos, was a dithyrambist in the second half of the sixth century BCE. Two significant innovations affecting Attic tragedy were attributed to him. Aristotle says that Thespis invented the prologue and set speeches of tragedies.[12] He also introduced dialogue, himself emerging from the dithyrambic chorus to engage in dialogue with it. Thespis is thus said to have invented the first dramatic protagonist and, some also said, Attic tragedy itself *c.* 535/534 BCE.[13]

Whether Thespis actually "stepped out" of the dithyrambic chorus to "invent" Attic tragedy or introduced other innovations, Athens was *the* place in Greece where tragedy developed in the later sixth century BCE. Choirilos of Athens presented tragedies in the early 520s, according to a late source; he competed in the early fifth century BCE.[14] Pratinas of Phlious near Corinth competed with Aischylos and Choirilos and was credited with inventing the satyr-play for the *Dionysia*. Phrynichos, a pupil of Thespis and famous for *The Capture of Miletos* produced in 494 BCE, won a tragic competition sometime between 511 and 508 BCE.[15] He is said to have been first to introduce female characters into tragedy. Aischylos, the first of the great fifth-century BCE Attic tragic poets, trained under Lasos of Hermione; he may have been influenced by Thespis. The performance of tragedy at Athens' *City Dionysia* was well established by the end of the Archaic period.

Performances of tragedy were part of the ritual worship of Dionysos Eleuthereos. In early Classical Athens, tragedies in sets of three (trilogies), followed by a lighter satyr play, were performed over three days of the *City Dionysia*. Poets competed with each other to be named best in the annual festival by a panel of Athenian judges. Tragedies centered on stories involving the gods or heroes and other mythic human characters of the Bronze Age. There are some few instances of contemporary historical tragedy, such as the *Capture of Miletos* and the *Persians* by Aeschylos produced in 472 BCE, but these were far outnumbered by tragedies inspired by myths and legends. Some scholars have linked the development of tragedy to the increasing participation of citizens in civic life and so to democratic Athens. While tragedies were designed for large audiences after all and the *City Dionysia*, like the *Panathenaia*, provided an occasion for Athenians to come together as a community in worship of Dionysos, the development of early tragedy at Athens seems to have been fostered by the Peisistratid tyrants.

With its roots in the *Rural Dionysia*, tragedy was meant to convey lessons of truth to spectators through actors serving as mediums for the god. In Attic tragedy, a larger-than-life hero or admirable mythical person is tested and usually fails due to a weakness in character, going too far and offending the gods. That character is subsequently punished severely, thus providing an example of wrong conduct to the audience. Early Attic tragedies are in some ways like stern sermons that warn against arrogance and disrespect to the gods. As Attic tragedy developed through the fifth century BCE, tragic poets became more interested in portraying how recognizably human beings might react in difficult, indeed no-win situations set up for them by fate or the gods. Tragedy's potential for emotional engagement with audiences was immense and increasingly better realized by Aischylos, Sophokles, and Euripides who learned from their forebears and each other. Progressively, the subjects of tragedies became more real and their characters more human – and, consequently, far less noble and admirable.

10.6 Summary

Local festivals allowed *politai* to come together to reaffirm community and identity. The most notable *polis* example, the *Panathenaia*, centered on Athens, Athena, and being Athenian; village celebrations affirmed local identities and bonds with neighbors. The greatest Greek festival of all, the Olympic, began locally in Elis, but expanded to become the foremost of Panhellenic celebrations. Processions, sacrifices, and ritual feasting elevated the occasions with pageantry and solemnity; release and refreshment from the mundane were afforded by entertainment, eating, drinking, and socializing. Competition, however, whether in song, music, or athletics, was at the heart of the greatest of the Archaic Greek festivals and games and account for their growing popularity and proliferation. The Olympics began as a one-day affair, but were lengthened to five days by the Classical period to include more and more competitions. The spectacle of the games coupled with the drama of competing – something dear to Greeks in all periods of their history – was so compelling that new Olympic-style festivals came into being in mainland Greece rather suddenly in the earlier sixth century BCE. Victors in these games became tangible, living substitutes for the storied, but long-dead heroes of old. Archaic and Classical Greeks apparently wanted heroes they could see excelling before their eyes and not just hear about.

Festivals provided other stimulations. Contemplation of ritual, religion, and the gods, the performance of poetry and music in one form or another, the sheer physical presence of huge and diverse crowds of Greeks from many different places at the Panhellenic festivals encouraged new thinking and imagining. Such a vast commingling of sights, sounds, tastes, smells, conversations, ideas, and contemplations goaded Greeks into considering the new, the unaccustomed, sometimes the uncomfortable, and occasionally even the frightening. If the process of intellectual, social, and artistic maturation of the Archaic Greeks is to be measured in the changing art and literature of the period, their increasing interests in athletic competitions, struggle, triumph, and defeat, portrayed sometimes horrendously in their games and festivals, must be counted as integral to further understanding who the Archaic Greeks were.

Notes

1 Miller, *AGA*, 20 ff. Achilles may have been "cleaning out" his wealth in order to dispose of it before his imminent death.
2 Greeks may have been wrong about the foot race as the only competition until 708 BCE: see H. Lee, "The 'First' Olympic Games of 776 B.C.," in Raschke, pp. 110–118.

3 The *dolichos* may have been as much as 24 *stadion* laps amounting to *c.* 9 kms.: cf. Miller, *AGA* p. 32.

4 Odysseus temporarily topples and pins the mightier Aias in the "Funeral Games" (*Iliad* 23.727–728).

5 Tityos was a lawless giant in Greek myth famous for his size and strength.

6 *Anth. Pal.* vol. ii. p. 851; *Suida s.v.* Phaÿllos; see M. Golden, *Sport in the Ancient World from A–Z* (London, 2008), pp. 130–131.

7 Though the date of the gruesome match is not fixed, R. Brophy ("Deaths in the Pan-Hellenic Games: Arrachion and Creugas," *AJP* 99 [1978] 382), places it around *c.* 400 BCE.

8 M&L, 17–18; D. Kyle, *Sport and Spectacle in the Ancient World* (London, 2008), p. 144.

9 Miller, *AGA* p. 139.

10 Kyle, *op.cit.* p. 156.

11 Plutarch, *Mor.* 527d.

12 Themistius, *Or.* 26. 316d.

13 *Marm. Par.* Ep. 43 (*FrGrHist* 239 A); *Suida s.v.* Thespis.

14 *Suida s.v.* Choirilos.

15 *Suida s.v.* Phrynichos.

Further Reading

Games and Festivals

R. Hard, *The Olympic Games and Other Greek Athletic Festivals* (London, 2004).
S. Miller, *Ancient Greek Athletics (AGA)* (New Haven, CT, 2006).
P. Valavanis, *Games and Sanctuaries in Ancient Greece: Olympia, Delphi, Nemea, Isthmia, Athens* (Malibu, CA, 2004).

Olympia

W. Raschke, ed. *The Archaeology of the Olympics: The Olympics and Other Festivals in Antiquity* (Madison, WI, 2002), pp. 35–118.
N. Spivey, *The Ancient Olympics* (Oxford, 2004).

Pythia

O. Picard, "Delphi and the Pythian Games," in O. Tzachou-Alexandri, ed. *Mind and Body: Athletic Contest in Ancient Greece* (Athens, 1989), pp. 69–81.

Isthmia

C. Morgan, "The Origins of the Isthmian Festival," in O. Tzachou-Alexandri, ed. *Mind and Body: Athletic Contest in Ancient Greece* (Athens, 1989) pp. 251–271.

Nemea

S. Miller, "Excavations at the Panhellenic Site of Nemea: Cult, Politics, and Games," in W. Raschke, ed. *The Archaeology of the Olympics: The Olympics and Other Festivals in Antiquity* (Madison, WI, 2002), pp. 141–151.

Athenian Festivals

E. Simon, *Festivals of Attica* (Madison, WI, 1983).
C. Sourvinou-Inwood, *Athenian Myths and Festivals*, edited by R. Parker (Oxford, 2011), esp. pp. 263–339.

Panathenaia

N. Evans, *Civic Rites: Democracy and Religion in Ancient Athens* (Berkeley, CA, 2010), esp. pp. 50–58.
J. Neils, *Worshipping Athena: Panathenaia and Parthenon* (Madison, WI, 1996).

Dionysia

H. Parke, *Festivals of the Athenians* (Ithaca, NY, 1977), pp. 100–103, 125–136.

Origins of Greek Tragedy

S. Scullion, "Tragedy and Religion: The Problem of Origin," in J. Gregory, ed. *A Companion to Greek Tragedy* (London, 2005), pp. 23–37.
I. Storey and A. Allan, *A Guide to Ancient Greek Drama* (London, 2005), pp. 1–70.

11

Cultural Identity, Social Forces, Values, and Behaviors

11.1   Introduction

According to Aristotle, man is by nature a "political" or "social animal." He regarded anyone who does not "socialize" with others as either beneath or above humanity, that is to say, either a beast or a god (*Politics* 1253a). Although Aristotle's statement was much later than the Archaic period, sociocultural forces influencing attitudes and behaviors remained largely the same in Greece from the Archaic period through the Classical. Greeks led public lives, what they did or did not was judged by their fellow Greeks, and they attained or lost status depending upon those judgments. Community standards and expectations informed community judgments and so prescribed roles, actions, and responses for men and women, young and old alike. To deviate from the group expectation was to risk negative evaluation, lowered standing, marginalization, or even loss of community – all of which Archaic Greeks wanted very much to avoid.

What others in the community expected could, however, be contradictory. On the one hand, Greeks were obliged to observe boundaries and be restrained: they were to behave in ways conducive to community cohesion. Law-breaking, injustice, and *stasis* destroyed the fabric of the *polis*, according to Solon. As we have seen, laws were codified in the seventh century BCE in many places in Greece to specify statutes, crimes, and punishments because of new forces and interests clashing with old standards and practices. The aim was to bring order to communities in turmoil. Yet Archaic Greeks contradictorily deemed violence and criminal action appropriate, indeed obligatory ways to redress wrongs, especially those affecting honor. Depending upon the affront, a person's reaction was expected to be summary and violent.

The paradox is explained by antagonistic social forces. One encouraging personal honor was based essentially upon the individual and social immaturity. It was premised on an understanding that men and women owed more to themselves and their immediate families than to their broader communities. It encouraged competition for status, comparison with others, abhorrence and avoidance of being bested, and, at its worst, vengeful response for wrongs or even verbal slights, actual or inferred. The other required submerging individuality for what was conducive to broader community interests and well-being. Though social responsibility was much discussed even early in the Archaic period, shame and honor remained significant forces affecting behavior. Individual aims and social responsibility continued to create tension in Greek communities through antiquity and even until rather recently in remoter parts of Greece.

Archaic Greece: The Age of New Reckonings, First Edition. Brian M. Lavelle.
© 2020 Brian M. Lavelle. Published 2020 by John Wiley & Sons Ltd.

What kind of lives were Archaic Greeks supposed to lead? What were the values that informed a person's conduct? Since Greeks took these for granted and there is no clear-cut sociological or anthropological data from the Archaic period, the evidence we have is much less straightforward than we would like. Yet, values imply motivations and actions, and analyzing these can help us to better comprehend Archaic Greek behaviors. As always, we approach the evidence carefully, a good deal of which derives from later periods.

11.1.1 *Philochoria*

Whether dwelling in larger or smaller communities, Greeks developed a sense of *philochoria* ("attachment to location") and identity from, among other things, living near one another, participating in shared community worships and celebrations, working toward common interests, and, of course, their differentiation from Greeks dwelling elsewhere. (Boundaries between distinct regions, Attika and Megara, for example, were sometimes set with definite markers.[1]) The *oikos*, the essential unit of ancient Greek society, was the core around which ringed the concentric spheres of kinship. An Archaic Greek's primary attention was directed to home and family (*oikos*), clan (*genos*), and nearer location, whether hamlet, village or *polis*.[2] He was further connected to *phyle* ("tribe") and so extended region, and *ethne* ("nation").

In the Archaic period, a Greek male's most profound shared experiences were war-related. Wars were waged for common interests, whether to acquire more land or moveable property or to keep others from taking them. Warriors congregated in masses to fight early on, then in phalanxes alongside members of their immediate families and clans. Clan units were mustered into tribal divisions. Warriors bonded through war experience, which cemented allegiances not just to family or place, but also to fellow warriors. As we have seen, participation in war qualified the warrior for political involvement in the *polis*. Excluded from politics were those who did not fight for the community: women, *xenoi* ("strangers, foreigners"), and, of course, slaves.

Shared religious beliefs and ritual practices also reinforced community identity. Local cults were complemented by regional ones as *poleis* coalesced and increased in size. Artemis, for example, was worshipped locally in eastern Attika at Brauron, at Athmonon (Marousi), and at Halai (Loutsa/Artemida), all with different epithets and somewhat different cult-rites. The focus for all citizens of Attika, however, was upon the Athenian *akropolis* and Athena. Exclusory cult-worship, such as that of Athena *Polias*, fortified Athenian identity. Presumably, Artemis worship at Athmonon was initially for Athmononians only, Brauron for Brauronians, etc.[3]

There were, however, counterweights to narrow community-orientation. Fundamental beliefs about the gods and right and wrong conduct, what a man and woman should and should not be, the need for positive community regard, and materialism, among other things, were all fairly uniform among Greeks. In the Archaic period, a Dorian Greek of the Peloponnesos could easily recognize and readily revere, if he could not actually worship, Athena at Athens or Apollo at Didyma as Ionians did. *Xenia* ("hospitality") – from the same root as *xenos* – might be extended to a Greek traveling away from home, even as he might extend it to foreign visitors arriving at his door. All Greeks would know that Zeus approved such behavior. A Dorian, who spoke essentially the same language as a Milesian and valued the same trade goods, could – and did – make common cause against others. Archaic Greeks generally appreciated the wisdom of Solon of Athens, Pittakos of Mitylene, Thales of Miletos, and Lykourgos of Sparta. Achilles from Thessalian Iolkos, Diomedes from Argos, and Odysseus from Ithaka were Panhellenic heroes, not simply regional or ethnic ones. Indeed, just about every Greek, it seems, claimed some connection to the Dorian Herakles. Archaic Greeks were most active in their local worlds, but well aware of and frequently active in the larger Greek one and even outside of it.

11.2   Honor, Fame, and Good Repute

11.2.1   *Kleos* and *Arete*: Old Standards and New Benchmarks

To acquire signal honor and outstanding repute were common aims for Archaic Greek males, but attaining them did not come easily. Achilles was best in battle, the consummate warrior, and far superior to other Homeric heroes: he was the paragon of *arete* and enjoyed the utmost community esteem. Achilles provided a benchmark, albeit an impossibly high one for any Greek male to attain. Possibilities for demonstrating individual valor in battle were curbed anyway by the dynamics of hoplite warfare. Indeed, the best citizen-warriors in Archaic Greece would seem to be those who fit in among rather than stood out from their comrades and communities: so Tyrtaios would say. Then again, who but the most god-favored and god-gifted could become an Olympic victor? In fact, Greek males could achieve and maintain status through more realistic, scaled-down standards of behavior, although they remained very much aware of the old heroic ones. In fact, Archaic males sought after what honor was available to them in their communities. Most of all, they wanted to avoid dishonor.

The dynamics of "shame" and "honor" in Archaic Greece are most vividly depicted in Homer's *Iliad*. The initial drama of the *Iliad* devolves upon two Greek males who seek to maintain their honor in the eyes of other Greeks. When Agamemnon takes Achilles' own war-prize as compensation for giving up his, Achilles responds destructively to his loss of honor. He first thinks to murder the king, then rashly calls down Zeus' anger upon his comrades-in-arms who have witnessed and – he imagines – condoned his shaming. In fact, Achilles *must* do something, for the entire Greek army, including Agamemnon, expects a reaction from him.

The opinion of the warrior-mass actually counts most in the *Iliad*. For Agamemnon and Achilles, being deprived of what was apportioned them *by the community* is what kindles their quarrel. Enflamed by immaturity, the emotion of the occasion, but also the consciousness that the army is witnessing how they behave, they lose sight of anything but personal dishonor. The upshot is that Achilles, Agamemnon, and the Greek army subvert their own best interests. Both Agamemnon and Achilles are goaded by group pressure and expectation – and their own overly emotional desires to maintain community esteem – to go too far and so to harm themselves and the army.

The transgression and harm are specified in the words and actions of others. Nestor states how destructive the quarrel of Agamemnon and Achilles is for the army and urges the men to leave off before it gets worse. Later, after many Greeks are killed and the entire expedition is in peril, when Agamemnon relents, sending a conciliatory embassy to Achilles and offering rich compensation for the earlier affront, the sulking hero will not accept it. Aias, the noblest warrior after Achilles, says that a reasonable man would take compensation and end the quarrel, but Achilles' pride has taken him beyond the boundaries of reasonable conduct – something Achilles actually acknowledges. Yet while Achilles is thus self-situated outside the society of the

Greek army, he is still admired by Greeks for standing up for his own honor in his way. Homer is well-aware of the paradox of individual and group interest in the case of Achilles.

The implications of shame, honor, community-awarded "trophies," excessiveness, and destructive behaviors are further illustrated in the causation of the Trojan War itself. When Paris absconded with Helen, he did not simply break the law of *xenia* guaranteed by Zeus, but also deprived his host of honor as husband and holder of Helen, the ultimate "trophy" wife for Greek males. *Xenia* obliged a host to receive and treat a guest well, but also the guest to recip-rocate. Paris broke the convention, offending both Zeus and Menelaos, his host. Possession in marriage of the most beautiful woman in all the world bestowed ***time*** ("honor") and *kleos* upon Menelaos: her presence and beauty betokened his standing. Deprived of Helen, Menelaos simultaneously lost fame, honor, status, wife – and, in essence, his home. His community expected him to react violently to the affront.

Other myths similarly illustrate the connections between a man's honor, his possessions, and a wife's fidelity. The driving emotional force of the *Odyssey* is the hero's implied anxiety about Penelope and the consequences of her loss to Odysseus. If Penelope marries one of the Suitors, Odysseus will be deprived of his home and his identity. Reclaiming his home, his possessions, his wife, and so his honor is a visceral, but also social imperative for Odysseus. His disguise as a beggar signifies several things in the epic, but it is above all a reminder of who he is at present and will remain – a humiliated, penniless, marginalized non-entity – unless he retakes what is his and acts as the Greeks expect him to do.

There is a historical example of a similar dynamic involving family-related honor that must be redressed by violence. According to Thucydides (6.54 ff.), the Athenian tyrant Hipparchos insulted Harmodios, a *polites*, by implying that his sister was not a virgin and so unworthy to carry a basket honoring the goddess Athena in the upcoming Panathenaic procession of 514 BCE. The implication amounted to a grave insult that stained the entire family's honor, but Harmodios, her brother, most of all. The boy had to act. Together with his kinsman Aristogeiton, Harmodios set upon Hipparchos as he was marshaling the procession and slew him. Although Harmodios and Aristogeiton paid with their lives for their violent act, their behavior was prescribed by community expectation. Of course, murder by its very nature is a crime against the community.

Efforts to maintain community esteem were frequently self-destructive. Near the end of the *Iliad*, Hektor faces the choice of losing his honor or his life (Box 11.1). In a practical, rational sense, he was best to enter the walls of Troy and save himself, even as his mother and father plead with him to do. He is called the "bulwark" of Troy, and surviving to fight another day would preserve both his life *and* his *polis*. But though it actually harms the community and means his death, Hektor's confrontation with Achilles is forced upon him by the very Trojans who need him to resist the Achaians.

Hektor acknowledges that too much pride brought him to this pass. He must atone for the flaw that an imagined inferior would taunt him with. That would humiliate him unbearably. Better to risk death and preserve honor and standing. In the passage, Hektor is very conscious that all of Troy will be watching and witnessing his bravery or cowardice. While no one can deny Hektor's ultimate valor, its expression is reckless and irresponsible and will destroy both himself and his community.

Archaic Greeks accepted such contradictory motivations and actions as part of being human. While Hektor's self-destruction is foolish, the manner of his death and the attainment of *kleos* make him immortal. Harmodios and Aristogeiton achieved martyrdom and were heroized as

---

Box 11.1 Hektor Ponders Outside Troy's Walls as Achilles Closes In

> Deeply troubled, (Hektor) spoke to his great-hearted spirit:
> "Ah me, I know that, if I go within the gates and the walls,
> Poulydamas first will lay blame on me
> who commanded me to lead the Trojans to the city
> during the night, the awful night when godlike Achilles rose up.
> But I did not heed him. Oh, how much better that would have been!
> As it is, I have destroyed the host because of my recklessness.
> I feel ashamed before the Trojan men and the women
>   with their long-trained gowns,
> lest someone much inferior to me will say:
> 'Hektor trusted in his own strength and destroyed the host!'
> So they will say. Far better for me will it be
> to meet Achilles face to face and either kill him
> or die by his hand gloriously in front of the *polis*."
>
> *(Homer,* Iliad *22.98–110)*

---

patrons of Athenian democracy for acting both rashly and bravely. Foolishness drove Hektor to ignore Poulydamas' advice to lead the army within the safe walls of Troy; blind anger motivated Harmodios. Yet such self-destructive emotions and actions are the very stuff of Greek heroes, as they are of heroic human beings. Homer and other Greek authors recognize the nature of heroism and are, as we all are, in awe of it: chosen consciously, heroism entailing certain death amounts to a triumph over the deepest fear of human beings.

Achilles' anger crescendos with his refusal to allow burial for Hektor's body – an atrocity. It subsides when Achilles experiences sympathy. Homer seems to be saying that, while self-centered and distancing emotions like stiff-necked pride and anger are destructive and human, shared and interactive emotions like sympathy and caring are redemptive because they are socially creative and beneficial. Achilles' ultimate sympathy for the father of the enemy who slew his best friend is, in many ways, far more impressive and ennobling than any feat of arms by any hero in the *Iliad*. He has at last reached a maturity that overcomes his former childish self-centeredness.

Needless to say, questions among the Greeks about human conduct will persist through the Classical period. What *is* right conduct after all? Should a man aspire to be like the heroes who gained undying *kleos*? Or should he be more community-conscious and responsible? What exactly *does* one owe one's community, what to one's self? Honor is a standard, but should one pursue it even as Achilles and Hektor had? At Athens, popular poetry advocated that *politai* act "just as Harmodios had" – murderously, but also patriotically.

11.2.2 Adjustments and Modifications to Standards and Expectations

Honor and glory from war remained in the minds of Archaic Greek males, although evolving consciousness about war's realities and their own places in their communities modified the Homeric standards. Though Tyrtaios drew upon those standards in his poetry of encouragement for the Spartans (Box 11.2), he implies that the old ideals and standards had failed to ignite the fighting spirits of Spartan youth. More practical considerations involving community must alter Homeric prescriptions for valor if Sparta were to survive in the Second Messenian War.

Tyrtaios recasts the hero as one who serves the community more than himself, giving his life for his country and his fellow-citizens.[4] A Spartan warrior's aims *must* be shaped by the collective, not by the individual, if the *polis* is to win the war. These verses promoted the kind of discipline that was needed for hoplite formation fighting – something the Spartans adopted with a will by the mid-seventh century BCE and brought to near-perfection by the mid-sixth.

One aspect of Homeric warfare served especially to reinforce the message of discipline – its focus on armor, especially the shield. Armor was part of a warrior's clothing, a signifier of his prowess and so his most precious possession. Such equipment was often inherited and so had further meaning because of its connection to ancestors who provided more personal benchmarks for warriors' behaviors. In the *Iliad*, when a warrior is killed by another, the victor strips the armor to profit from it, but also to make the victory total. For a warrior to abandon his armor was to cast away the warrior persona, his own being, and to lose all honor. When raging Achilles meets Lykaon (*Iliad* 21.34 ff.), the Trojan youth is armor-less, naked, and abject: he is not a warrior anymore and can only throw himself at Achilles' knees for mercy. He has lost everything and can only beg for his life.

Box 11.2 Esteem for the Brave Spartan Warrior

He who falls in the forefront of battle and loses his dear life there,
   brings honor upon his *asty*, the masses, and his father,
struck many times through the breast and the well-bossed shield
   and through the breastplate from in front.
Him young and old alike mourn,
   and with painful longing the entire *polis* is troubled,
and his grave and his children are marked conspicuously among men,
   and the children of his children and his clan thereafter.
His noble *kleos* never perishes nor the name of him,
   but even though he is beneath the earth, he is deathless,
that man who excelling in valor stands fast and struggles
   for his land and children, that man whom rushing Ares destroys.
But if he should flee the doom of death which is endless,
   if he conquers and acquires the glistening pride of the spear,
everyone will give him honor, young and old alike,
   and having experienced many pleasant things, he goes down to Hades.
As he grows old, he shines as an ornament to the townspeople.
   No one wants to harm his respect nor what is rightfully his,
but, all in the assemblies, those who are younger,
   yield their places, and even those who are older than he is.

(Tyrtaios F 12, 23–42)

Spartans were indoctrinated with special regard for their shields, the most significant element of hoplite armor. In other *poleis*, warriors often drew heraldic devices on their shields as expressions of personality (see Figure 4.3 on p. 59). In Sparta, shield-devices would become uniformly the Lakedaimonian lambda after the Archaic period in keeping with the unit-ideal first emphasized by Tyrtaios.[5] Spartan women sent their menfolk off to battle, admonishing them to come home with their shields on their arms or dead upon them and so respectable in death. The Spartan shields amounted to the honor of a warrior and his family, but also to the collective honor of Sparta. Punishment for "shield-discarding" in many other Greek *poleis*, while undoubtedly conceived of as a deterrent to cowardice in battle, also points to a shared sense of the shield's symbolism for the community.

Yet, there were contradictions. As we have seen, Archilochos discarded his shield to save his life. He then took the Homeric principle head on by declaring that a shield was really not a symbol of valor, but an eminently replaceable tool of war. Archilochos' challenge came in the wake of changes affecting Archaic Greek society and re-evaluation of standards. Tyrtaios' own verses show that young Spartan contemporaries needed to have Homeric values of *time* and *kleos* redefined and made relevant in order to motivate them. Tyrtaios invoked community which became most important at Sparta. From his verses, Archilochos seems to have been a man whose community was really not a *polis*, but rather his warrior-brethren and those who would listen to his verses.

The creation of mercenarism in the Greek world in the early seventh century BCE worked against both *philochoria* and traditional ideas about warrior-honor. When Ionian marauders became paid warriors for the Egyptian pharaoh, the incentives really had nothing to do with honor, glory, or protecting one's own community. Rather, regular pay was what these newly-minted Egyptian mercenaries were after. For these – and there appears to have been many of them – loyalties were not tethered to *polis*, but up for sale to the highest bidder. Such was the increasingly real, but cynical environment in which Archilochos and his fellow-warriors now dwelt.

11.2.3   Right Conduct: Constructive and Destructive

So far our discussion has centered on male war experience and expectations of conduct in battle. But what was "right conduct" for Greek males and females in civilian circumstances? Naturally we assume that "right conduct" in Archaic Greece amounted to conforming to community standards and expectations conducive to good order. It was prompted by *dike*, whose guardian was Zeus. In the last section, however, we observed how community expectations involving "right conduct" could actually promote divisive, destructive, and even deadly outcomes in the worst cases.

Hesiod says that *dike* harmonizes nature and society and promotes *polis* well-being and prosperity; its opposite, *hybris*, ruins it. Hesiod complains about the corrupt judges in Askra, who, he says, "eat" bribes, render "crooked" decisions, and so pervert *dike*. Hesiod reminds his audience that those who perpetrate such *hybris* will be punished by Zeus. On the other hand, those who keep their oaths, avoid envy, lies, and deceit, render just decisions, speak straightly, and honor family and others contribute to community harmony and the good of those in it.

Other poets condemn unjust rulers and individuals alike. Solon says that *Eunomia* which is founded upon *dike* "quickly claps fetters round the unrighteous ... soothes the rough, stops wealth-insolence, eclipses *hybris* ... by her all things that are man's are right and reasoned" (F 4, 33–34, 39). Like Hesiod and Solon, Theognis of Megara (*c.* 550 BCE) cites the evil affecting his *polis*. Corrupt leaders pervert justice which leads to strife (43–52); a trustworthy man is "worth [his] weight of gold and silver" in times of *stasis* (77–78). Lying, cheating, and deception injure both the individual and the *polis*; it is in righteousness that true *arete* resides (147). Indeed "every man is estimable who is a just man" (148). Theognis redefines *arete*, detaching it entirely from war and martial prowess. These poets oversimplify to strengthen their assertions: Hesiod, Solon, and Theognis want to emphasize for their fellow *politai* what should and should not prevail in their *poleis*. Hearing such voices, Archaic Greeks were made constantly aware that they should be just and ethical, especially in relation to one another, for their own good and that of the community.

Archaic Greek conceptions about "right conduct" were not as complex as they would become in the Classical period, it seems. So, **euethes**, which later meant "simple-mindedness, naïveté," or even "foolishness," seems to have connoted "good-heartedness, simplicity," and "straightforwardness" to an Archaic Greek. In one famous passage of the *Iliad* (9.312–13), Achilles, himself a model of straightforwardness, marks with strong disapproval, the sly or calculating man, saying that he hates the man "like the gates of Hades" who says one thing, but hides another in his heart. Theognis repeats the sentiment nearly verbatim (91–92). Thucydides (3.83.1) says that it was only after the start of the Peloponnesian War, spurred by *stasis* that engulfed the Greek world in the later fifth century BCE, that the old way of interacting with others, *euethes*, "in which a sense of honour has so large a part,"[6] was being, literally, scoffed out of existence in his day.

Despite these constant reminders, the paradoxical counterpoint to righteous conduct and *dike*, socially condoned violence, was valid in Greek society. As we have seen in the case of Harmodios, an Archaic Greek male's honor depended upon his own comportment, but could also depend upon that of female relations. Athenian females at least sought not to be talked about – the exact of opposite of what men sought: the estimation of women was based most upon *what they did not do* and *how their conduct was not appraised*. Chiefly at stake for a woman was her reputation for chastity, married or not. In fact, it was all important for females to maintain good repute, since a charge of sexual misconduct would redound upon her and her family, and bring social ruin.

Myths about goddesses and mortal women alike provided examples of comportment. Hera was a model wife: she was a faithful spouse whose reputation was unsullied. Aphrodite, on the other hand, was disdained by the other gods for sexual incontinence. In the song of Demodokos (*Odyssey* 8.266–366), when Aphrodite is caught *in flagrante* with Ares in the net of her husband, Hephaistos, she is instantly the object of ridicule and humiliation by the Olympian male gods. (The goddesses keep away from the sight of such shame, as human women were also supposed to do.) The gods laugh at the pair derisively, heaping scorn upon both (8.326). Ares and Aphrodite run away out of sight of the others, humiliated. Of course, the scene is drawn from Greek community reaction to adulterers caught in the act.

On the mortal plane, Penelope, Helen, and Clytemnestra reinforce the polarity of good and bad sexual behavior. The latter two sundered their marriages, destroyed their homes, and shattered their families by committing adultery. Helen succumbed to Paris, the desire for whom was aroused by Aphrodite, the force of sexual indiscretion. Clytemnestra conceived of evil for her husband because of his sacrifice of their daughter, Iphigeneia, conspiring with her lover

Aegisthos to kill Agamemnon and take his power. Their opposite is Penelope. Though alone and without a male protector, with the outlook for husband's return very dim indeed, surrounded by aggressive Suitors, Penelope remains chaste and devoted to her husband through the *Odyssey*.

A similar polarity appears in Semonides F 7, who names only one type of woman as a worthy mate for a man – the "bee"-woman. Industriousness is implicit in the characterization, but Semonides focuses more on her disposition and dutiful relationship with her husband. This type of woman avoids sex-talk with other women – and so trouble. She earns esteem for her *genos*, is "very distinguished among all other women, a godly grace surrounding her" (88–89). The "donkey"-woman, on the other hand, will not work at all, eats and eats, and will have sex with anybody that comes along. For Semonides, "good" or "bad" behavior for women devolves upon sexual conduct and whether wives are faithful to their husbands.

Actually, sexual behavior of specific females was not a proper topic for discussion in many places in Greece. Any shadow cast upon the conduct of a wife, mother, daughter, or sister must result in violent response and retribution from the family. Harmodios' response to his sister's insult was swift and deadly. Inaction was tantamount to admission: whether the misconduct occurred or not, the substance of the insult would have been accepted as true. Such strictness did not obtain everywhere in ancient Greece: the lives and conducts of Spartan women, for example, were considerably less restricted than in Athens and Ionia. (We return to this topic in Chapter 12.)

Some types of collective violence seem almost institutional in Archaic Greek *poleis*. *Stasis*, of which we hear a great deal, spawned its own set of expected actions and responses, especially among family and clan members who were required to act violently. No community can exist in such conditions for long, and it appears that widespread *stasis* was only intermittent in Archaic Greece. When *stasis* ended, Greek communities apparently returned temporarily to peace and quiet. But feuds and vendettas, the bases for social conflict and *staseis* in the Archaic period, could break out again at any time and widespread violence with it.

11.2.4 *Philia*

The duty to protect one's self and one's own from injury was deeply engrained in Archaic Greeks. Although the sentiment, "helping friends and harming enemies," was most famously stated in the fifth century BCE, it must have been very old by then. **Philia** ("friendship" or "affinity") is perhaps best defined as a non-erotic bond between individuals. It began with one's *oikos* and *genos* but could extend to others with whom one shared *philia*. Affinities and friendships were cemented through action and interaction – marriage and common cause and interest. While affection and emotional attachment may have played a part in Archaic Greek *philia*, it was also informed by practicality and the advantages that a mutually supportive alliance could produce.

One of the expressions of Archaic Greek *philia* was dining together. Drinking and eating are conspicuous preliminaries even to dialogue in Homer. A good host offers **philoi** ("friends") all they can eat and drink before talking meaningfully with them. So Achilles on the beach near Troy offers food and drink to ambassadors from his enemy Agamemnon before speaking with them (*Iliad* Book 9). His hosting is courtly and correct. Penelope's Suitors, on the other hand, are uninvited and unwanted, eating and drinking riotously: they burn through Odysseus' possessions daily. They provide the negative example of what such occasions should be: hosted, cultured, structured, and finite.

Good befalling a *philos* is cause for rejoicing, but for an enemy to encounter evil seems to bring greater happiness. Homer's heroes regularly exalt in an enemy-warrior's death, vaunting over the corpse. They rant about the pain they will inflict on Trojan warriors by taking their womenfolk in addition to their lives. Theognis (337–340) prays that he may repay his friends, but even more his enemies, and says that a heart shrunken from great suffering grows again when revenge occurs (361–362). Enemies were by no means merely those who attacked one physically. They were also those who scorned or ridiculed by word or deed, who diminished esteem by insult or slight. Archilochos (F 23, 14–16) knew well how to hate with words and even took lives with his poetic invective.

The tension of opposing social and anti-social forces was unremitting in Archaic Greece. Order, based upon right conduct, respect for others, and basic standards of justice and non-violence were praised by all because they were indispensable for any community. Exceptions to order, however – individuals taking the law into their own hands for their own reasons – were not only condoned but encouraged because of more visceral standards of power, pride, and primacy that were rooted in earlier, much rougher times when social conditions were more primitive.

11.3 Excess and Moderation

Archaic Greeks were constantly cautioned against excessiveness. Solon spoke directly to the *demos*, saying that moderate wealth is best and that greed and the desire for excessive wealth lead to ruin. The antidotes for excessiveness are sobriety and prudence. In the famous story of Solon and Kroisos in Herodotos (1.29–33), the lawgiver tries to dissuade Kroisos from infatuation with wealth by teaching him about the real "wealth" of insight and understanding. Solon employs the bittersweet stories of Tellus of Athens and Kleobis and Biton of Argos. Both tales end in "beautiful" deaths that not only demonstrate exemplary lives, but also stress that they had ended in the best possible way – at the peak of good fortune when it could not be undone. Indeed, all three achieve fame and avoid ruin. The lesson is lost on Kroisos who is besotted with his own riches. In fact, the Lydian king's blindness to the truth is utter and his incapacity for insight as profound as his wealth is great. The story, a myth really, is didactic and a warning to Greeks who might be subject to obsessive materialism. But how many Archaic Greeks would actually have understood the story's point or agreed with Solon?

How should a Greek live if not to gain materially? The pain of poverty leading to beggary – a hideous thing to Homer and Hesiod – and the dream of wealth compelled a man to work hard, to take to the treacherous seas to profit from trading, colonizing, and even fighting for a pharaoh, really to do anything he could do to survive first and then prosper. Theognis says (181–182) that it is better to be dead than to be a poor man ground down by poverty. But Solon was not advocating for poverty or privation: wealth, he says, he himself desires (F 13, 7). Rather he cites the disruptive effects of ill-gotten and immoderate wealth which creates *hybris* and so destroys the *polis* (Box 11.3).

Box 11.3 Solon's Contentment

Blest is he who has loving children and solid-hooved horses
and coursing hounds and a friend in another land.
(Solon F 23)

Equally wealthy are they who have much silver
and gold and a field of grain-bearing land
and horses and mules, and they that have only these things:
to be well-fed, well-clothed, and well-shod …
(Solon F 24, 1–4)

For Solon, enough *is* enough. Excessive wealth is unnecessary for a happy life.

Solon says that overly wealthy Athenian leaders are overbearing and intolerable because of their wealth (F 4c); *koros* ("glut, surfeit" but also "insolence deriving therefrom") is the root cause of the problem. He orders them to moderate their "big mindedness," since it alienates them and subverts orderliness. For Solon, *koros* automatically created *hybris* when a man's character was defective (F 6, 3–4). Self-restraint was the best way to achieve harmony in a *polis*. The haughtiness of the "haves" should not stoke the discontentment of the "have-nots."

Even the unconventional Archilochos counsels moderation in behavior, telling his audience to be neither too elated by victory nor too weighed down by defeat. Rather be measured, realizing that life is made up of both ups and downs (F 128). About a century later, Theognis tells his friend Kyrnos to hold firm in bad times, since good times return (355–360). Moderation, not excess, is the best way to endure the ebb and flow of fortune, even as Solon had tried to impress upon an uncomprehending Kroisos. Constant reminders like **meden agan** ("nothing too much") notwithstanding, Archaic Greeks persisted in being immoderate. Wealth and the status it provided were very powerful goads in Greek society. We return to the subject of wealth in Section 11.4.1.

11.3.1 The Seven Sages and the Delphic Maxims

The "Seven Sages" of Archaic Greece were so reputed for teaching their fellow Greeks practicality, common sense, truth, and better ways to live their lives. According to Plato, the Seven were Solon, Thales, Pittakos, Bias of Priene, Chilon of Sparta, Myson of Chen, and Kleoboulos of Rhodes.[7] Their lessons may have been conveyed in longer discourse, but became famous – and have come down to us – mostly in the form of pithy sayings. For example, when Thales was asked what man is "fortunate," he replied: "He whose body is sound, whose spirit is agile, and whose nature is refined." Thales' aim was dissociation from material standards of "happiness," just as it was Solon's. Others offered more direct advice. Chilon said, "Do not let your tongue outstrip your thought" and "Choose loss over disgraceful gain." Pittakos offered, "Not even the gods contend with the inevitable." And Bias: "Gain with persuasion, not force."[8] The general drift of the sayings is about moderation and recognizing and respecting boundaries. While the sayings reminded Greeks about how to lead their lives, they also raised their consciousness about right and wrong. Though the Seven Sages were greatly admired, their sayings are devoid of encouragement to materialism.

The appearance of this Archaic collection of sages, all of whom were roughly contemporary, was not fortuitous. With social values and standards pulling in conflicting directions and new economic and political realities unmooring from once fixed boundaries, Archaic Greeks were willing to heed the wisdom of the Seven. The ideology of moderation was sensible, attractive as egalitarian, practicable for all, and conducive to community coherency and success; their words to live by were easily remembered. While the sayings of the Sages were what we might regard today as elementary, obvious, and even simplistic, they were taken quite seriously and even cherished as veritable beacons of perceptiveness and guidance by Archaic Greeks. In fact, what the Sages advocated seems to be akin to what Ionian scientists were seeking in the *kosmos*, that is, universal laws and principles of, in their case, social and political harmony. As for the *kosmos*, so for the *polis*: social order was an extension of the universe which, as the Ionian scientist-philosophers suggested, was itself harmonious.

Many of their sayings were associated with Delphian Apollo; that they seemed in sync with the divine only added to their authority and celebrity. Perhaps the most famous of the Delphic maxims – one also attributed to Thales – was **gnothi seauton** meaning "know yourself" and where you stand in the *kosmos*. In other words, "be circumspect," humble, and very considerate of what you are and are not. Together, the Seven Sages and Apollo promoted consciousness of forces outside of human control, a lessening of ego, and a deeper engagement with natural *and* social environments. Such consciousness and engagement worked for a broader understanding of one's self and others. The Delphic maxims and sayings of the Seven might then be interpreted as much appreciated signposts for Greeks in a fast-changing, less certain Archaic Greek world, distilling how they themselves could better live and navigate the times in community with others.

11.4 Competition

Competitiveness is fueled by a need to demonstrate superiority, but also for approval in the wake of that demonstration. While battle-conduct and athletic competitions figured prominently as ways for Archaic Greeks to display superiority and obtain honor, wealth and political power also played a part. Wealth earned community approval, but many could acquire it. Singular political power, however, was granted by the *polis* because an individual was judged to be better than all others – at least temporarily. Wisdom, as it was ascribed to Solon and Pittakos, or successful war-leadership as demonstrated by Peisistratos, could garner such power. It was also frequently conceded to victors in Panhellenic Games, since these were judged to be god-favored. Indeed, Archaic Greeks believed that a man outstanding for wealth, accomplishment in war, or at the Games was blest by the gods and that the good fortune that attended him could transfer to them.

Competition was a constant in the lives of Archaic Greeks. Casual athletic contests for young men and boys were daily occurrences, with older men looking on approvingly or disapprovingly as youths competed. Craftsmen and merchants, too, contended in an open market for patrons and buyers. As we have seen, even Athenian potters and painters of the Archaic period, striving for market share, but also standing, inscribed their vases to publicize their superior proficiencies. The potters' names alone on vases, but more explicitly their declarations, and the names of sculptors on statues or statue-bases dedicated in sanctuaries throughout Greece were vaunts as well as challenges. To be recognized not simply as excellent among many, but as superlative was a driving force in Archaic Greek society.

11.4.1 The Pursuit of Wealth

Before the Archaic period, Greek *aristoi* seem to have monopolized local wealth, even as they did leadership and governance. The source of their wealth – and their power – was land-ownership. Sarpedon's words to Glaukos, that the community surrenders the best of everything to the best fighters, including the choicest lands, seem to reflect a time when the *aristoi* defended communities and so were conceded land, power, and status for their services (*Iliad* 12.310–314). Changes in the Archaic period enabled non-aristocrats to accumulate wealth and so to aspire to political power. At Athens, Solon altered the qualifications for office from birth and landed wealth to wealth including land-equivalencies rather than land itself in the early sixth century BCE.

In the *Works and Days* (20 ff.), Hesiod says that a lazy man seeing a neighbor working to become wealthy is stirred to work himself. "Neighbor strives to emulate the neighbor striving after wealth" (23–24). The payoff amounts to more than material possession. If one works "the idle will envy you as you get wealthy. Excellence and fame attend upon the man who is wealthy" (*Works and Days*, 312–313). Alkaios of Mytilene re-stated the words of Aristodemos, a sage of Sparta, in a poem in the late seventh century BCE: "wealth is the man: no poor man can obtain esteem or honor."[9] For the Athenians, the pursuit of wealth seems to have been all-engrossing, as Solon notes (F 13, 71–74): "There is no clear goal of wealth that is established for men,// for those of us now who hold the most//seek after double. What could satisfy all?// The immortals grant gain to men." Solon cites the greed of all Athenians, leaders and *demos*, but, as we have seen, condemns really only the immoderate and unjust pursuit of material gain. Notwithstanding, his words had little effect, since the Athenians kept seeking after wealth and leaders who would deliver upon promises to them of enrichment. Just how important status tied to wealth, especially landed wealth, was to the Athenians is illustrated by the Athenian colonies called **klerouchies**, the first of which seems to have been established in the late sixth century BCE.[10] The Athenian landless sought to become landed through the *klerouchies* and so to achieve higher status even where those colonies were most unwelcome among the natives into whose lands they intruded.

The Athenians were by no means the only Greeks caught up in the pursuit of wealth. Theognis gauges the appetite of his fellow Megarians, deploring it to his friend Kyrnos (129–130): "Do not pray for *arete*, son of Polypais, nor to be prominent//nor for wealth." These were three things Kyrnos and others obviously wanted very much. Theognis goes on to note how class in Megara was being eroded by wealth (185–192):

> Untroubled by the baseness in marrying a base woman, //the noble man is – provided she gives him much wealth.//Nor does a woman refuse to be the spouse of a base man// – who is a rich man, but rather wishes wealth instead of nobility.// Wealth is what they honor. Good stock marries base//and base marries noble. Wealth confounds the stock.

From what Theognis says, being affluent had become a kind of benchmark for basic honorable status in the Megara of his day.

The subtext of Herodotos' story of Kroisos and Solon (*Histories*.1.29–33) offers further evidence about the valuation of wealth. As we have seen, when after Kroisos had asked Solon whom he thought was "most blest" of men and Solon named three relatively impoverished Greek nobodies who had died "happily," the Lydian dismissed him summarily. The luster of Lydian gold, which persisted into the mid-fifth century BCE when Herodotos told the story and either repeated or invented the moral – and indeed tragic – lesson of excess, must have been far greater in the sixth century BCE. To Archaic Greek subsistence farmers, however, Kroisos must have seemed in fact the "most blest" man in the world.

Speaking at Sparta before the Peloponnesian War in 432 BCE, Athenian ambassadors say that the Athenians are motivated to keep what they have gotten, that is, their empire, because of "honor, fear, and material gain."[11] Honor and gain are, of course, closely related, desire for one driving desire for the other. Their empire had produced unprecedented wealth for the Athenians, but also prestige among the rest of the Greeks because of their *polis'* singular power. In the eyes of the Athenians and even other Greeks, their empire made them superior to other *poleis*. They were in fact greatly envied for that superiority. It was also because of that power and position that Athens was called by other Greeks a tyrant-*polis*.

11.4.2 The *Agon* of Politics and Display

As we have seen, leadership in the Dark Ages depended upon competency in war, but changing conditions altered things dramatically. Leaders who could do little or nothing other than lead in war were incapable of solving issues created by the new circumstances beginning in the early Archaic period. The inclusion of new political participants, their demands for justice, stability, and a larger share in governance created the need for lawgivers and other resourceful aspirants to leadership to deal with the new conditions. As we have also seen, the old order did not leave without resistance.

Once again, Solon's career and its context exemplify the new political conditions. The clashing of *demos* and "the powerful and wealthy" brought Athens to a standstill. One side wanted better leaders, a greater say in governance, and shares of the wealth only too apparent around them. The *aristoi* resisted concessions. Solon was chosen as arbitrator by both sides. He tried, but failed to solve the crisis. Competitors for power outbid him for the allegiance of the *demos* and, by competing, not only outdid him, but raised the bar for their contemporaries and those who came after them.

Solon stopped short of seizing tyrannical power for himself, refusing those telling him to take it. But others both in Athens and elsewhere in Greece aspired to tyranny, impressing *politai* as capable in crisis. Peisistratos, acquiring great popularity and credibility as victor in the war with Megara, became tyrant at Athens after Solon. In fact, the *demos* conceded power to him because of what it judged to be his fitness to rule.

Crises addressed, Archaic Greek tyrants had to maintain the consent of the *politai* to hold on to their power. While they were envied for their talents and their achievements, tyrants maintained lasting allegiance by sharing their good fortune. Peisistratos seems to have distributed the first Athenian coins strategically as tokens of his wealth and good fortune. Moreover, he, Kypselos and Periandros of Corinth, and others sponsored colonization and, along with Polykrates, further means of enrichment. Displays of wealth and power through control of festivals and games burnished the image of tyrants as blest, advertised their superiority, and urged continuing assent to their leadership.

Second-generation *tyrannoi* raised the ante, sometimes spectacularly competing for the attention not just of their *polis*, but of the Greek world. Periandros was famous for, among other things, attempting to cut through the Isthmus of Corinth to facilitate ship traffic. He settled instead for a "drag-through" upon which ships could be conveyed from one side of the Isthmus to the other. He kept the famous dithyrambic poet Arion at his court, signifying his wealth and power, but also that of Corinth. Polykrates was the most dazzling of all Archaic Greek tyrants. He sponsored the last and greatest of temples to Hera on Samos, which by his design, was the largest of any Greek temple. His coterie of poets included Ibykos of Rhegion and Anakreon of Teos. In a gaudy display, Polykrates linked the island of Rheneia to Delos with a golden chain as a tribute to the god Apollo. Not to be outdone, the sons of Peisistratos at Athens contrived to build the largest temple ever erected on the mainland. The colossal temple of Olympian Zeus was begun in the later 520s BCE. The famous poets patronized by the younger Peisistratids included Lasos of Hermione, Simonides, and Anakreon. The Peisistratids seem to have had Polykrates' examples clearly in view. Panhellenic contests remained excellent venues for tyrants for ostentation, competition, victory – and publicity. The wealthiest entered teams for chariot-racing, the most glamorous of events. Victories were publicized first by Olympic proclamation and then by Pindar and other poets whose epinikian odes praised them and made them the talk of the Archaic and Classical Greek worlds.

11.5   Old Allegiances and New Realities

11.5.1   *Aristoi* and *Demos*

The *aristoi* seemed to have monopolized political power and governance during the Dark Ages. Dissent from that may be found, however, as early as the epic poets. That government should be more subject to the will of the entire community and not just the self-interest of Greek aristocrats was realized in the codification of laws in *poleis* both big and small in the seventh century. In fact, a political evolution may be traced from the very early Archaic period to the establishment of democracy in Athens in 507 BCE.

The first prominent dissenter is Thersites who vehemently criticizes Agamemnon, the "great king," for deficient leadership (*Iliad* 2.212 ff.). What Thersites says is true and, although he receives summary punishment when he goes too far, he has the undeniable right to speak out and be heard by others in his community. Archilochos echoes Thersites' criticism of aristocracy, contrasting the "all-for-show" aristocratic-looking war leader with the better commander who seems reminiscent of Thersites himself.

Hesiod complains bitterly about the "bribe-eating" *basileis*, who may have been among the last of the abusive "old guard" in such places as Askra. The appearance of law codes, which were meant to correct such abuses, is symptomatic of the growing divide between the *demos* which demanded laws be fair and constant and the *aristoi* who apparently controlled the dispensation of law theretofore. It is also a sign of the *demos'* power to obtain such concessions from aristocrats who could not prevent them. The potency of the *demos*, growing through the sixth century BCE, eventuated in the establishment of democracy at Athens.

Notwithstanding, aristocrats nevertheless retained privileged positions in most Greek *poleis*, whether they governed or not. A part of that retention was due to their implication with ages-old religious cults and rituals that had become part of the *polis'* fabric. At least in Athens, part was due to the successful adaptation of some *aristoi* to new political conditions: the preeminent example is Kleisthenes, scion of the noble Alkmeonidai and founder of Athenian democracy.

Athenian *aristoi* retained their disdain of the *demos* nonetheless. Pseudo-Xenophon, also called the "Old Oligarch," demonstrates quite vividly that, while the Athenian *aristoi* in the mid-fifth century BCE accepted the democracy, they continued to resent it bitterly. In fact, the ancient gulf between *aristoi* and the *demos* seems never to have narrowed in ancient Greece.

11.6 Summary

Archaic Greeks lived and interacted within two systems of opposing values. One prescribed strict roles for men and women based upon an honor code. Self-consciousness stemming from judgments made by others, competitions to get and keep status within the community, the desire for honor, fear of its loss, humiliation, and the loss of status all weighed daily upon males and females in *poleis*, villages, and *oikoi*. To be reckoned a "man," a Greek male must live up to his community's conception of manliness. For a warrior to turn coward in battle may not have been as damaging in Athens as it was in Sparta, but it was a charge every Archaic Greek male wanted to avoid. Acquiring wealth and power, being the object of admiration if not envy, all amounting to esteem and higher status, were compelling aims for males during the Archaic period. For an Athenian woman, not acquiring any reputation would, somewhat paradoxically, earn her community esteem. Oppositely, just the hint of misconduct, especially sexual misconduct, could drain the honor and status of a woman and her family irrevocably. Antagonism and violence were natural concomitants of this system: even inferred slights had to be avenged.

What the community expected of individuals in regard to honor was contradicted by what was actually known to be good for that community. Expectations of retribution for insults or other losses of honor or even being bested in competition could result in feuding and violence and envelop a *polis* in general disorder and *stasis*. Hesiod and Solon are not concerned with "manliness," but "justice," "right and wrong conduct" – all of which are conducive to social responsibility and orderliness. Solon condemns excess: for him, the most "blest" of mortals achieved their status through moderation and piety – and really for not being outstanding in the traditional ways.

Archaic Greeks, like their descendants of Classical Greece, were fundamentally conflicted in many of their values and the questions of personal responsibility and public good. One of the greatest Attic tragedies of the fifth century BCE, Sophokles' *Antigone*, deals with the clash between individual rights and public standards, ages-old ritual beliefs and man-made laws, honor and cynicism. As great as it is, *Antigone* left the issues it raises unresolved, even as they had been during the Archaic period.

Notes

1 Theseus is said to have set up a *stele* at the Isthmus of Corinth demarcating "Ionia" and "the Peloponnesos" (Plutarch, *Life of Theseus* 25.3).
2 In Attika, one's fundamental geographical connection was to one's ***deme*** ("village, district, neighborhood").
3 Peisistratos seems to have transferred worship of Brauronian Artemis to Athens, and the cult at Brauron became part of Athenian *polis*-cult thereafter (Pausanias 1.23.7).
4 Similar sentiments are to be found in Kallinos of Ephesos F 1.
5 N. Kennell, *Spartans: A New History* (London, 2010), p. 154.
6 A.W. Gomme, *A Historical Commentary on Thucydides, Books II–III* (Oxford, 1962), p. 380.
7 Plato, *Protagoras* 343a.
8 Literally: "Having persuaded, take, not having forced." All of these "sayings" come from the very late and rather dubious Diogenes Laertios.
9 *S&A* Z 37 (12) 3–4 (p. 315). (Diogenes Laertios I.31).
10 Cf. M. Hansen and T. Neilsen, *An Inventory of Archaic and Classical Poleis* (Oxford, 2004), p. 638.
11 Thucydides 1.76.2.

Further Reading

Values and Behaviors

A. Adkins, *Merit and Responsibility: A Study in Greek Values* (Oxford, 1960).
V. Farenga, *Citizen and Self in Ancient Greece: Individuals Performing Justice and the Law* (Cambridge, 2006).

Greek Lyric Poetry and Society

S. Hornblower, "Greek lyric and the politics and sociologies of archaic and classical Greek communities," in F. Budelman, ed. *The Cambridge Companion to Greek Lyric* (Cambridge, 2009), pp. 39–57.

Localism/Regionalism

J. Hall, "Polis, Community, and Ethnic Identity," in H. Shapiro, ed. *The Cambridge Companion to Archaic Greece* (Cambridge, 2007), pp. 40–60.
C. Morgan, *Early Greek States Beyond the Polis* (London, 2003).

Honor and Shame

D. Cairns, *Aidos: The Psychology and Ethics of Honour and Shame in Greek Literature* (Oxford, 1993).
N. Fisher, *Hybris: A Study in the Values of Honour and Shame in Ancient Greece* (Warminster, UK, 1992).
B. Lavelle, "The Nature of Hipparchos' Insult to Harmodios," *American Journal of Philology* 107 (1986) pp. 318–331.

Competition and Politics

N. Fisher, "The Culture of Competition," in K. Raaflaub and H. Van Wees, eds. *A Companion to Archaic Greece* (Oxford, 2009), esp. pp. 536–540.

L. Kurke, "The Economy of Kudos," in C. Dougherty and L. Kurke, eds. *Cultural Poetics in Archaic Greece: Cult, Performance, Politics* (Oxford, 1998), pp. 131–163.

Wealth

J. Davies, *Wealth and the Power of Wealth in Classical Athens* (Salem, NH, 1984).

D. Tandy, *Warriors into Traders* (Berkeley, CA, 1997).

Justice

M. Gagarin, "*Dike* in Archaic Greek Thought," *Classical Philology* 69 (1974). pp. 186–197.

The Seven Sages

R. Martin, "The Seven Sages as Performers of Wisdom," in C. Dougherty and L. Kurke, eds. *Cultural Poetics in Archaic Greece: Cult, Performance, Politics* (Oxford, 1998), pp. 108–130.

The *Aristos/Demos*

W. Donlan, *The Aristocratic Ideal and Selected Papers* (Wauconda, IL, 1999), esp. Chapters 1 and 2, pp. 1–75.

P. Rose, "Class," in K. Raaflaub and H. Van Wees, eds. *A Companion to Archaic Greece* (Oxford, 2009), pp. 468–482.

Thersites

N. Postlethwaite, "Thersites in the '*Iliad*,'" *Greece and Rome* 35 (1988), pp. 123–136.

12

Gender and Sexuality in Archaic Greece

12.1   Introduction

According to Perikles, the fifth-century BCE Athenian statesman, an Athenian woman should not be spoken of whether for good or evil.[1] Perikles' pronouncement alludes to the disparity between how Greek males and females were expected to behave and thus to the repressive Athenian attitude toward girls and women. While Greek youths and men must court attention for their behavior to be approved of, girls and women were judged most positively for being inconspicuous. At Athens, attention was paid especially to a woman's sexual conduct, before *and* during marriage. Chastity was the all-important basis of honor or dishonor not only for women, but also for male relatives, and so women's lives, especially after reaching child-bearing age, were rigidly monitored and very circumscribed.

Other parts of Archaic Greece actually offer some contrast to this picture at Athens. Sappho, perhaps the most renowned voice from the Archaic period, composed erotic poems which were well-known and apparently well-received in her lifetime and after in her community and the broader Greek world. That reception suggests that expectations of women's conduct were not as repressive in some places in Archaic Greece as they were elsewhere in Greece. In fact, contemporary evidence implies that the lives of Archaic Greek women in some communities were rather different from those in places like Athens. In Sparta and Lokris, women could own land in their own right – a singular source of empowerment different from Athenian women who could not.

12.2   Archaic Greek Females

12.2.1   The Problem of Male Sources: Pandora, Helen, Clytemnestra, Penelope

A good deal of the evidence about Archaic Greek women derives from male authors. Several project such a pronounced negativity as to suggest that what they say is quite distorted. There are few female sources from the period and, while they are indispensable, they tell us much less than we would like to know about them and their lives. Because of that, we supplement what little evidence we have with that from other periods.

Archaic Greece: The Age of New Reckonings, First Edition. Brian M. Lavelle.
© 2020 Brian M. Lavelle. Published 2020 by John Wiley & Sons Ltd.

Hesiod's works seem overcast with a disapproval of women. Pandora is the product of Zeus' anger and requital for Prometheus' theft of fire: she is imagined as punishment for mankind (Box 12.1). The gods contribute various features to her when she is created, all of which, while attractive, are pernicious. Not only is Pandora designed by Zeus to be a bane to man, she brings about all of the evils in the world.

The Pandora-myth explains the genesis of women, but also the gap between human and divine and how evils came into the world of man. The explanation is similar to that in the Old Testament involving Adam and Eve. Eve is blamed for disobeying God, eating from the Tree of Knowledge, and then getting Adam to do the same. In Genesis, all troubles seem to begin with Eve, as they seem to do in the *Theogony* with Pandora. For Hesiod, there is no paradise to lose, but he implies that the world was relatively trouble-free until the "beautiful evil" was created. On closer inspection, though, things are not so black-and-white. Pandora is actually not more responsible for what happens to mankind than Zeus, for it is he who from spite and anger commands that Pandora be fashioned into a "deadly trap." After all, the troubles she unleashes are "gifts" from the gods. Like Eve, Pandora is scapegoated for the flaws in man that, in other myths, explain the separation of God/s and Man.

Pandora's "evil" really comes down to her physical attractiveness. Regarding her, males are overwhelmed by lust and blinded to what lies beneath the beautiful surface. Of course, these are the same charges leveled at Aphrodite – or Helen of Sparta – in whose presence males are utterly disarmed. Pandora is adorned as a bride for her debut: she actually stupefies Epimetheus, Prometheus' much less crafty brother. He cannot resist her charms and so disobeys

---

Box 12.1 Pandora

"To them for fire I shall give an evil, in which
all will delight in their spirit, though they are embracing evil."
So [Zeus] spoke. And the father of men and gods laughed out loud …
And Hephaistos, the famous one, he commanded as quickly as possible
to mix earth with water, and to put in it the voice of a person
and the strength, and to liken it in face to the immortal goddesses
and the beautiful desirable form of a maiden girl. And [he ordered] Athena
to teach her skills, to weave on the intricate loom.
And golden charms [he ordered] Aphrodite to pour around her head,
and painful desire and sorrows that eat at the limbs.
And he ordered Hermes, the Messenger, the Dog-Slayer,
to put into her a dog-mind and a thieving way.
So he spoke. And they obeyed Zeus, the son of Kronos, the lord-king.
…. and [Zeus] called this woman
"Pandora," because all the gods who have homes on Mount Olympos
gave her a gift, a misery for men who labor for their bread.
(Hesiod, Works and Days *57–69, 80–82)*

In the *Theogony*, Pandora is called the "beautiful evil" (line 585). Zeus conceived of her as a deception, concealing evil. She was Zeus' punishment for Prometheus' thievery and deceit, like for like.

Prometheus' directive not to accept any such "gift" from the gods. Pandora's adornments, which include crowns and flowers, emphasize her fertility and readiness for marriage. In the *Homeric Hymn to Aphrodite* (6.6 ff.), Aphrodite is similarly adorned by the Seasons.

Hesiod describes an unsavory paradox for men who would avoid women. He who marries gets only trouble, but he who does not has no caretaker in old age nor heirs to inherit his property. A man who marries a bad wife never sees *any* good, but the man who gets a good wife, gets no better than good and evil mixed. Women stay at home, doing nothing, and yet are fed by their husbands. A woman is not a complete loss, however: she works some – or at least has the capacity to work – and above all is beautiful and so alluring. For Hesiod, though, attractiveness alone is not enough to compensate for the evil with which the gods fashioned Pandora.

Like Pandora's, the "evil" of Helen of Sparta is her beauty – or, rather, the trouble it causes men. From maidenhood, Helen is the center of male competition. Every Greek hero of the Trojan War era wants her for his own. Married to Menelaos, she runs away to Troy with Paris, beguiled by *eros* and Aphrodite. Far more for pride than anything like love, Menelaos must have her back. Consequently he and his brother Agamemnon launch the "thousand ships" to get Helen back and punish the Trojans. After ten years of fighting and the deaths of countless warriors, Greeks and Trojans, and the disruption of thousands of lives, when Troy is in ruins, Helen is finally recovered and Menelaos' male honor salvaged. Surprisingly, for the response she generates, Helen has little *actual* form or feature in the Greek myth and poetry that survives. She seems unwitting of her own power, the placid eye of the storm around which the storm of *eros* spins.

Back in Sparta, Helen and Menelaos are visited by Telemachos, Odysseus' son, who arrives seeking news of his long-lost father (*Odyssey* 4). When Helen sees Telemachos and Menelaos weeping, she thinks to alleviate their sorrow by drugging their wine. Homer says that the very unnatural potion is so powerful that it would prevent even a man who witnessed his brother or son being murdered in front of him from crying. While Helen's intentions may be good, the implications of her action are not entirely so: her powerful drug reminds us of Kirke and her potion which made Odysseus' men powerless by turning them into swine. The potent drugs of Kirke and Helen are in fact metaphors for women's intoxicating power over men, which renders men helpless. Like Pandora, Kirke and Helen are both fascinating and fearful to Greek males because of their attractiveness and what it does to males.

Greek males also suspected that wives could be unfaithful and league with their lovers to destroy them. Clytemnestra, Helen's adulterous half-sister, loathes her husband, Agamemnon, because he murdered their daughter Iphigeneia at Aulis before the Trojan War. While Agamemnon is away at Troy, Clytemnestra takes up with Aegisthos, Agamemnon's enemy. When her husband returns, Clytemnestra slays him, thus realizing the nightmare suspicion of Greek males. Of course, Clytemnestra is punished in turn, but Agamemnon's very dismayed ghost bemoans his lot in the Underworld in the *Odyssey*, comparing his wife unfavorably with Penelope. Although the crime of Clytemnestra and Aegisthos is best known from Aischylos' *Agamemnon*, produced in the mid-450s BCE, Homer mentions it several times in the *Odyssey* as a counterpoint to Penelope's conspicuously good conduct. As Penelope seems to be the best of wives, so is Clytemnestra the worst because she is treacherous.

Yet, even Penelope raises some suspicion in the *Odyssey*. To appearances, Penelope resembles Semonides' "bee"-woman – industrious, devoted to her husband, and chaste. She awaits Odysseus' return faithfully for 20 years, her fidelity apparently never flagging. Penelope's ostensible devotion amounts to a statement of Odysseus' worth: she is the "good woman," the fulfillment of the male fantasy of absolute fidelity. Yet the implicit sense of male distrust of females actually creates the primary drama of the *Odyssey*. There is an implied sexual tension between Penelope and the Suitors who want to replace Odysseus as master of house and kingdom, but also as Penelope's husband. The possibility seems to exist that Penelope might just succumb, especially near the end of the epic.

The female characters of Homer and Hesiod come down essentially to "bad" and "good," defined in terms of male valuations of their beauty and conduct. Pandora epitomizes the negative effect of women upon males in a man's world, inasmuch as she is the embodiment of Zeus' punishment for fire. She deceives, but also captivates by her physical charms. Helen is dangerous because of the trouble she causes by her allure. The powers of captivation which she shares with Kirke can ensnare men, cause them to lose self-control and their gender-identity. Helen and Clytemnestra provide the worst examples as wives, because they betray their marriages, the latter in the worst conceivable way. Penelope, their opposite, is the best of women precisely because she acts in accordance with male wishes. There is much in Homer's Penelope that is over-idealized and drawn from a male perspective. It is worth noting though that Penelope is also "good" because, as we have seen, there is a balance between her and Odysseus. She is intelligent, shrewd, and crafty and out-tricks the trickster in the end. (See Section 12.2.4.)

12.2.2 Voices of Archaic Greek Women

12.2.2.1 Sappho

Sappho's poetry offers rare insight into the thoughts and emotions of an Archaic Greek woman.[2] Her sophisticated skills suggest that she was well-educated and well-trained in poetic composition, and obviously marvelously gifted. Despite the candid content of her personal poetry, she was not marginalized or excluded from her *polis* because of her candor. Sappho composed wedding and ritual songs for her community, which suggests that she was a well-respected member of it.

Relationships are of profound consequence to Sappho. What she says about them seems to be drawn from her own experiences and feelings and appears very real. The poet wants her audience to witness not only the events of her life, but also the intensity of her emotion, inasmuch as her narrative frequently seems to be unfolding in real time (Box 12.2). That intensity is enhanced by the economy of her expression.

Sappho reveals herself as no other Archaic Greek poet had done before and few would do after. She had many female friends with whom she seems to have laughed, danced, loved, and celebrated together. Sappho was also involved in Mytilenaian politics, and perhaps these were discussed when she and her friends got together. She was later exiled from Mytilene for political reasons, proving that although women could not vote in assemblies, they could and did participate in politics.

The evidence about Sappho does not support the idea that Archaic Greek women were always and everywhere confined to homes and limited to domestic and ritual roles. A less well-known female poet, Corinna of Tanagra, composed songs for local festivals for choruses of males or females. She was also a teacher of Pindar.[3] Later, during the Classical period, Praxilla of Sikyon and Telesilla of Argos became famous for composing dithyrambs for community performance. While Sappho, Corinna, Praxilla, and Telesilla are the

Box 12.2 Sappho and Relationships

Kyprian One and Nereids, unharmed to me
grant that my brother come here
and all those things he wants for his spirit,
bring them all to pass.

All those wrongs he did before, let him undo them
and become a welcome friend to friends
and a plague upon his enemies, and may no one become
a grief to us.
And his sister, let him want to bestow
honor [upon her].

(F 5, Campbell)

Oh, I was in love with you, Atthis, a long time ago.
You were to me just a little child – and without charm …

(F 49, Campbell)

"I wish I was dead – I mean it!"
She went away from me crying
so many tears and said this to me:
"Oh my, how awfully we have fared,
Sappho, and I leave you all unwilling."
But I said this back to her:
"Go now with a smile and remember
me. You know how I took care of you.
but if you don't [remember], I want
to remind you …   10
…. and the lovely things we did.
[…]
And on a soft couch   21
delicate …
You loosed your desire …"

(F 94, Campbell)

"Sweet mother, I can no longer weave on the loom,
for I am overcome with longing for a youth by slender Aphrodite."

(F 102, Campbell)

The moon has set,
and the Pleiades, it's the middle
of the night, the hours pass by,
and I sleep alone.

(Fr. Adesp, 976, Campbell)

> F 5 is about Sappho's brother, Charaxos, who had become involved with a courtesan of Naukratis named Rhodopis ("Rosey"). Sappho wants him to leave Rhodopis and come home to Lesbos. The fragment illustrates the close and affectionate bond between Greek brothers and sisters.
>
> F 49 seems to be a parting shot directed at Atthis, who is mentioned elsewhere in Sappho's poems.
>
> F 94 is a tenderer parting, with Sappho's lover in tears. Physical intimacy seems to be mentioned in it.
>
> It is questionable whether, in F 102, Sappho is speaking for herself or for a persona.
>
> F 976 is a beautiful lament about the loneliness of an empty bed. Sappho makes what might seem commonplace extraordinary and very emotionally evocative. (Some scholars do not take the fragment to be by Sappho.)

names of female poets we know, there were surely others whose names we do not know. Their craft and roles as poets made them integral to the lives of their communities. In what other important community roles may Archaic Greek women have functioned routinely? Among others, as priestesses, farm-owners, and farm-workers certainly; as experts in childbirth and child-rearing surely; as practitioners of medicine and healing, and artists and musicians very likely.

12.2.2.2 The *Parthenion* of Alkman of Sparta

While the ***Parthenion***, "the maiden song," was reputedly authored by Alkman, it nevertheless appears to offer a unique glimpse into the lives of Spartan girls of the seventh century BCE. The poetry of Alkman, who may not have been a Spartan by birth, was nevertheless inextricably linked to Sparta. He composed wedding-and other communal songs, but was apparently especially focused on Spartan women. He authored two books of *parthenia* and either one or several on "swimming women." The "maiden song" is remarkable for preserving what purports to be exchanges between Spartan girls vying in song and dance.[4]

The fragment we possess was composed in the second half of the seventh century BCE and performed at a Spartan festival, perhaps that of Artemis Orthia. A chorus of Spartan girls begins by singing of the many sons of the Spartan king Hippokoön who were killed by Kastor and Polydeukes. It turns away from that myth and its warning against *hybris*, however, to what seem to be much lighter topics, including praise for two beautiful Spartan girls, Agido and Hegesichora (Box 12.3). This portion of the song is delivered in a breezy, rambling, almost conversational manner.

While the maidens offer an episode of Spartan mythic history and a moral at the beginning of the poem, they change to remark on – and even express – their feelings for one another as the song goes on. They seem to speak freely about infatuations and charms: there may in fact be an erotic overtone with Hagesichora as a fantasy focus.[5] Alkman's *Parthenion* suggests that in Sparta young girls were not only free to engage in such infatuations, but also to sing about them in performance before the entire community. Choruses, which were so vital to social and religious functions in Archaic Greek *poleis* and villages, brought boys, girls, men, and women together to sing and dance and others to watch them.

Box 12.3 Alkman's *Parthenion*

[...]
But I sing
the radiant light of Agido: I see   40
her like the sun, which for us
Agido calls forth
to shine. But our brilliant chorus-leader
permits me neither to praise
nor to blame her at all.   45
For she herself seems to be
matchless as if one were
to set a horse among herd animals,
a courser, a wind-swift thunderer
from the dreams you dream beneath rock-shade.   50

Don't you see her? The swift
Enetic one? The hair
of my cousin
Hagesichora blossoms forth
like gold unmixed,   55
her silvery face …
Why should I speak so obviously?
That is Hagesichora.
second after Agido in appearance,
as a Kolaxian to an Ibenian she would run.   60
For the Pleaides rise up and fight with us
bearing the plough to Orthia through the ambrosial night
just as the Sirius Star rises.

Our purple cloth
isn't good enough to save us,   65
nor our dappled snake-shaped bracelets
all of gold, nor the hairband
from Lydia, for girls
with violet eyes an adornment,
nor Nanno's hair   70
nor again the goddess-look of Arete,
nor Sylakis or Kleësisera,
nor running to Ainesimbrota's [house] will you say:
"Let Astyphis be mine"
or "Let Philylla look toward me"   75
or "Damareta" or "lovely Wiantehmis."
But Hagesichora wears me out (or guards me).

Yet she of the beautiful ankles
Hagesichora is not here   80

> but by Agido …
> …. and looks approvingly on our rites.
> But you receive their prayers, you gods:
> for their fulfillment and accomplishment
> are of the gods. Dance-leader,
> I can say that, I a maiden, am   85
> hooting like an owl
> from the roof-beams, but Aotis especially
> I will sing to please.
> For from pain
> she is our healer.
> Because of Hagesichora, girls   90
> come to their desired peace.
>
>   (F 1, 39–91 *PMG*)

12.2.2.3 Documentary Evidence

Documentary evidence about Archaic Greek women is sparse indeed. What little survives derives mainly from votive or funerary inscriptions which more often reflect the sentiments of loved ones than of the women themselves. Nevertheless, we gain valuable information about relations between women and their families from them.

The inscription on the Nikandre *kore* (Chapter 8.3.5, Figure 8.19) names a woman from a wealthy and notable Naxian family:

> Nikandre dedicated me to the far-shooter who delights in arrows, the daughter of Deinodikes of Naxos, far above others, sister of Deinomenes, wife of Phraxos.

Nikandre's connections to father, brother, and husband are highlighted in the inscription but her name is the first to appear and most prominent. It is *her* dedication to the goddess, not theirs: their pride derives from connections to her "far above others."

Similar in its highlighting is Phrasikleia (Chapter 8.3.5, Figure 8.21). Upon the statue-base the following is written:

> The tomb-marker of Phrasikleia: "*kore*" I shall be called always instead of "married woman," taking that name by the will of the gods. Aristion of Paros made me.

The inscription calls out to the passer-by to stop and think about Phrasikleia and her fate. It is meant to evoke pity because the maiden did not live to see her marriage day, the happiest ancient Greeks could imagine for a girl or woman. Such markers and inscriptions were not rare in ancient Greece.

An inscription from the base of the Phaidimos *kore*, *c.* 540 BCE, from Attika (NM 81), says that Phile's father set up the monument, "beautiful to behold," for his daughter. Still another inscription (*CEG* 119) from the early fifth century BCE in Thessaly was set up by a grieving father and mother for their infant daughter, Thessalia:

> A mere baby, I died, nor yet did I take the flower of my youth
> but I came early to Acheron of the many tears.
> This memorial, her father, Kleodamos, the son of Hyperanor,
> stood up for their daughter Thessalia, and Korona, her mother.

And finally, again from the early fifth century BCE from Thasos (*CEG* 161):

> Look you, this beautiful monument her father stood up for the dead Learete: for on her
> still living we shall look no more.

The emotional connection of father and daughter is evident in the doting of King Alkinoös upon Nausikaa, who addresses her father as "daddy dear" (*Odyssey* 6.57). When she asks for a mule-cart to take her to the river so that she might wash clothes, Alkinoös responds (6.68): "Neither will I deny you the mule-cart, my child, nor anything else."

Archaic Greek mothers and daughters seem to have been deeply emotionally connected. A brief, very beautiful poem of Sappho (F 132 Campbell) is about her daughter, Kleis:

> I have a child as beautiful as golden flowers
> and she has such a lovely form, my so beloved Kleis.
> For her I would not take all of Lydia …

Archaic Greek girls spent perhaps most of their time before marriage with their mothers (Hesiod, *Works and Days* 520).

The law of Lokris, dating from the last quarter of the sixth century BCE, involves inheritance and partition of lands.[6] While the son of a family is given primacy to inherit land, if there is no son, the inheritance goes to the *kore*. Of significance, too, is the fact that the land initially apportioned does not belong solely to the father, but "to the parents," that is, both mother and father. Women could thus be landowners in Lokris, just as they were in Sparta. Citizenship and status in communities were based on land-ownership; choice and freedom also attend it. A Spartan or Lokrian woman was free to marry, but also free *not* to marry if she chose. We note, however, that, on the evidence, women were not allowed to be voting citizens in any Archaic Greek *polis*.

If we had only the evidence from such as Hesiod and Semonides, our vision of the lives and relationships of Archaic Greek girls and women would be quite distorted. In fact, there is further literary evidence to the contrary. Theognis, for example, says to his friend (1225–1226): "Nothing, Kyrnos, is sweeter than a good wife.//I know. Witness my truth for yourself." "Wedded bliss" even for the crabby Megarian! On the other hand, Hesiod and Semonides were not just "outliers": social practices affecting ancient Greek women especially in places like Athens were distinctly repressive.

12.2.3 Childhood and Maidenhood

Archaic Greek mothers bore children at home presumably with family women and neighbor-women attending. The physical condition of the child – and the financial situation of the parents – influenced whether it would live or die after birth. Greeks exposed infants as birth control and, if it was so decided, a baby could be abandoned to die. At Athens, five to seven days after birth – when the child was seen to be viable by its parents – it was ritually introduced into the household and presented to the *genos* and wider community for approval. A hearth ceremony occurred inside the home with the father of the children presiding, while a strip of wool or olive sprig was hung outside to announce the birth to the neighbors. Babies were named then, and a girl might be named after a relative, perhaps the maternal or paternal grandmother.

Very early childhood for girls was not so different from that of boys. Children were primarily under their mothers' care. Some like Sappho and the others, however, must have received extraordinary education perhaps very early on. Girls also participated in religious rituals from an early age.

Menarchy brought restrictions to the lives of girls. Activities were more closely monitored, and what a girl was permitted before, such as fetching water from a public fountain house or spring or even being alone, was now chaperoned. Between menarchy and marriage, unmarried girls played important roles in community rituals. Anything that drew attention to the girl's physical and sexual maturity was avoided except, it seems, on specified occasions.

12.2.3.1   Archaic *Korai* and the Idealized Maiden

Archaic Greek conceptions of female youth, fertility, and physical attractiveness inform the *kore*-type. Sculptors aimed to capture what was considered the acme of a person's physical life, that is, just after puberty. Many *korai* seem dressed as for a wedding, even as Pandora is depicted in Hesiod. The sexuality of later *korai* especially is intensified by increasingly diaphanous clothing and the drawing of the *chiton* tightly round the lower body, thus enhancing the shape of the legs and buttocks. The sculptors appear to be aiming at portraying an idealization that incorporated aesthetics, "sex appeal," and a kind of abstraction or mystique, if not divinity.[7]

Some Archaic Greek literature focuses similarly on the physical appearance of maidens. In the *Parthenion*, the female chorus praises the superlative forms, hair, faces, and even the ankles of Agido and Hegesichora. Hesiod interrupts his description of the harsh winter month of Lenaion in the *Works and Days* (519–523) to describe what a maiden does within the house then:

> [Boreas' force] does not blow through the tender-skinned virgin-girl //who stays beside her loving mother within the house, not yet knowing the works of very golden Aphrodite.// Washing well her delicate skin and anointing herself with sleek oil she lies down to sleep deep within the house.

The same kind of voyeuristic fascination seems in play in the description of Nausikaa who cavorts with maid-servants by the river where they have gone to wash clothes (*Odyssey* 6.96–98): "When they had washed and anointed themselves with sleek oil, then they ate their lunch beside the bank of the river, waiting for the clothes to dry by the sun's ray." Nausikaa leads the maidens in singing and dancing and is compared to the beautiful, but untouchable Artemis (*Odyssey* 6.101 ff.). Such male fascination portrayed at a distance is partially explained by social standards: maidens were off-limits to males and could only be seen from afar before marriage in most places in Archaic and Classical Greece. The *Parthenion*, however, shows that maiden beauty may have had ritual significance for the community of Sparta.

As the praises for Hagesichora and Agido, *korai* may represent an effort to gain favor from the gods for individuals, but also perhaps for the community in general. The statues were sacred dedications after all: most of the Archaic Athenian *korai* discovered were votives to

Athena on the *akropolis*. Notwithstanding their connection to the virgin goddess, Athenian *korai* become increasingly more sensual in appearance through the Archaic period. What can account for these changes?

12.2.4 Marriage and Family

Around the age of 7, a girl began actively to assist her mother with domestic chores and so learn what Archaic Greeks must have considered essential for females. These included spinning, weaving, and cooking. Evidence from the fourth century BCE suggests that further "training" for a girl occurred in her husband's household. In Xenophon's *Oikonomikos* (7.4–6), Ischomachos, an Athenian, converses with Sokrates who asks: "Did you yourself instruct your wife to be such as she must be, or did you get her from her father and mother already knowing the things she must to keep house properly"? To which Ischomachos replies, "And what could she have known when I took her to wife, Sokrates? She came to me not yet fifteen years old and before that lived under great supervision, such that she saw, heard, and said as little as possible." Ischomachos goes on to say that the unnamed girl knew only spinning, weaving, and how to check her appetite. According to the girl, she learned only to be chaste from her mother. Hesiod in *Works and Days* (699) urges Perses to marry a virgin "so that you may teach her 'discreet habits.'" The implication is that such male "training" included topics of household management, but also of sexuality. Girls were not to hear any talk about sex before their marriages – a topic that older women discussed a great deal – and it was apparently left to the girl's husband to inform her. This agrees with Herodotos' story of the maiden wife of the Athenian tyrant Peisistratos who apparently knew nothing about sexual intercourse upon marrying him (1.61.1–2): she had certainly not discussed the subject with her mother!

Girls were married soon after menarchy, *c.* age 13–15. Hesiod (*Works and Days* 698) urges Perses to marry a girl "in the fifth year" after menstruation, that is, about 17 or 18, but Ischomachos' wife was only 14 at marriage. A law from Gortyn in Crete, dated around the mid-fifth century BCE, implies that girls there were marriageable at the age of 12. Males were much older when they married.

Marriages were arranged between male members of households. In the time of Homer, a groom would literally buy his bride by offering wedding gifts to the father proving his worth and the seriousness of his suit (Box 12.4). The memory of competitions for particularly desirable brides even in the Archaic period is preserved in the story of the contest for Agariste, the daughter of Kleisthenes, tyrant of Sikyon (Herodotos 6.126–130), although it seems to be mostly fictitious. Practical advantages undoubtedly won out in the end and the pact between *oikoi* was formalized by oaths. The bride entered her new household with a dowry of some type.

How much participation the maiden had in the choice of her marriage partner is unclear, but indications are that it was very little.

The wedding ritual marked a fundamental transition for bride and groom. The wedding began at the bride's family home with feasting, moved to the groom's house, and finished there with the bride ritually accepting her new role and status as wife. The transition was symbolized in different ways. When the final feast occurred at her family's house, before she left it, the bride cut a lock of hair, an offering of mourning, but also of separation from maidenhood. The couple made its way through the *polis* with much singing and dancing to the home of the groom, with the groom leading the bride. The bride was veiled, but the veil was raised at the appropriate

---

Box 12.4 Weddings

> In one [*polis*], there were weddings and banquets
> and brides from the chambers under the sparkling torchlights
> they were leading up through the town, and the wedding song rose loudly,
> and the young men-dancers were whirling, and among them
> the flutes and harps kept up the music. And the married women,
> standing in their doorways, were enraptured, each one of them.
>
> *(Homer, Iliad 18.491–496)*

A substantial portion of the community seems to participate in the wedding celebration in Homer's *Iliad*, if only as passive witnesses to the nuptial procession. Certainly loud and demonstrative parades through the *polis* were meant to draw attention and so publicize and legitimize the union before the community. The description of dancing matches many Archaic vase-paintings: several show men and women dancing together in a circle as if for a wedding – one of the rare occasions apparently when such integrated dancing could occur.

---

time to signify her new status as wife. At the groom's house, rituals of arrival preceded the marriage's consummation which was marked by a crowd singing and shouting outside the marriage chamber (Box 12.5).

Child-bearing and child-rearing were primary focuses of marriage for ancient Greek women. There is little information about conditions affecting pregnancy and childbirth in the ancient world, but pregnant women were not helped in gestation, labor, and birth by lack of hygiene, drugs, or extensive medical knowledge. A famous pronouncement by Medea in Euripides' *Medea* (250–251) underscores the rigors of childbirth for ancient Greek women: "Three times beside a shield I would rather stand than give birth once!" A woman's best helpers were other women of the family and community who were experienced and could act as midwives.

Women were responsible for the household in general. They brought water from fountain houses, springs, or rivers to their homes in the early morning for use during the day. Presumably that is also when they washed clothes, as Princess Nausikaa did before encountering Odysseus on the riverbank. Penelope's primary task seems to have been weaving. There are several vase-paintings from the Archaic period that depict women weaving everything from small things to what appear to be sizeable cloths.

While women in places like Athens were essentially prohibited from moving about outside of their homes as they pleased, they were allowed the company of other women. Athenian vase-paintings of the Classical period show women together apparently in the homes of each other (Box 12.6). See current Boxes 12.6 and 12.7. Sappho certainly had female friends frequently about her, and the girls of the *Parthenion* seem to know each other pretty well.

The *Odyssey* highlights the ingredients of the best marriage in the words of Odysseus to Nausikaa who wants him to stay and marry her (*Odyssey* 6.180–185):

> May the gods give you all those things that you long for in your heart,// a husband and a household and a like-mindedness//which is excellent. For there is nothing stronger or better//than when those united in thought and purpose hold a household,// a husband and wife. Many griefs they give to their enemies,//many joys to those who are their friends. They know it especially.

Box 12.5 Wedding Procession: Bride and Groom Riding to Groom's House

Figure 12.1 Wedding procession, Attic B-F *lekythos*, attributed to the Amasis Painter, *c.* 550–530 BCE.

Bride and groom ride in a cart accompanied by others. Out in front, a woman with torches precedes the cortege. The groom's mother waits in the doorway of the groom's house to welcome her new daughter-in-law to her home to-be.

Harmony, Odysseus' wish for Nausikaa and her husband-to-be, is generally prescribed in Greek literature as the basis for a good marriage.

12.2.5 Ritual and Religion

While a good deal of the evidence for the participation of women in rituals concerns Athens, women elsewhere in Greece will have participated significantly both privately and publicly. In Athens, in the fifth century BCE, girls took part in religious rites on behalf of the *polis* from the age of 7 to maidenhood with basket-carrying in the Panathenaic procession. Although virginity was an important element in rituals involving girls, ritual participation did not end with marriage. A festival restricted to Athenian women, the *Thesmophoria* honoring Demeter, occurred in November, around the time for planting. A piglet's remains formerly deposited in the clefts of the Pnyx were retrieved, mixed with grain, and planted in the fields to increase their fertility. Female participants were the necessary mediums between Athenians and the earth for making the magic work. During the *Anthesteria*, in late February, in a very ancient ritual, the ***basilinna***, the wife of the archon *basileus*, attended by Athenian women, became the wife of Dionysos by ritually mating with the "god" in the *Boukoleion* near the *prytaneion*.[8] It is presumed that the part of Dionysos was played by none other than the archon himself!

Women were also cult-priestesses. Athena's "house" on the *akropolis* was stewarded by a priestess, as was the cult of Athena *Nike* there. The priestess of Athena's "house" was literally its protector. It was she who forbade Kleomenes of Sparta entry because he was a Dorian. Such custodians of goddess-shrines are found elsewhere in Greece. Some cults required that priestesses be virginal. At Delphi, an older woman who became the *Pythia* had to be celibate from the beginning of her service.

12.2.6 Summary

The statements of Hesiod and Semonides about women might lead us to believe that Archaic Greek males were misogynists. The former seems to blame Pandora – and all women – for the evils in the world, while the latter likens females to animals. Counter-evidence shows

---

Box 12.6 Women at the Fountain House

Figure 12.2 Women at fountain house, Attic B-F *Hydria*, attributed to the class of Hamburg 1917.477, *c.* 510–500 BCE.

Women meet and converse with one another as they come and go from the fountain house. The woman on the right watches as her hydria fills with water issuing from a bronze lion's head spout embedded in the fountain house-wall.

that such negativity was not pervasive. Contemporary inscriptions demonstrate that fathers, brothers, and husbands proudly and affectionately proclaimed their affinities to daughters, sisters, and wives. Moreover, at least some women like Sappho were very conspicuous in their communities and apparently highly respected. This is not to say that women in Archaic Greece did not encounter misogyny or were not maltreated, but rather that the picture is not as grim as we might infer from Hesiod and Semonides and social practice at Athens. Sappho candidly revealed her own emotions, erotic feelings, and intimate connections to other women but remained the poet of Mytilene (see Box 12.7). See current Boxes 12.6 and 12.7. She was one among perhaps other female poets in the Archaic period.[9] Helen's knowledge of concoctions meant to allay pain might suggest that women were practitioners of medicine; they were certainly midwives. While it is true that women could not hold office or vote, voting and office-holding were reserved in fact for those who fought for the community and no one else. Women performed indispensable roles in cults implicated with the *polis*. While

---

Box 12.7 Wedding-Songs of Sappho

> High up the roof beam!
> Sing Hymenaios!
> Raise it high, builder men!
> Sing Hymenaios!
> The bridegroom comes in, the equal to Ares,
> much greater than the greatest man!
> (F 111, S&A)

> Blest bridegroom, the wedding you begged the gods for
> is made! You have the girl you prayed for.
> Your body is so charming, your eyes …
> are gentle, desire is all over your face.
> Aphrodite honors you like no man.
> (F 112 S&A)

> "Maidenhood, my maidenhood, where have you gone
> after you left me?"
> "Never again will I come to you, never again."
> (F 114 S&A)

The bittersweet nature of marriage for Archaic Greeks is portrayed in the last lines. Marriage is sad because a girl is leaving behind her innocence and family, closing one portion of her life forever. But it is also joyful because she is entering upon a new life that should bring its own happiness with a home that is her own, a husband, and children – apparently all that Archaic Greeks imagined happiness to be for a woman. The marriage ritual thus seems symmetrical: the leave-taking from the family home resembles the death ritual with its lock-cutting by the bride; the arrival is punctuated by happy songs and reminders of a new life as if the girl was thought to have been reborn.

repressive conditions are in evidence in Classical Athens, and Archaic Athens is likely to have been much the same, at Sparta, Lokris, Mytilene, and elsewhere in Greece, things were rather different.

12.3 Archaic Greek Males

12.3.1 Childhood and Youth

In Athens, inclusion for males depended upon community recognition and the approval of a boy as legitimately Athenian. Presentation of a child to the family and community soon after birth was an important initial step, but really only the first of the rituals leading to full citizenship – the age when the boy could take his place in the phalanx. Eligible male infants, along with newlywed women, whose community status was vital for birth legitimacy, were recognized at Athens at the once-yearly festival of the *Apatouria*; boys were presented and recognized as citizens by their *demes* at 17 or 18. Such presentations were in fact common throughout ancient Greece.

Age seven seems to have been a watershed for Greek boys more generally. Formal education could begin then, although, with the exception of Sparta, it does not appear to have been institutionalized in the Archaic period. Rather, schooling seems have depended upon individual *oikoi*. Phoinix, a fugitive in the house of Peleus, the father of Achilles, and surrogate parent in his own estimation, remarks in the *Iliad* (9.442) that he was appointed Achilles' teacher by Peleus. In myth, Achilles' tutor and that of many other mythical heroes was the centaur Cheiron. Of course, special circumstances attended Greek heroes, and Archaic Greek boys were more likely educated by males of the household or *genos*.

Apart from learning about livelihood from fathers, whether farming, sailing, fishing, merchantry, crafts, or something else, education seems to have focused on proficiency in war-training and public-speaking. Such proficiency was in fact superlatively located in Achilles, the idealized, indeed, impossible model for all ancient Greek boys. In the Archaic period, becoming a warrior entailed acquiring general dexterity, facility with weapons, and experience moving in unison with others in the phalanx. To gain them, youths assembled on designated grounds, such as the precincts of Hekademos and Kynosarges just outside of Athens, first to exercise together – running, throwing, and wrestling. Older ones then learned to wield the shield, spear, and sword. Such training was most intense in Sparta where, from the age of seven, boys were trained primarily for war. Aristotle (*Politics* 1338b, 25 ff.) observed that Spartan superiority in hoplite warfare was due not to their differences in training methods, but to the fact that they trained *all the time*.

Young men at Sparta, Athens, and elsewhere in Greece also learned singing and dancing (Box 12.8). Some of the movements, such as the pyrrhic dance, were directly war-related, but others helped with agility and endurance. Spartans were required to sing war-songs as they marched into battle, some of which originated in the verses of Tyrtaios. Such training was by no means limited to Sparta. Hippokleides, an aristocratic Athenian, is said to have excelled all other Greeks of his time in singing, dancing, and performing athletic feats. Hippokleides might represent more an ideal aristocratic model than an ordinary Athenian, but such skills remained at the core of Greek male education through the Classical period. Young men

---

Box 12.8 Youth Playing a Lyre

Figure 12.3 Youth playing a lyre, Attic Red-Figure *chous*, attributed to the Berlin Painter, *c.* 510–500 BCE.

A youth plays a lyre while a boy looks on. Perhaps the boy is being instructed in how to play the instrument.

---

became full warriors at 20 and served actively to the age of 60 when, like the Trojan elders, they were physically unable to fight effectively.

Public speaking was not particularly prized at Sparta in the Classical period; it was said the word "laconic" derives from Lakonia, the region where Sparta was located. But it was very important elsewhere. In the *Iliad* and the *Odyssey*, proficiency in speaking is already linked to prestige and power: the *agora*, where *politai* speak and listen to others, is "honor-bestowing" (*Iliad* 1. 490). Solon attests to competitions among speakers for political power as early as 600 BCE at Athens. After the introduction of democracy there, skill in oratory was essential for anyone aspiring to political office, prestige, and honor. Sparta's devaluation of public-speaking may in fact have been overstated, since decisions about policy were being made in the assembly long after the Second Messenian War.

12.3.2 Marriage and Family

Around 30 seems to have been the ordinary marriage age for Greek males, although Homeric heroes and others seemed to have married rather earlier.[10] Waiting to marry allowed a man to establish himself and his household and so to become more attractive as a bridegroom to the bride's father or guardian. Men were responsible for the viability of the *oikos*, but also for its status in the community. Fathers presented children to neighbors and relations and made the ultimate decisions that affected the household, including life or death ones. Yet sources do not seem to imply a one-sided domestic "tyranny."

Respect and regard for parents were expected. When Telemachos, trying so hard to come of age in the *Odyssey*, is about to string his father's bow for the contest proposed by Penelope, Odysseus signals him to hold off. The boy stops immediately, thus demonstrating utmost respect for his father (*Odyssey* 21.125–129), for he could clearly have strung the bow of Odysseus. (Of course, the plot also requires him to desist!) Heroes and even "bit players" in the *Iliad* are many times compared to their fathers and warned that they should do them proud by excelling them. Hektor's famous prayer for his son Astyanax is that the boy will outshine his father (*Iliad* 6.476–481). The potency of father-figures and the respect given them generally are demonstrated in the characters of Priam and Nestor, and echoed by Alkaios of Mitylene, *c.* 600 BCE: "... and let us not shame [by cowardice] //excellent fathers who [lie] beneath the earth."[11] Sons were responsible for taking care of fathers.[12] Although, by contrast, Telemachos seems rather sharp with his mother, Penelope, in *Odyssey* Book 1, his impertinence is really more a sign of his unnaturally prolonged adolescence than it is indicative of usual conditions. Hektor in the *Iliad* is very respectful and deferential to his mother Hekabe.

12.3.3 Ritual and Religion

Greek boys and men functioned in myriad cults and rituals affecting both household and *polis*, some involving gods, others heroes. Priesthoods were family- or clan-owned and hereditary; some cults were at least as old as the Bronze Age. In Book 3 of the *Odyssey*, Nestor, home from the Trojan War, presides over a massive bull-sacrifice to Poseidon on the beach at Pylos. Such sacrifices and feasting continued at major festivals such as at Olympia and at Athens for the *Panathenaia*. Priests of Athena, Dionysos and Apollo at Athens were significant functionaries in *polis* cults which brought with them considerable prestige and honor.

12.3.4 Social Life: *Philia* and *Symposia*

The *symposion* was a formal drinking-party for males, never females, of the community. For it, couches for reclining were brought together in the male quarter of the house, garlands distributed to guests, and a hymn sung to Dionysos. The symposiasts drank wine mixed with water according to the host's wishes. Greek wine was very strong when unmixed, so the usual proportion was one measure of undiluted wine to three of water. There were drinking games like **kottabos** – throwing the dregs from one's shallow drinking cup into a vase or urn set up between couches – which, as drinking games do, encouraged inebriation. In his F 93, the Classical comic poet Euboulos has Dionysos say that three drinks is quite enough at a *symposion*.[13] Abstemiousness was not the rule, for Dionysos alludes to symposiasts drinking up to ten draughts of wine, which if served in a capacious cup of the period would amount to nearly 2.5 liters! Many vase-paintings of the late Archaic period, such as those of Euphronios (Munich 8935), Smikros (Brussels 200102), and Euthymides (Munich 2307), celebrate inebriation.

During the drinking, conversation could turn to political, social, intellectual, or business topics. *Symposia* were also venues to hear and sing poetic verses and drinking and other songs.

There was also flute-playing by slave girls and, as the drinking continued, sex with paid sex workers, sometimes including the flute-girls or others.

Imported into Greece from the east, the *symposion* seems to have been the province of the *aristoi* to begin with. By the second half of the sixth century BCE, however, even householders of moderate means, it seems, could convene *symposia*. Attic pottery of the late Archaic period through to the early fifth century is full of symposiastic scenes, including highly charged sexual ones.

12.3.5 Summary

While the lives of Greek men were more self-determined and freer than those of Greek women, they were also restricted by community expectation. The possibilities for social recognition and reward were much greater: a male could advance in estimation if not in social station. The risks, however, were high. War dominated the lives of Archaic Greek men, and the real test of a man's worth was what he did in battle. For an adult male to gain and keep status in his community – to be a citizen – he must stand and fight with others to protect the *polis* or advance its interests. Those who did not do so lost status in the *polis*.

12.4 Sex, Gender, and Archaic Greek Society

12.4.1 Introduction: "Secret Sex" and Open Encounters

Though Archaic Greek standards regarding sexual behavior seem to have been strict, they do not appear to have been strictly followed. Adultery is a common theme in Greek myth: the stories involving Aphrodite, Helen, and Clytemnestra, among others, might be taken to reflect its frequency.[14] Illicit sexual "encounters" are also mentioned in Archaic poetry. Mimnermos' mention of "secret sex ... and bed" implies that clandestine trysts occurred regularly: Archilochos' seduction of Neoboule's apparently maiden sister (F 196a) seems furtive and inappropriate, if not criminal.[15] Tales of the misdeeds and punishments of mythical characters were reinforcements of moral and ethical standards, which were apparently easily broken.

As in Greek village society until recently, much could be gotten away with provided it did not become public. Common knowledge of sexual misconduct, especially for females, could result in permanent and dire consequences. Even an unsubstantiated rumor could ruin the reputation and so the honor of a girl, her family, and even her entire *genos*. Since the sexual conduct of females reflected on males and their honor, the latter were required to avenge any dishonor, as was the case for Harmodios and his sister.

There was certainly a double standard as males seem to have been encouraged to engage freely in sex and to talk about it. While Penelope sits at home and waits, Odysseus beds two demi-goddesses, Kirke and Kalypso. Kalypso promises him immortality if he will stay with her and have sex every night, while Kirke finds him so irresistible that she wants him almost immediately after he arrives. Archilochos' publication of his encounter with Neoboule's sister was a boast, but it may also have been part of the invective directed at the family. Did Archilochos' desire to vaunt over and so ridicule Neoboule and her family result in a fictionalized "encounter"?[16] That would certainly be in keeping with the psychology of an adolescent-minded male.

Greek females were powerful in gauging the manliness of Greek males. Hektor feared that, if he did not face Achilles, he could become a laughingstock among the Trojan women. Of course, diminution of the manliness of Menelaos is all-but-explicit in Helen's flight with Paris: the Trojan seems the "better man." But that implication is only temporary, for Helen's withering disdain for Paris' manliness (*Iliad* 3.428 ff.) reinstates Menelaos as the "better man." Spartan women were in fact the most conspicuous and powerful judges of manliness in Archaic and Classical Greece.

12.4.2   *Eros*

Sappho's very frank list of symptoms of love-sickness (F 31) aligns with others observed by later Greek poets. Euripides' famous portrayal of a fevered Phaedra prostrate and dying because of unrequited passion for her step-son Hippolytos seems, in some ways, an elaboration on Sappho F 31. As with Phaedra, Helen's erotic attraction to Paris was created by Aphrodite. Helen knew better than to run off with Paris, but did so anyway as a prisoner to her lust. When she sees Paris in bed, brought clear from battle with Menelaos by the intervention of Aphrodite, "like a groom new from the wedding dance," Helen is revulsed and insults him. But then, quite suddenly, she reverses herself, succumbing to Paris' physical appeal and her own desire, and joins him in bed.

The power of *eros* was not confined to Greek females. In fact, Pandora, like Helen, Aphrodite-on-earth, personifies male lust-objectification. Hesiod states that the sight of Pandora, costumed and adorned by Aphrodite, so captivated both gods and men that they were hopelessly smitten (*Theogony* 588–589). Homer indexes Helen's famously disarming beauty similarly. When Helen approaches the wall of Troy and the Trojan elders, they say in reaction: "It is no outrage that the Trojans and well-greaved Achaians//suffer so many griefs for such a long time for the sake of such a woman.//For terribly like the immortal goddesses is she in beauty of face" (*Iliad* 3.156–158). Their aged pulses beat more quickly at the approach of this earthly Aphrodite. It is of course lust that beguiles and misleads – the old men of Troy quickly collect themselves, since lust is only a fleeting memory for them. That female beauty could produce such lack of control thoroughly frightened Greek males of the Archaic and Classical period.

Warnings about lust are voiced to prevent men from erring and falling into the "deadly trap" of *eros*. Hesiod admonishes (*Works and Days* 373–374): "Don't let a woman with her hips decked out deceive you,//a wily coaxer, a seeker after your grain." The connection between Hesiod's reference and the garments of Archaic *korai* drawn tightly round their hips is here noticeable.[17] Sappho, too, is said to have been very vexed that her brother Charaxos was enthralled sexually by the courtesan Doricha of Naukratis (F 15b Campbell). Charaxos was hardly alone among ancient Greek males in squandering his wealth upon *hetairai*.

Although some courtesans were renowned, like Doricha, there were many other anonymous female sex-workers. Symposium flute-girls and other **pornai** ("prostitutes") worked for little recompense by comparison. Some very graphic vase-paintings of the late Archaic period depict what appear to be such prostitutes in a variety of sexual acts; many of these depictions were apparently intended to stimulate male *symposiasts*. Prostitutes, like slaves and foreigners, were unclassed as citizens and lived on the margins of society presumably in larger *poleis* and ports like Corinth, Peiraios, and Miletos.

The paths for men to pursue their lusts were far more numerous than for women. In fact, Greek women were prohibited such pursuits. The famous complaint of Medea about a woman's confinement to one man as husband, the "master of [her] body," was composed much later than the Archaic period, but could apply to it (Euripides, *Medea* 244–247): "Whenever a man is discontented with those inside the house//he can go abroad and stop his heart from distress.// But we women are forced to look to one [man], one alone." Social convention mandating "married chastity" precluded women from even suggesting lust for a man, even her husband. Yet some Greek women seem to have spoken freely about sex. If we were to judge by the content of her poetry, Sappho and her coterie in Mytilene were uninhibited; so, too, the Spartan girls in the *Parthenion* who might allude to sex in their song. At Athens and other places in Greece, unmarried girls were not permitted to hear or know about sex before their marriages.

There are many Greek myths that portray adultery, and adultery laws suggest its actual frequency. What did not come to law, however, may have far exceeded what did. The nurse in Euripides' *Hippolytos* (462–463) asks her *eros*-stricken mistress Phaedra: "How many men, who hold a good measure of common sense, see their marriage-beds defiled, but *seem* not to see it?" The nurse implies that what is contrary to standard cannot be prevented but can at least be kept hidden and that the marriage can go on (466). Later sources indicate that cuckolded husbands were less put off by the actual adultery of their wives than by the risk that their bloodline might be tainted by illegitimacy or that they might lose their wives' affection.

12.4.3 Same-Sex Relationships

Segregation of males and females in Archaic and Classical Greece and the association of sexually mature men with men or boys and women with women or girls encouraged same-sex encounters. As we have seen, Sappho freely discussed erotic attractions to other females. Again, the girl-chorus of the *Parthenion* declare unabashedly the physical attributes of other girls and might allude very briefly to sexual gratification. Such female relationships were safe because they entailed no real social consequences and did not involve male competition or honor.

Male same-sex relations in Archaic and Classical Greece appear to have been predominantly pederastic with temporary erotic unions formed between older men and youths. Such unions were said to be conducive to the education and training of boys in middle adolescence. The focus of some Archaic Greek homoerotic verse and art on the physical aspects of pederastic sex, however, suggests that, although there were said to be other loftier aspects to such relationships, the erotic ones were actually paramount. The idealized late adolescent type seems to be represented in the Archaic *kouroi*.

Attachments of the **erastes** ("lover") to the **eromenos** ("beloved") began when the former was between the ages of 20 and 30 and the latter from about the age of puberty to 17. The *erastes* pursued the *eromenos* with gifts and attention; *eromenoi* were apparently flattered by the pursuit and gratified by the gifts. The older male's role was to be dominant and so masculine; the younger, yielding but not to the point of submissiveness. Indeed, there are Archaic Greek vase paintings which depict couples gazing at one another face to face, the *erastes* touching the genitals of the boy with one hand and his chin with the other. Sanctioned copulation was inter-crural, that is, between the thighs. It was important for the future *polites*, the *eromenos*, not to be "womanly" by allowing actual penetration. Should it occur, it was not to be mentioned; it was never to be desired. In some places in Archaic Greece, male same-sex courtship could be ritualized and resemble pre-marriage practice. In Dorian Crete, the *erastes* abducted the *eromenos*, remaining with him away in the mountains for an extended period. Such abduction finds mythical parallel in the story of Zeus' abduction of Ganymede. Same-sex relationships in Archaic and Classical Greece were limited in most places it seems. For the *erastes*, marriage, which brought with it different focuses of home, wife, and family, ended the relationship. For the *eromenos*, maturity reversed the role as he might become an *erastes*.

Same-sex relationships that carried on into adulthood were not sanctioned in places like Athens, but were in others like Sparta. Conditions there prolonged the period of males being almost exclusively in the company of other males. The Spartan practice of stealing into the marriage-chamber in the darkness, having a new wife wear her hair short and wrapped in a man's cloak, suggest that the primary sexual partners of Spartan males were other Spartan males.[18]

Achilles and Patroklos are often cited as same-sex lovers. The extravagant grief of Achilles in the wake of Patroklos' death in the *Iliad* has been taken to depict his deep emotional attach-ment to Patroklos. There are some indications in Archilochos' poetry of male same-sex rela-tions, but most evidence comes from later Archaic poets. Solon (F 25) says: "... while one still wants a boy in the lovely flowering of youth// longing for thighs and sweeter lips." Theognis states (1335–1336): "Fortunate the man who when he lusts goes home and 'exercises'// bedding a comely lad all day long." Archaic poets, including Mimnermos, Anakreon, and Ibykos, among others, celebrate the physicality of pederasty, not its effects on the formation of youth.

There are many depictions of same-sex episodes in Archaic Greek art and myth. One is the very late Archaic/early Classical terracotta statue of Zeus and Ganymede dedicated at Olympia *c.* 480–470 BCE. The small painted piece portrays Zeus running off to Olympus with his arm wrapped round the pre-adolescent boy. The boy holds a rooster, a love gift from Zeus, in his left hand. Vase-paintings from the later Archaic period depict the moments of seduction or couples engaging in sexual acts.

The most famous story of Archaic Greek same-sex *eros* comes from Thucydides in the later fifth century BCE (6.54–59). Harmodios and Aristogeiton, *eromenos* and *erastes* respectively, killed Hipparchos, the son of Peisistratos, at the Panathenaic festival of 514 BCE. Harmodios was motivated by an insult to his sister – Hipparchos' reprisal for Harmodios' turning him down as *erastes*. Aristogeiton acted in concert with him to preserve his hold on Harmodios. Much in this story was later embellished. In fact, Harmodios and Aristogeiton became symbols of Athens' democracy in the first instance because they struck the first blow for it and against tyranny, not because they were involved in an erotic triangle. Yet, though the basis of the story may be fictionalized, it was deemed plausible by no less an authority than the estimable Thucydides.

Pederastic relationships were common even among non-aristocrats. Thucydides describes Aristogeiton as a "middling citizen" and, in the fifth century BCE, Sokrates, a mere stone-cutter's son, became renowned for his preferences for the company of younger males. The proliferation of homoerotic scenes on Greek vase-paintings might suggest that pederastic relations were common in Athens by the end of the sixth century BCE.

12.5 Summary

Some modern scholars have concluded that ancient Greeks were freer in the expression of their sexuality than we are today. It is very true that Sappho and others declare erotic feelings openly and that Archaic Greek vase-paintings are very graphic in what they portray. Yet poets and artists need not have spoken for the general public, and sexual art does not necessarily depict what is common. In fact, the ancient Greeks seem to have been somewhat conflicted about sexuality. A law in Classical Athens prohibited men who had received gifts in exchange for sex even as some *eromenoi* did from holding any offices of the state (Aeschines 1.19). The fact that the laws existed at all suggests a divided attitude toward same-sexuality.

Such conflict about sexuality is in fact more generally evident in Archaic Greek literature. Helen knows what right conduct is but cannot master her body's impulses to do the opposite. Penelope's extraordinary demonstration of faithfulness might be taken to emphasize its ordinary opposite, unfaithfulness. She also might be taken to waver near the end of the *Odyssey*. Sappho and Archilochos discuss sexual encounters and *eros* – and these may have lent some kind of permission for others to do the same – but these discussions oppose the Delphic maxims of restraint and moderation that were invoked generally by the Greeks as finger-pointers for successful social interaction.

It would be much too simple to think of ancient Greek society as simply sexually open and unconflicted between their sexuality and community standards mandating restraint. Most humans navigate between moderation and excess in any case, realizing the benefits of the one, while attempting to control the power of the other. Archaic erotic poetry and sexually graphic vase-paintings, most of which were created for special purposes and occasions, provide only partial evidence for Archaic Greece sexuality.

Notes

1 Cf. Thucydides 2.45.2.
2 It should be noted that skeptics disbelieve that the emotions Sappho represents in her poems are her own: cf. Foxhall (2009), p. 491.
3 That Corinna lived during the Archaic period is disputed: see Campbell, pp. 408–409.
4 How Alkman came to know the very personal words that the chorus of girls sings is not at all clear.
5 The Greek word *teirei* ("wears out" or "rubs away") might carry an erotic connotation, but cf. Campbell, p. 209, argues for *terei* ("guards, protects").
6 M&L, 13; Dillon & Garland 1.48 (pp. 32–33).
7 The idea that at least Athenian *akropolis korai* offerings might represent Athena (C. Keesling, *The Votive Offerings of the Athenian* Acropolis [Cambridge, 2003], pp. 97–161) seems belied by the increasing sensuality of the figures as well as a conspicuous lack of definitive Athena-markers on them (cf. W. Furley, "Life in a Line: A Reading of Dedicatory Epigrams," in M. Baumbach, A. Petrovic, and I. Petrovic, eds. *Archaic and Classical Greek Epigram* [Cambridge, 2010], p. 162).

8 *CA* 3.5; W. Burkert, *Greek Religion* (Oxford, 1985), pp. 237–42.

9 Cf. M. Skinner, "Corinna of Tanagra and her Audience," *Tulsa Studies in Women's Literature* 2 (1983), pp. 9–20.

10 Hesiod, *Works and Days*, 696 provides the age for male marriage. Cf. M. West, comm. *Hesiod. Works and Days* (Oxford, 1978), p. 327.

11 *S&A* A 6, 13–14 (p. 183).

12 Plut. *Sol.* 22.1 and 4 imply maintenance of parents by sons.

13 Athenaios 2.3.

14 Cf. Theognis 457–460 on "wandering" younger married women.

15 M.L. West, *Greek Lyric Poetry* (Oxford, 2008), pp. 3–4.

16 Cf. L Swift, "Negotiating Seduction: Archilochus' Cologne Epode and the Transformation of Epic," *Philologus* 159 (2015) pp. 2–28, who suggests that the epode might be interpreted as a "a travesty of an epic seduction scene."

17 Cf. M. West, comm. Hesiod, *Works and Days* (Oxford, 1978), pp. 250–251.

18 Plut. *Lykourgos* 15.3.

Further Reading

Gender

L. Foxhall, "Gender," in K. Raaflaub and H. van Wees, eds. *A Companion to Archaic Greece* (Oxford, 2009), pp. 483–507.

Childhood and Youth

M. Golden, *Children and Childhood in Classical Athens* (Baltimore, MD, 1990).

J. Neils and J. Oakley, eds. *Coming of Age in Ancient Greece: Images of Childhood from the Classical Past* (New Haven, CT, 2003).

Women's Lives in Ancient Greece

M. Lefkowitz and E. Fant, *Women's Life in Greece and Rome: A Source Book in Translation*[4] (Baltimore, MD, 2016).

Marriage in Athens

C. Patterson, "Marriage and the Married Woman in Athenian Law," in S. Pomeroy, ed. *Women's History and Ancient History* (Chapel Hill, NC, 1991), pp. 48–72.

Women in Archaic Greece

H. Foley, S. Pomeroy, and H. Shapiro, "Women in Archaic Greece: Talk in Praise and Blame," in E. Fantham, H. Foley, N. Kampen, S. Pomeroy, and H. Shapiro, eds. *Women in the Classical World* (New York, 1995), pp. 10–55.

Literary Sources

P. Brule, *Women of Ancient Greece*, trans. A. Nevill (Edinburgh, 2003) esp. Chapter 2, "Women of the Epics," pp. 43–73.

N. Loraux, *The Children of Athena*, trans. C. Levine (Princeton, NJ, 1993), especially Chapter 1.2: "On the Race of Women and Some of its Tribes: Hesiod and Semonides," pp. 72–110.

Sappho

E. Greene, ed. *Reading Sappho: Contemporary Approaches* (Berkeley, CA, 1999).

Alkman's *Parthenion*

A. Dale, "Topics in Alcman's *Parthenion*," *Zeitschrift für Papyrologie und Epigraphik* 176 (2011), pp. 24–38.

Material Evidence

M. Dillon and L. Garland, *The Ancient Greeks: History and Culture from Archaic Times to the Death of Alexander* (London, 2013), pp. 139–146.

I. Morris, "Archaeology and Gender Ideologies in Early Archaic Greece," in M. Golden and P. Toohey, eds. *Sex and Difference in Ancient Greece and Rome* (Edinburgh, 2003), pp. 264–275.

Korai

S. Blundell, *Women in Ancient Greece* (Cambridge, MA, 1995): Chapter 9: "Women in Stone," pp. 92–94.

Women and Religion

M. Dillon, *Girls and Women in Classical Greek Religion* (New York, 2003).

Males in Archaic Greece

J. Roisman and J. Yardley, (trans.) *Ancient Greece from Homer to Alexander: The Evidence* (Maldon, MA, 2011) pp. 165–175.

Symposia and Other Entertainments

R. Garland, *Daily Life in Ancient Greece* (New York, 2008), pp. 171–208.

O. Murray, "The Culture of the Symposia," in K. Raaflaub and H. van Wees, eds. *A Companion to Archaic Greece* (Oxford, 2009), pp. 508–523.

Masculinity

D. Graziosi and J. Haubold, "Homeric Masculinity ἠνορέη and ἀγηνορίη," *JHS* 123 (2003), pp. 60–76.

Sex/Sexuality in Archaic Greece

M. Skinner, *Sexuality in Greek and Roman Culture*[2] (Maldon, MA, 2013), pp. 29–138.

Eros in Literature

C. Calame, *The Poetics of Eros in Ancient Greece*, trans J. Lloyd (Princeton, NJ, 1999).

Homosexuality and Pederasty

K. Dover, *Greek Homosexuality* (Cambridge, MA, 1989).
E. Lear and E. Cantarella, *Images of Ancient Greek Pederasty: Boys Were Their Gods* (London, 2008).

13

Epilogue

The Common and the Extraordinary

In villages, towns, and even cities throughout Greece today, crowing roosters still herald the sunrise. Anywhere near the sea, dusk-to-dawn fishermen steer their small boats into harbors to dock and lay their night's catch out on the quayside to sell. In the countryside, farmers head to the fields. When the sun is fully up, shop awnings clatter open, grocers tilt boxes of bright fruits and vegetables on tables in front of their shops, hawkers begin to bleat out locations and wares. Marketing is done early on, business conducted to just after noon. By then, the noises begin to die down and people are sparser in the streets. The morning's bustle is over, and most head home for dinner – what we call lunch. Not everything stops, nor does everyone sleep after dinner: modern markets, bars, and *kapheneia* stay open. But the quiet is noticeable, and those who work into the afternoon are far fewer. Tranquility lasts until late in the afternoon when the streets begin to fill again and Greeks find time for a little business still. The pace is more leisurely, however, and, business concluded, walkabouts and conversations end with supper. After that, except for the young, energetic, and adventurous, most Greeks go home to sleep. While there are breaks in the routine – weekends, festivals, name-days, weddings, deaths, political demonstrations – in the main, the next day, Greeks rise and do it all over again. But that is now. What about then? How different were the lives of the Archaic Greeks?

Up at dawn, a married woman or a servant-girl went to fetch the day's water from a river, well, or, in more fortunate Archaic *poleis* like Athens or Megara, a tyrant's fountain house. Here women could chat with other women while doing laundry or before carrying water back home in large earthen *hydriai*. After a simple breakfast of yesterday's bread dipped in a little watered wine, olives, cheese, and fruit, when her husband was off to the field, a craft, or a trade, a married woman tended the household, cleaning, weaving clothes for the family, and minding the children. The midday meal was followed by a quiet time.[1] Supper was eaten around sunset, it seems, and there was probably some leisure time before and after it. Late-day fare was simple: goat, lamb, or fish if available, cheese, olives, figs, vegetables, and wine. The Spartan warriors' common mess with its staple of "black broth" – a concoction of pig's blood, salt, and vinegar – was to other Greeks much grimmer than their own simple food. A man from Sybaris who had eaten black broth said that it explained Spartan bravery: any reasonable person would rather die 10,000 times than eat Spartan black broth once![2] Daily routine was interrupted by festivals, assemblies, and, for men, *symposia*, which could go on through the night. Of course, war was a common occurrence in the lives of ancient Greeks and could alter routines for men and women drastically. Otherwise, with work done, an Archaic male was free to go about in the *agora*, if he lived in or near enough to the *polis*, or in fact wherever he pleased. A woman's focus, however, remained home and family, although it shifted to participation in rituals and important community festivals when required.

Archaic Greeks were both the same and different to one another, region to region, *polis* to *polis*, village to village. While they shared a common language, beliefs, values, and aspirations to a "blest" life, and a sense that they were united in the struggles imposed by their unique environment, they were also divided by identification with their own locales. Every Greek was a "Greek" compared with a "barbarian," but family interests came first, then extended family, clan, tribe, and region. Things are not so different today: a Greek anywhere in the world still identifies herself or himself by "my village" in Greece.

Archaic Greeks were real people leading real lives, just as we do. Their basic needs were seen to first of all, just as ours are today – food, shelter, clothing, and security. They were then also interested in the basic questions of existence – just as we are today. The majority were simpler people, not renowned as originators or innovators, politicians or warriors, memorable athletes or even the self-named potters familiar to us from the Archaic period. We actually know relatively few names of Archaic Greeks, and many of those are no more than names.

Yet the mainly anonymous Greeks who constituted the *demos* were arguably the most important single component of Archaic Greek culture and society. The "people" *were* the community: they set and maintained community standards, judged who was and was not a *polites* or honorable among them, and kept or rejected leaders. Significant changes in Archaic culture and society had to have involved the *demos*' own changing conceptions about itself, stimulated of course by new and different social, economic, and intellectual conditions and the realization of its own collective power. The Archaic *demos* not only permitted but encouraged Archilochos' rebellious affronts, Sappho's startlingly intimate discourse, the astonishing assertions of Thales and the other Milesians, Xenophanes' provocations, and of course the new political scheme of Kleisthenes. The changes were by no means logical progressions: while Archaic Greeks had done with kingship in many places in Greece early in the period, they allowed the tyrannies of Polykrates, Pittakos, Peisistratos, and even the evil Phalaris of Akragas.

The interrelationship between the *demos* and the *aristoi* was very old by the Archaic period. The meager evidence we have about them from Bronze Age Greece suggests that the Mykenaian ruling class and *damos* were implicated in religion, law, and economy. Communal worships are attested in the Homeric poems, parts of which are plausibly dated to the Bronze Age. In the *Iliad*, Agamemnon is described as a *wanax*, the name for a Mykenaian high king. If the evidence of the *Iliad* offers any veritable reflection of Bronze Age realities, the status and authority of one such as Agamemnon, although said to derive from Zeus himself, may well have depended on those who were led by him.

Post-Bronze Age *basileis*, who ruled in villages in the aftermath of the Mykenaian collapse, were primarily responsible for protecting their communities. Evidence derives from Homer, whose ideas about local monarchies will have been more informed by Dark Age kingship – the period of *basileis*' sovereignty in ancient Greece. Sarpedon says to Glaukos that *basileis* like themselves are obliged to risk their lives in the forefront of battle in return for rank, privilege, and material wealth from their fellow Lykians. He implies that, if they don't do their part, these rewards will be reallocated to others who will do what's expected of them. The prehistory of Athens, though affected by myth, supports the implication. The Athenian *polemarchos* supplanted the *basileus* as war-leader because the latter became "faint-hearted when it came to war." How replaceable a *basileus* could be is demonstrated in Books 1 and 2 of the *Iliad*. When the *laos* leaves the assembly suddenly, Agamemnon is a king without subjects – and so is no longer a king. The dynamic is perhaps more vividly depicted in *Oedipous Tyrannos*, wherein the *basileus* must prove before the *demos* his effectiveness as ruler. If he does not, he will be deposed in favor of another who will be effective in the current crisis. The *demos'* growing sense of its own political power and of the inadequacies of aristocratic leaders paved the way for the advent of Archaic Greek tyrants by the early seventh century BCE. Homer's heroic kings and warriors, whose portrayals were surely strongly influenced by Dark Age models of *basileis* and *aristoi*, if not by Mykenaian ones, could still fire the imaginations of Archaic Greeks, but were politically dispensable by the time of Archilochos – and his contemporary, Pheidon, the first known tyrant of Greece.

Basileis and *aristoi* also lost their monopolizing grip on the formulation of law and the dispensation of justice. In the *Iliad*'s "Shield of Achilles," Homer's judge-elders, who seem to function in the same way that Hesiod's "crooked" *basileis* do, render their decisions one after the other. But in Homer's "*polis* of Peace," the *laos* approves the best decision, suggesting that, unlike the "crooked" *basileis* of Askra, the *demos* determined what was just. Discontent with the actions and decisions of "bribe-eating" aristocratic judges and rulers led to the writing down of laws through the seventh century BCE.

The publication of the laws deprived judges of the freedoms of interpretation that they had apparently enjoyed theretofore. Term limits as set out in the Law of Dreros and elsewhere, including the institution of annual offices, stopped *aristoi* from acquiring too much power by holding them for too long. These measures favored the *demos* and further indicate its increasing political power. Of course, the ultimate result of this increase at Athens was Kleisthenic democracy and the outright "rule of the people."

Some scholars have coupled the rise of the *demos* – and tyranny – in the Archaic period with the introduction of hoplite warfare. In the Dark Ages, smaller numbers of warriors fought each other in melee fashion, it appears. The most proficient and heavily armed then were the *basileis*, the *aristoi*, and their closer adherents who engaged their enemy counterparts one-on-one, just as they do in scenes from the *Iliad*. Men of lower class, much less proficient and less well-armed, clustered behind the formidable fighters in front of them. In the later eighth century BCE, new style hoplite armor appears in Greece, proving that by then such warfare was already known and practiced by Archaic Greeks. The Chigi Vase gives evidence that it was widespread in Greece by *c.* 650 BCE.

Hoplite warfare required numbers of men to march and fight in formation, quite unlike the old-style combat of the Dark Ages. Warriors had to work together with their shields overlapping to maintain battle-order. The individual bravery of the *Iliad*'s heroes was of no use in such warfare; numbers and discipline mattered more than birth, wealth, or self-centered acts of valor. There were only so many *aristoi* with adherents anyway, and new sources of manpower had to be found to fill the formation's ranks. But risking death in battle must have entailed incentives for the phalanx's new fighters. Why should they fight, after all, if their lot was to be the same whether they did or didn't? It is from the mid-seventh century BCE really that we witness a greater sharing of political power in Archaic Greece between *aristoi* and *demos* – the latter, of course, the logical pool for the new warriors needed. A *polites* now was any adult male who took his place in the battle-line with spear and shield, held his position like every other fighter, and defended his *polis* and home. Although the "old order" strived to maintain its prerogatives in the face of these changes, nothing was ever the same after the seventh century BCE.

The (re)discovery of science further contributed to the empowerment of the non-aristocratic. Thales was not the first objective observer of the natural world – that honor went to unnamed Near Eastern or Egyptian scientist-forebears perhaps ancient even in Thales' day. But he was the first of whom the Greeks knew to reject received "wisdom" about the *kosmos* in favor of observation. Thales was also the first to posit water as the primal source, thus decoupling it from divinity. His successors, Anaximandros and Anaximenes, offered other rationalizations and speculations about the *kosmos* and primal substances that further undermined the gods' authority.

Thales was also first in Greece to attain renown for demonstrating that science could bring practical benefits, something to which Archaic Greeks were much attracted. Herakleitos implies that Hesiod's pre-scientific "almanac" was well known to and much appreciated by "the masses," and that his reputation for wisdom was established by Archilochos' time – well before Thales. Science (and scientific methodology) could be learned and applied by any one: it proceeds from intelligence, not birth or wealth. By its very nature, scientific enquiry questions accepted beliefs and discards the untrue. Its language is logic and reason, which form bridges to further knowledge and understanding.

While Milesian science signaled a new valuation of and belief in human intellectual potential, the Panhellenic Games, beginning with the Olympics, celebrated human physical possibilities and achievements. The latter began as a religious event, but, by the end of the Archaic period, the ritual aspects of the Olympic festival had taken second seat to a much expanded roster of competitions, apparently in response to popular demand. Archaic Greeks also flocked to Delphi, Nemea, Isthmia, and even Athens to witness the Hellenic *agones*, to watch athletic and other events, and to acclaim victors. While such festivals ostensibly honored the gods whose presence was acknowledged in several ways, Archaic Greeks really attended to participate in the drama of human competition and so to experience through competitors the euphoria of victory and the pathos of defeat. Olympic and other Panhellenic victors surpassed the physical limitations of other athletes to become, if ever so briefly, like the gods themselves. To win an event at one of the Panhellenic Games was to earn undying fame and admiration in the eyes of all Greeks. So enraptured were the Greeks by human competition that they made the game-sites places of worship for superlative athletes and athleticism as well as for the gods.

Xenophanes objected strenuously to such adulation, saying that it should not go to such victors, but to the wise men of the *polis*. It was not the gleaming athlete who made the *polis* "blest": such a man did not fill its coffers. No, said Xenophanes, it was the man of wisdom who produced wealth and prosperity for the community. It was wrongheaded indeed to think that a community would prosper merely by the presence of a "god-favored" athlete or an aristocrat.

Some voices sought not to reject, but to revise old paradigms to bring them into line with new realities. In his poetry of encouragement for hard-pressed Spartans during the Second Messenian War, Tyrtaios redefines heroism, exhorting his fellow citizens to be brave and fight in the forefront not for their own individual glory, but because it saves the army and the *polis*. Don't be an Achilles or a Diomedes; be a Spartan, he says. Discipline yourselves, hold the line. Old-style heroes are self-centered, unmeasured, excessive, and so prone to error: they can cause disaster to themselves and the army. It is that man who knows and holds his place among others who is the true hero for the community.

In fact, it is the person who knows his place who is the real hero for the Archaic period. The most esteemed personages of the time, models of moderation themselves, uniformly promoted the "middle way." "Know who you are" and "nothing too much" were prescriptions for Archaic Greeks to live by, sanctioned by Apollo, but repeatedly stated in the words and exemplified in the conduct of Solon and other Archaic sages. Solon observed that fortune could change abruptly, pushing the lowly to unimagined heights and hurtling the rich and famous to destitution or destruction. Moderation, of which Archaic Greeks were constantly reminded and which anyone could practice, was not only best, but also ennobling. Solon scolds the wealthy *aristoi* of Athens for excessiveness, unbridled greed, and arrogance, ordering them to quell their proud hearts: they bring disorder to the community. Solon praises the moderate and the simple life – a way by no means difficult for the *demos*. The maxims reinforced new definitions of superlativeness: the "best" were those who lived their lives best – morally, righteously and moderately – not those who had merely been born *aristoi*. Yet though many times repeated, the message of the sages achieved no real traction among the Archaic Greeks. Kroisos and Greek tyrants, the callow epitomes of materialism and excess, remained fascinating and admired figures even for the *demos* precisely because of their immoderate wealth and power. "Hard it is to be good," said Pittakos, who was both sage and tyrant.

There were other levelers. Many poets of the Archaic period focus in upon thoughts, feelings, values, behaviors, and especially human interaction without regard to wealth or poverty, high or low status. While Archilochos' father, Telesikles, was an *aristos*, Archilochos is of the *demos*. He dwells defiantly in a vulgar, but very real world. Archilochos observed that war was neither glorious nor ennobling, but actually sordid and dirty. He abjured the aristocratic dictum that one must die with one's shield, judging, like Achilles in the Underworld in the *Odyssey*, that it was far better to be among the living, even in disgrace, than to rule among the "glorious" dead.

Sappho's frank disclosures of her most intimate feelings are unprecedented and remarkable. She communicates what she observes about herself and others, but also unabashedly reveals her emotions and, in so doing, exposes for the first time the realities – and complexities – of erotic attachment. An aristocrat herself, Sappho's truths are basic and oblivious to class, status, or wealth. Her poems provide deeply personal glimpses into Sappho, her life, and her loves that nevertheless apply equally to anyone who has experienced such feelings. Yet Sappho's poetry, which sometimes addresses Aphrodite as a familiar, elevates what is all too human to the level of the divine.

The desire to achieve a fusion between mortal and immortal is also evident in Archaic Greek art, especially in sculpture. Prototypical Egyptian statues of humans inspired *kouroi* and *korai*. Early examples like the Sounion and the New York *kouroi* are angular, disproportionate, and even alien-looking, and, yet in them, we detect sculptors striving to portray the human body as something more than human. While, gradually, these sculptures soften and come more accurately to represent human males and females, sculptors continue to endue their representations with youth, beauty, and symmetry, the ingredients of human perfection – and divinity – to the Archaic Greeks. There is no drama or emotion in the *kouroi* and *korai*, but there is, especially as they evolve through the sixth century BCE, a sense that the beings they represent might just possess that Promethean spark within them.

Archaic Greek vase-painters seek to engage the viewer with their art as poets do with their verses. From the Nessos Painter's capturing of the near-death moment of the suppliant-centaur at the hands of Herakles to that supremely ironic instant of love and death achieved simultaneously by Achilles and Penthesilea, Archaic Greek vase-painters many times freeze a moment of supreme drama. By doing so, they animate a continuing story in effect, for the "snapshot" calls upon the viewer to supply "the before" and "after," that is, the further frames of the "moving picture." Yet the snapshot by its very nature also fixes the action in a brilliantly static fashion that encourages emotional and intellectual engagement at the same time. By the Archaic period's end, scenes typical of human life and drama seem to be preferred to mythical ones. The Brygos Painter's menacing drunken reveler grasping the arm of a recoiling *hetaira* confronts us with sexual tension and alarm, but also seems to offer a dark visual pun: it is a "marriage no marriage." The portrayal was created at least partially from observance of real life; the Brygos Painter adds his own invitation to disquiet. Indeed, his notice and then depiction of human *eros* as having two faces simultaneously prompt the viewer to consider more deeply the nature of desire.

The relationships between males and females are prominent in Archaic Greek literature. In the *Iliad*, Andromache's primary role is that of non-combatant wife. She is conflicted emotion-ally, both wanting and not wanting her husband to stay with her and away from war behind the walls of Troy. Hektor may actually desire such safety, but he fears above all the ridicule of Trojan women who would think him cowardly and deride him were he to shrink from battle. Greek males dreaded the negative judgment of women, their "unmanning," and the defection of a wife to a "better" man. In the *Odyssey*, the hero's life – who he is and will be – hinges on whether Penelope will remain faithful to Odysseus. His manly worth is on a razor's edge before he violently reasserts his presence and reclaims his own household. His worth soars finally because Penelope's extraordinary loyalty places him above all other males contending for her. Penelope fulfills the male fantasy of absolute fidelity, the negative counter to which is the deadly treachery of Clytemnestra, sister of Helen and murderer of her husband.

While Agamemnon and Clytemnestra provide perhaps the worst examples of husband and wife in Greek mythology, Odysseus and Penelope offer better ones. Clytemnestra destroys the household by taking up with Aegisthus and then killing her husband: the ramifications sweep up her children in the cycle of vengeance-killing in which they are obligated to participate. Though literally besieged by the Suitors, Penelope resists their coercions, holding out for Odysseus for nearly two decades. But it is her canniness and equality with Odysseus that des-ignate the pair a model. Their marriage is in fact the fulfillment of Odysseus' prayer for Nausikaa for a good marriage (*Odyssey* 6.180–185).

Negative models, involving erotic misadventure, over-the-top emotional or sexual attrac-tion, attachment, or betrayal, are featured quite often in Greek myth. Helen's extreme attrac-tion to Paris is depicted in her instantaneous changeover from contempt to lust in the *Iliad*. It is that lust that ruined her marriage to Menelaos, and Helen is only moments before succumb-ing to *eros* painfully aware that she has destroyed her Spartan household and irreparably shamed herself. But, then again, Helen is a prisoner of Aphrodite. Sappho's erotic poems sometimes seem to be more about the exquisite pain of desire and loss than they are about harmony or happiness. Are the wounds self-inflicted or are Eros and Aphrodite actually to blame? Anakreon is rejected – and unmanned – by a Lesbian girl who is not interested in him because he is an aged male. But shouldn't he know better than to lust after a girl much younger than himself? Or can't he help himself? Such questions recur in Greek literature and thought: are individuals *always* responsible for their indiscretions? Should they *always* have to pay a price for excess?

To want to exceed boundaries, Archaic Greeks realized, was perfectly human, but to do so would almost inevitably invite retribution. The deterrents were self-control, commitment to social and emotional balance, and careful regard for boundaries. Yet they also observed that something bad could happen even to an ostensibly good person for no apparent reason. Observing such misfortune, seeking to rationalize it, Greeks worked backwards, assuming that current suffering must have originated in some ancient transgression perpetrated by an ancestor. The sins of the past could play out in punishment for otherwise innocent descendants. But where is the justice? The Chorus in *Agamemnon* cries out in despair, when Agamemnon through no fault of his own, but because of the barbarous deed of his father, Atreus, is forced by the goddess Artemis to sacrifice his own completely innocent daughter to atone. Archaic Greeks had reasons enough to be mystified, pessimistic, dissatisfied, and even enraged about life's often painful contradictions and injustices.

The lives of Archaic Greeks were full of contradictions. They feared the gods, while harboring resentful, subversive thoughts about them. They found affinity in each other, but were also circumspect, suspicious, and frequently hostile to one another. They were generally more hopeful than cynical, especially in comparison with their descendants, but they could also be quite glum about their existence. Less experienced, but less jaded; less cocky perhaps and more conventional than Classical Greeks, Archaic Greeks may perhaps be likened in some ways to adolescents whose turbulent lives are alternately governed by emotion and reason, by fear and hope, and by restraint and abandon. They seek experience from curiosity and the need to know. More often than not though, the lessons are not really learned, mistakes are made again and again. On the other hand, the Archaic Greeks were in other ways sophisticated beyond our comprehension. Beauty and the wondrousness of humanity could be expressed in a few deft brushstrokes by a Red-Figure pottery painter, in the subtle smile of a downward-looking *kore* of the late sixth century BCE, or in the moonlight musings of a love-struck Lesbian poet.

Notes

1 Herodotos (1.63.1) mentions some Athenians playing games or napping after their midday meal.
2 Athenaios 4.138d.

Glossary of Greek Terms

adikia   wrongdoing, injustice p. 115.
agoge   Spartan training program p. 25.
agon/agones   athletic contest/contests p. 180.
agora   market-place/assembly-place p. 5.
akon   javelin p. 187.
akoniti   by default, uncontested (in the games) p. 180.
akousmatikoi   Pythagorean "listeners" p. 121.
akropolis   high settlement-center p. 18.
alloglossos/alloglossoi   foreign-tongued one/ones p. 57.
Altis   "Grove": the *temenos* of Olympia p. 181.
amphiktyonia   league of neighbors p. 18.
amphora/amphorai   two-handled jug/jugs p. 195.
aoidos/aoidoi   singer/singers, epic poetry singer/singers p. 9.
apeiron   the "boundless" p. 115.
arche   primal source, first principle of all things p. 97.
arete   excellence, virtue p. 9.
aristos/aristoi   the best person/the best people, nobles p. 6.
aspis   round shield p. 53.
Athenaion Politeia   "Constitution of the Athenians" p. 10.
Atthis/Atthides   local chronicle/chronicles of Athens p. 10.
autopsia   seeing, verifying with one's own eyes p. 101.
barbaros/barbaroi   foreigner/foreigners, a non-Greek p. 18.
basileus/basileis   king/kings p. 20.
basilinna   the wife of the Athenian archon *basileus* p. 234.
boule   council; at Athens of 500 *politai* p. 44.
daimon/daimones   spirit/spirits, animate force/forces p. 114.
damios/damioi   he/those of the people p. 6.
damos   the people (variant of *demos*) p. 6.
deme   town, village, district, neighborhood p. 219.
demokratia   rule of the people p. 27.
demos   the people p. 6.
diaulos   two-*stade* race p. 183.

Archaic Greece: The Age of New Reckonings, First Edition. Brian M. Lavelle.
© 2020 Brian M. Lavelle. Published 2020 by John Wiley & Sons Ltd.

didaskalos   teacher p. 94.

dithyrambos   dithyramb, a choral song for Dionysos p. 197.

dike   justice p. 12.

dokos   opinion, belief pp. 117–118.

dolichos   24- (or 48-) *stade* race p. 183.

dory   spear p. 53.

doulos/douloi   slave/slaves p. 23.

ekklesia   assembly p. 27.

emporion   trading station p. 19.

ephors   overseers p. 41.

erastes   male lover p. 242.

eris   strife p. 120.

eromenos   male beloved p. 242.

eros, Eros   sexual desire, Lust (Greek god) p. 9.

ethne   nation p. 204.

euethes   simplicity, straightforwardness p. 210.

Eunomia   Good Order, p. 166.

genos/gene   clan/clans p. 35.

gnomon   sundial p. 100.

gnothi seauton   "know yourself" (Delphic maxim) p. 214.

helots   Spartan serfs p. 25.

hetaira/hetairai   female companion/companions, courtesan/courtesans p. 135.

hoplite   shield-man, warrior p. 21.

hoplitodromos   full hoplite armor race p. 184.

hoplon/hopla   round shield/round shields; weaponry p. 21.

hybris   arrogance, sin caused by arrogance p. 22.

karyatis/karyatides   column/columns shaped as maidens p. 138.

kithara   a stringed instrument p. 192.

kleos   fame, glory p. 9.

klerouchy/klerouchies   Athenian garrison colony/colonies, p. 215.

kore/korai   clothed maiden-statue/statues p. 83.

koros   glut, surfeit; insolence from surfeit p. 213.

kosmos   the universe p. 112.

kosmos/kosmoi   arranger/arrangers (at Dreros) p. 6.

kottabos   drinking game at *symposion* p. 239.

kotyle   small, two-handled cup p. 3.

kouros/kouroi   nude male youth statue/statues p. 12.

laos/laoi   mass/masses, frequently synonymous with *demos* p. 32.

lochos   army unit, division p. 55.

logographoi   chroniclers p. 8.

logos/logoi   stories, accounts, p. 101.

mathematikoi   Pythagorean "learned" p. 121.

meden agan   "nothing too much" (Delphic maxim) p. 213.

menis   furious anger pp. 153–154.

naos/naoi   temple/temples p. 83.

naukraria/naukrariai ship-guild/ship-guilds p. 67.

naukraros/naukraroi ship-guild member/ship-guild members p. 36.

nike, Nike victory, Goddess of Victory p. 188.

nous mind p. 114.

oikos/oikoi household/household; family/families, p. 44.

Panathenaia all-Athens festival p. 87.

pankration "all-in" athletic event p. 187.

parthenion/parthenia maiden song/maiden songs p. 226.

pentathlon "five contests" athletic event p. 184.

phalanx massed formation of hoplites p. 21.

pharmakon/pharmaka drug/drugs, healing or harming p. 106.

philia friendship, affinity p. 211.

philochoria attachment to location p. 204.

philos/philoi friend/friends p. 211.

phyle tribe p. 204.

physis nature p. 99.

polemarchos annually elected "war-leader" at Athens p. 35.

polis/poleis settlement-center/settlement-centers p. 5.

polites/politai citizen/s of a *polis* p. 21.

porne/pornai prostitute/prostitutes p. 241.

prytaneion town-hall p. 36.

prytaneis ton naukraron leaders of ship-guild members (at Athens) p. 36.

prytanis/prytaneis originally lord/lords, later presider/presiders, leader/leaders p. 36.

rhapsodos/rhapsodoi lit. "song-stitchers," oral poetry performer/performers p. 153.

rhetra saying, covenant; the Great *Rhetra* is Sparta's Constitution p. 25.

sophia wisdom beneficial to the *polis* p. 118.

sophoi wise men p. 118.

stade Greek unit of measurement (= 185 m) p. 104.

stadion footrace of one *stade*; place where footraces and other competitions occurred p. 180.

stasis/staseis civil strife p. 10.

stele/stelai upright stone slab/slabs p. 5.

strategos/strategoi army leader/leaders, general/generals, war-leader/leaders p. 42.

stratos army p. 55.

symposion/symposia male convivial drinking-together p. 4.

synoikesis settling-together p. 34.

Synoikia Athenian festival celebrating founding of *polis* p. 34.

Taraxippos "Horse-Frightener," *daimon* of chariot-racing p. 188.

teirei he, she, it wears or rubs p. 243.

temenos/temenoi precinct/precincts (of temples, sanctuaries) p. 83.

terei he, she, it guards or protects p. 243.

tetractys Pythagorean mystical-symmetrical figure of ten components p. 122.

thesmothetai annually elected "law-establishers" at Athens p. 35.

thetes landless, impoverished citizens p. 42.

thiasos circle of women, especially linked to Sappho p. 163.

time   honor p. 206.

tragoidia   p. 198.

tyrannis   tyranny, the rule of one man p. 21.

tyrannos/tyrannoi   tyrant/tyrants p. 21.

wanax   Mykenaian "high king" p. 31.

xenia   hospitality p. 204.

xenos/xenoi   stranger/strangers, foreigner/foreigners p. 204.

xiphos   sword p. 53.

xoanon/xoana   crude wooden statue/statues of a god or goddess p. 146.

Index: Literary Citations

a

Aischines
  1.19   243
Aischylos *Agamemnon*
  107 ff.   85
  160-182   114
Alkaios
  A 6 (*S&A*, 183)   244
  Z 37 (12)(*S&A*, 315)   219
Alkman, *Parthenion*
  F 1, 39-91 (*PMG*)
      226-228
Anakreon
  F 358 (*PMG*)   168
  F 417 (*PMG*)   169
Anthologia Palatina
  ii. p. 851   200
  vii.664   175
Apollodoros *Library*
  3.6.7   91
  3.12.5   91
Archilochos
  F 1   9, 54
  F 2   54
  F 3   54, 55, 64
  F 4   55
  F 5   54
  F 21   55
  F 23.1-6   212
  F 105   158
  F 114   55

F 116   55
F 118   159
F 119   159
F 120   159, 198
F 122   98, 158
F 128   160, 213
F 172   159
F 188   159
F 189   159
F 196a   239
F 216   20, 56
Aristotle
  Metaphysics.983b.6-12   17
  986b.18-27   124
  On the Heavens
      294a.28-33   124
  On the Soul
      411a.7-8   124
  Poetics
      1449a   198
      1460b 34-35   176
  Politics
      1253a   203
      1259a.5-21   98
      1265b   40
      1273b   40
      1274a   40
      1274b.3-6   40
      1305a.19   36
      1310b, 26-27   38
      1338b.25 ff.   236

Archaic Greece: The Age of New Reckonings, First Edition. Brian M. Lavelle.
© 2020 Brian M. Lavelle. Published 2020 by John Wiley & Sons Ltd.

Athenaios *Deipnosophistai*
2.3 244
4.138d 253
10.4 185
(*Song of Hybrias*)
15.50.24 (*PMG* 909, pp. 478–479) 53, 71

c

CEG
119 228
161 229
Clement *Miscellanies*
5.115.1 (Graham 147, pp. 176–177) 124
5.109 (Graham 35, pp. 110–111) 117
Constitution of the Athenians (*CA*)
3.1 47
3.2 35, 248
3.3 35
3.5 35, 36
8.3 67
13.2 38

d

Diodoros Sikulos *Bibliotheca Historica*
1.98.5-7 105
9.19.1 47
Diogenes Laertios, *Lives of Eminent Philosophers*
1.31 219
1.33 99
2.22 124
8.36 124

e

Euboulos (Athenaios 2.3)
F 93 238
Euripides
Hippolytos
462-463, 466 241
Medea
244-247 241
250-51 232

g

Galen, *On Philosophical History*
7 (Graham 80, pp. 126–127) 124

h

Hekataios *FrGrHist* 1
F 1 108 (101)
F 22 108
F 26 108
F 27 108
Herakleitos
22 B53, (D-K) 51
Herodotos *Histories*
1.21-22 23
1.23 198
1.23-24 71
1.29-33 212, 216
1.31 149
1.32.5 22
1.59.3 42
1.61.1-2 231
1.63.1 253
1.74.2 97
1.74.3 98
1.75.4-6 97
1.141.3 23
1.164-65 23
1.168 23
1.170.3 108
1.171.4 57
3.60 104, 105
3.125 108
3.129-37 108
3.130.3 108
4.87-88 105
4.88.1 87
4.161 86
5.36 100, 101
5.49.1 100
5.66.2 44
5.69.2 44
5.71 36
5.72.3 87
6.77 ff. 86
6.81 87
6.103.2-3 47
6.125.2-5 22
6.126-130 231

Hesiod
  Theogony
    1-35   11
    585   77, 222
    588-589   240
    590-612   160
    824 ff.   78
  Works and Days
    20 ff.   215
    38-40   20
    42-44   74
    57-69   222
    60-69   77
    80-82   222
    83 ff.   78
    90-95   160
    109 ff.   79
    213   113
    216-218   113
    238-247   113
    267-269   113
    312-313   215
    373-374   240
    383 ff.   94
    458-463   95
    473-478   95
    519-523   230
    520   229
    585   222
    618 ff.   68
    624-629   69
    631-32   17
    696   244
    698-699   231
Hippolytos, *Refutation*
  9.10.2 (Graham 19, pp. 144–145)   108, 124
  9,10.5 (Graham 79, pp., 144–145)   108, 124
  9.10.7 (Graham 56, pp. 156–157)   124
Homer
  Iliad
    1.490   237
    1 and 2   152, 249
    2.92-95   33
    2.211 ff.   33, 217
    3.156-158   240
    3.173-176   252
    3.428 ff.   240
    3.433   252
    4.51-53   86
    4.204-219   106
    4.473 ff.   51, 132
    6.476-481   238
    8.302-308   51
    9.1 ff.   211
    9.42   236
    9.312-13   210
    9.382   96
    11.514   107
    11.632-37   3
    11.670 ff.   64
    11.842-848   106
    12.310 ff.   52, 53, 81, 215, 248
    12.322-328   154
    15.190-191   89
    17.365   52
    18.478 ff.   90
    18.490-1   32
    18.491-496   232
    18.497-508   32
    18.520 ff.   55
    21.34 ff.   208
    21.461-467   80
    22.98-110   207
    23.1 ff.   179
    23.306-348   179
    23.709   180
    23.727-728   200
    23.757-760   185
    23.763-775   185
    23.778-779   185
    24.527-33   87
  Odyssey
    1.1-2, 4-5   80
    2.7-10   33
    2.16   33
    2.25-34   33
    3.1 ff.   238
    4.1 ff.   223

Homer (*cont'd*)
    5.249 69
    5.270-277 108
    5.291 ff. 70
    6.57 229
    6.68 229
    6.96-98 230
    6.101 ff. 230
    6.180-185 232, 252
    6.262-69 32
    8.100 ff. 179
    8.109 180
    8. 266 ff. 90, 210
    8.326 210
    8.390-391 47
    9. 1ff. 211
    9.323 69
    14.245 ff. 67
    19.455-458 106
    20.18 ff. 158
    21.125-129 238
Homeric Hymn, to Aphrodite
    6.6 ff. 223
Horace *Odes*
    4.2 173
Hybrias, Song of (*see* Athenaios)

k

Kallimachos
    F 380 Pf 176
Kallinos
    F 1 219

m

Mimnermos
    F 1 163
    F 2 162
    F 14 162

p

Parian Marble (*MP*)
    Ep. 43 200
Pausanias
    Hellados Periegesis
        1.23.7 219
        1.44.1 183

        3.17.2-3 149
        4.5.10 47
        4.15.1 47
        4.15.6 176
        5.4.5 182
        5.9.3 182
        5.16.2,4 181
        8.14.8 105
        8.40.2 187
        8.40.3-5 194
Pindar
    Olympian Odes
        1.1-24 174
    Pythian Odes
        1.95-96 39
        2.55 176
        F 5 [1].6 193
        F 110 52
Plato
    Protagoras
        343a 219
    Theaitetos
        174a.4-8 99, 108
Pliny
    Natural History
        2.20 124
        7.57 149
        18.213 98
        36.21 103
Plutarch
    Lykourgos
        6.1-2 41
        6.3 40
        6.4 41
        15.3 244
    Moralia
        147a 108
        298c 47
        404d 124
        527d 200
    Solon
        22.1, 4 244
    Themistokles
        2.4 124
    Theseus
        25.3

Propertius
  1.9.11   162

q
Quintilian
  Institutio Oratoria
    10.1.59-60   175
    10.1.61   173

s
Sappho
  F 1 (*S&A*)   165, 168
  F 2 (*S&A*)   164–165
  F 5 (Campbell)   225, 226
  F 15b (Campbell)   240
  F 31, 1-15 (*S&A*)   163, 164, 240
  F 49 (Campbell)   225, 226
  F 94 (Campbell)   225, 226
  F 102 (Campbell)   225, 226
  F 111 (*S&A*,120)   235
  F 112 (*S&A*,122)   235
  F 114 (*S&A*,122)   235
  F 132 (Campbell)   229
  F *Adesp*. 976 (Campbell)   225, 226
Semonides
  F 7   160, 211
Sextus Empiricus, *Against the Professors*
  7.49.110 (Graham 74, pp. 126–27)   118
  7.132-33 (Graham 8, pp. 140–43)   119
Simonides
  F 83 D (Campbell)   172
  F 92 D (Campbell)   172
  F 542.11-20, 33-40 (*PMG*)   170
  F 543.1-22 (*PMG*)   171
  F 579 (*PMG*)   171, 173
Simplicius *Physics*
  22.22-24 (Graham, 42, pp. 114–115)   124
  23.11-12, 20 (Graham 37–38, pp.
    110–111)   117
  24.18-21 (Graham 8, p. 50)   115
  25.1 (Graham 3, p. 74)   116
Solon
  F 4.1-10, 26-39   166, 176
  F 4.4   83
  F 4.33-34, 39   210
  F 4a.37, 38   213
  F 4c   37, 38, 213

F 6   37, 213
F 11   37, 38, 176.
F 13.7   212
F 13.7-14, 17, 25-32   167
F 13.71-74   215
F 22.1 and 4   244
F 23   213
F 24.1-4   213
F 25   242
F 34.4-6   37, 38
F 36   37
F 36.1-2, 15-17   37, 38
Sophokes *Elektra*
  698-704   190
  709-740   190
Strabo *Geographika*
  10.1.11-12   64
Suida s.v.
  Choirilos   200
  Phaÿllos   200
  Phrynichos   200
  Thespis   200

t
Themistios *Orations*
  26.316d   200
Theognis
  43-52   210
  53-58   36
  77-78   210
  91-92   210
  129-130   215
  147-148   210
  181-182   212
  185-192   215
  193-96   36
  337-340   212
  355-60   213
  361-362   212
  457-460   244
  1225-1226   229
  1335-1336   242
Theokritos
  Epigrammata 21   175
  Idylls
    22.80-106   186

Thessalus, *Oratio in Hippocr. Opera*, vol. iii,
    p. 836   109
Thucydides
  The War Between the Peloponnesians and
    the Athenians
    1.4-5   66
    1.5   17
    1.13.3   69
    1.13.4   68
    1.15.3   64
    1.16   23
    1.17.1   39
    1.49.1-2   68
    1.76.2   219
    2.15.1-2   34
    2.15.6   47
    2.45.2   243
    3.83.1   210
    4.101   66
    5.71   58
    6.54 ff.   206, 242
    6.54.6   38
Tyrtaios
  F 4   41

F 6   62
F 10.1-10, 13-18   161
F 11   63
F 12.23-42   208
Tzetzes, *On the Iliad*
  126 (Graham 86, pp. 162–163)   124

V

Vitruvius, *De Architectura*
  10.2.11-12   103

X

Xenophanes
  F 2   118, 187, 188
  F 7a   122
  F 8   23
  F 11 (D–K)   82
  F 14 (D–K)   81, 82
  F 15 (D–K)   82
  F 16 (D–K)   81
  F 18 (Campbell)   27
Xenophon *Oikonomikos*
  7.4-6   231

Index

a

Achaia/Achaians   3, 26, 33, 52, 152, 155, 182, 185, 190, 206

Achilles (*see also "Iliad," "*Troy/Trojan War")   9, 52, 79, 80, 87, 88, 90, 106, 132–133, 134–135, 149, 153–155, 156, 157, 172, 179, 180, 185, 199, 204, 205, 206, 207, 208, 210, 211, 236, 240, 242, 250, 251, 252

  anger (*menis*) of   79, 80, 81, 153–155
  knowledge of his own mortality   81, 153–155
  "Shield of,"   32, 34, 36, 52, 90, 249
    polis of Peace   32, 36, 249

Aegean Sea   16, 17, 20, 23, 26, 27, 66, 68–70, 76, 108, 147, 158

Aischylos   85, 114, 198, 199, 223
  Agamemnon   85, 114, 198, 223, 253
  Persians   198
  Prometheus Bound   88

Agamemnon (*see also "Iliad"*)   52, 79, 85, 114, 134, 153, 154, 180, 198, 205, 211, 217, 223, 248, 249, 252, 253

  as deceptive leader/speaker   33, 38

agora/agorai (*see also* "assembly/assemblies")   5, 19, 32, 33, 34, 40, 45, 46, 64, 108, 180, 195, 237, 248

  Bronze Age   32
  and communities   34

Aias   44, 52, 90, 132–134, 154, 180, 185, 200, 205

Aegisthos   211, 223

Aigyptios   33

Alkaios   215, 238

Alkinoös   156, 179, 229

Alkman   226, 227, 243, 245
  Parthenion   226–228, 230, 232, 241, 245
    Agido/Hagesichora   226–228, 230

Alkmeon/Alkmeonids (*see also* "Kleisthenes of Athens")   8, 22, 43, 218

Al Mina   15, 19, 29, 96

alphabet   15, 19, 96

Alpheios River   174, 181

Alyattes   23, 30, 162

Ameinokles   69

Amyklai   25, 27

Amykos   186

amphiktyonia/amphiktyones   18, 64
  Delphic   107, 192

Anakreon   10, 15, 24, 163, 167–169, 173, 175, 177, 217, 242, 252

Anatolia/Anatolian   20, 21, 23, 24, 96

Anaximandros   93, 100–102, 107, 109, 111, 115–116, 117, 118, 120, 124, 250
  apeiron   115, 116, 117
  "coming-into-being/passing-away,"   115
  gnomon   100, 102, 107
  map   100–102, 107

Anaximenes   93, 111, 115–116, 124, 250
  air   115, 116
  "rarefaction/condensation,"   115, 116

Andromache   52, 154, 252

aoidos/aoidoi   9, 151, 152, 153, 175

Aphrodite (*Kypris*)   3, 73, 78–80, 90, 93, 105, 132, 137, 163, 164, 165, 168, 210, 222, 223, 225, 230, 235, 239, 240, 251, 252

Archaic Greece: The Age of New Reckonings, First Edition. Brian M. Lavelle.
© 2020 Brian M. Lavelle. Published 2020 by John Wiley & Sons Ltd.

Apollo (*see also* "Delphi," "Dreros," and
        "Corinth")   5, 6, 8, 12, 18, 22, 64, 74,
        79, 80, 83–86, 90, 93, 102, 103, 106,
        112, 119, 138, 139, 140, 143, 154, 160,
        180, 182, 191, 192, 193, 196, 197, 204,
        214, 217, 238, 251
    Daphnephoros   12
    Delphinios   12, 102, 103
    epithets   12, 25, 138
    and law   86
    and prophecy   85–86
archaeology/material remains, (*see also*
        "burials/graves," "inscriptions//
        graves," and "pottery")   1–8, 11–12
    evaluation/interpretation   7–8, 11–12
    historical significance   11–12
arche   97, 99, 112, 114–118, 120
Archilochos (*see also* "Ionian warriors," and
        "early Archaic warfare")   8, 9, 10, 11,
        15, 17, 19, 20, 30, 51–56, 61, 64, 67,
        151, 153, 158–160, 163, 164, 175, 176,
        198, 209, 212, 213, 217, 239, 242, 243,
        248, 249, 250, 251
    antiheroic   55, 158–159
    eclipse (*see also* "eclipse" and
        "Thales")   97–98
    and Homer   54
    Lykambes and Neoboule   158–159, 239
    and the Muses   9, 158
    "servant of the War-god"   53–56
    and shield-discarding (*see also* "social forces:
        honor: community esteem:
        armor")   54–55, 209
Ares   35, 54, 73, 74, 79, 90, 143, 144, 208, 210
arete (*see also* "Homeric heroes," and "social
        forces:repute and esteem")   9,
        51–52, 63, 155, 171, 172–173, 205,
        210, 215
Argos/Argive   18, 25, 29, 38, 46, 60, 61, 63, 65,
        83, 85–87, 89, 143, 171, 191, 194, 204,
        212, 224
Arion   70, 198, 217
    and the dolphin   70
Aristion   147, 228
Aristogeiton (*see also* "tyrannicides")   40, 206,
        242

aristos/aristoi   6, 7, 20, 21, 31, 34–38, 42, 43,
        45, 46, 47, 52, 55, 56, 60, 61, 65, 100,
        151, 172, 179, 180, 195, 215–218, 220,
        239, 248, 249, 251
    diminishing power/influence of   36–38, 216
    intransigence in the face of change   36–38, 216
    political role in *polis*   35–38
Aristotle   10, 98, 99, 117, 124, 159, 176,
        198, 203
Arkadia   138, 187
art, pre-Archaic/Archaic   127–149
    architecture
        columns   83, 87, 103, 104,138, 141
        temples   102–104
    Egyptian influence on   103, 127, 137, 138, 142,
        145, 146, 148, 150
    funerary   128–131, 143–144, 147
    Minoan   179
        "Boxer Fresco," 179
        bull-leaping frescoes   179
    pottery   2–4, 5, 7–8, 15, 96, 215
    sculpture   5, 12, 15, 20, 27, 83, 84, 88, 93, 96,
        103, 127, 137–148, 150, 215
        "archaic smile,"   142, 143, 144, 145, 146, 147
        architectural (relief)   138–142
            Dioskouroi (Delphi)   138–139, 141
            Gigantomachy (Delphi)   141
            Herakles/hind (Delphi)   140–142
        Daedalic   146
        free-standing
            female figure, ivory (Athens)   137
            Mantiklos   137–138
            Charioteer of Delphi   193
        kore/korai   83, 84, 127, 137, 142, 145–148,
            150, 228, 229, 230, 240, 243, 245,
            251, 253
            Berlin goddess   146–147
            Kore 674   147–148, 149
            Nikandre   83, 146–147, 228
            Phrasikleia   147–148, 228
        kouros/kouroi   12, 20, 84, 108, 127, 137, 138,
            142–145, 147, 148, 149, 150, 241, 251
            Anavysos *kouros* ("Kroisos")
                143–144, 145, 146, 147
            Aristodikos *kouros*   144–145
            Kleobis and Biton   143–144, 146

Kritios boy   145, 148
New York *kouros*   142–143, 251
Sounion *kouros*   251
Severe style   75, 141, 145
vase-painting/-painters   2, 4, 15, 18, 24,
        128–137, 251–252
    early Archaic   4, 129–31
        Chigi vase   59–61, 129
        Corinthian   129–130
        Nessos amphora   130–131, 133, 149, 251
        Orientalizing style   15, 18, 24, 129
        Proto-Attic style   4, 127, 129–130
        Proto-Corinthian style   127, 129
    Black-Figure (B-F) painted pottery   2,
        4, 74, 131–135, 150, 184, 188, 189,
        196, 233, 234
        Achilles/Penthesilea (Exekias)
            134–135, 149
        François Vase (Kleitias/
            Ergotimos)   131–133
        "Suicide of Aias" (Exekias)   133–134
    Geometric   127, 128–129, 131, 137, 143
        Dipylon amphora   128–129, 143, 146,
            149, 150
    Red-Figure (R-F) painted pottery   2, 4, 24,
        134–137, 150, 237, 253
        "Three Old Revelers" (Euthymides)
            135–136, 149
        "Young Revelers" (Brygos Ptr.)
            136–137, 149
Artemis, (*see also* "Ephesos, *Artemision*")   18, 23,
        24, 83–85, 87, 90, 119, 139, 146, 196,
        204, 219
Asklepios   106, 107
Askra (Mount Helikon) (*see also* "Hesiod")   11,
        68, 69, 209, 217, 249
assembly/assemblies (*ekklesia*)   5, 21, 25, 27,
        31–34, 37, 38, 40, 41, 42, 44, 45, 46,
        47, 64, 65, 208, 224, 237
    Homeric   32–34
    speakers/speaking in (*see also* "Aigyptios,"
        "Thersites,"   33–34, 44–46, 216, 217,
        237
    deceptive speaking in (*see also*
        "Agamemnon," "Solon")   33, 36, 38
Astyanax   52, 154, 238

Athena   18, 27, 34, 41, 74, 76, 77, 79, 80, 81, 83,
        87, 89–90, 128, 132, 133, 134, 155, 156,
        162, 166, 180, 185, 194, 195, 196, 199,
        201, 204, 206, 222, 231, 238, 244, 245
    epithets   27, 41, 146, 234
    Polias   34, 83, 194, 195, 204
Athens/Athenian/s (*see also* "Athena," "Solon,"
        "Peisistratids," "tyrannnicides," etc.)
        2, 5, 6, 8, 10, 11, 12, 13, 18, 20, 21, 22,
        23, 24–25, 26–27, 29, 30, 32, 34, 35,
        36, 37, 38, 39, 40, 41–45, 46, 47, 49,
        65, 66, 76, 96, 97, 100, 128, 129, 132,
        133, 134, 137, 140, 141, 144, 145, 147,
        148, 149, 150, 153, 165, 166, 167, 168,
        169, 170, 171, 173, 176, 184, 189, 190,
        191, 193, 194–196, 197–199, 200, 201,
        204, 207, 211, 212, 215, 216, 217, 218,
        219, 220, 221, 229, 230, 232, 233, 236,
        237, 238, 241, 242, 243, 244, 247, 248,
        249, 250, 251, 253
    akropolis,   18, 26, 30, 32, 34, 35, 38, 39, 83,
        84, 87, 90, 147, 166, 195–197, 204,
        221, 231, 234, 243
    archon-list   11, 13
    archons/archonships   11, 34–36, 38, 41, 43,
        234, 243
    aristoi   35–38, 42–45, 65
    autochthony   18, 26
    boule   44
    burials, Geometric   5, 6, 14
    Council of the Areopagos   35
    demos   36–38, 42–46, 166, 176, 212, 215,
        216, 217, 218
    demokratia (*see also* "Kleisthenes of
        Athens")   44–46, 207, 218, 249, 251
    festivals/games (*see* "festivals: local:
        Panathenaia")
    Mykenaian Athens   32, 34, 194
    naukraroi (*see also* "ship/s: ship-guilds")   67–68
    pottery (*see also* "art: vase-painting,
        pottery")   2, 4, 15, 24, 239
    stasis   36–38, 42, 46, 166
        "parties" of Attika   42–43
    tyranny (*see also* "tyrants/tyranny,"
        "Peisistratids")   38–40, 42–43,
        46, 67

Attika/Attic   2, 4, 5, 19, 24, 26, 29, 30, 69, 83,
        84, 89, 132, 134, 135, 136, 142, 144,
        146, 150, 184, 188, 189, 195, 197, 198,
        199, 201, 204, 218, 219, 228, 233, 234,
        237, 239
Aulis   85, 223

b

Babylon/Babylonian   12, 93, 96, 97, 99,
        100, 108, 120
barbaros/barbaroi   18, 22, 23, 99, 100
basileus/basileis   20, 31, 33–36, 38, 44, 45, 52, 53,
        60, 65, 67, 73, 180, 217, 234, 248, 249
Black Sea   16, 19, 70, 96, 101, 105
Boiotia/Boiotian   26, 54, 58, 66, 182, 197
Bosporos (*see also* "Mandrokles")   86, 97, 105
Brauron/Brauronian   83, 84, 204, 219
Bronze Age   9, 18, 19, 20, 25, 26, 31–32, 34,
        45, 47, 48, 58, 75, 90, 91, 95, 102, 127,
        151, 179–181, 198, 238, 248
burials/graves   2, 4–5, 7–8
    Phaleron   5

c

calendar   94, 96
Chaos   76, 112, 114, 115
Charaxos   226, 240
chariots/charioteer/s   4, 39, 179, 180, 182, 184,
        188, 189, 190, 192, 193, 195, 196
Cheiron   106, 236
Chigi vase (*see also* "hoplites/hoplite warfare,"
        and "art:vase-painting: early
        Archaic")   53, 57, 59–61, 129, 249
Clytemnestra   157, 210, 221, 223, 224, 239, 252
coins/coinage   39
colonies/colonists/colonization   2, 4, 7, 15, 16,
        19–20, 43, 45, 46, 67, 68, 70, 96, 100,
        212, 215, 216
    and oracles   86
Corinna   224, 243, 244
Corinth/Corinthian (*see also* "art: early Archaic:
        Corinthian")   19, 24, 34, 35, 36, 38,
        39, 40, 46, 66, 67, 68, 69, 86, 89, 90,
        182, 193, 194, 198, 216, 217, 219, 240
    Temple of Apollo   103
cosmogony   112, 114, 116, 123

Crete/Cretan   5, 7, 19, 28, 57, 67, 69, 89, 96,
        102, 103, 165, 179, 231, 242
cultural identity   204–205
    and *philochoria*   204–205
    and religious beliefs   204
    and warring together   204
"Cup of Nestor,"   2–8, 11, 15, 29
Cyclades/Cycladic   26, 147, 149, 196
Cyprus   73, 90

d

Damasias   38, 42
Danae   171–172
Dareios   24, 87, 105, 107, 109
Dark Age/s   31, 34–36, 45, 47, 67, 70, 73, 96,
        127, 152, 195, 204, 216, 217, 248, 249
Deianeira   130
Delos/Delian   11, 18, 27, 30, 68, 83, 90, 146, 217
Delphi/Delphic (*see also* "Apollo," "festival and
        games, Pythia/Pythian," and "Seven
        Sages")   8, 12, 16, 18, 22, 25, 39, 40,
        41, 64, 83, 84, 85, 90, 138, 139, 140,
        141, 143, 149, 182, 190, 191, 192, 193,
        195, 200, 234, 243
    maxims   86, 213, 214, 243, 251
    oracle of   40, 64, 85–86, 91, 92, 119, 182, 191
    Python and   85, 191, 192
    Temple of Apollo   102, 192
    Treasury of the Athenians   140–141
    Treasury of the Sikyonians   138, 139, 187
    Treasury of the Siphnians   138, 139, 140,
        141, 149
deme/s   197, 219, 236
Demeter   76, 83, 89–90, 139, 147, 158
Demokedes   107, 109, 121,
demokratia (*see also* "Athens: demos,
        demokratia")   27, 30, 42–45
demos/damos (*see also* "*laos/laoi*," Athens,
        demos")   6, 7, 20, 21, 24, 26, 27,
        31–38, 61, 217–218, 220, 248, 249,
        251
    Mykenaian *demos*   31–32
    role in the development of the *polis*   31–46,
        217–218
Diomedes (*see also* "Homeric heroes")   52, 79,
        180, 204, 250

Dionysos   84, 90–91, 158, 159, 197–198, 234, 238
   Eleuthereos (*see also* "festivals: local: Dionysia")   197–198
   maenads/bacchai   91
Dodona   85
Dorian/Doric   18, 25, 27, 87, 173, 174, 204, 205, 234, 242
Drakon   12, 20, 26, 30, 40, 42
  law code   42
Dreros
  Law of   5–7, 11, 12, 14, 19, 21, 30, 35, 36, 40, 41, 47, 86, 103, 249
  Temple of Apollo *Delphinios* at (*see also* "Apollo *Delphinios*")   5–6, 12, 102–104

e
eclipse/s (*see also* "Archilochos," "science: astronomy: *saros* cycle," and "Thales")   96–98, 115
Egypt/Egyptian   11, 12, 15, 17, 18, 20, 28, 30, 55, 56, 57, 67, 69, 70, 83, 95, 96, 97, 98, 100, 101, 103, 104, 105, 107, 108, 120, 127, 137, 138, 142, 145, 146, 148, 150, 158, 165, 209, 250, 251
  opening to Greeks (*see also* "war: mercenaries")   15, 20, 30, 55–56, 93, 96, 209
  science   93, 96–98, 100, 107
  technology   93, 96, 103–105, 127
Elea/Eleatic   23, 111, 116
  philosophy (*see also* "Xenophanes")   116
Eleusis   89
Eleutherai   197
Elis   182, 183, 199
Enyalios/Enyo   54, 55
Ephesos/Ephesian   23, 24, 51, 83, 87, 90, 108, 118, 119, 121, 162, 219
  Artemision (Temple of Artemis)   23, 24, 83, 87, 102–105, 119, 127
Eretria/Eretrian   12, 36, 47, 64, 66, 67, 68
Ergotimos   133
Eris   73, 120
eros (*see also* "sex/sexuality")   9, 162, 163, 165, 168, 223, 240–241, 242, 243, 246, 252
Eros   73, 76, 93, 168, 252

Euboia/Euboian   19, 26, 29, 38, 54, 64
Euripides   12, 119, 128, 159, 199, 232, 240, 241
  Hippolytos   241
  Medea   232
Eupalinos   104–105, 110
  Mole of   105
  Tunnel of   104–105
Euphronios   238
Eurotas River   25, 41
Euthymides   135, 136, 149, 238
Exekias   133–135, 149

f
farmers/farming, (*see also* "Hesiod: farming advice")   8, 9, 16, 17, 18, 24, 42, 46–47, 62, 87, 93–95, 102, 107, 108, 109
  almanac   93, 94–95
  cycle of seasons   88–89, 93, 94, 95, 97, 98
  militia   60, 65
  sailing to trade (*see also* "sailors/sailing")   68–69, 70
festivals/games, Archaic Greek   179–200
  local/regional   194–199
    Anthesteria (Athens)   234
    Apatouria (Athens)   236
    Arrephoria (Athens)   76
    Delia (Delos)   196, 198
    Dionysia (Athens) City   197–199
     komos   197
     tragedy   24, 197–199, 201
    Rural   197–198
    Karneia (Sparta)   197
    Panathenaia/Panathenaic (Athens)   87, 194–196, 198, 199, 201, 233, 238, 242, 250
     Greater *Panathenaia*   194–196, 199
     origins   194–195
     prize amphora/s   184, 189, 195–196
     procession   195, 206, 233
     victors   195–196
    Panionia (Mykale)   196–197
    Thesmophoria (Athens)   76, 233
  Mykenaian/Dark Age   179
    "Funeral Games for Patroklos" (*Iliad*)   179–180, 185, 191, 195, 196

festivals/games, Archaic Greek (*Cont'd*)
    Panhellenic   10, 16, 39, 118, 170, 173, 182,
            188, 189, 191, 193, 194, 195, 199, 201,
            214, 217
      ideal   191
      Isthmian   18, 185, 191, 193, 194, 200, 250
      Nemean   18, 185, 191, 194, 250
      Olympic/s   18, 39, 83, 118, 121, 170, 173,
            174, 179, 180, 181–191, 192, 193,
            194, 195, 199, 200, 201, 205, 217, 250
      Pythian   39, 118, 170, 185, 190, 191–193,
            194, 195, 200, 250
    events for boys   188
    events for men
      boxing   179, 180, 185–187, 188, 194,
        195, 196
      chariot-racing   179–180, 182, 184,
        188–190, 192, 193, 195, 196
      equine competitions (see also "chariot-
        racing")   188, 193, 194, 195
      pankration   187–188, 191, 194, 195
      pentathlon   184, 187, 188, 195
      running   179, 180, 182–184, 185, 187,
        188, 195, 196, 200
      wrestling   179, 180, 184–185, 187, 188,
        195
    victors/victory (*nike*)   118, 170, 173, 180,
        182, 183, 184, 185, 187, 188–191, 192,
        193, 194, 195, 196, 199, 250
First Sacred War (*see also* "Delphi")   64,
    107, 192
fish/fishing   16, 32, 68–69
"Five Ages of Man" myth   79, 157
food   16, 247, 248

g

Gaia and prophecy (*see also* "oracles/
    prophecy")   76, 77, 84–85, 101, 112,
    113, 114
Ganymede   242
gender   12
    female (*see also* "social values/beliefs, etc." and
      "Archaic Greek religion: women in")
      childhood and maidenhood   229–230
      depictions of maidens (*korai*)   230–231
      choruses (*see* "Alkman: Parthenion")

      documentary evidence about   228–229
      education   230
      "good woman"/"bad woman,"   160,
        210–211, 221–224
      male sources and accounts of   160,
        221–224
      restrictions on freedoms   232
      women together   247
      depictions of (vase-paintings)   236
    male
      education   236–238
      warfare   236
        gymnastics   236
        singing, dancing   236
        pyrrhic dance   236
        speaking (*see* "assemblies")   237
genos/gene   35, 44, 47, 65, 239
Geometric Period   3, 4, 15, 29, 45, 52, 66, 127,
    128, 131, 137, 143, 180, 196
Giants/Gigantomachy   88, 139–141
Gitiadas   128
Glaukos (*see also* "Sarpedon," "Homeric heroic
    code")   53, 154, 215, 248
gnomon (*see also* "Anaximandros")   100, 102,
    107
gods, Greek (*see also* "religion," "temples,"
    "Hesiod and," "Homer and," "Ionian
    philosophy," and "Xenophanes")
    5, 8, 9, 11, 73–82, 86–91, 93, 250, 253
    appearances   80
    conceptions of   73–82, 114–118, 120
    science and   108
    depictions   73–75, 89–91, 127, 139–141, 142
    immortality   80, 81
    implicit superiority of humans to   80, 88
    Olympian gods   9, 11, 18, 19, 22, 73–91,
      95, 98, 108, 113, 114, 116, 120, 139,
      140, 141, 210, 217
      and *poleis*   83, 86, 87
gorgon/s/(Medousa)   58, 130
Gyges   21, 22, 29, 162

h

Hades   89, 208, 210
Halikarnassos   7, 108
Halys River   21, 23

Harmodios (*see also* "tyrannicides")   40, 206, 207, 210, 211, 219, 239, 242

Hekabe   52, 238

Hekataios   100–102, 107, 120

Hektor   52, 80, 81, 154–155, 206, 207, 238, 240, 252

Helen of Sparta/Troy   25, 80, 90, 154, 156, 157, 175, 206, 210, 221–224, 234, 239, 240, 243, 252

helots (*see also* "First Messenian War")   25, 62

Hephaistos   32, 77, 79, 90, 132, 139, 194, 210, 222

Hera   23, 76, 81, 83, 84, 85, 86, 87, 89, 90, 106, 132, 181, 210

　Heraion, Argive   83, 86, 102

　Heraion, Samian (*see also* "Polykrates")   12, 23, 39, 83, 84, 87, 105, 127, 217

　Temple of Hera, Olympia   182

Herakleitos   15, 51, 94, 102, 111, 112, 116, 117, 118–120, 121, 122, 123, 125, 250

Herakles   63, 74, 77, 88–90, 101, 130, 131, 141, 180, 181, 182, 193, 194, 205, 251

herald/s   32, 33, 36, 65

Hermes   74, 78, 81, 90, 156, 222

Herodotos/*Histories*   1, 8, 10, 12, 18, 22, 23, 42, 43, 44, 54, 86, 99, 101, 102, 105, 108, 212, 216, 231

Hesiod (*see also* "*Theogony*" and "Works and Days")   8, 9, 11, 12, 15, 16–17, 18, 20, 24, 29, 32, 35, 36, 45, 46, 54, 74, 76–82, 87, 88, 90, 91, 93–95, 98, 101, 102, 107, 108, 109, 112, 113, 114, 115, 116, 117, 118, 120, 122, 123, 124, 157, 160, 161, 164, 166, 172, 174, 176, 209, 210, 212, 215, 217, 218, 222–224, 229, 230, 231, 234, 240, 244, 245, 249, 250

　basileis (*see also* "*basileus/basileis*")   35, 36, 45

　and *dike*   12, 115

　farming advice/science   93–95, 109

　and the gods (*see also* "gods: Olympians")   76–79, 81, 87–88, 102, 115, 118

　and good order   95, 113–114

　Muses and   11, 80, 84

　and Zeus   112–114

Hipparchos (*see also* "Peisistratids" and "tyranncides")   40, 43, 167, 168, 206, 219, 242

Hieron   169, 174

Hippias (*see also* "Peisistratos/ Peisistratids")   39, 40, 43

Hippias of Elis   182, 183

Hippokleides   195, 236

Homer/Homeric (*see also* "*Iliad*" and "*Odyssey*")   1, 3, 4, 9, 17, 18–19, 20, 32–34, 36, 45, 46, 48, 51, 52, 53, 54, 61, 69, 76, 79–81, 82, 89, 90, 91, 108, 112, 114, 117, 118, 122, 132, 151–157, 158, 159, 161, 162, 168, 172, 174, 175, 176, 179, 180, 185, 191, 185, 191, 195, 205, 206, 207, 208, 209, 211, 212, 223, 224, 231, 232, 237, 240, 245, 246, 248, 249

　and the gods   79–81, 87–88, 114, 118, 155, 157

　heroic code (*see also* "Sarpedon")   52, 81, 152–155, 205, 209

　heroes and heroic obligations   3, 9, 51–53, 81, 108, 151, 152, 155, 156, 157, 158, 172, 205, 223, 248–249

　Hymns   8, 223

　warfare (*see also* "war/warriors")   51–53

house/s   7, 16, 25, 36, 83, 87

Hybrias and the Song of   52–53, 54

hybris see "social forces: pride/arrogance (*hybris*)"

Hysiai   25, 29, 38, 60, 61

i

Ibykos   169, 217, 242

Iliad (*see also* "Homer," "Troy/Trojan War," etc.)   3, 4, 7, 9, 32–33, 48, 51, 52, 53, 62, 64, 79, 80, 81, 86, 88, 90, 96, 106, 108, 132, 144, 151, 152, 153–155, 156, 157, 159, 168, 175, 179, 205–208, 210, 220, 232, 236, 248, 249, 252

　date   4

　gods   79, 80

Ino   156, 193

Ionia/Ionian (*see also* "philosophers," and "scientists")   8, 12, 15, 16, 18, 20, 21, 22, 23, 24, 26, 27, 28, 30, 55, 56, 68, 93, 95, 96, 97, 99, 100, 102, 104, 105, 107, 108, 109, 162, 167, 195, 196, 197, 204, 209, 211, 214, 219

Ionia/Ionian (*Cont'd*)
  Athens as "oldest land of," 37
  conquest by Persians   12, 15, 23
  Enlightenment (*see also* "Miletos")   93
  revolt   23, 30, 100, 197
  warriors (*see also*: "Archilochos," "war/warriors:
      mercenaries")   55–57, 70, 96, 108
inscriptions, evaluation and significance
      of   5–8, 13
Iphigeneia   85, 210, 223
Ischia   2, 3, 7, 17, 19
Isthmus/Isthmia/Isthmian   18, 68, 182, 185,
      191, 193, 194, 200, 217, 219
  Temple/sanctuary of Poseidon   89,
      103–104, 108
Itea   192, 193
Ithaka   33, 80, 81, 155, 156, 204

j

justice/injustice (*dike/adikia*) (*see also* "law"
      and "social forces: pride/arrogance,
      right conduct, and honor/shame")   9,
      12, 20, 77, 87–88, 112, 113, 114, 115,
      120, 123, 150, 157, 166, 167, 170, 171,
      203, 209, 210, 218, 219, 220

k

Kalchas (*see also* "oracles/prophecy")   65, 85
Kallimachos   98, 158, 176
Kallinos   162, 219
Kalypso   81, 156, 157, 239
Kalydonian Boar Hunt   132, 133
Karia/Karian (*see also* "war/warriors:
      mercenaries")   16, 18, 20, 30, 55,
      56–57, 70, 96, 97
Kassandra   52, 85, 90
Keos   10, 169
Keratea   146, 147
Kerberos   101, 108
Kerkyra/Kerkyran   68, 71
Khalkis   64, 66, 67, 68
Khersiphron   103, 104, 109, 127
Kimon   39, 189
Kirke   90, 156, 157, 223, 224, 239
Kirrha   64, 107, 192

Kleisthenes of Athens (*see also* "Alkmeon/
      Alkmeonids")   27, 30, 43–45, 46,
      218, 248
  reforms   43–45
Kleisthenes of Sikyon (*see also* "tyrants,"
      "festivals/games, Pythian," "Delphi,"
      and "First Sacred war")   39, 64, 84,
      192, 193, 231
Kleitias   131–133
Kleoboulos   38, 213
Kleomenes   86, 87, 100, 234
kleos (*see also* "Homeric heroes" "social values:
      fame")   9, 80, 151, 154, 155, 174,
      205–209
Kolophon   23, 81
kosmos (*see also* "Ionian philosophy/
      philosophers")   86, 87, 97, 112, 113,
      114, 115, 116, 117, 119, 120, 121, 122,
      123, 157, 214, 250
Kroisos   12, 22, 23, 30, 83–84, 86, 97, 162, 212,
      213, 216, 251
  of Anavysos (so-called)   143–145
  and oracles (*see also* "Delphi, oracle of")   86
  wealth of   22, 212–213, 216
Kronos   76, 77, 89, 112, 113, 174, 222
Kylon/Kylonian pollution   26, 30, 39, 42, 43,
      67, 189
Kyrnos   213, 229
Kyros   22, 23

l

Lakonia /Lakedaimonia   25, 26, 29, 61, 62,
      100, 209, 237
laos/laoi (*see also* "demos/damos")   32, 36,
      38, 249
Lasos   173, 198, 217
law (*see also*, "Dreros, law of,"and "justice/
      injustice")   5, 6, 12, 19, 20, 26, 28, 30,
      32, 34, 35, 40–42, 45, 49, 241, 243, 249
  adultery   241
  Chios   11, 13, 35, 36
  codes   12, 17, 20, 26, 30, 40–42, 60, 118, 217
  Eretria   36
  Gortyn   47, 231
  homicide law   20, 32, 35, 42

judge/s/judge-elders   32, 34, 35, 36, 45, 249
lawgivers (*see also* "Drakon," "Lykourgos,"
          etc.)   10, 12, 20, 26, 27, 40–42, 49, 86
   Lokrian   229
Lelantine War   64, 72
Leonidas   26, 30, 172, 197
Lesbos/Lesbian   9, 19, 20, 46, 69, 70, 163, 168,
          175, 198, 226
literacy   4, 5–7, 15, 96
literary sources, problems affecting
          interpretation   1, 8–12
Lokris   221, 229, 236
Lydia/Lydian   12, 15, 16, 18, 20, 21, 22–23, 29,
          30, 83, 84, 98, 162, 174, 193, 212, 216,
          227, 229
Lykia/Lykians   52, 81, 154, 248
Lykourgos (*see also* "law" and "lawgivers")   12,
          20, 25, 30, 40, 41, 204
   reforms   40–41, 62, 86

m

Mandrokles and the bridge over the
          Bosporos   87, 105
map/s (*see also* "Anaximandros" and
          "Hekataios")   100–102, 107
Marathon   24, 27, 30, 40, 68, 140, 197
mathematics/mathematicians (*see*
          "Pythagoreanism")
Medes/Media   22, 23, 98, 172
Mediterranean   2, 15, 16–17, 18, 19–20, 27, 101
Megara/Megarian   36, 39, 42, 46, 47, 86, 166,
          182, 183, 204, 210, 215, 216, 229, 247
   war with Athens   26, 37, 39, 42, 43, 47, 64, 68
Megistias (*see also* "oracles/prophecy")   65, 172
Memory (Mnemosyne)(*see also* "Muses")   11
Menelaos   106, 134, 154, 156, 180, 206, 223,
          240, 252
Messenia   12, 36, 62, 103, 182
   First Messenian War   25, 29, 40, 61, 62
   Second Messenian War   20, 25, 29, 30, 40,
          60–62, 161, 208, 237, 250
Metagenes   103, 104
metal working   2, 17
Methymna   70, 198
Metis   89, 157

metropolis/metropoleis   19, 20, 26
Miletos/Milesian (*see also* "science/
          scientists")   20, 23, 28, 30, 36, 37, 46,
          93, 95–98, 99, 100, 101, 102, 108, 109,
          204, 240, 248, 250
   "forever sailors," 67
   prytanis   36
Milon   121, 185, 189
Mimnermos   162–163, 168, 169, 177, 239, 242
Minos/Minoan   90, 179
Muses (*see also* "Hesiod, Muses and")   9, 11,
          80, 84, 112, 152, 158, 166, 167
Mykale   23, 197
Mykenai/Mykenaian   19, 25, 83, 85, 86, 90, 95,
          101–103, 127, 151, 179, 194, 248, 249
   citadel/s   31, 32, 34, 45
   megaron   83, 102
Mytilene   20, 37, 38, 163, 175, 204, 215, 224,
          236, 241

n

naukraria/naukraria (*see also*
          "ship/s, ship-guilds")   66–68
Naukratis   11, 96, 105, 226, 240
Nausikaa   32, 156, 229, 230, 232, 233, 252
Naxos   83, 138, 142, 228
Near East/Near Eastern   5, 17, 18, 20, 76, 94,
          95, 122, 127
Nereus/Nereids   70, 193, 224
Nessos, Nessos amphora   130–131, 133, 149
Nestor   3, 4, 7, 64, 107, 156, 179, 180, 205, 238
Nichoria ("chieftain's house")   36, 103
Nikandre, insription (*see also* "art, Archaic:
          korai")   11, 13, 83, 146–147, 228
Nile River   56, 57, 67, 96, 97

o

Odysseus   9, 32, 34, 66, 67, 69, 70, 79–81, 90,
          96, 106, 134, 153, 155–157, 158, 161,
          175, 180, 184, 185, 200, 204, 206, 212,
          223, 224, 232, 233, 238, 239, 252
   suffering of   81, 153, 156–157
Odyssey (*see also* "Homer")   9, 32, 33, 35, 67,
          151, 155–157, 158, 180, 206, 211, 223,
          224, 232, 237, 238, 243, 251, 252

Oedipous   193, 249

oikos   44, 204, 211, 218, 231, 237

Oinomaos   182, 188

olive oil/olive presses (*see also* "Thales")   96, 98, 99, 108

Olympia (*see also* "festivals: Panhellenic: Olympics")   7, 16, 38, 39, 82–84, 89, 180, 181, 182, 183, 185, 187, 188, 189, 191, 192, 193, 194, 195, 200

   Altis (*see also* "Hera: Hera temple at Olympia")   181–183, 191

Olympeion (Temple of Olympian Zeus, Athens)   39, 217

Olympos, Mount   78, 79, 81, 89, 222,

oracle/s and prophecy (*see also* "Delphi: oracle of" and, "Dodona," "Olympia," and "Teiresias")   18, 22, 84–86, 91, 92, 182

Ouranos   76, 77, 90, 112

p

Pandora   75, 77–79, 90, 157, 160, 221–224, 230, 234, 240

Parnassos, Mount   83, 191

Paris   79, 80, 88, 90, 129, 154, 206, 210, 223, 240

Paros/Parian   8, 19, 20, 30, 54, 56, 98, 108, 138, 140, 147, 158

Parmenides   102, 116, 117, 120

Patroklos (*see also* "Achilles")   58, 106, 132, 154, 155, 179–180, 181, 195, 196, 242

Pausanias   105, 181, 182, 191

Peisistratos/Peisistratids (*see also* "Hippias," "Hipparchos")   24, 26, 27, 30, 38, 39, 40, 42, 43, 44, 46, 68, 168, 169, 173, 195, 197, 198, 214, 216, 217, 219, 231, 242, 248,

Peleus   132, 152, 236

Peloponnesian War   64, 66, 210, 216

Peloponnesos   16, 18, 25–26, 27, 29, 63, 82, 90, 174, 181, 204, 219

Pelops   174, 180, 181, 182, 188

Penelope   81, 155–157, 206, 210, 211, 221, 223, 224, 232, 238, 239, 243, 252

Penthesilea   134, 135, 149, 252

Periandros (*see also* "tyrants/tyranny")   39, 216, 217

Persephone   76, 89, 139, 146, 147

Perses (*see also* "Hesiod"and "Works and Days")   8, 9, 17, 20, 93, 113, 157, 172, 231

Perseus   101, 130, 171–172

Persia/Persian   12, 15, 18, 22–25, 26, 27, 29, 30, 40, 64, 68, 86, 100, 101, 105, 106, 107, 140, 147, 167, 169, 171, 172, 191, 197

Persian War   10, 24–27, 30, 40, 64, 68, 70, 169, 172, 191

pessimism   18, 79

Phaiakia/ Phaiakians   32, 81, 156, 179, 180

Phaedra   240, 241

Phanodikos inscription   11, 13

phalanx (*see also* "war/warriors/warfare")   21, 28, 52, 56–61, 65, 66, 70, 236

Phalaris (*see also* "tyrants/tyranny")   38, 39, 248

Phaleron graves (*see also* "burial/graves")   5, 13

Pheidon (*see also* "tyrants/tyranny")   38, 39, 60, 61, 249

philosophy/philosophers, Archaic Greek (*see also* "Thales," "Pythagoras," etc.)   18, 111–124

  epistemology   116–118, 120

  Ionian philosophy/philosophers   114–16, 118–20

    Milesian philosophy/philosophers   99, 111–112, 115, 117, 120

  monism/monists   116, 117

Phoenicia/Phoenician   15, 17, 19, 20, 27, 69, 70, 73, 90, 94, 96–99, 108, 137, 193

Phoinix   180, 236

Phokis   7

Phokaia/Phokaian   23

Phrasikleia and inscription (see also "art, Archaic: *korai*")   147, 158, 228

Phrynichos   198

  Capture of Miletos   198

Pindar   10, 39, 52, 158, 170, 173–174, 175, 176, 177, 193, 217, 224

Pisa   174, 182

Pithekoussai   2, 3, 19

Pittakos (*see also* "tyrants/tyranny")   20, 38, 39, 170, 175, 204, 213, 214, 248, 251

Plataia/Plataian   24, 25, 26, 30, 64, 172

Plato   128, 219

Pleiades   94, 98, 225
Pliny   98, 103, 122, 124
Plutarch   1, 8, 10
poetry/poets, Archaic Greek (*see also* "Hesiod,"
          "Sappho," etc.)   8–9, 10, 11, 34, 36,
          39, 47, 151–176
     choral/chorus   159, 170, 173, 175, 176, 224,
          226–228, 230, 241, 243
          Parthenion (*see also* "Alkman")   226–228,
               230, 232, 241, 245
     dithyramb (*see also* "festivals: local:
          Dionysia")   159, 197–198, 224
     elegiac   157–163, 165–167, 170, 172
     epic   18, 151–157, 161, 168, 175, 176, 195,
          217, 224, 244, 245
     epinikian   170, 173–174, 175, 193, 217
     epigram   169, 170, 172, 243
     erotic   162–165, 168, 169
     iambic   158, 160, 163
     lyric   1, 8–10, 24, 128, 157, 163, 172, 173, 175
     sympotic   165, 168
polis/poleis (*see also* "*polites/politai,*"and
          "law")   5–8, 10, 12, 15, 19–21, 22, 23,
          24, 25, 26, 27, 28, 31–47, 55, 60, 61,
          63–68, 70, 71, 76, 83, 86, 87, 92, 96,
          97, 100, 103, 104, 107, 113, 114, 115,
          118, 121, 161, 162, 165–167, 170, 175,
          182, 189, 191, 192, 194, 195, 196, 197,
          199, 203, 204, 206, 207, 208, 209, 210,
          211, 212, 213, 214, 216, 217, 218, 219,
          224, 226, 229, 232, 233, 238, 239, 240,
          247, 248, 249, 250
     not "city-state" 34
     deceit, political   37, 38
     emergence of   5–6, 31–47
     origins in Bronze Age   31–32
     and Panhellenic games' victors   118
     religion and   86–87
polites/politai (*see also* "*polis/poleis*")   21, 27,
          33, 34, 38, 39, 42, 44, 45–47, 60, 64, 87,
          104, 112, 118, 127, 166, 167, 189, 199,
          206, 207, 210, 216, 237, 242, 248, 249
Polydeukes   186, 226
Polykrates (*see also* "tyrants/tyranny")   23, 39,
          69, 84, 87, 104, 105, 107, 121, 167,
          216, 217, 248

Poseidon (*see also* "Isthmus/Isthmia")   32,
          75, 81, 84, 89, 93, 156, 175, 186,
          193, 196
Priam (*see also* "*Iliad,*" and "Troy/Trojan
          War")   52, 81, 85, 155, 175, 238
Prometheus (*see also* "Hesiod," and
          Aischylos")   74, 75, 77, 79, 88, 157,
          222, 223, 251
Protagoras   116, 171
Proteus   70
prytaneion/prytanis/prytaneis   36, 234
prytaneis ton naukraron   36, 43, 67–68, 70
Psammetichos I   55, 56, 67
Pythagoras   15, 111, 112, 120–123
     "Pythagoreans/Pythagoreanism"
          121–122, 148
     mathematics/mathematicians   120–122
     music/tones   122
     numbers   122
     "Pythagorean theorem," 120–122
     sayings   121
Pythia/Pythian (*see also* "Delphi, oracle," and
          "festivals: Panhellenic:,
          Pythian")   85–86, 234

r

religion, Archaic Greek (*see also* "gods:
          Olympians," "oracles/prophecy,"
          "festivals/games," and
          "temples")   73–91
     cult/ritual   82–87
          sacrifices/sacrificing   76, 77, 84, 85, 87
          statues   83–84
          boys, youth, men in   238
          girls, youths, women in   233
               basilinna (Athens)   234
          and *poleis*   86–87
          prayer   74, 76
          sacred space   82–84
          votives   83–84
rhapsodos/rhapsodoi   153, 175, 195
Rhea   76, 77, 89, 113
rhetra (*see also* "Sparta: Great Rhetra")   35,
          41, 89
Rhodes/Rhodian   2, 213
Rhoikos   105, 127

S

sailors/sailing (*see also* "ship/s")   16, 17, 19, 20,
    32, 55–56, 67–70, 107, 212
  piracy/pirates   17, 66, 67, 70, 87, 96
  navigating (*see also* "Thales:
      navigation")   70, 96, 98, 102, 107
  rowing   70
Salamis   24, 26, 27, 30, 68, 70, 172
Samos/Samian (*see also* "Hera," and
      "Polykrates")   12, 23, 39, 69, 83, 84, 87,
      89, 103, 104, 105, 106, 107, 110, 120,
      121, 127, 167, 217
Sapphic meter   163, 164, 165
Sappho (*see also* "poetry, lyric")   9, 10, 15,
      30, 90, 163–165, 168, 175, 176, 177,
      221, 224–226, 229, 230, 232,
      235, 240, 241, 243, 245, 248, 251,
      252, 253
Sardis   22, 23
Sarpedon (*see also* "Homeric heroic
      code")   52, 53, 81, 154, 215
Scheria (*see also* "*Odyssey*," "Nausikaa")   32,
      70, 71
  science/scientists, Archaic Greek (*see also*
      "Egyptian science," "technology,"
      "Thales," etc.)   11, 15, 18, 20, 27,
      93–109, 127, 250
    astronomy   94, 95, 96, 97, 108, 109
      calendar   94, 96
      eclipses and the saros cycle   97
    Ionian science/scientists   8, 15, 18, 93,
        95–109, 214
      Milesian science   96–102
      and practical ends   93
      primary aim   102
    mathematics   18, 97
    medicine   96, 106–107, 110
      anatomy   107
      physicians   106–107
seer/s   65, 84–86
Semonides and poem on women   12,
      158, 160, 176, 177, 211, 223, 229,
      235, 245
Seven Sages   39, 99, 112, 123, 167,
      213–214, 220, 251

sex/sexuality (*see also* "social forces/values/
      behaviors")   160, 163, 164, 168, 221,
      224, 230, 231, 239–242, 246
  adultery   210, 239, 241, 243
  depictions:, vase-paintings and
      statuary   241–243
  double standard/male anxiety   239, 252
  eros (lust)   223, 240–241, 242, 243, 246,
      251, (252)
  female chastity/promiscuity   159, 210–211,
      218, 221–224
  "married chastity" (*see also* "gender: female:
      "good woman/bad woman")   210–211,
      241, 243
  public and private   239–240
    same-sex relationships   241–242
    pederasty   241–242
      erastes/eromenos   242
      Zeus and Ganymede   242
    "secret sex,"   163, 239
    sex work/workers (female)   240, 252
  unsanctioned sex and its consequences   159,
      239–240, 252
ship/s   16, 17, 18, 27, 30, 32, 33, 66, 96
  cargo   68–69
  design/construction   68–70
  fifty oared   69
  large and small craft   68–70
  maneuvering   70
  Phoenicians and Greek ships (*see also*
      "trireme/s")   69–70
  ship-guilds (*see also* "*prytaneis ton
      naukraron*")   36, 66–67, 70
  trireme/s   68, 69, 96
    design from Phoenicians   69–70
Sicily/Sicilian   15, 19, 29, 38, 40, 46, 66, 70, 86,
      169, 173, 174, 193
  tyranny   40, 173
sibyl/sibyls   84–86
Sikyon/Sikyonian (*see also* "Kleisthenes of
      Sikyon")   187, 192, 193, 224
Simonides   10, 17, 24, 169–173, 175, 177, 217
Skopadai   39, 168, 169
Smyrna   9, 162
social forces/values/behaviors   203–219

aristos and demos   217–218

community consciousness/identity
      (*philochoria*)   204–211

competitiveness   9, 214–217

daily living   247–248

display   216–217

excess and moderation   212–214, 251, 252

obligations and adjustments, (*see also*
      "Homer:, heroic code," "Sarpedon,"
      "Tyrtaios")   207–209

overabundance (*koros*) as cause for
      stasis   166, 213

fame (*kleos*)   80, 81, 205–209

honor (*timē*)/shame (*atimia*)   9, 203,
      205–211, 214, 215, 216, 218

   and armor (*see also*
      "Archilochos")   54–55, 208–209

   and community esteem   64, 205–207, 218

   and Sparta (*see also* "Spartans, shields
      and")   208–209, 218

hospitality (*xenia*)   204, 206

friendship (*philia*)/hostility   211–212, 239

marriage and family   221, 223, 224, 228, 229,
      230, 231–236, 237–238, 241, 242, 244

   child-bearing and–rearing   232

   weddings   32, 231–235

positive/negative emotion   205, 206, 207, 211

pride/arrogance (*hybris*)   9, 22, 36, 37, 39,
      45, 64, 113, 166, 167, 205, 206, 207,
      209, 210, 211, 212, 215, 213, 219,
      226, 251

repute and esteem (*arete*)   81, 205, 206, 208,
      210, 215, 218

right conduct   166, 207, 209–211, 251

   female (*see also* "sex/sexuality: female
      chastity/promiscuity")   210–211, 218

   male   205–211, 218

ritual presentation of children   235

simplicity (*euethes*)   210

status   9, 35–38, 64

symposion/symposia   4, 157, 169, 238–239

wealth (*see also* "Solon: *Eunomia*")   166–167,
      169, 172, 173, 174, 175, 212–213,
      214–216, 218

Sokrates   66, 111, 119, 123, 128, 231, 242

Solon   5, 8, 10, 12, 13, 22, 26, 30, 36–38, 40,
      42, 43, 46, 48, 49, 64, 165–167, 170,
      175, 176, 177, 203, 204, 209, 210,
      212, 213, 214, 215, 216, 218, 237, 242

   and *dike*   12, 166

   Eunomia   166, 209

   political poetry   37–38, 165–166

   scolds *demos*   37–38

   seeks to curb Athenian extravagance and
      greed   5, 42, 166, 167

   reforms   38, 42–43, 46

sophia/sophos   118, 167

sophist/s   170, 171

Sophokles   159, 190, 199, 218

   Antigone   218

Sounion   84, 89, 143

Sparta/Spartan (*see also* "Messenia," and
      "Lykourgos")   10, 12, 18–20, 24,
      25–26, 27, 29, 30, 31, 36, 38, 40, 41,
      43, 44, 45, 61–64, 86, 90, 100, 128,
      156, 160, 161, 172, 175, 176, 182, 186,
      190, 197, 204, 208, 209, 211, 213, 215,
      216, 218, 219, 221, 222, 223, 226, 229,
      230, 236, 237, 240, 241, 242, 247,
      250, 252

   coalescence   34

   constitution (*see also* "Lykourgos," and
      Sparta: Great *Rhetra* [and
      "Rider"])   20, 25

   damos   40–41, 61

   ephors   41, 45

   Great *Rhetra* (and Rider)   25, 40–41, 61, 86

   kings   31, 36, 40, 41, 45

   war/warrior (*see also* "Tyrtaios," and "war/
      warriors/warfare")   60–64

      agoge   25, 41, 62, 63, 237

      reputation for victory   64

      shields and   54–55

      unit consciousness   62

      values   62

stasis   10, 19, 21, 26, 27, 35–38, 42, 46, 60,
      165, 166, 203, 210, 211, 218

stele/stelai   5, 219

strategos   42, 44, 65

stone working   17, 20, 96, 104, 107, 108

Sybaris   121, 247
Syrakusa/Syrakusan   19, 29, 169, 174
Syria/Syrian   2, 15, 19, 96

t
Taras   19, 20, 37, 121
Tartaros   76–78, 113
Taygetos, Mount   25, 61
technology (*see also* "science")   20, 83, 93, 94,
        96–97, 102–108, 127
    engineering/architecture   97, 102–106,
        109, 110
Teiresias   85
Telemachos   33, 81, 155–156, 223, 238
temple/s, pre-Archaic and Archaic (*see also*
        "Mykenaian megaron," "religion:
        sacred space," "gods
        Olympians")   5–6, 7, 12, 15, 18, 20,
        23, 24, 25, 30, 38, 39, 41, 43, 47,
        82–84, 86, 87, 93, 96, 102–104, 105,
        107, 108, 109
    evolution of   102–104
    treasuries (*see also* "Delphi, treasuries")   84
Teos/Tean   10, 23, 97, 167
Thales (*see also* "science: Ionian," and
        "Seven Sages")   93, 97–100, 101,
        102, 108, 109, 111, 112, 114, 115,
        116, 118, 123, 124, 167, 170, 204,
        213, 214, 248, 250
    navigation   98, 102
    and the olive presses   97–99
    and water as the *arche*   99, 114, 116
Thasos/Thasian   19, 55, 229
Theagenes   36, 38, 39, 47
Thebes/Theban   10, 66, 85, 137, 138, 173, 174,
        193, 194, 224
Themis   139, 140
Themistokles   68
Theodoros   103, 105, 127
Theognis   36, 47, 166, 210, 212, 213, 215, 216,
        229, 242
Theogony (*see also* "gods," and "Olympian
        gods")   9, 76–79, 80, 88, 112, 113,
        114, 157, 160, 222
    origins of the gods   76

Theokritos   158, 186
Thermopylai   26, 30, 172, 197
Thersites (*see also* "*Iliad*")   33, 34, 42, 52, 217, 220
    assembly speaker (*see also* "assembly:
        speakers")   33–34, 217
Thespis   197, 198, 200
Thetis (and the "marriage of")   79, 132, 133, 154
Theseus   34, 132, 141, 193, 196, 219
Thessaly/Thessalian   16, 39, 106, 168, 169,
        190, 204, 228
Thrace/Thracian   19, 43, 54, 70, 81, 90, 158,
        167, 169
Thucydides   17, 23, 34, 64, 66, 101, 206, 210,
        219, 242, 243
Titan/s   76, 77, 88, 89, 94, 113
Tityos   186, 200
trade/trader/trading   2, 4, 15, 16–17, 19, 20,
        66–70, 96, 204, 212
tragedy/tragic poets   12, 24, 197–199, 201
Triton   70
Troy/Trojan War (*see also* "Homer" and
        "*Iliad*")   3, 4, 9, 33, 51, 52, 65, 80,
        81, 85, 88, 90, 106, 132, 134,
        153–155, 175, 180, 185, 206, 207,
        208, 211, 212, 223, 237, 238, 240
Tynnondas   38
Typhoeos   77–79, 88, 113
Tyrannicides (*see also* "Harmodios,"
        "Aristogeiton")   40, 148, 149
tyrannis/tyrannos/tyrannoi   21, 38, 39, 73
tyrants/tyranny, Archaic Greek (*see also*
        "Peisistratos/ Peisistratids." "Pheidon,"
        "Polykrates,"etc.)   10, 15, 18, 20, 21,
        23, 24, 26, 28, 29, 36, 38–40, 42, 43,
        46, 47, 49, 60, 84, 100, 104, 167, 168,
        169, 171, 173, 216, 217
    general attitudes toward   39–40, 216–217
        conditions favoring   38–39
        elected   38
        and games   217
        perceptions of Athenian demos (*see also*
            "Peisistratos/Peisistratids,"and
            "tyrannicides")   40
Tyrtaios   10, 12, 59, 61–63, 160–161, 175, 176,
        177, 205, 207–209, 236, 250

u
Underworld   89, 156, 223, 251

v
violence (*see also* "sailing: piracy," "*stasis*," "war/warriors/warfare")   36, 64–66, 112

w
wanax   31, 248
war/warriors/warfare (*see also* "Spartan warriors" and "phalanx")   9, 10, 15, 18, 19, 20, 21, 22, 23, 24, 25, 26, 27, 28, 33, 35, 37, 38, 40, 41, 42, 43, 46, 47, 48, 51–71, 223, 236, 239
    attitudes toward   64
    battle   51–61, 64–66
        plunder   60, 66
        seers/augury, (*see also* "oracles/prophecy," "Kalchas," and "Megistias")   65
        causes of war   64
        cavalry   66
    early Archaic war (*see also* "Archilochos")   53–56
    Homeric   51–53
    hoplite/hoplite warfare (*see also* "Sparta, war/warriors")   15, 18, 21, 25, 28, 56–61, 65, 66, 68, 70, 71, 129, 139, 205, 208, 209, 249
        adoption of by Greeks   60–61
        "shoving,"   59, 71
    mercenaries, (*see also* "Egypt: opening, of," and "Karian, warriors")   20, 30, 55–57, 70, 96, 108, 209
    naval combat (*see also* "ship/s, triremes")   68
    non-combatants   52
    promachoi ("front-fighters")   59, 60
    seers before battle (*see also* "seers")   65
    shield-abandonment, (*see also* "Archilochos," and "Spartan warriors:, shields and")   54
    training   65
    war and local identity   204

warriors in Egypt (*see also* "Egypt, opening of and "Ionian warriors")   20, 56–57, 96, 209
weapons   53–61, 65, 66
    shield (*aspis*)   53–56, 58–59
        heraldic devices   58, 65
    spear (*dory*)   53, 57, 61, 65
wealth   37, 43
writing   5–7, 15, 29
Works and *Days* (*see also* "Hesiod")   8, 9, 15, 16, 18, 20, 24, 29, 45, 74, 76–79, 88, 93–95, 108, 109, 112, 113, 114, 123, 157, 215, 230, 231

x
Xenophanes   23, 81, 82, 102, 111, 114, 116–118, 119, 120, 121, 122, 124, 125, 187, 189, 191, 248, 250
    abstract conception of "God,"   117
    and *arche*   117
    complaint about Homeric/Hesiodic gods   81–82, 117
    complaint about Panhellenic games' victors   118, 250
    epistemology   116–118

z
Zeus (*see also* "Hesiod and Zeus" and "gods: Olympians")   11, 33, 41, 74–79, 80, 82, 84, 85, 87–90, 93, 95, 98, 112, 113, 114, 120, 154, 158, 160, 166, 167, 175, 180, 181, 182, 186, 188, 189, 191, 193, 194, 204, 205, 206, 209, 217, 222, 224, 242, 248
    as cultural hero   77–78
    establishes supremacy   77
    fear of displacement   89
    and justice (*see also* "justice/injustice")   88, 114
    and order/disorder   87–88, 112, 113, 114
    and prophecy   84–86
    (or Poseidon) of Artemision   75